GENERAL ELECTIONS IN SOUTH AFRICA
1943–1970

GENERAL ELECTIONS IN SOUTH AFRICA

1943–1970

Kenneth A. Heard

Department of Political Science
Dalhousie University

London
Oxford University Press
Cape Town New York Toronto
1974

*Oxford University Press, Ely House, London W.*1
GLASGOW NEW YORK TORONTO MELBOURNE WELLINGTON CAPE TOWN IBADAN
NAIROBI DAR ES SALAAM LUSAKA ADDIS ABABA DELHI BOMBAY CALCUTTA MADRAS
KARACHI LAHORE DACCA KUALA LUMPUR SINGAPORE HONG KONG TOKYO

ISBN 0 19 215643 8

PRINTED IN THE REPUBLIC OF SOUTH AFRICA BY
THE RUSTICA PRESS, PTY., LTD., WYNBERG, CAPE

272

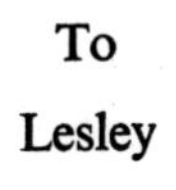

To

Lesley

Contents

Preface

This is a book about the struggle for power within the formal political structures of South Africa. Because of the nature of those political structures the actors on stage are white; but the non-whites, or Blacks as they are beginning to call themselves, are not just an audience, even a participant audience; for their destinies are at least in part decided upon by what goes on on the stage. Consequently they, too, want to mount the stage—some, to replace the white actors, others, to share the stage with them. While the play goes on then, there is at the same time a continuing dispute between the actors and audience about who should be playing what roles, about what the play should be about, and indeed what stage or stages should be used. While this book focuses on the play itself, these on-going conflicts need to be kept in mind—if for no other reason than that the play is constantly, in greater or lesser degree, responsive to them. Neither the scene of the play nor the site of the stage is Atlantis: if it were, the play would be a completely different play.

This analogy, while helpful up to a point, is misleading, however, if taken beyond that point. While it may be true that some of the 'actors' may from time to time come to be trapped within their roles—and my hunch is that this is increasingly the case of the present National Party leadership—on the whole the major participants have a real conviction that what they do and say *matters*, that they concern real issues, and that the determination of those issues will have far-reaching consequences. While there are elements of ritual, of role-playing, in South African politics, the electoral conflicts do reflect the clash of opposing convictions. To try to explain what the bases of these convictions are and how they have come into being would require an historico-sociological analysis beyond the scope of this present study. That is a task which the author hopes to undertake in the near future. For the present, however, we may reflect on the fact that the ideological divide among the parties and their respective supporters has come substantially to correspond to the linguistic divide. The greater part (but by no means all) of Afrikaner voters have thus come to support the National Party, and the greater part (but, again, not all) of English-speaking voters have come to support the United Party. A brief outline of the history of party conflict in South Africa may help to explain this phenomenon, or at least to provide a perspective for the better understanding of the chapters that follow. At the outset a tabulation of election results from 1910 to 1938 can help to depict the shifts of party fortunes.

	S.A.P.		*N.P.*[1]	*Unionists*		*Labour*	*Others*
1910 .	68		—	37		3	13
1915 .	54		27	39		4	6
1920 .	41		44	25		21	3
1921 .	79		45	—		9	1
1924 .	52		63	—		18	2
1929 .	61		78	—		8[2]	1
1933 .	61		75	—		4[3]	10
1934 .		*U.P.*			*Dominion*		
1938 .	—	111	27	—	8	3	1

Notes: [1] After 1934 Purified N.P.
[2] After a split in the Labour Party five continued to support Hertzog while three went over in support of Smuts.
[3] Including two 'Independent Labour'.

Throughout the first fifty years of South Africa's history as a union, three major themes dominated political debate: South Africa's relationship with Britain, the relationship between the two major white groups, the Afrikaners and those of British descent, and the policies to be pursued towards South Africa's 'non-white' groups—the Africans, Coloureds, and Indians (in South African terminology, 'Asiatics'). Other issues have, of course, arisen—for example, the labour question, the debate in the 1930s over the gold standard—but, by and large, perspectives on these other issues have been coloured by the particular views held on the three major themes. Inevitably, therefore, party divisions have formed around these questions. The original South African Party, led by Botha and Smuts, was primarily committed to the healing of the wounds left by the Anglo-Boer War—to the reconciliation of Dutch and English (as Afrikaans- and English-speaking South Africans were still usually called)—through an over-arching commitment to South African unity on the one hand, and co-operation with Great Britain and the Empire on the other. In this endeavour, however, they initially lacked the support of the more extreme British element of the population, who found their home in the Unionist Party. At the same time, and on the other flank, there were Afrikaners who came to the conclusion that Botha and Smuts were more concerned to win over the English-speakers and to support Britain than they were to protect the interests of Afrikaners and to give primary loyalty to South Africa. It was largely on these grounds that General Hertzog split from his former colleagues and in 1914 formed the National Party—a party committed, in its turn, to gaining an effective equality for the Afrikaner in South African society and to asserting the primacy of South African interests vis-à-vis Great Britain and the Empire.

South Africa's participation in the First World War, and the decision to send a South African force to South West Africa (later extended to East Africa and to Europe) exacerbated the conflict between the South African Party and the National Party, reinforcing the latter's image of the former as the subservient tool of imperialism. At the same time, the National Party further sharpened its own image as the party that would free South Africa from its allegedly subordinate status by adopting the goal of an independent republic, outside the Empire, in which the Afrikaner could achieve his full identity. With the National Party gaining increasing Afrikaner support, General Smuts found his power base shrinking and was forced to woo the Unionists. They, in turn, were alarmed on the one hand by the upsurge of Afrikaner nationalism, and reassured on the other by Smuts's firm position on the imperial connection. They were ready, therefore, to succumb to Smuts's wooing, and in 1920 merged with the South African Party. But this marriage in turn further underlined, as far as the Nationalists were concerned, Smuts's betrayal of his 'own' people. In current terminology he would be accused of being the complete neo-colonialist.

At this point, moreover, economic depression gave rise to serious labour problems, and urban white workers reacted against not only the exploitation of their capitalist masters, but also against the threat of having their wages undercut by the immense reservoir of black labour. The Smuts Government not only offended these workers by appearing to side with the mine-owners in the Rand miners' strike in 1922, but it then went on completely to alienate them in the harsh, even brutal, suppression of the 'Rand Revolt'. Having allowed the conflict to escalate to that point in the first instance, it then called in the armed forces to crush it, with the consequent loss of some 230 lives. Predictably, the Labour Party reaped the fruits of this alienation, and, predictably again, although largely English-speaking in support it was happy to enter into an alliance with Hertzog's Nationalists to fight the common enemy. What was of immense significance in this 'Pact' was that the salient issue on which they united was the 'colour question', that is, race. Consequently, the emphasis in inter-party conflict shifted away from questions of status (the status of Afrikaners, the status of the Union) to questions of racial policies. And although Hertzog was impelled by the logic of his own position and by the aspirations of his followers to press for such 'status' measures as the Balfour Declaration, 1926, and the Statute of Westminster, 1931, and although these status questions have continued since then to enjoy periods of salience, nevertheless, on the whole, since the victory of the Nationalist–Labour Pact in 1924, race has continued to be the major preoccupation of South African politics.

The Pact victory in 1924 enabled Hertzog to form his first ministry, and in 1929 he achieved an even greater electoral victory. For the first time the National Party obtained an over-all majority in the House of Assembly; but Hertzog remained loyal to his Labour supporters, and although the Labour Party had meanwhile split on the question of continued co-operation with the National Party, he still included two Labourites in his Cabinet.

The new ministry, however, soon ran into difficulties. The acute financial crisis facing the Union, largely due to its stubborn insistence on remaining on the gold standard (another 'status' issue), forced for the first—and so far the only—time economics into the top priority issue. In response to this crisis, and to an apparently growing public demand, Hertzog and Smuts sank their differences and agreed to the formation of a national government. The 1933 election was, in a sense, a non-election; for virtually all candidates were pledged to support the coalition. With the election over, the two major parties took the final step of joining together, in the so-called 'Fusion', to form a single party, the United South African National Party (henceforward referred to as the United Party). The elements, then, that came together under this umbrella were the larger part of the English-speaking citizens and the 'moderate' Afrikaners (from the old South African Party), and the larger part of Afrikaner nationalists (from the National Party). Some of both sections, however, preferred to remain outside. The more extreme ('loyal') British section, deeply suspicious of Hertzog's republicanism, concluded that Smuts had changed his colours and consequently declined to follow his lead. These, then, formed the Dominion Party, a resurrection in spirit of the old Unionists. At the other extreme, there were Nationalists, predominantly in the Cape, who, under the leadership of the unbending Dr Malan, saw Hertzog as abandoning the true cause and submitting to the corrupting embrace of the arch-imperialist, General Smuts. In reaction they formed the 'Purified' National Party (later to become the Herenigde [Re-united] Nasionale Party—not to be confused with the Herstigte [Re-constituted] Nasionale Party formed in 1969 by General Hertzog's son, Dr Albert Hertzog). It might be noted, in passing that the Dominionites and the Purified Nationalists were almost equally conservative on race issues although they were at opposite poles on status issues.

These parties, however, remained numerically unimportant. For the major part, politics during the period 1933–9 returned in some measure to the honeymoon days of 1910–12, the mainstream of both 'Boer' and 'Briton' finding a common political home in the United Party. There was nevertheless a strong contrast between the two periods; for one thing, it was General Hertzog, not General Botha, who was now Prime Minister, and for another, in so far as the mantle of conciliation had fallen on Smuts, it was the Hertzogite elements in the Party that Smuts was mostly called upon to conciliate. In the process, the United Party Government continued to move in the general direction set by the former National Party's administration. Three pieces of legislation illustrate this trend. The Status of the Union Act, 1934, affirmed (or reaffirmed) the sovereignty of the South African Parliament. The Representation of Natives Act, 1936 (see Chapter 1 below), projected Hertzog's segregationist policies into the constitutional arena by removing African (i.e. 'Native') voters from the common roll in the Cape and substituting instead a minimal form of separate representation. Thirdly, the Native Trust and Land Act, 1936, in demarcating the 'Native Reserves' in effect laid the foundations for the present Government's Bantustan policies. Reference to the Representation of Natives Act permits one to suggest parenthetically that the initial preoccupation of the National Party with the concept of status cast its thinking within that mould, so that when the direct 'status issues' were resolved the same cast of thought came to be extended to race issues. As a result, they too have come to be perceived as status issues, thus adding a further dimension of rigidity to race policies.

The outbreak of the Second World War shattered the unity of the United Party. General Hertzog's personal defeat in Parliament (see Chapter 2), and the subsequent resignation from the United Party of himself and his followers, created the opportunity for re-establishing Afrikaner unity within the National Party. But the Purified Nationalists under Malan had moved in the direction of a much narrower and a much more militant Afrikaner nationalism than had been the case under Hertzog. In consequence, in the end, the gulf between him and the new party proved too great to bridge and Hertzog retired from politics, a defeated man. His followers, under his former lieutenant, Havenga, formed themselves into the Afrikaner Party, in opposition to the Malanites. And other divisions arose: Pirow's 'New Order', the Ossewa Brandwag, the Greyshirts, all claimed their adherents, and Afrikanerdom was in patent disarray. Nevertheless, despite the conflicts and the confusion, the binding conviction persisted that Afrikaners *should* be united, that there was, indeed, deeply embedded in their 'soul' a fundamental unity that called out for political expression. The importance of the 1943 election is that in it Malan's Herenigde Nasionale Party established its credentials as the Afrikaner body that provided that expression. The subsequent task of the National Party was to bring all straying Afrikaners within the fold of National Afrikanerdom. Since the Afrikaners form approximately 58% of South Africa's white population success in that endeavour would inevitably bring as well success at the polls. And so, indeed, it has proved.

The period covered by this book is the period, then, in which National Afrikanerdom established its political hegemony in South Africa. The symbol of its success was the establishment of the Republic of South Africa on 31 May 1961. The referendum in 1960 that provided Parliament with its mandate for that act is, therefore, a central part of the story, and Chapter 6 is concerned with it.

On the other hand, while this is the dominant theme of the period, it is by no means the only one. Given the cultural diversities, or more accurately cleavages, in South African society, almost any period of South African history, and ours is no exception, may be viewed in terms of action, interaction, and reaction. And this applies not only to the relationships between groups, but also to that between the various facets of public life, such as politics and economics. Any analysis of South African society must, if it is to be successful, be correspondingly complex and subtle. This book, however, does not attempt such an analysis although it may provide much of the material for one. What it does set out to do is to provide insights, firstly, into the relevant (as defined by contemporary perceptions) environing circumstances of each election, secondly, to present the major issues of each campaign and the various parties' respective positions on them, and thirdly to examine the voters' responses to these issues and policies. The triad of action, interaction, and reaction is, indeed, brought into play, but the elements involved are events, party policies, and voter response.

In order to facilitate cross-reference, each chapter broadly, but not slavishly, follows the same pattern. The material establishes the format, not vice versa. Consequently, where it seems appropriate, the pattern has been modified. Again, I have attempted to keep the chapters to approximately the same length; but the attempt had to be abandoned in the chapter dealing with the 1970 election. There are several justifications for this: as the most recent general election it commands the most interest and therefore demands a rather more detailed treatment; moreover, and more important, it publicly exposed for the first time since 1943 the divisions within Afrikanerdom itself. Since Afrikaner solidarity, as exhibited in the intervening years, has rested upon (*a*) a common Afrikaner mythology, (*b*) a homogeneous ideology, and (*c*) an integrated institutional structure, and since the events of 1968–70 threatened each one of these supports, their implications for the future of politics in South Africa are far-reaching, perhaps crucial. From this point of view, Chapter 9, which deals with these events, is, indeed, too brief.

If the above paragraph may be construed as an apology to the general reader, perhaps another is due to a specific class of potential readers. South African political terminology has a number of idiosyncrasies, and many terms are politically loaded. Even the term 'Afrikaans-speaking South African' (as against 'Afrikaner') has come to have political overtones. I myself use 'Afrikaans-speaking South Africans' and 'Afrikaners' interchangeably; and when I wish to refer to those who are in the political and cultural mainstream (members and supporters of the National Party, members of the Dutch Reformed Church, supporters of the Broederbond, and members of at least one of the cultural organizations, be it the Rapportryers or the Afrikaans Taal- en Kultuurvereniging or whatever), I refer to them as 'national-minded Afrikaners' (a translation of '*nasionaal-gesind*'), and to that group collectively as 'National Afrikanerdom'. But that is not the subject of my apology. The apology grows out of the problem of how to refer to Africans, Coloureds, and Asians collectively. The term I have used is the traditional South African term, and one which was generally acceptable to the groups themselves during the period covered in this book: 'non-whites'. More lately, however, at least certain sections of these groups have adopted as their chosen self-appellation the term 'Blacks', and certain newspapers (e.g. the *Rand Daily Mail*) and associations (e.g. the South African Institute of Race Relations) have followed their lead. It is not clear to what extent this is a preference that extends beyond the élites (e.g. the South African Student Organization, representing black students) that have been articulate in voicing the demand, so that acting in accordance with their preference may well offend others. There is a real dilemma here; and I have, perhaps, taken the easy way out in adopting the position that I have stated. It is not intended to imply a *political* position on the question.

In general, indeed, I try in this book to avoid taking political positions. That is not to say that I do not have one, or that I expect my political preferences not to show; but if I express opinions on and criticisms of certain policies from time to time, my main object is to present the facts as fairly as possible.

There is one other politically contentious issue on which I have had to make a decision. Throughout this study I have excluded South West Africa from my analysis of results, although South West Africa has been represented by six representatives in the House of Assembly since 1950. This exclusion is primarily based on the fact that both in terms of international law and in terms of South African law, whatever else the status of that territory is, it is not part of the territory of the Republic of South Africa: it is a distinct juridical unit. In consequence, the inclusion of South West Africa would, in my view, require more stringent justification than its exclusion. That was the argument that was decisive to my mind; but two subsidiary points support it. In the first place, South West Africa has for the greater part lain outside the mainstreams of South African history and politics, and the interplay of party and voting in that territory really requires separate examination (something, incidentally, which it has not yet received). In the second place, since it was not given Parliamentary representation until well into our period of study, its inclusion from that stage would diminish to some extent the comparability of results over the whole period.

With regard to the statistical analysis of the results, I have been confronted with two major problems. The first arises from the periodic redelimitation of constituencies. Four delimitation commissions sat in the period under review, and in each case constituency boundaries were redrawn, new constituencies were created, and old ones disappeared. As a result, it becomes impossible to follow through the support given to the respective parties in specific constituencies for the whole period. To compensate for this difficulty I use rather larger areas as the basis of comparison. Following the divisions contained in the official publication of results in the *Official Yearbook of the Union*, No. 30, 1960, I divide the Cape Province into four regions (Cape Town, Port Elizabeth, Border, Rest of Cape), the Transvaal also into four regions (Johannesburg, Witwatersrand, Pretoria, Rest of Transvaal), Natal into two (Durban–Pietermaritzburg, and Rest of Natal), but the Orange Free State I have retained as a single region. This categorization of regions approximates very roughly, but still for our purposes sufficiently, to the distinction between urban and rural areas. It is only a rough approximation, because there are urban centres of relatively substantial size, particularly in the Rest of Transvaal and in the Orange Free State. On the other hand, the towns in these areas do tend to take on the socio-cultural coloration of their surrounding rural environments; moreover, as we shall see, the divisions do produce distinctively different patterns of voter response.

In spite of the difficulty noted above with respect to changing constituency boundaries, I do make use of the 'swing' as an index of change of voter response, with respect to specific constituencies as well as with respect to aggregated totals. But I do so with caution, and I am careful to explain in each chapter the extent to which the calculation is possible for the election concerned. I might add that

I use the term 'swing' irrespective of the direction of change: for example, continued, but increased, support for the National Party is described as a continuing swing towards the National Party. An instance, taken at random, should make this procedure clear. In 1948 in the seat of Pretoria West, the National Party gained 50,3% of the votes cast, and the United Party 48,7%. In 1953 the National Party won 57,2% of the votes and the United Party 42,0%. The National Party gain, therefore, was 6,9% and the United Party loss 6,7%, which, averaging these two figures, means a continued swing to the National Party of 6,8%. (In 1948, it might be added, there had been an 11,2% swing to the National Party.)

The second major problem bearing on the comparison of election results arises from the fact that in every election a number of candidates are returned unopposed. Since the seats in which this happens, as well as the number of seats affected, vary from election to election, gross voting figures provide only a poor basis for comparison. In each election, therefore, I attempt to make allowances for these uncontested seats in projecting the *total* estimated vote for the respective parties. In making these allowances, I do not follow the same procedure throughout (in particular, there is a major departure in dealing with the 1961 election), because the procedure most generally used is not always the most appropriate in particular circumstances. Unless otherwise stated in the text, the general method used takes into account with respect to a given election the following factors: The number of registered voters in the constituency, the average per cent poll in the region in which the constituency is situated, the average percentage of spoilt papers in the relevant region, the percentage of the vote that went to the respective parties in the constituency concerned in the general election nearest in time to the one under examination, and the average swing in the relevant region for the period between those two elections.

Finally I come to the pleasant task of thanking those who have helped me in one form or another in this undertaking. Their number is legion, and some indeed in casual conversations have assisted me unawares. In particular, however, I would thank Professors Edgar Brookes, Jeffrey Horton, and Mark Prestwich, all of the University of Natal, and Professor Gwendolen Carter of Northwestern University for their helpful comments and encouragement, indeed for their assistance in a variety of ways. I am also deeply grateful to those members and officials of all the major parties who have given me generously of their time, granting me extended interviews and providing me with much useful material. Since some wished to remain anonymous, perhaps it would be invidious to mention any by name, but I am deeply appreciative of their help even if they are left unnamed. I can, however, mention Mr M. Collins of Microfile (Pty) Ltd, Johannesburg, and Mr G. J. van Rensburg, Librarian of *Die Burger*, Cape Town, both of whom helped me in their various ways with a courtesy and friendliness that equalled their generosity, and I thank them most sincerely.

I am particularly grateful to Canada Council for the award of a research grant that enabled me to return to South Africa for the collection of essential material, and also to Dalhousie University for the grant from its Research and Development Fund to meet secretarial costs. Mr Jim Oliver, a graduate student in the Political Science Department, Dalhousie University, ably served as my research assistant in connection with part of my work, and I would thank him for that and wish him well in his career. I would also thank Mrs R. Serfontein who ably and cheerfully typed part of my manuscript, and, especially, Miss Joan Connolly who bore the brunt of the typing work, not only for the high level of professional skill that she brought to the task and the assistance she gave me in other more tedious tasks, but also for remaining a very good friend through all the stresses and strains unfortunately associated with working with me over an extended period of time.

1

The Rules of the Game: Who Plays, How, Where, and When?

FRANCHISE

The question of the franchise was at the time of the National Convention (1908–9) a critical one. In the first place, and in the most fundamental sense, it established the foundation for all subsequent politics in South Africa; and in the second place, and more immediately, it was an issue that nearly produced a deadlock in the Convention, and that, in turn, might have deferred indefinitely the establishment of the Union of South Africa. Prior to Union, of the four colonies the Cape Colony was the only one that had a franchise that approximated to a multiracial one, in that a common qualification was laid down applying to all male British subjects regardless of race or colour. In Natal, under a franchise law that imposed more stringent qualifications, there were a few, but not very many, Africans and other non-whites who were entitled to the vote. The Transvaal and the Orange River Colony (as it then was) rigidly restricted the vote to whites. The final compromise reached at the National Convention was incorporated in the South Africa Act in sections 35, 36, and 152. In effect, it placed the political future of all citizens other than the whites in the hands of the white voters. By enacting that the qualifications existing in the colonies prior to Union should continue in effect after Union,[1] and by further providing that Parliament, as elected on that basis, might by law prescribe the qualifications for the vote,[2] it ensured that additions of non-white voters to the voters' list would occur only if the predominantly white electorate agreed.

Those non-white voters who were already, or who would become, qualified to vote under the Cape and Natal franchise laws, would, of course, under these provisions continue to enjoy that entitlement. And indeed, on the insistence of the Cape delegates to the Convention, they were given some constitutional protection in the enjoyment of their rights. Section 35(1) provided that no person in the Cape 'who is or may become capable of being registered as a voter' could be disqualified unless by an Act passed at its third reading by a two-thirds majority of the total membership of both Houses of

Parliament sitting together. And section 35(2) provided further and generally that no person who at the time of the passing of 'any such law' was registered as a voter might be removed from the register on grounds of race or colour only. Section 152, finally, prescribed that section 35 (and section 137, establishing the equal status of both official languages) might be amended or repealed only in accordance with the procedures as described in section 35(1). These sections, then, did offer some protection against disfranchisement on racial grounds. Nevertheless it was not an absolute protection and, in view of the composition of Parliament, it was one which could be, and subsequently was, rendered ineffectual; for there were more than enough members coming from exclusively white seats to satisfy the two-thirds majority requirement.

Parliament has exercised its powers with respect to the franchise on several occasions. On each occasion that the law was changed for white voters it involved an extension of voting rights; on each occasion, with one partial exception,[3] that it was changed for non-whites it involved a contraction, a restriction, or even a total withdrawal. In 1930 the vote was extended to all European women over the age of twenty-one, without any qualification requirements.[4] This Act had the effect, of course, of relatively depreciating the voting strength of African and Coloured voters, particularly in the Cape. It created a further anomaly in that males in the Cape and Natal still had to meet the stipulated qualifications before they could vote. To overcome this anomaly the law was changed in the following year, removing these qualifications for white male voters.[5] In that the qualifications were retained for non-white voters, this Act, again, involved a relative loss in the voting strength of non-whites and consequently was, in a negative sense, discriminatory.

The Cape franchise, implying, as it ultimately did, an integrationist approach to race relations, had never really won the acceptance of the northern Nationalists. General Hertzog, the first Nationalist Prime Minister, made his first attempt to introduce a separate system of representation for Africans in the Cape in 1926, his second year of office. He failed, however, to gain the necessary two-thirds majority. Again he tried in 1929, and again he failed. In 1936, however, now at the head of a United Party Government, he finally secured the passage of the Representation of Natives Act[6] in accordance with the procedures prescribed in sections 35(1) and 152 of the South Africa Act. This Act resulted in the removal of Africans in the Cape from the common voters' roll and in the creation of a separate voters' roll for them for the election of three white 'Natives' Representatives'.[7] The abortive exception to the general process of restricting the voting rights of non-whites in the Union was, as noted above, the Asiatic Land Tenure and Indian Representation Act, No. 28 of 1946, which *inter alia* provided for the election of three members of Parliament by Indians voting on a separate roll. This provision was, however, boycotted by the Indians and was repealed by the Malan Government in 1948 without having been put into effect. The concept of separate representation in Parliament was finally applied to the Cape Coloured voters in the Separate Representation of Voters Act, No. 46 of 1951, which provoked the constitutional storm briefly described in Chapter 4, and which required the passage of the South Africa Act Amendment Act, No. 9 of 1956, in order to revalidate it. In terms of this Act, the Coloured voters in the Cape were removed from the common roll and placed on a separate register for the purpose of electing four members to the House of Assembly and two provincial councillors.

In 1959 a new turn was given to the Nationalist ideology of *apartheid*; for in that year the principle of separate representation for non-whites (other than Asians) was jettisoned in favour of a system of separate political structures. The Act embodying this new concept was the Promotion of Bantu Self-Government Act, No. 46 of 1959, which laid the foundations for the system of Bantustans, and which at the same time abolished the system of Natives' representatives in Parliament. This principle was extended to Indians, although in considerably modified form, with the creation of the National Indian Council in 1964, and to Coloureds with the passage of the Coloured Persons' Representative Council Act, No. 49 of 1964. From the time that this last Act was passed, the fate of the system of separate representation of Coloureds in Parliament was virtually sealed. The quietus to this system was finally given in the Separate Representation of Voteıs Amendment Act, No. 50 of 1968, which provided that no further Coloureds' representatives would be elected to the Assembly or to the Cape Provincial Council.

Meanwhile two Acts had further enhanced the voting strength of whites. In 1949 the white voters of South West Africa, in spite of the fact that that territory was not legally part of the territory of the Union, were given the right to elect six members to the House of Assembly.[8] And in 1958 the voting age for whites (and only for whites) was reduced from twenty-one to eighteen years.[9]

The effects of these Acts on the composition of the general register of voters is shown in Table 1.

COMPOSITION OF THE HOUSE OF ASSEMBLY

According to the original provisions of the South Africa Act, the House of Assembly when it first met was to consist of 121 members elected by a plurality of votes in single-member constituencies.

Table 1

REGISTERED VOTERS ACCORDING TO RACE, 1909–65[1]

	CAPE				NATAL				TRANSVAAL	O.F.S.
Year	*White*	*African*	*Asian*	*Coloured*	*White*	*African*	*Asian*	*Coloured*	*White*	*White*
1909	121 336	6 637	783	13 611	29 259[3]		186[3]		97 772[4]	38 261[4]
1921	156 501	14 282	2 429	24 361	34 041	2	45	389	140 583[5]	47 481[5]
1929	167 184	15 780	1 737	23 881	42 584	1	16	329	151 604	49 357
1931	352 658	12 271	1 680	24 698	87 671	1	15	326	311 466	98 384
1935	382 103	10 628	1 401	23 392	91 762	1	10	343	349 400	101 089
1937	396 237	—	1 462	25 238	98 026	1	8	333	391 850	105 413
1945	493 910	—	1 849	52 285	126 427	1	2	787	584 929	119 257
1948	515 041	—	—	47 329[2]	138 458	—	—	1 163	628 355	121 827
1953	547 078	—	—	47 677[2]	164 852	—	—	1 337	711 045	137 880
1958	530 286	—	—	—	167 167	—	—	660	706 983	140 815
1960	591 298	—	—	—	193 103	—	—	—[6]	818 047	160 843
1965	596 017	—	—	—	203 814	—	—	—[6]	875 245	165 454

Notes: [1] These figures are compiled from *Official Yearbooks of the Union* (No. 26—1950; No. 29—1956–7; No. 30—1960), and from the *Government Gazette Extraordinary*, Vol. 19, No. 1364, 7 February 1966.
[2] These figures include Asians.
[3] These figures are for 1911. Non-white voters were then not differentiated according to race.
[4] These figures are for 1908–9.
[5] These figures are for 1919.
[6] Such Coloured voters as remained in Natal were not separately counted.

It further distributed the membership among the provinces on an arbitrary basis as follows: the Cape 51, the Transvaal 36, and Natal and the O.F.S. each 17. The Act, however, also provided that as from 1911 a census should be taken every five years, and as the population increased so the membership of the Assembly should be expanded, subject to the proviso that the representation of no province should be increased until the increase in its adult white male population entitled it to additional seats.

Two points in these arrangements deserve comment. In the first place, in terms of population the two smaller provinces were over-represented. This was clearly a political compromise intended to allay their fears of domination by the two larger provinces; but it also intended that this should be a transitional arrangement with the two larger provinces as the major beneficiaries of the increased membership that would follow their growth in population. Once the total membership reached the stipulated maximum of 150, the allocation of seats to the respective provinces would be strictly pro rata to its adult white male population; and then, and only then, could decreases occur in the representation of the smaller provinces. A further change in the law in 1952 provided that the census might be taken at intervals of up to ten years.[10]

The second noteworthy point is that although, as we have seen, the franchise in the Cape included non-whites, the basis for allocating seats was the number of white adult male population, not the total number of voters. In consequence, in terms of its share of total *voters*, the Cape was, and continued until 1958 to be, under-represented. This remained true even after the Electoral Laws Amendment Act, 1952, shifted the basis of calculation to voters rather than population, for only *white* voters were to count for this purpose.

The first major change in the membership of the Assembly took place in 1936 with the passing of the Representation of Natives Act, already referred to, which added three members to represent the Africans of the Cape. As the number of members had by then already reached 150, the Assembly thereafter increased its size to 153. In 1949, this number was increased again to 159, with the addition of six members to represent the white voters of South West Africa, resulting, it might be noted, in a spectacular over-representation of those voters. Consequent to the revalidation of the Separate Representation of Voters Act in 1956, four more members were added to represent the Coloured voters of the Cape. But three years later again the Promotion of Bantu Self-Government Act abolished the system of Natives' representatives—a fate that in turn befell the Coloureds' representatives in 1968.

Meanwhile in 1965 a major revision in the composition of the Assembly had taken place. This took the form of an amendment to section 42 of the Republic of South Africa Constitution Act, 1961.[11] According to this amendment, the ordinary membership of the Assembly (i.e. excluding South West Africa's and Coloureds' representatives) was increased from 150 to 160. Perhaps even more far-reaching changes were those relating to the distribution and size of seats, as will be seen in the next section.

The changing structure of the House of Assembly as it has been briefly outlined is shown more clearly in Table 2.

Table 2

REPRESENTATION IN THE HOUSE OF ASSEMBLY

Years	*Cape*	*Natal*	*Transvaal*	*O.F.S.*	*Natives' Reps.*	*Coloureds' Reps.*	*S.W.A.*	*Total*
1910–15 .	51	17	36	17	—	—	—	121
1915–19 .	51	17	45	17	—	—	—	130
1920–24 .	51	17	49	17	—	—	—	134
1924–29 .	51	17	50	17	—	—	—	135
1929–33 .	58	17	55	18	—	—	—	148
1933–38 .	61	16	57	16	3	—	—	153
1938–43 .	59	16	60	15	3	—	—	153
1944–48 .	56	16	64	14	3	—	—	153
1948–53 .	55	16	66	13	3	—	6	159
1953–58 .	54	15	68	13	3	—	6	159
1958–61 .	52	16	68	14	3	4	6	163
1961–66 .	52	16	68	14	—	4	6	160
1966–70 .	54	18	73	15	—	4	6	170
1970– . .	54	18	73	15	—	—	6	166

This table, taken together with Table 1, clearly exhibits the growth of the Transvaal ascendancy in South Africa's political life, particularly since World War II. Nor are there any signs to indicate that this trend will do anything but continue. This trend indeed reflects the demographic consequences of the Transvaal's, and particularly the Witwatersrand's, role as the economic growth centre of South Africa. Table 3 serves to demonstrate this in terms of the white population only, although the trend is not confined to whites. In 1911, for example, there were approximately one and a half million Africans living in the Cape compared with one and a quarter million in the Transvaal. By 1960 the African population in the Cape had

Table 3

GROWTH OF THE WHITE POPULATION PER PROVINCE, 1911–70
(in 000's)

Year	*Cape*	*Natal*	*Transvaal*	*O.F.S.*	*S.A.*
1911 . .	582	98	421	175	1 276
1921 . .	651	137	545	189	1 521
1936 . .	791	191	821	201	2 003
1946 . .	870	237	1 063	202	2 372
1951 . .	935	274	1 205	228	2 642
1960 . .	1 001	337	1 466	276	3 080
1970 . .	1 102	442	1 890	296	3 751

grown to just over three million (an increase of 98%), while in the Transvaal it had risen to over four and a half million (or a 280% increase).

THE DELIMITATION OF CONSTITUENCY BOUNDARIES

By the beginning of the period covered by this study, the membership of the House of Assembly, as far as the ordinary members were concerned, had reached its prescribed maximum of 150. Accordingly, the allocation of seats to the various provinces was no longer subject to special provisions designed to 'protect' the smaller provinces. Basically the system of allocation and delimitation was as laid down in the South Africa Act (sections 39 to 43), as amended by the Electoral Laws Amendment Acts of 1940, 1946, and 1952.[12]

The responsibility for the delimitation of constituencies was placed in the hands of a judicial commission, referred to as the delimitation commission, which since the establishment of Union has been appointed by the Governor-General and since 1961 by the State President.[13] As we have already seen, the distribution of seats was related to white population, and the basis on which the delimitation commission has worked has been the census, which up to 1952 was to be taken every five years and since 1952 is taken at intervals of not less than five and not more than ten years. The intervals at which delimitation commissions are to be appointed has consequently been similarly altered. It was as a result of this change that the constituencies as determined by the Twelfth Delimitation Commission in 1965 remained the same in both the 1966 and 1970 general elections.

(i) *Delimitation system prior to 1965.* Before 1965 the work of the delimitation commission was carried out in two phases. The first determined the number of seats per province, and this was done on a strictly arithmetical basis. The commission was required

> . . . [to] divide each province of the Union [Republic] into so many electoral divisions that their number bears, as nearly as possible, the same ratio to one hundred and fifty as, in terms of the current voters' lists, duly corrected up to the latest possible date, the number of white voters in the province in question bears to the total number of white voters in the Union.[14]

It should, parenthetically, be re-emphasized that a province's share of the seats in the Assembly depended on the number of *white* voters in that province, and until the Coloured voters in the Cape were removed from the common roll, this resulted in a relative depreciation not only of their vote but also of the voting strength of the Cape as a whole.

At all events, to clarify this part of the commission's work, we may express it in the following formula:

$$\text{no. of seats in province} = \frac{150}{1} \times \frac{\text{no. of white voters in province}}{\text{total no. of white voters}}$$

Having obtained the number of seats in each province, the commission's next task was to divide the number of voters (in this case without specification as to race or colour) in the province by the number of seats allocated to it in the manner just described. This average number of voters per constituency is termed the provincial quota. The commission is then directed to divide the province into constituencies, each having 'a number of voters, as nearly as may be, equal to the quota of the province'.[15] Nevertheless, the Act having thus stressed the primacy of the principle of equality immediately proceeds to qualify the principle. The commission, in drawing the boundaries of constituencies, is *required* to give 'due consideration' to five further principles:

(*a*) community or diversity of interests;
(*b*) means of communication;
(*c*) physical features;
(*d*) existing electoral boundaries;
(*e*) sparsity or density of population.[16]

Under these considerations, the commissioners may then 'whenever they deem it necessary' depart from the quota by increasing or decreasing the number of voters in a constituency but by no more than 15% of the quota. This provision therefore allows a maximum variation of 30% of the quota at the time of the delimitation. This is the system generally referred to in South Africa as the 'loading' and 'unloading' of seats.

Opposing views have been expressed on the merits of this system. There are those, for example, who have argued in effect that the fifth factor (sparsity or density of population) makes it mandatory that sparsely populated areas be unloaded and densely populated areas be loaded. The Ninth Delimitation Commission disposed of any such notion in these words:

> . . . the grant of an unload or the imposition of a load is, in the view of the Commission, not a right but merely a means entrusted to the Commissioners' discretion of giving effect to one or a combination of more or all of the five specifically mentioned factors.[17]

Perhaps the most impressive attack on the system of loading and unloading constituencies, and particularly on the general practice of loading urban and unloading rural constituencies, was the submission made by Mr Arthur Suzman, Q.C., to the Tenth Delimitation Commission on behalf of the Torch Commando. The Commission, however, remained unimpressed:

The line taken in the document and the whole argument amounted to this that sparsity and density of the population were the only reasons for loading and unloading by previous commissions. . . . There is no justification for this contention of the Torch Commando.[18]

Earlier in its report the Commission had prepared the ground for this rebuttal by asserting, 'In loading and unloading the various constituencies in the Union your Commission took into account all the factors referred to in section *forty* (3).'[19] The Tenth Commission, in making this assertion, was undoubtedly gilding the lily; the correct interpretation of the Act was that given by the Ninth Delimitation Commission in the passage cited. One would think indeed that it would be rare that *all* the factors were relevant to a constituency's boundaries.

There can be little doubt, however, that the general practice has been to load urban and unload rural constituencies. Other factors may have been present; but sparsity or density of population has been a constant factor. The Tenth Delimitation Commission itself at one point tacitly admitted this when it wrote: 'where a province has an equal number of densely and sparsely populated electoral divisions, it is easier to effect the *desired* loadings and unloadings. . . .'[20] Perhaps the last word (especially as it confirms what has been said) may be allowed the last commission to report up to the time of writing:

. . . there can be no question of a law of the Medes and the Persians concerning the extent of loading and unloading of each particular electoral division or type of electoral division. Since the factor 'sparsity or density of population' must, like all the other factors, be taken into due account, the result is—and previous delimitation commissions assumed this point of view—that densely populated electoral divisions have to be loaded and sparsely populated electoral divisions unloaded. The extent of loading and unloading depends on the circumstances of each particular electoral division.[21]

The general effect of the system, of course, is to increase the representation of the rural areas at the expense of the urban areas. Since, moreover, there is always a time-lag between the compilation of the register of voters as used by the commission and the following general election(s), some shifts in population as well as additions to and deletions from the register occur. Consequently, the differences in size in constituencies have tended to be much greater at the time of elections than those allowed for by the delimitation commission. This is manifest from the figures given in Table 4.

Table 4

VARIATIONS IN SIZES OF CONSTITUENCIES, 1943–70[1]

Province	*Year*	*Quota*	*Maximum*	*Minimum*	*Actual*[2] *largest*	*Actual*[2] *smallest*
Cape . .	1943	8 905	10 241	7 569	11 468	7 225
	1948	8 508	10 954	8 082	12 464	8 412
	1953	11 132	12 802	9 462	12 877	9 395
	1958	9 949	11 441	8 457	12 052	8 490
	1961	9 949	11 441	8 457	14 953	9 100
	1966	11 503	13 228	9 778	14 239	9 709
	1970	11 503	13 228	9 778	17 244	9 753
Transvaal .	1943	7 515	8 642	6 388	12 277	6 857
	1948	8 402	9 662	7 142	13 355	7 620
	1953	10 477	12 049	8 905	12 023	9 228
	1958	10 026	11 530	8 522	12 163	8 535
	1961	10 026	11 530	8 522	16 119	9 061
	1966	11 503	13 228	9 778	14 305	9 702
	1970	11 503	13 228	9 778	19 019	9 530
Natal . .	1943	7 956	9 149	6 763	9 930	6 382
	1948	8 769	10 084	7 454	10 058	7 290
	1953	10 193	11 721	8 665	11 867	9 020
	1958	10 009	11 510	8 508	11 658	8 803
	1961	10 009	11 510	8 508	13 621	9 768
	1966	11 503	13 228	9 778	13 393	9 908
	1970	11 503	13 228	9 778	18 220	11 007
O.F.S. . .	1943	7 846	9 023	6 669	9 557	7 480
	1948	8 909	10 245	7 573	11 268	8 393
	1953	10 509	12 085	8 933	12 330	9 299
	1958	9 754	11 217	8 291	11 737	8 711
	1961	9 754	11 217	8 291	15 904	11 133
	1966	11 503	13 228	9 778	13 518	9 716
	1970	11 503	13 228	9 778	16 236	9 81[illegible]

Notes: [1] The figures for the quotas and for the maxima and minima are taken from the reports of the relevant delimitation commissions. The maxima and minima figures refer to the maximum and minimum number of voters permissible in terms of the 15% load and unload respectively. In 1966 the quota was fixed for the Republic as a whole; hence the figures in the 'Quota', 'Maximum', and 'Minimum' columns are constant for all provinces in both 1966 and 1970.

[2] The figures in the last columns are taken from the official election returns. They include the electorates for uncontested seats except for the 1961 figures, since the official returns for that year did not provide updated numbers of registered voters in the uncontested seats. The 'smallest' constituencies for 1966 and 1970 do not include the special rural constituencies that were allowed an unload of up to 30%.

It will be noticed that, for reasons already discussed, there was considerable variation in the size of the quota from province to province. In 1943, for example, the largest provincial quota (in the Cape) exceeded the smallest (in the Transvaal) by 18,5%. In 1948 the difference was 13,2%; in 1953 it was 9,2%; but in 1958 it fell to a difference of 2,8%. Particularly for the years 1943–53 this resulted in an even greater discrepancy for the Union as a whole between the largest and smallest constituencies; and again this discrepancy was magnified by the time the elections took place. Table 5 provides illustration of this, as it shows the differences in size for the country as a whole at the time of the respective elections.

Table 5

DIFFERENCES BETWEEN LARGEST AND SMALLEST CONSTITUENCIES: S. AFRICA AS A WHOLE, 1943–70[1]

Year	(*a*) *Largest*	(*b*) *Smallest*	(*c*) *Difference*	(*d*) (*c*) *as % of* (*b*)
1943 . . .	12 277	6 382	5 895	92,4
1948 . . .	13 355	7 290	6 065	83,2
1953 . . .	12 877	9 020	3 857	42,8
1958 . . .	12 163	8 490	3 673	43,3
1961[2] . . .	16 119	9 061	7 058	77,9
1966 . . .	14 305	9 100	5 205	57,2
1970[2] . . .	19 019	9 530	9 489	99,6

Notes: [1] The figures under (*b*) for 1966 and 1970 again exclude the special rural constituencies. If these were included, columns (*b*) and (*d*) for 1966 and 1970 would be 8 383 and 70,6, and 7 997 and 137,8 respectively.

[2] It should be remembered that there were no new delimitations prior to the elections in these years.

Since the National Party has tended to enjoy a virtual monopoly of the rural areas apart from Natal and the Transkei, the relative over-representation of these areas has resulted in an over-representation of the National Party. This will be examined in more detail in the chapters that follow.

(ii) *The 1965 changes in the delimitation system.* Act No. 83 of 1965 introduced substantial changes in the law relating to the composition of the Assembly, and more particularly the system of delimitation. In the first place, it increased the number of 'ordinary' seats from 150 to 160, which, with the S.W.A. and Coloureds' seats added, resulted in a total membership of 170. This figure was, however, subsequently reduced by four when Act No. 50 of 1968, abolishing Coloured representation in Parliament, came into effect. The growth in the white population (as shown in Table 3) and hence in the number of white voters, no doubt justified this increase. It will be seen from Table 4 that even with this increase in the number of seats, the Republican quota in 1966 was still considerably larger than the largest provincial quota in 1958–61.

The second major change was the abandonment of the system of provincial quotas in favour of a single quota for the Republic as a whole. This was to be arrived at simply by dividing the total number of white voters in the Republic by 160. This change might be expected to reduce the gap in numbers between the largest and the smallest constituencies across the country. Nevertheless, as the figures for 1966, 1958, and 1953 show in Table 5, this expectation, if it existed, was not realized. Of rather deeper significance is the intention which some have alleged to exist behind this change. In the view of these critics the change represents a further step in the direction of the centralization of the political system by diminishing the status of the provinces in the representative structures. That there is such a centralizing trend in South African politics, and that this change is at least in line with that trend are hardly disputable. Nevertheless the practical effects of the change are mitigated by the requirement that every constituency should lie wholly within one province. In terms of the effect of the change on the actual work of the commission, the Twelfth Delimitation Commission summarized the change as follows:

> Contrary to the position at previous delimitations . . . the allocation of electoral divisions to the provinces is no longer determined by a purely mathematical calculation. Now the Republic has to be considered as a whole, and the number of electoral divisions allocated to each province in terms of the amended Act is actually a result of the delimitation of the Republic as a whole.[22]

As the system worked out in 1965–6, it was to the benefit of the Cape and the O.F.S., at the expense of the Transvaal. If the provinces had been allocated seats on the basis of the old system, the Cape would have had 52 seats and the O.F.S. 14 as against the 54 and 15 respectively that they actually were given; while the Transvaal would have had 76 as against the 73 it was allocated. Natal, on the other hand, would have remained unaltered at 18 seats.

The third major change in the Act was the addition of two further factors to the list of factors to which the Commission was required to give 'due consideration' in the delimitation of constituencies. These two factors were:

(*f*) probability of increase or decrease of population;
(*g*) local authority and magisterial district boundaries.[23]

With regard to the former of these two factors, the Commission had this to say:

> It stands to reason, and it was in fact in this way that your Commission interpreted this consideration, that where an area is developing rapidly it should contain fewer votes and where there is a decline in development the electoral division should be given more votes.[24]

What is not clear, however, from its report is the criteria used by the Commission in applying this principle or even what weight it carried with the Commission in determining particular constituency boundaries.

The second of the two additional factors was also one which the Commission, on its own admission, sometimes found difficult to apply, largely because magisterial boundaries and the existing electoral boundaries diverged, thus making it impossible to implement both principles at the same time. It would appear that in general the Commission tended to give existing electoral boundaries precedence over magisterial district boundaries; but it did recommend that the Departments of the Interior and of Justice should consult with one another in future alterations of boundaries.

The fourth important amendment provided that the number of voters in constituencies with an area of 10 000 square miles or more might be reduced to 8 000 or 70% of the quota, whichever was the greater. Since the quota for the Republic for 1966 (and 1970) as calculated by the Commission was 11 503 and 70% of that number is 8 052, in effect the Commission in these constituencies worked on the basis of a maximum unload of 30%. In the event, there were in 1965–6 ten constituencies in the Cape with areas of over 10 000 square miles, three in the Transvaal, and one in the O.F.S. It was at least in part in order to accommodate the relatively large number of constituencies in the Cape in this category with their heavy unloads that the Commission found it necessary to allocate 54 seats to the Cape.

DURATION OF PARLIAMENT

Under the South Africa Act (section 45) it was laid down that every House of Assembly 'shall continue for five years from the first meeting thereof, and no longer, but may be sooner dissolved by the Governor-General'. The maximum permitted life of a Parliament under this section could, of course, have been extended by an Act of Parliament in so far as this section could be amended by ordinary legislative procedures, but in fact it never has been. The constitution was silent, however, on what restraints, if any, operated in this area of the Governor-General's discretionary power.

The Republic of South Africa Constitution Act in section 47(1) repeats the old provision of the South Africa Act except for the substitution of 'State President' for 'Governor-General'. It does, however, go slightly further than the South Africa Act in delimiting the President's discretionary powers. In section 7(5), for example, it states that 'The constitutional conventions which existed immediately prior to the commencement of this Act shall not be affected by the provisions of this Act'. In section 16(1) it is stated that 'The executive government . . . is vested in the State President, acting on the advice of the Executive Council', and subsection (2) of the same section states: 'Save where otherwise expressly stated or necessarily implied, any reference in this Act to the State President shall be deemed to be a reference to the State President acting on the advice of the Executive Council.' Nevertheless in subsection (3) it is stated that the above two sections shall not apply *inter alia* to the dissolution of the House of Assembly and of the Senate. All this subsection states, of course, is that the State President is not bound by the advice of the Executive Council when it comes to dissolving Parliament. In this area, however, existing conventions apply. All one can say, at any rate briefly, on the subject is that there has been only one occasion when the Governor-General has refused a Prime Minister's request for a dissolution, and that was in the exceptional circumstances of 1939. In fact, of the fourteen Parliaments from 1910 to 1970 only five served for less than their full five-year term of office.

2

The General Election of 1943: The United Party Triumph

INTRODUCTION

The dominant issue of the 1943 election, dwarfing all others, was the issue of war or peace. South Africa's entry into the Second World War on 6 September 1939 had been determined by the slender majority in the House of Assembly of 13 votes out of a total of 147 votes cast. By that margin on 4 September had General Hertzog's 'neutrality' motion been rejected. The same evening Hertzog requested the Governor-General to dissolve Parliament in order that the electorate might itself pronounce upon the issue. The Governor-General, however, declined on the following grounds: that such an election would lead to great bitterness and possibly violence, that the House had given its decision and he saw no reason why he should revoke that decision, and that General Smuts should be in a position to form a government having the support of the House.[1]

Consequent to the Governor-General's refusal, Hertzog had no alternative but to resign. Smuts was, in fact, able to form a government in coalition with the Dominion and Labour parties, and, with the further support of the three Native Representatives, maintained a slender, but working, majority in both Houses. Nevertheless, the Opposition continued to argue that Smuts had committed the country to a war which had broken out purely as a result of treaty arrangements between Great Britain and Poland, in which the vital interests of the Union were not involved, and for which the Government had no mandate. Indeed, it was argued, had the issue been put to the people, they would probably have voted against it.

This was the controversy that still governed the debate in the 1943 elections, for now Smuts was asking the electorate to approve what the Government had done, to give it a further mandate for the prosecution of the war, and to strengthen its hand in the peace talks that were to come. That Smuts was able to talk in terms that looked forward to peace was due, of course, to the much more favourable turn of events in the war itself. By now the Allies were on the offensive, and the victory that in darker days had seemed so remote could now more plausibly be believed to be certain. The new tide of confidence swept not only the armed forces but the civilian population itself. This no doubt worked powerfully on the side of the Government, particularly since the electoral law had been amended to enable the soldiers serving outside the Union to vote.

The *gesuiwerdes*, or 'purified', Nationalists,[2] on the other hand, argued, as they had argued throughout, that South Africa's involvement in the war was contrary to her interests, and that the only way whereby South Africa might in the future avoid being dragged into 'England's wars' was to declare herself an independent republic. But with victory in sight, even if still only rather distant sight, this argument was robbed of much of its emotional appeal. And in so far as the appeal still applied, it was likely not to extend beyond those whose hearts were already pure. In the prevailing mood of the country it could hardly be expected to win converts.

THE CONTESTANTS

(*a*) *Major parties*

The issue between the United Party and the H.N.P. was, therefore, clear and clean-cut. In addition, of course, the election represented for them the first real trial of strength since the disintegration of the Fusion Government, and thus attention was also directed to the future; for it would give them some indication of their prospects in a post-war election. Moreover, as we shall see, the H.N.P. was determined to establish itself as the orthodox party of Afrikaner nationalism and to crush all rivals within that movement. Indeed, this was perhaps the H.N.P.'s primary electoral task. The known dispositions of strength, the favourable turn of events in the war, and the likelihood of strong support for the Government from the armed forces,[3] all tended to the conclusion that the Government would be returned with an increased majority. Not that this assessment of the situation resulted in, or required, a campaign aimed at the 'enemy within' rather than at the Government; on the contrary, it demanded that the H.N.P. attack the Government more vigorously than any other party or group. But it also required that the party, as far as possible, contest every seat contested by one of its rival claimants to the title of the true champion of Afrikanerdom.

The United Party strategy was also quite clear: to extend its political grip on the country as widely and as firmly as possible, so that it might demonstrate a nation-wide support for the war effort (and for this purpose votes were as important as seats) and so that it might advance its prospects of continued electoral victories when the war was over.

In the event, 132 out of the 150 ordinary constituencies (i.e. excluding those for the Native Representatives) were contested. Of the unopposed seats, 12 were in the Cape, 11 going to the United Party, and 1—the only unopposed Nationalist seat in the Union—to the H.N.P., that of Piketberg, the seat of Dr Malan, Leader of the H.N.P. and of the Opposition. In the Transvaal a further 5 United Party candidates were returned unopposed, and in Natal 1 Dominionite was also unopposed. In all, then, the United Party and its allies nominated candidates for every seat except Dr Malan's; and the United Party itself, besides its 16 unopposed candidates, had 115 candidates in the field. The H.N.P. for its part mustered 109 candidates in addition to Dr Malan; and while this meant that it left 40 seats without an official party candidate, it nevertheless represented a considerable effort for a party which in 1938 had secured only 27 seats, and which, prior to dissolution, had only 41 members in the House. By the extent of its effort the H.N.P. demonstrated the earnest of its intention to present itself to the electorate as an alternative government.

(*b*) *Minor parties and independents*

The 1943 elections were remarkable for the number of minor party and independent candidates. All together there were 85 such candidates seeking election. In consequence 43 constituencies[4] had three or more candidates—almost one-third of the total number of contested seats. In part, this situation reflected the splintered nature of the House prior to dissolution; for in that House had sat sixteen followers of Pirow's New Order, eight Dominionites, four Labour Party members, and two independents (one supporting the Government, and the other, the Opposition).[5]

The price which Smuts had paid for his coalition government was a 'standstill' electoral agreement with the Dominion Party and Labour Party respectively. He honoured this agreement by granting eight seats[6] to the Dominion Party: the Durban seats of Berea, Central, Musgrave, Point, and Umlazi; Pinetown; Pietermaritzburg District;[7] and East London North. With the Labour Party, however, Smuts went beyond the terms of the agreement and allocated five additional seats to it, giving it a total of nine seats: six in the Reef (Fordsburg, Mayfair, Benoni, Germiston, Krugersdorp, and South Rand), two in Natal (Durban North and Umbilo), and one in the Cape (East London City). What induced Smuts to this act of political generosity is not known; but it still left the Labour Party unsatisfied.

It was in the Durban–Pinetown–Pietermaritzburg complex of seats that the tensions of the coalition most clearly manifested themselves. The Dominion and Labour Parties were joined together in the coalition only through a common support for the war effort; for the rest, there was a radical difference in outlook. And in these seats, comfortably free from the possibility of affording any success to the H.N.P., they felt free to express these tensions. The Labour Party appears to have taken the initiative in contesting Dominionite seats, but the Dominionites were not slow in retaliating.[8] Originally, the Labour Party proposed to contest, in addition to the two seats allocated to it, the Dominionite seats of Durban Musgrave, Umlazi, Durban Central, Pinetown, and Pietermaritzburg District; but it later withdrew its candidates in the first two.[9] The Dominion Party, for its part, apart from an abortive intervention in Durban North, opposed the Labour Party only in Durban Umbilo.

Adding to what the *Natal Mercury* termed these 'unnecessary "dogfights" ' were seven independents in the nine seats contested in this region.[10] The United Party reacted to this situation by designating the candidate of the party which held the seat before the outbreak of war as the 'official Candidate', and by further asserting that a vote against an official candidate was a vote against the war effort.[11] However vehemently this was repeated, it was still not likely to persuade the voter while the opposing candidates remained undenounced by their respective party leaders, who, for their part, continued to sit, if not happily at least decorously, together in the Smuts Cabinet.

Of far greater and more enduring significance was the contest between the H.N.P. and its nationalist rivals.[12] Neither Pirow's New Order nor Van Rensburg's Ossewa Brandwag officially participated in the elections, but the loyal followers of Hertzog, Havenga's Afrikaner Party, entered hopefully into the contest. Throughout the Union it contested 22 seats, although it concentrated primarily on the Orange Free State and, to a lesser extent, the Transvaal. In the Free State it supported 13 candidates, in the Transvaal 8 (originally 11), and in the Cape 1 (in remote Kuruman).

As between the Afrikaner Party and the H.N.P., there was no electoral alliance, in the end because Malan just was not interested. And this of course placed the former at a serious disadvantage. The United Party was in effect the Government party, the H.N.P. the official Opposition—and each had to pit its strength against the other, opposing the other wherever there was any prospect of securing a substantial vote. Under these circumstances the H.N.P. was not likely to stand aside in order to allow the Afrikaner Party an opportunity to oppose the United Party in a straight fight, especially as it was determined to demonstrate its predominance over its younger rival. In consequence the Afrikaner Party was forced to appear as a 'third party' in every contest in which it took part; and it suffered the almost inevitable consequence.[13]

One other party contested the elections, and that was the Communist Party. It entered nine candidates, all in urban areas: three in Johannesburg constituencies and another in Springs, three in Cape Town constituencies, one in Durban Point, and one in East London North. No doubt it hoped to capitalize on the Russian successes in the war and the apparent amity between the Allies, and also on dissatisfaction in South Africa over food supplies. It achieved, as we shall see, some local successes as far as votes were concerned; but on the whole it made a negligible impression on the electorate.

Perhaps the most remarkable feature of this aspect of the election, however, was the very large number of independents. Altogether 38 independents were named on the ballot papers, although in fact 5 of these had previously withdrawn. Of the effective candidates, 9 stood in the Cape, 15 in the Transvaal, and 9 in Natal. Generally speaking, it is true to say that the independents tended to cluster in areas where Nationalist strength was particularly weak. This was true of all the Natal candidates, it was true of the Border area, where 5 independents stood in three constituencies, and it was broadly true of the Transvaal in that 6 out of the 13 Johannesburg seats were contested by independents. Nevertheless there were several exceptions to this general rule. There was, for example, an independent (admittedly no very strong contender: he polled just over 1 per cent of the votes) in the closely fought Paarl constituency; and in the Transvaal there were 6 independents (plus 4 who withdrew) in the rural constituencies.

These divergencies arose from the mixed nature of the candidates: some would fall in the category of 'cranks'; some were ex-party men who had been disappointed in the nomination contests;[14] others were party men in all but name;[15] and a substantial number were dissident Afrikaners not yet prepared to accept the claims of the H.N.P.[16]

THE TURN-OUT

With the war issue as the critical issue of the electoral campaign, the Government insisted that votes were just as important as seats. In other words the Government sought to treat the elections as much as a referendum as an election. It was therefore of paramount importance to 'bring out' the vote. The endeavour met with only moderate success. The total number of registered voters in the 132 contested seats was 1 114 110; and of these 885 623, or 79,5%, cast their vote.[17] At first sight this appears to be a more than reasonable turn-out; but on closer inspection it is much less impressive. As far as the overall percentage is concerned, the main depreciating factor is that, for a variety of reasons, the number of voters registered was probably significantly low. Consequently the percentage of those who were *qualified* to register who actually voted would have been clearly less than 79,5%.

Participation varied considerably, moreover, from province to province and from region to region, as Table 6 shows.

Table 6

PERCENTAGE POLL IN THE MAJOR REGIONS

Area	*Electorate*	*Votes Cast*	*% Poll*
Cape Town area	49 260	37 236	75,6
Port Elizabeth area	41 068	31 961	77,8
Border	28 617	19 174	67,0
Rest of Cape	279 674	237 957	85,1
Total Cape	398 619	326 328	81,9
Johannesburg	119 767	88 346	73,8
Witwatersrand	134 686	108 594	80,6
Pretoria	69 619	52 877	76,0
Rest of Transvaal	163 364	133 457	81,7
Total Transvaal	487 436	383 271	78,6
Durban–Pietermaritzburg	74 279	52 333	70,5
Rest of Natal	39 285	29 102	74,1
Total Natal	113 564	81 435	71,7
Total O.F.S.	114 491	94 589	82,6

What is particularly striking in the provincial figures is the low percentage poll in Natal, the most 'English' and loyalist of the provinces. That this was due not to apathy or indifference over the war issue but to the absence of any real excitement in the electoral contests is demonstrated first by the overwhelming support which Natal gave to the Government, and secondly by the particularly low poll in the constituencies where there were few or no Nationalists to vote against. This was indeed a general phenomenon throughout the Union.[18] With the rather odd exception of Pretoria, the regions in which relatively low polls were recorded were those in which the clash of party battle was most muted, with the Cape Border and the Durban–Pietermaritzburg regions the most notable examples. For the elector in 1943 it would seem that the appeal to treat the election as a referendum was at any rate partly disregarded. The contest in his own constituency was apparently far more significant in determining participation.

There was then a clear tendency for the percentage poll to vary according to whether the contest involved both major parties or not, and, although to a lesser extent, according to the closeness of the contest between those parties. There were, however, deviations from this tendency, and these bring to mind the existence of a further possible factor: the effectiveness of party organization. A comparison of the percentage poll in seats won by the Coalition with the percentage poll in seats won by the H.N.P. gives some support for this suggestion.

Table 7

A COMPARISON OF VOTER-PARTICIPATION ACCORDING TO PARTY WINNING THE SEAT

Region	*Coalition seats*	*H.N.P. seats*
Cape	79,8%	85,3%
Transvaal	78,4%	81,0%
Natal	71,7%	—
Orange Free State	80,9%[1]	82,9%
Union	77,8%	83,4%

Note: [1] 1 seat only.

THE RESULTS

(*a*) *In terms of seats*

The final election results were published on 30 July, 23 days after the elections had taken place.[19] They could hardly have been more satisfactory from the Government's point of view, generally exceeding the expectations even of the supporters of the Government.[20] Excluding the three Native Representatives, the Government forces now stood at: 89 United Party members, 9 Labour Party, 7 Dominion Party, and 2 independents. Against them the 43 H.N.P. members represented the total force of the Opposition. This gave the Government 71,3% of the seats, the Opposition only 28,7%; and where its majority had been only 20, it now had the enormous majority of 64, again not counting the three Native Representatives. Smuts happily claimed that the Government's action in 1939 'has now been overwhelmingly endorsed by the people in an almost two to one majority'.[21]

Table 8

PARTY DISTRIBUTION IN THE HOUSE OF ASSEMBLY AFTER THE 1943 ELECTION

Area	*Coalition Numbers*	%	*H.N.P.*	%
Cape Town area	13	100	0	0
Port Elizabeth area	5	100	0	0
Border area	5	100	0	0
Rest of Cape	14	42,4	19	57,6
Total Cape	37	66,1	19	33,9
Johannesburg area	17	94,4	1	5,6
Witwatersrand area	15	100	0	0
Pretoria area	6	75,0	2	25,0
Rest of Transvaal	15	65,2	8	34,8
Total Transvaal	53	82,8	11	17,2
Durban–Pietermaritzburg area	10	100	0	0
Rest of Natal	6	100	0	0
Total Natal	16	100	0	0
Total O.F.S.	1	7,1	13	92,8
Total Union	107	71,3	43	28,7

It will be seen from Table 8 that in six regions, including one province, and totalling in all 54 seats, the H.N.P. gained no representation at all. In the Transvaal rural areas it did less well than

Table 9

PARTY STRENGTHS ACCORDING TO SIZE OF CONSTITUENCY

	Cape		*Transvaal*		*Natal*		*O.F.S.*		*Union*	
	U.P./ L.P./ D.P.	H.N.P.	U.P./ L.P./ D.P.	H.N.P.	U.P./ L.P./ D.P.	H.N.P.	U.P./ L.P./ D.P.	H.N.P.	U.P./ L.P./ D.P.	H.N.P.
10 000 upwards .	18	—	3	—					21	—
9 000–9 999 .	11	4	19	2	3	—	1	1	30	7
8 000–8 999 .	8	11	15	1	5	—	—	8	36	20
7 000–7 999 .	4	4	12	5	1	—	—	4	17	13
6 000–6 999 .			4	3	7	—			11	3

expected, so that the United Party and its allies gained a firm grasp over the province. As far as the Cape as a whole was concerned, this was broadly true there as well, although the H.N.P. did gain a majority in the Cape rural areas. In Natal the Nationalists lost their only seat; but in the Orange Free State the H.N.P. advanced its position, winning every seat except Bloemfontein City.

In the Cape the United Party gained five seats from the Nationalists and one from the New Order, and in addition won two new seats, the Labour Party gained one seat, given to it by the United Party, and the H.N.P. gained one seat, Calvinia.

In the Transvaal the United Party won six new seats, and gained

Table 10

VOTES CAST IN CONTESTED SEATS, 1943

Area	*Reg. Voters*	*Votes Cast*	%	*Spoilt*	%	*U.P.*	%	*L.P.*	%
Cape									
(W.P.) . . .	49 260	37 236	75,6	446	1,2	25 720	69,1	—	
(P.E.) . . .	41 068	31 961	77,8	326	1,0	22 250	69,6	—	
(Border) . .	28 617	19 174	67,0	301	1,6	3 715	19,4	4 696	24,5
Rest of Cape. .	279 674	237 957	85,1	2 470	1,0	118 797	49,9	—	
Total Cape .	398 619	326 328	81,9	3 543	1,1	170 482	52,2	4 696	1,4
Transvaal									
Johannesburg .	119 767	88 346	73,8	1 005	1,1	58 095	65,8	7 617	8,6
Witwatersrand .	134 686	108 591	80,6	1 088	1,0	50 345	46,4	18 309	16,9
Pretoria . . .	69 619	52 877	76,0	393	0,7	31 356	59,3	—	
Rest of Transvaal	163 364	133 457	81,7	1 202	0,9	65 999	49,5	—	
Total Transvaal . . .	487 436	383 271	78,6	3 688	1,0	205 795	53,7	25 926	6,8
Natal									
Durban–Pietermaritzburg .	74 279	52 333	70,5	906	1,7	5 130	9,8	12 770	24,4
Rest of Natal .	39 285	29 102	74,1	334	1,1	16 295	56,0	—	
Total Natal .	113 564	81 435	71,7	1 240	1,5	21 422	26,3	12 770	15,7
O.F.S.									
Total . . .	114 491	94 589	82,6	889	0,9	33 472	35,4	—	
Total Union	1 114 110	885 623	79,5	9 360	1,1	431,171	48,7	43 392	4,9

(w/d) = withdrawn

seven seats from the New Order, one from the Nationalists, and one from the Afrikaner Party; Labour was given an additional seat, and won a seat from the Nationalists; and the H.N.P. won five former New Order seats and gained one from an independent.

The United Party gain of Vryheid in Natal was offset by the loss of Frankfort in the Orange Free State; and in that Province the H.N.P. further succeeded by capturing five Afrikaner Party seats.

The distribution of party seats can also be viewed in a different way—in terms of size of constituency (see Table 9).

This form of presentation becomes of rather greater significance in subsequent elections. Nevertheless even in 1943 it is of interest in demonstrating the pro-Government hold on the more populous constituencies.

These figures may be amplified by reference to the average electorate in constituencies won by the United Party and its allies and by the H.N.P. respectively. In the Cape the average Government seat was 9 391 as against the average H.N.P. seat of 8 580. In the Transvaal the corresponding figures were 8 416 and 7 590; in Natal all seats went to the Government candidates (average 7 571); and in the Orange Free State the single United Party seat was 9 246 against the H.N.P. average of 8 096. In short, it is clear that the United Party's predominance was most marked in the urban areas, and that the Nationalists' strength was mainly in the rural areas. And since the

D.P.	*%*	*H.N.P.*	*%*	*A.P.*	*%*	*Inds.*	*%*	*C.P.*	*%*
—		6 062	16,3	—		1 174	3,2	3 834	10,3
—		8 815	27,6	—		570	1,8	—	
5 743	30,0	—		—		4 375	22,8	344	1,8
—		112 654	47,3	238	0,1	3 798	1,6	—	
5 743	1,8	127 531	39,1	238	0,1	9 917	3,0	4 178	1,3
—		16 059	18,2	777	0,6	3 185	3,6	1 608	1,8
—		38 104	35,1	(w/d) 85	0,1	202	0,2	458	0,4
—		20 338	38,4	500	0,9	290	0,5	—	
—		57 134	42,8	2 095	1,6	7 027	5,3	—	
—		131 635	34,3	3 457	0,9	10 704	2,8	2 066	0,5
19 570	37,4	843	1,6	—		12 550	24,0	564	1,1
3 710	12,7	6 852	23,5	—		1 914	6,6	—	
23 280	28,6	7 695	9,4	—		14 464	17,8	564	0,7
—		49 459	52,3	10 769	11,4	—		—	
29 023	3,3	316 320	35,7	14 464	1,6	35 085	4,0	6 808	0,8

urban areas were loaded, and the rural areas generally unloaded, this meant that the United Party and its allies tended to win the larger constituencies, while the seats won by the H.N.P. tended to be below average in size. In all, throughout the Union, this gave the H.N.P. an advantage of 7,75%; but in the conditions of 1943 this was still not particularly significant.

(*b*) *The results in terms of votes*

The measurement of party strengths according to seats won, given the single-member system of constituencies, is at best crude, and can be, as we shall see, grossly misleading. It is far more accurate to look at the actual votes cast for the various parties, and at the percentages of the total poll which these votes represent. These figures are given in Table 10. It will be seen from the figures given there that the Nationalist strength was rather greater in the urban areas than is suggested by the figures given in Table 8. The most outstanding example is the Witwatersrand where the H.N.P. failed to gain even one of the 15 seats, although in that region it polled 35,1% of the votes.

Further comparison between seats won and votes cast reveals the same kind of exaggeration. Taking just the Coalition on the one hand, and the H.N.P. on the other, we find that in the Cape Province the Coalition candidates polled 55,4% of the votes, but gained 66,1% of the seats; while the H.N.P. polling 39,1% of the votes won only 33,9% of the seats. In the Transvaal the Coalition won 82,8% of the seats with 60,5% of the votes, while the H.N.P. gained only 17,2% of the seats with 34,3% of the votes. But in the Free State the United Party fared even worse, for there, although it gained 35,4% of the votes it won only 7,1% of the seats (i.e. one seat).

If seats won had been in direct proportion to votes cast, the results for each province and for the Union would have been as shown in Table 11.

Table 11

DISTRIBUTION OF SEATS PROPORTIONATE TO VOTES CAST
(Actual figures are given in brackets)

Region	*Government*	*H.N.P.*	*A.P.*
Cape	31 (37)	22 (19)[1]	—
Transvaal.	39 (53)	22 (11)[1]	—
Natal	15 (16)[2]	1 (—)	—
O.F.S..	5 (1)	7 (13)	2 (—)

Notes: [1] These figures are short of the provincial totals because independents are left out of account.
[2] The major independents are here, however, included.

The over-all difference is of a kind familiar to students of electoral systems; nor is it of such dimensions as to occasion particular comment. Nevertheless, within the total picture there were disturbing details. Two of these are apparent in the above figures: the Nationalists were grossly under-represented in the Transvaal in general, and the Witwatersrand in particular, as was the United Party in the O.F.S. But the rural areas both of the Cape and of the Transvaal also produced strange results. In the Cape rural areas, the H.N.P. won 19, or 57,6% of the seats, although it polled only 47,3% of the votes as against the 49,9% polled by the United Party. In the rural areas of the Transvaal, however, the situation was reversed. There the Government gained 15, or 65,2%, of the seats, with only 49,5% of the votes; while the H.N.P. was not much more than half as successful with 42,8% of the votes.

The true significance of these figures lay not so much in the light they shed on the deficiencies of the electoral system, as in the indication they gave, concealed though it was by the small number of seats won, of the considerable strength of the H.N.P. in all regions of the Transvaal except that of Johannesburg.

(*c*) *Minor parties and independents*

(i) *The Labour Party*

The effect of the 'standstill' agreements between the United Party and the Dominion and Labour Parties respectively was to cloud the assessment of the strengths of the minor parties. As we have seen, the Labour Party contested twelve seats; of these, nine had been allocated to it by General Smuts, and in the remaining three it intervened in order to fight the Dominion Party.

In every seat that the Labour Party opposed an official Government candidate it lost; its average percentage of the poll in these constituencies being only 32,3. Every seat, on the other hand, in which it officially represented the Coalition, it won; although in the single seat in which it provided the official candidate in a contest with the Dominion Party, its victory was gained with only 49,9% of the poll, an independent candidate having drawn off 9,3% of the vote. It was, however, uniformly successful in its contests with the H.N.P., its share of the vote here ranging from 51,8% in Mayfair (which was to be lost to the Nationalists in 1948) to 78,4% in Benoni. In these contests it is doubtful whether the fact that the candidates were members of the Labour Party rather than of the United Party had any bearing on the results.

(ii) *The Dominion Party*

The outstanding feature of the results as far as the Dominion Party is concerned is the defeat of its candidates in the officially allocated seats of Durban Berea and Durban Point by independent candidates. It is true that in Point its opponent was independent only in name, that he was both the sitting member and in fact a member of the United Party.[22] And in Berea the successful independent, J. R. Sullivan, was a man of high local standing whose proposals for 'Social Security' had gained considerable favourable publicity. Nevertheless, there is the suggestion in these two results that had the Dominion Party been opposed by the United Party it would hardly have repeated its successes of 1938. Indeed the split between Smuts and Hertzog and the entry of South Africa into the war in support of the Commonwealth had removed its *raison d'être*, and it is probable that a more flexible leader than Col. Stallard would by this time have sought a merger with the United Party. Although, therefore, the 29 023 votes cast for the Dominion Party amounted to 53,4% of the votes in the seats it contested, there was nothing in these results to suggest that they reflected approval for distinctively Dominionite policies.

(iii) *The Afrikaner Party*

The Afrikaner Party was the only party which made any significant attempt to establish itself as a 'third force' in South African politics. In all it had 22 candidates in the field (plus three who had withdrawn): one rather forlorn candidate in the Cape, the stronghold of Malan; 9 in the Transvaal; and 13 in the O.F.S. Deprived of the benefits of an electoral alliance, the Afrikaner Party candidates were everywhere involved in three-cornered fights.

These results decisively crushed any serious ambitions which the Party might have cherished. With a total poll of 14 300 in the 22 seats it contested, and an average percentage of 10,2% of the vote, its weakness was patent. Moreover, its candidates lost their deposits[23] in 10 of these seats; indeed, in constituencies outside the Free State, in 6 out of 9 seats. In every contest, even in Jeppe where there was also an independent candidate, the Afrikaner Party candidate was at the bottom of the poll. Only in the Orange Free State did it look even faintly respectable; but even there the best it could do was to gain 22,5% of the votes cast in Frankfort and in Hoopstad. Yet Frankfort, one of its two most successful attempts, perhaps most clearly demonstrated its lack of support; for its candidate here was Mr Havenga, Hertzog's 'heir', a veteran of the Anglo-Boer War, a Nationalist M.P. since 1915, and Minister of Finance from 1924 to September 1939. Not even Havenga could raise support for his party above little more than one-fifth of the votes polled in his constituency.

Yet, despite its general failure, the intervention of the Afrikaner Party was not without effect. In five of the seats it contested it occasioned minority victories: Pretoria District, Middelburg, Frankfort, Hoopstad, and Kroonstad. If we assume that all its supporters would otherwise have voted for the H.N.P., the Afrikaner Party 'let in' the United Party in Pretoria District and Middelburg; and, perhaps most galling of all to the H.N.P., the withdrawn candidate in Heidelberg still had 79 votes recorded against his name, and the United Party sidled in with a majority of 57.

The Afrikaner Party had come into existence as a result of the Nationalists' rejection of Hertzog; it represented a protest, a challenge to the H.N.P., and an expression of Hertzog's more temperate political ideals. Its defeat at the elections was, as Roberts and Trollip have said, 'smashing, total, definitive—the rebels against Malan's leadership had been simply annihilated'.[24] And they go on to comment:

> Meanwhile, Malan's long-term policy had attained its goal. The Hertzogites, the Pirowites, the O.B., had all challenged the claim of himself and the H.N.P. to be the sole representatives of Nationalist Afrikanerdom. The challenge had been met, and from the electoral battle the H.N.P. had emerged victor. It had made good its boasted monopoly. It stood now, the sole effective organ of Afrikanerdom, compact, purified, and beyond the reach of revenge.[25]

The Afrikaner Party did, in fact, survive, not as a challenge to the H.N.P., but as a tolerated junior party, and only at the cost of the sacrifice of its ideals. In 1951 it finally merged with the H.N.P. to form the National Party which was to prove still to be the old H.N.P., quite undiluted, under another name.[26]

(iv) *The Communist Party*

The Communist Party stood apart from the other minor parties. With the U.S.S.R. also at war with Germany, it now gave full support to the war effort. It remained, however, as opposed to the doctrines and policies of the Coalition parties as it did to those of the Opposition.

In general, the result marked a shattering defeat for its hopes. In only two seats, Cape Flats and Woodstock, did their candidates save their deposits; and if it had not been for their showing in those two seats the average percentage of the poll gained by Communists in the seats they contested would have been considerably lower than 10,8.[27] Moreover only in East London North, where the doubtful distinction fell to one of the two independent candidates, did the Communists avoid coming at the bottom of the poll.

Clearly, even at a time when the Western world was most favourably inclined to the U.S.S.R., Communism failed to attract more than a handful of the electorate.[28]

(v) *Independents*

If the nature of the independent candidates showed considerable variation, so also did their results. Two of the independents were successful: J. R. Sullivan at Durban Berea (with 72,6% of the vote), and Dr Shearer at Durban Point. At the other end of the scale, 16 independents lost their deposits, and, of these, 7 secured less than 5% of the votes in their constituencies.

In 5 constituencies the intervention of independent candidates resulted in minority victories: Brits, Lichtenburg, Wolmaransstad, Soutpansberg, and Durban Umbilo. Of these seats it is probable that only in Soutpansberg would the results have been different if there had been no independent.

(*d*) *Estimated adjustments for uncontested seats*

The intrusion of minor party and independent candidates, while it was extensive and resulted in 11 seats being won on a minority vote,[29] still constitutes a less serious problem in the assessment of the state of public opinion than the 18 uncontested seats; for, in the final view, the main interest in the election lay not in the dwindling strength of lost causes, but in the over-all strength of the two major parties.

Table 12

ESTIMATED TOTAL VOTES, 1943

	Cape	*Transvaal*	*Natal*	*O.F.S.*	*Union*
Reg. voters .	518 034	539 217	123 494	114 491	1 295 290
Total votes .	422 077	422 147	88 386	94 589	1 027 199
U.P. votes .	245 065	239 863	21 422	33 472	539 822
% . .	58,1	56,8	24,2	35,4	52,5
L.P. votes .	4 696	25 926	12 770	—	43 392
% . .	1,1	6,1	14,4	—	4,2
D.P. votes .	5 743	—	29 883	—	35 626
% . .	1,4	—	33,8	—	3,5
H.N.P. votes	148 697	136 443	8 043	49 459	342 642
% . .	35,2	32,3	9,1	52,3	33,4
A.P. votes .	238	3 457	—	10 769	14 464
% . .	0,1	0,8	—	11,4	1,4
Ind. votes .	9 917	10 704	14 464	—	35 085
% . .	2,3	2,5	16,4	—	3,4
C.P. votes .	4 178	2 066	564	—	6 808
% . .	1,0	0,5	0,6	—	0,7

Notes: Figures for the Orange Free State are the same as in Table 10, because there were no uncontested seats in that province. Nor, for the reason stated in the text, are any adjustments made in the cases of the L.P., D.P., A.P., or independents.

In Table 12 voting figures have been adjusted to allow for probable voting strengths in the uncontested constituencies. Except for the uncontested Dominionite seat of Durban Musgrave, no attempt has been made to estimate the possible strengths of minor party candidates in seats which they did not contest, primarily because any such attempt could be made only on the basis of the most tenuous of hypotheses, but also because, in the context of 1943, it is hardly likely that such candidates would have gained significant success in those seats which they preferred not to fight.

On the strength of these figures it seems probable that the United Party and its allies represented the support of some 60% of the voters of the Union, as against an estimated 33,4% for the H.N.P. Looked at in the light of these figures, the disparity between votes and seats becomes less serious. The conversion of 60% of the votes into 71% of the seats is by no means unusual given the single-member constituency type of electoral system, which has the general tendency of exaggerating voting strength. At least there could be no argument that the United Party majority in Parliament represented only a minority of voters.

By and large, then, the results of the 1943 elections gave comfort and encouragement to the Government. Its majority had been substantially increased, and its support was apparently broad-based. Yet there remained certain disquieting features that made doubly dangerous the United Party tendency to succumb to the temptation of complacency.

(*e*) *Disparity in size of majority: the key to the future*

A further defect of the single-member constituency 'first past the post' system of elections besides that already noted is the 'wastage' of votes due to the piling up of large but fruitless majorities in a limited number of constituencies. This defect was certainly observable in the 1943 elections. In 18 constituencies the U.P. and its allies secured majorities of over 3 000 votes, a number that would have been increased to 35 if their 17 unopposed seats had been contested. On the other hand no H.N.P. candidate achieved a majority of this magnitude. At the other end of the scale, however, 49 seats were won by majorities of under 1 000, and of these 28 were Government seats. And on the long view this fact was perhaps the most important of all the minor features of the election; for it meant that, taking these 28 Government seats alone, an alteration in the allegiance of 14 000 voters out of an electorate of some 1,3 million would place the Government's majority in jeopardy, cutting it down to a mere 8 seats. In all the United Party jubilation, these facts were quietly ignored; but they were there to be seen: the greater part of the party's voting strength lay in its relatively small number of safe seats, while in a critical number of seats its hold was precarious. Quite how precarious it was, was to be decisively demonstrated five years later.

3

The General Election of 1948: Indecisive Victory

INTRODUCTION

When Parliament was dissolved on 15 April 1948, it was in many ways a different age from that in which it was elected. In 1943 the United Nations was a military alliance poised for a victory that was still a long way off, but yet discernible; the Commonwealth was still the British Commonwealth, and the British Commonwealth and Empire were fighting in unison both in Europe and Asia; and in South Africa the squabbles of a disunited Opposition—indicative as they were of an Opposition that did not expect victory—and the rallying effect of the war effort had combined to sweep Smuts back into power.

In 1948 the war was over; but the inheritance of austerity remained, particularly in the form of economic controls, housing shortages, and sub-abundant food supplies, and it was widely resented, not least in South Africa. By 1948 the Commonwealth of Nations had taken on a startlingly new character. In 1947 India and Pakistan had become independent members, and in February 1948 they had been joined by Ceylon, while also in 1947 Burma had gained her independence outside the Commonwealth. By the admission of India, Pakistan, and Ceylon into the Commonwealth, it had been transformed into a multiracial association in which the old ties of kinship, language, family sentiment, and loyalty to the Crown were no longer exclusive qualifications for membership. It marked, too, the end of the formerly powerful, although unarticulated, concept of white hegemony in the British Commonwealth and Empire. Even in Africa (particularly in the Gold Coast) events were moving in the same direction and contributed not a little to the anxieties of white South Africans. But overshadowing it all was the development of the Cold War which, in one of its aspects, saw Communism as a grave international menace: it had conquered Eastern Europe, and in allying itself with the independence movements it was apparently sweeping through Asia, while the discovery of Communist agents in Canada and the U.S.A. spread alarm in the West.

These were some of the more obvious of the general currents that disturbed the minds of men, and that were in the end perhaps to be decisive in the overthrow of the United Party Government. For if there is one thing that is antipathetical to the disturbed it is the appearance of complacency in those in authority; and it was just this appearance that, rightly or wrongly, the Government tended to convey. The Nationalists, on the other hand, in spite of their continued difficulties with the Ossewa Brandwag, stood as an effective fighting force in alliance with the Afrikaner Party,[1] in militant mood, and with answers to the problems of the day that matched the anxious mood of the electorate at least to a degree sufficient to bring them into power.

In South Africa itself events came to the aid of the Opposition, particularly with regard to South Africa's Indian population and to South West Africa. The Government's attempts to resolve the political conflicts that centred upon the Indians were both unpopular and unsuccessful. Bowing on the one side to popular emotions at home, particularly in Natal, it made permanent the restrictions, first imposed by the 'Pegging Act' of 1943, on the sale and purchase of land by Asians. This part of the Asiatic Land Tenure and Indian Representation Act, 1946, provoked a passive resistance campaign by the Indians in South Africa and aroused the indignation of the newly independent countries of Pakistan and India. It was Mrs Pandit Nehru who inflicted a humiliating defeat on Smuts in the United Nations General Assembly in moving a resolution that condemned South Africa's treatment of her Indian citizens—a defeat that seriously damaged Smuts's reputation back home. But in deference to the kind of opinion that was thus aroused, and in part no doubt in response to Hofmeyr's influence, Chapter II of the Act extended a limited degree of representation to the Indians in Natal and the Transvaal by granting them two senators (one elected by the Indians voting on a communal roll, and one nominated by the Government) and three members in the House of Assembly, also elected on a communal roll. It further provided for the separate election of two Indians to the Natal Provincial Council. These provisions undoubtedly strengthened the cause of the Nationalists and sharpened their attack on Hofmeyr; they also succeeded in splitting both the Dominion and Labour Parties, their opponents among the former forming the South African Party still under the leadership of Col. Stallard, and those among the latter forming the Central Group. At the same time, while these provisions considerably exacerbated white opinion, they were completely rejected by the Indians themselves and did nothing to placate external opinion.

The Indian reaction to the Land Tenure Act played no small

part too in the United Nations' rejection of Smuts's proposal to incorporate South West Africa into the Union. Instead the United Nations called upon the Union to place South West Africa under United Nations Trusteeship. Smuts 'flew home', records Eric Walker, 'smoothing his ruffled plumes to find even the most liberal white South Africans seething with indignation at the stream of "unjustifiable odium" that had thus been poured upon them by Hindus and Communists of all people'.[2]

At the same time the focus of attention on racial issues was maintained by the strike and procession to the Johannesburg City Hall of the African Mineworkers' Union in August 1946, some 70 000 Africans being involved in all,[3] and by the voluntary suspension of further proceedings by the Natives Representative Council.

Aware at the same time of its helplessness at home and the growing movement of support for its cause outside, the non-white population was growing in determination and in assertiveness, becoming increasingly resolved not to allow its fate to be controlled by the governing white minority. For its part, that white minority drew together in alarm at what it saw and heard both at home and abroad. And the weapon of defence that it chose for itself was the shining new policy of 'Apartheid'. White nationalism, with Afrikaner nationalism as its vanguard, was putting itself in battle array in defence against the gathering threat of black nationalism.

If this brief survey of the background to the 1948 elections implies a certain inevitability in the Nationalist victory, this was far from evident at the time. The signs were undoubtedly there, but few read them dispassionately and clearly. The prevailing mood of the Government's supporters indeed was one which simply assumed victory, while speculation confined itself to the extent of that victory. The general attitude is perfectly illustrated by this passage from a leading article appearing in the pro-Government press:

> It is notorious that the principal opposition, the Nationalists, are at sixes and sevens about leadership, between the Provinces, and about slogans and policies. Political strategists have advanced that [*sic*] present victory would embarrass them more than defeat. . . . All these things added together: The inevitability of victory for General Smuts. The confusion of the oppositions [*sic*], the overwhelming complications of affairs overseas, are being subtly used to dampen United Party zealousness, to make the election appear a side-show lacking real and lasting significance.[4]

Indeed, one of the recurrent themes of Government speakers was the danger of over-optimism.

THE CONTESTANTS

(a) Major parties

The election campaign officially began with the dissolution of Parliament on 15 April 1948, nomination day being set for 26 April and polling day for 26 May. In effect, however, the opening of the campaign can be identified with the opening of Parliament. On the eve of that event, Smuts had reshuffled his Cabinet, the major political significance of the changes being the appointment of J. H. Hofmeyr as Deputy Prime Minister and Leader of the House of Assembly[5]—this at a time when Hofmeyr was running into heavy attack on account of his liberal tendencies. But this was only the prelude to the opening salvo. That came with Malan's reply to the speech from the Throne. Instead of moving a 'no confidence' motion that ranged the gamut of governmental policy and activity, Malan delivered what was in effect an election manifesto, a demand for the implementation of a policy of apartheid.

In this speech he attacked the element of representation, meagre though it was, accorded to Indians by Chapter II of the Asiatic Land Tenure and Indian Representation Act, 1946, and promised the repeal of that Chapter; he urged that African representation in the House of Assembly be abolished, leaving Africans representation only in the Senate, and that the admittedly moribund Natives Representative Council be replaced by 'representative native governing bodies for the various native territories set up on the basis of tribal and language affinity and with powers of government under European trusteeship granted gradually in relation to the degree of development of the groups concerned and their ability to bear responsibility for self-government'.[6]

The H.N.P. Election Manifesto, published exactly three months later, was mainly an elaboration of the speech's major theme: that the U.P. government was weak and pusillanimous in its defence against the twin menaces of Communism and 'the black sea of South Africa's non-European population'. It gave advance notice of the apartheid programme that it proposed to implement with regard to the three major non-white groups—the 'Natives', Coloureds, and Asians. It promised to 'purify our State and public services of Communists and Communist influences'. As well, it hit hard at the weaknesses of the United Party's administrative record and its mismanagement of the economy.

The United Party Manifesto, issued a few days later, was over-elaborate—running on to twenty-one points—and tame in its over-all tone: 'weary, stale, flat, and unprofitable' indeed! It was also, of course, unexceptionable. It proclaimed the ideal of national unity[7] and promised the preservation of the Commonwealth connection and the promotion of international co-operation and goodwill. It declared the United Party's stand in defence of individual rights and the system of private enterprise, and undertook to procure the advance of the nation's prosperity. On the issues of colour, it proposed to develop the Natives Representative Council and other African governing bodies 'subject to the authority of Government and Parliament', to recognize the Coloureds' special position 'as an appendage to the Whites', and to apply the Asiatic Land Tenure Act to the Indians. In response to the H.N.P. apartheid plans the U.P. leaned heavily on the Fagan Report,[8] which had rejected the concept of separate development, at least territorially, as impracticable and had regarded as inevitable the permanent residence of Africans in white areas. In this vein Smuts declared, 'The idea that the Natives must all be removed and confined in their own kraals is in my opinion the greatest nonsense I have ever heard'.[9]

Throughout the campaign it was the H.N.P. that made the most direct, the simplest, and the most consistent appeal to the electorate's fears, as well as to their sense of grievance. In consequence the U.P. was put on the defensive and at the same time its policy statements became increasingly amorphous.

The H.N.P. campaign extended beyond the realms of ideas and philosophies to surely one of the most concentrated, indeed one of most scurrilous, personal attacks to be found in the Union's lively political history. The target of this attack was J. H. Hofmeyr, the Deputy Prime Minister. The H.N.P.'s charge was that Smuts was planning to retire soon after the election and to hand power over to Hofmeyr—the arch-Kaffirboetie[10] of the U.P.—who would surely bring about the destruction of 'White Civilization' in South Africa. Here again the U.P. was put on the defensive. 'This was really a war against Hofmeyr,' Smuts said, 'and Hofmeyr is one of the best men we have ever produced in the country. They are trying to wound him in advance. If you want me to carry on I shall go on, but I do hate these attacks on Hofmeyr.'[11] While Hofmeyr himself was driven to declare, 'I am supposed to be in favour of equality between Europeans and non-Europeans. That of course is nonsense. It is just as wrong as other allegations the Nats have made about me in the past.'[12]

So the contending forces, the United Party–Labour Party alliance on the one hand, and the National Party–Afrikaner Party on the other, marched to the election which, as Smuts with true prescience said, would mark one of the turning-points of the history of the nation: 'Long years afterwards the effect of this election will be felt here in South Africa.'[13]

The Government alliance all told put 147 candidates into the field, 139 of these being United Party members and 8 being Labour Party. Eleven of these candidates were returned unopposed, five in the Cape and six in the Transvaal (all the latter in the Johannesburg area). In its turn, the Government alliance failed to put up candidates in Mossel Bay, where Dr Van Nierop was opposed by an independent; in Oudtshoorn, where the Nationalist candidate was returned unopposed; and in the Free State seat of Bethlehem, where Dr Van Rhijn was returned unopposed.

The Opposition alliance, on the other hand, entered the lists with only 102 candidates, of whom 10 represented the Afrikaner Party. It thus virtually presented the Government with 48 seats; but although some Government spokesmen and some sections of the pro-Government press attempted to make some capital of this, claiming that it represented an Opposition confession of defeat, in fact it was quite without prognostic value; for hardly even the wildest Nationalist optimist expected it to win many seats, if any, in Johannesburg and the urban areas of the Cape and Natal. In fact it needed, at the barest minimum, and taking into account the three Native Representatives, to win 78 seats if it was to come into power. It had, therefore, candidates enough; but the task of wresting 35 seats from the United Party, requiring as it did an improvement of more than 80% over its 1943 performance, was certainly formidable and, on paper, gave some ground for United Party optimism.

(*b*) *Minor parties*[14]

Compared with 1943, there was a marked decline in the number of candidates standing as representatives of minor parties or as independents. Exclusive of the Labour and Afrikaner Parties which had entered into electoral alliances with the United and National Parties respectively, there were only 55 candidates in this category, or, if we include the Labour and Afrikaner Parties, there were 73, still 10 short of the 1943 figure. More strikingly, where there had been 43 constituencies in 1943 contested by three or more candidates, in 1948 there were only 12. All together, minor party and independent candidates contested 43 seats in the Union.

The most important of these minor parties were the South African Party and the Central Group. As we have seen, the former party was the old Dominion Party operating under a new name, while the latter comprised, in the main, dissidents from the Labour Party. Both had gone into opposition to the United Party in reaction to the Government's non-European policy, particularly with regard to the representative rights given to the Indians. Both accordingly were given the blessing of the H.N.P., which instructed its supporters to vote for them in seats where there were no Nationalist candidates.[15] But in two constituencies the S.A.P. and the C.G. opposed each other, and in Roodepoort Col. Stallard, the Leader of the S.A.P., was involved in a three-cornered fight with both the U.P. and the H.N.P.[16] Each of these parties put up eleven candidates: four each in the Cape, two each in the Transvaal, and five each in Natal. Their main function politically was to highlight the anti-Indian feeling so characteristic of Natal in general and of Durban in particular. In the end both were effectively eliminated at the polls, and the *Natal Daily News*, rejoicing at the defeat of the S.A.P. in the Durban constituencies, remarked, 'This election, whatever its outcome, marks Natal's full graduation into the larger South Africa.'[17]

The Communist Party, appearing for what was to be the last time in a South African general election, entered only a token force. It put three candidates into the field, and they polled a total of only 1 783 votes. Certainly as far as the white electorate was concerned it was apparent that it did not require legislation to wipe the party off South Africa's political map. Besides the candidates of these three parties, there were 30 candidates who may be classified as independents, although some of them attached party names to themselves, and others, as in 1943, were less independent in their political attachments than their labels suggested.[18] These 30 candidates contested a total of 25 seats, and once again they were more typically an urban phenomenon than a rural one, 24 of them contesting 20 urban seats; while in the rural areas only five seats were contested by six independents.

THE TURN-OUT

The delimitation of constituencies for the 1948 election had been based on the voters' list as it stood on 31 May 1947. By the time the election took place, on 26 May 1948, the total number of registered voters had grown from 1 351 920 to 1 459 670. Since twelve constituencies were uncontested, however, the total number of voters able to exercise their vote dropped to 1 338 543. Of these 1 075 328 actually voted—the first time in the history of the Union that the poll had topped the million mark. This figure represented 80,3% of the effective electorate—a reasonable turn-out by the standards of most democratic countries. Yet it was disappointing. It was the first post-war election in South Africa. There was not the difficulty of organizing the large 'soldiers' vote', and the issues before the electorate were clear, decisive, and of critical importance to the country's future development. In spite of all this, the gain in the percentage poll over the 1943 figures was only 0,8%.

As in 1943, however, the turn-out varied considerably from province to province.

Table 14

VOTER PARTICIPATION PER PROVINCE

Province	*Electorate*	*Votes cast*	*% Poll*
Cape	494 346	411 117	83,2
Transvaal	583 735	458 138	78,5
Natal	139 996	105 537	75,4
O.F.S..	120 466	100 536	83,5
Union	1 338 543	1 075 328	80,3

Once again Natal gained the unwanted distinction of the lowest percentage poll.

The outstanding feature of this election was the fact that the United Party and its allies secured a substantial majority in terms of votes, while suffering a narrow defeat in terms of seats. To this feature we shall have to pay more particular attention later, but in view of the narrowness of the United Party's defeat it is worth noticing that there was a substantially lower poll in seats won by the U.P. than in the H.N.P. seats.

Table 15

AVERAGE PERCENTAGE POLL ACCORDING TO PARTY WINNING SEAT

Province	*U.P./L.P.*	*H.N.P./A.P.*
Cape	78,6	87,1
Transvaal . . .	74,6	81,8
Natal.	73,1	87,5[1]
O.F.S.	85,1[2]	83,4

Notes: [1] Only 2 seats were won by the H.N.P./A.P. alliance.
[2] Only 1 U.P. seat.

The low poll in U.P. seats was principally a phenomenon associated with the absence of H.N.P. candidates. Thus in the Cape Town area where the aggregate percentage poll was 77,0%, there were only two seats contested by Nationalists, and in those seats the percentage polls were 83,9% and 85,1% respectively. In the Border area of the Cape, again, where there was no contest at all between the major parties, the percentage poll was only 77,9%, compared with the 87,1% poll recorded in the Cape rural areas, where both major parties contested every seat.

The same pattern is repeated in the Transvaal and in Natal. In the Johannesburg area, where the Nationalists contested only 5 of the 12 seats,[19] the average percentage poll was only 69,2%, compared with 79,6% in the Witwatersrand area, where only 3 of the 17 contested seats were fought by the United Party against a minor party or independent candidate, and 83,5% in the more rural area, in which all the seats were fought by both major parties. In Natal the Nationalist alliance contested only five seats, and in those seats the percentage poll ranged from 76,3%[20] to 88,6%[21]; while in the other seats the percentage poll ranged from 66,5% to 76,4%. In the O.F.S. every seat except Bethlehem was contested by the two major parties, and in Bethlehem, in which the H.N.P. fought an independent, there was a higher-than-average 84,4% poll.

The inference is inescapable that in general the electorate was not particularly interested in side-issues, in issues raised by minor parties and independents, and this, in the context of 1948, is only to be expected. But these figures also suggest that the supporters of the United Party may have been over-optimistic, too complacent, or insufficiently enthusiastic, or perhaps that the United Party itself failed to a significant degree 'to bring out the vote'. If the energy and drive that went into the United Party's 1953 campaign had been matched in 1948, it is possible that the final result might have been different.[22]

THE RESULTS

(*a*) *In terms of seats*

Viewed from the perspective of the past fifteen years, the 1948 elections can clearly be seen as having set the course of South African post-war politics: a course radically different from what it would have been if the Nationalists had remained in opposition. Yet rarely can a country have embarked on a new course on the basis of so indecisive an electoral victory, nor one so little expected. In the event, the H.N.P./A.P. alliance won the election by eight slender seats, and that majority is reduced to five if the three Natives' Representatives are added to the Opposition side. At the time, the Nationalists' exultant boast that they would hold power for twenty years seemed rashly optimistic. That period is now well over, and a new generation of voters has arisen that has known no other government than that of the National Party. And there is still no foreseeable end to their regime. If the Nationalist victory was narrow and indecisive, from the United Party point of view the results were nevertheless a shattering reversal of their previous position. All together the United Party and its allies lost 36 seats to the National and Afrikaner Parties, its share of the House dropping from 71,3% to 47,3%, while the Nationalist share soared from 28,7% to 52,7%.

In the urban areas the United Party more or less held its own, the major exceptions being the Witwatersrand and Pretoria. In the Cape urban areas the H.N.P. gained a seat in the new constituency of Parow, and the Afrikaner Party captured Uitenhage.

In the Transvaal the H.N.P. scraped home in the Johannesburg constituency of Mayfair with a majority of 388. In the urban seats of Natal and the O.F.S. the *status quo* was retained. If these had been the only Nationalist gains, they might have been regarded as significant, but not disturbing. What was both significant and disturbing from the United Party point of view was the Nationalists' capture of six of the urban Witwatersrand seats where previously they had held none, and of five out of the eight Pretoria seats, gaining Pretoria Central, Pretoria District, and Pretoria West. These were to prove fatal breaches of the United Party's defences in the Transvaal; for their majority there depended on a continuing hold over the urban seats. But where out of 41 such seats in 1943 they had held 38, now out of 43 seats they held only 30, while the Nationalists increased their holdings from three to thirteen seats.

It was, however, in the Cape and Transvaal rural seats that the United Party was defeated most decisively, as Table 16 shows.

Table 16

RESULTS OF THE 1948 ELECTION IN TERMS OF SEATS[1]

Area	*U.P.*	*L.P.*	*Total*	*%*	*H.N.P.*	*A.P.*	*Total*	*%*
Cape Town	13 (3)	—	13	92,9	1	—	1	7,1
Port Elizabeth	4 (1)	—	4	80,0	—	1	1	20,0
Border	5	—	5	100,0	—	—	—	—
Rest of Cape	5 (1)	—	5	16,1	25 (1)	1	26	83,9
Total Cape	27 (5)	—	27	49,1	26 (1)	2	28	50,9
Johannesburg	14 (6)	2	16	88,9	2	—	2	11,1
Witwatersrand	9	2	11	64,7	6	—	6	35,3
Pretoria	3	—	3	37,5	4	1	5	62,5
Rest of Transvaal	—	—	—	—	20	3	23	100,0
Total Transvaal	26 (6)	4	30	45,5	32	4	36	54,5
Durban–Pietermaritzburg	8	2	10	100,0	—	—	—	—
Rest of Natal	3	—	3	50,0	1	2	3	50,0
Total Natal	11	2	13	81,3	1	2	3	18,7
Total O.F.S.	1	—	1	7,7	11	1	12	92,3
Total Union	65 (11)	6	71	47,3	70 (1)	9	79	52,7

Note: [1] The figures in brackets are for uncontested seats.

In the Cape the United Party's hold on the rural seats dropped from 14 to 5, while the Nationalists gained 7 more seats, to rise from 19 to 25. But it was the Transvaal rural seats that provided the *coup de grâce*. In 1943 the United Party had won 15 out of 23 seats in this group. In 1948 all of these 23 seats went to the Nationalists.

In sum, the wind of change that blew the United Party out of power clearly reached gale force in the Transvaal. In 1943 there had been 64 Transvaal seats, of which the United Party had won 53 and the National Party 11. But in 1948 the Nationalists swept in with 36 seats out of a total of 66.

Over all, the picture that emerged was one which showed the United Party as primarily an urban party, 88,7% of its seats being found in the major urban areas, and the National Party as still primarily rural, only 21,5% of its seats being in the urban areas. This picture is perhaps given more detail if we look at the seats won by the various parties in terms of the size of the electorate, remembering that size of constituency tends to vary with density of population.

Table 17

THE RESULTS ACCORDING TO SIZE OF CONSTITUENCY

Registered Voters	*Cape*		*Transvaal*		*Natal*		*O.F.S.*		*Union*	
	U.P./ L.P.	H.N.P./ A.P.	U.P./ L.P.	H.N.P./ A.P.	U.P./ L.P.	H.N.P./ A.P.	U.P./ L.P.	H.N.P./ A.P.	U.P./ L.P.	H.N.P./ A.P.
13 000– 13 999 .	—	—	—	1	—	—	—	—	—	1
12 000– 12 999 .	—	1	—	—	—	—	—	—	—	1
11 000– 11 999 .	6	1	7	2	—	—	—	1	13	4
10 000– 10 999 .	15	5	14	8	1	—	1	1	31	14
9 000– 9 999 .	5	16	9	3	8	—	—	2	22	21
8 000– 8 999 .	1	5	—	18	1	—	—	8	2	31
7 000– 7 999 .	—	—	—	4	3	3	—	—	3	7

The kind of disparity revealed in this table obviously operated heavily in favour of the Nationalists. It meant that their 79 seats represented an electorate of 735 709; while the total electorate in

Table 18

VOTES CAST IN CONTESTED SEATS, 1948[1]

Region	*Reg. voters*	*Votes cast*	*% poll*	*Spoilt*	*%*	*U.P./L.P.*	*%*	*N.P./A.P.*	*%*
Cape									
Cape Town area .	119 501	91 998	77,0	726	0,8	66 037	71,8	10 345	11,2
Port Elizabeth .	44 851	36 264	80,9	285	0,8	20 987	57,9	11 500	31,7
Border . . .	50 704	39 521	77,9	267	0,7	28 506	72,1	—	—
Rest of Cape . .	279 290	243 334	87,1	2 069	0,9	100 665	41,4	135 261	55,6
Total Cape .	494 346	411 117	83,2	3 347	0,8	216 195	52,6	157 106	38,2
Transvaal									
Johannesburg .	125 003	86 477	69,2	630	0,7	56 287	65,1	18 299	21,2
Witwatersrand .	186 657	148 667	79,6	841	0,6	77 184	51,9	59 733	40,2
Pretoria . . .	78 956	61 790	78,3	298	0,5	31 254	50,6	30 192	48,9
Rest of Transvaal	193 119	161 204	83,5	1 023	0,6	64 093	39,8	96 052	59,6
Total Transvaal . . .	583 735	458 138	78,5	2 792	0,6	228 818	49,9	204 276	44,6
Natal									
Durban–Pietermaritzburg .	93 870	68 022	72,5	394	0,6	50 347	74,0	1 793	2,6
Rest of Natal .	46 126	37 515	81,3	231	0,6	22 533	60,1	11 962	31,9
Total Natal .	139 996	105 537	75,4	625	0,6	72 880	69,1	13 755	13,0
Total O.F.S. .	120 466	100 536	83,5	629	0,6	29 544	29,4	68 141	67,8
Total Union	1 338 543	1 075 328	80,3	7 393	0,7	547 437	50,9	443 278	41,2

Note: [1] All voting figures for 1948 are from the *Government Gazette Extraordinary*, Vol. CLII, No. 398 4 June 1948.

the 71 seats won by the United and Labour Parties was 723 962. In other words, with 8 fewer seats the Opposition 'electorate' was smaller than that of the Nationalists by only 11 747 voters—the size of a fairly typical Cape urban seat.

(*b*) *The results in terms of votes*

What the combination of geographical factors and the electoral system cost the United Party and its ally is shown by comparing table 16 with Table 18. Taking, first, only the contested seats, it is seen that while the United and Labour Parties won only 54 seats in the Union as a whole against 78 won by the National and Afrikaner Parties, they nevertheless polled 547 437 votes, or 50,9 %, of the total votes cast, against their opponents' 443 278 votes, which represented only 41,2 % of the votes cast. Moreover, whereas the United and Labour Parties were able to gain a majority of seats only in Natal, on actual votes cast they were headed at the polls only in the Free State. Perhaps the disparity between votes cast and seats won is seen at its most dramatic in the Transvaal, where, with a majority of over 24 000 votes over the Nationalists, the United and Labour Parties could muster only 30 out of 66 seats, and 6 of these were unopposed. In Pretoria they won only 3 out of the 8 seats, while polling more votes.[23] And all 23 rural seats in the Transvaal were won by the Nationalists with only 59,6 % of the votes.

C.P.	*%*	*C.G.*	*%*	*S.A.P.*	*%*	*Inds.*	*%*	*Majority*	*%*
1 009	1,1	1 392	1,5	2 223	2,4	10 266	11,2	55 692	60,5
—		—	—	—	—	3 492	9,6	9 487	26,2
—	—	3 451	8,7	2 241	5,7	5 056	12,8	17 758	44,9
—	—	—	—	—	—	5 339	2,2	34 596	14,2
1 009	0,2	4 843	1,2	4 464	1,1	24 153	5,9	59 089	14,4
774	0,9	2 257	2,9	831	1,0	7 129	8,2	37 988	43,9
—	—	2 605	1,8	267	0,2	8 037	5,4	17 451	11,7
—	—	—	—	—	—	46	0,1	1 062	1,7
—	—	—	—	—	—	36	0,02	31 959	19,8
774	0,2	5 132	1,1	1 098	0,2	15 248	3,3	24 542	5,4
—	—	3 859	5,7	5 169	7,6	6 460	9,5	48 554	71,4
—	—	1 626	4,3	1 163	3,1	—	—	10 571	28,2
—	—	5 485	5,2	6 332	6,0	6 460	6,1	59 125	56,0
—	—	—	—	—	—	2 222	2,2	38 597	38, 4
1 783	0,2	15 460	1,4	11 894	1,1	48 083	4,5	104 159	9,7

All these figures neglect the probable votes that would have been cast in the 12 uncontested seats, of which, as we have seen, 11 returned United Party members and one a Nationalist. Some account must be taken of these seats if a more accurate picture of party strength is to be drawn. Table 19 shows the adjusted voting

Table 19

ESTIMATED TOTAL VOTES FOR THE TWO MAJOR PARTY GROUPS

Region	*Reg. voters*	*Est. votes*	*Rej.*	*Est. H.N.P./ A.P.*	%	*Est. U.P./ L.P.*	%
Cape							
Cape Town area . . .	151 301	117 437	929	14 562	12,4	87 056	74,1
Port Elizabeth . . .	55 682	44 929	354	13 219	29,4	27 864	62,0
Border	50 704	39 521	267	—	—	28 506	72,1
Rest of Cape. . . .	298 000	259 238	2 196	143 395	55,2	108 308	41,7
Total Cape . . .	555 687	461 125	3 746	171 176	37,1	251 734	54,6
Transvaal							
Johannesburg . . .	184 790	134 309	965	23 442	17,5	98 639	73,4
Witwatersrand[1] . . .	186 657	148 667	841	59 733	40,2	77 184	51,9
Pretoria[1]	78 956	61 790	298	30 192	48,9	31 254	50,6
Rest of Transvaal . .	193 119	161 204	1 023	96 052	59,6	64 093	39,8
Total Transvaal .	643 522	505 970	3 127	209 419	41,4	271 170	53,6
Natal							
Durban–Pietermaritz-burg[1]	93 870	68 022	394	1 793	2,6	50 347	74,0
Rest of Natal[1] . . .	46 126	37 515	231	11 962	31,9	22 533	60,1
Total Natal[1] . .	139 996	105 537	625	13 755	13,0	72 880	69,1
Total O.F.S.[1] . .	120 466	100 536	629	68 141	67,8	29 544	29,4
Total Union	1 459 671	1 173 168	8 127	462 491	39,4	625 328	53,3

Note: [1] These figures are unchanged from Table 20, because all seats were contested.

strengths of the two major political groups with the estimated votes in the uncontested constituencies included in the totals. On the basis of these estimates the United and Labour Parties enjoyed a clear majority in the Transvaal (compared with 49,9% of votes in contested seats only), and a much firmer majority (53,3% *vice* 50,9%) in the Union as a whole than the figures for just the contested seats indicated.

(*c*) *The swing*

In spite of the limitations of the concept of the swing as noted in the Introduction, it provides an illuminating comment on the 1948 elections. It can be calculated for 81 out of the 138 contested seats, and it demonstrates the almost solid movement to the right that took place in South African politics in 1948. In only two of these 81 seats was there any swing at all in favour of the United Party: in Pretoria City with a swing of 1,2%, and in Marico with a swing of 0,2%. There was, however, considerable regional variation. In the Cape Province the average swing in 27 seats towards the Nationalists was 6,2%. In the Transvaal, on the other hand, in 40 seats there was an average swing towards the Nationalists of 10,4% —indicative again of the fact that the Transvaal formed the vanguard of the Nationalist advance to power. In Natal the average swing towards the Nationalists was 11,9%, but this clearly is a distortion in that the only 4 relevant seats were all rural seats, leaving out of account the 10 solidly United Party seats of Durban and Pietermaritzburg. In the Orange Free State there were 10 seats for which the swing can be calculated, but, except for only one of these, Bloemfontein City, in all the others in 1943 there had been three-cornered contests between the H.N.P., the United Party, and the Afrikaner Party. If we restrict our calculations to the votes gained by the H.N.P. and lost by the United Party, ignoring the votes cast for the Afrikaner Party in 1943, the average swing to the H.N.P. was 10,7%. It is, however, more realistic for these purposes to add the Afrikaner Party votes to the 1943 H.N.P. votes, and on this basis the swing towards the Nationalists in 1948 is reduced to only 3,3%. In the Orange Free State, in other words, it appears that the Nationalists won over the Afrikaner Party vote, but that the United Party support on the whole remained remarkably firm.

In the Union as a whole the average swing towards the Nationalists was 9,1%; but this figure is reduced to 8,2% if the Orange Free State figures are adjusted in the way suggested. This still suggests an impressive movement in opinion. Even the lower figure, however, is biased in favour of the Nationalists, because it leaves out of account many centres of United Party strength, including the seats in which there was no contest. If we calculate the swing on the basis of the total votes, including our estimates for the uncontested seats, we find that it is reduced to 5,75%; and this is probably a more accurate indication of the over-all movement of opinion. It is still, of course, a substantial swing; but the fact remains, as we have seen, that a clear majority of the voters still preferred the U.P. to the H.N.P.

(*d*) *The disparity between seats and votes*

The H.N.P./A.P. alliance formed the new Government in South Africa with 79 out of 150 ordinary (or 153 total) seats in the House of Assembly. With this slender majority it proceeded to initiate what amounts to a revolution in social and political terms. In the ensuing turbulent five years, however, it claimed with uninhibited fervour to represent 'the will of the people', and to have a clear 'mandate' for its proposals. These claims, viewed in the light of the voting figures, clearly deserved the scepticism with which they were received by the Opposition.

The distorting effect of the electoral system was the real source of the H.N.P.'s power, not the state of opinion at large. The degree of distortion is amply demonstrated by comparing the number of seats won with the effective voting support (including allowance for uncontested seats) for the respective parties. The H.N.P./A.P. alliance gained 52,7% of the ordinary 150 seats with 39,4% of the votes; while the United Party/L.P. alliance could win only 47,3% of the seats with 53,3% of the votes. If seats had been distributed in proportion to votes, the United Party alliance would have won 80 seats, the H.N.P. and A.P. only 59, with independents and minor parties holding 11 (of which the majority would have supported the United Party). In other words the United Party would have continued to enjoy a workable, though reduced, majority in the new Parliament.

A different, but equally revealing, index of the distortion is given in Table 20, which shows the number of votes that it cost the respective parties to win each contested seat.

Table 20

NUMBER OF VOTES REQUIRED TO WIN EACH SEAT

Province	*U.P./L.P.*	*H.N.P./A.P.*
Cape Province	9 827	5 819
Transvaal	9 534	5 674
Natal	5 606	4 585
O.F.S.	29 544	5 678
Union	9 124	5 683

(*e*) *Factors in the distortion of voting strengths*

(i) *The loading and unloading of constituencies*

For some time it was not considered necessary to look beyond this factor for an explanation of the H.N.P.'s return to power on a minority of votes both in 1948 and in 1953. Typical expression of this view is found in H. J. May's *South African Constitution*: 'The loading and unloading of constituencies . . . enabled the Nationalists to secure a majority in Parliament out of proportion to the number of votes cast in their favour.'[24] This view has, however, now been largely discredited. Professor Carter[25] admits loading and unloading to be 'partly' the cause of the disparity in 1953, but goes on to consider other factors 'which may be still more important', factors which we shall examine later. Lakeman and Lambert go rather further in their depreciation of loading as a factor: 'The "weighting" of electorates . . . can have been only a minor contributory factor, not the cause of Malan's victory in 1953. Still less could it account for the similar result in 1948, for the "weighting" then was smaller'[26] (owing to the absence of the very small South West Africa seats).

We have already seen that in fact the United Party seats were, by and large, concentrated in the urban and therefore loaded constituencies, whereas the H.N.P. successes were mainly in the unloaded rural constituencies,[27] and that this resulted in a much larger United Party 'electorate'. Taking into account the contested seats only, the average United Party constituency for the Union as a whole was 10 204, compared with the H.N.P. average of 9 312. In the critical Transvaal constituencies the difference was even more marked: an average United Party constituency being 10 539, compared with the average H.N.P. constituency of 9 189. It is nevertheless far from easy to determine the extent, if any, to which these facts contributed to the distortion of the vote. Indeed no certain answer is possible, since a more equal distribution of voters among the constituencies would obviously have required the redrawing of constituency boundaries, and the way in which this task was done could certainly have affected the outcome in a number of seats. Nevertheless the factor of geographical concentration was probably far more decisive in determining the outcome.

(ii) *The concentration of United Party support*

There can be little doubt that this has been, and still is, the greatest single electoral handicap that the United Party has to face.[28] The evidence of vast majorities, representing as it does so many 'wasted' votes, is impressive, as may be seen in Table 21.

Table 21

AVERAGE MAJORITIES WON BY U.P./L.P. AND H.N.P./A.P. RESPECTIVELY

Area	U.P./L.P.		H.N.P./A.P.	
	Gross[1]	%[2]	*Gross*[1]	%[2]
Cape Town	4 363 (10)	54,6	1 232 (1)	11,6
Port Elizabeth	2 229 (3)	25,8	691 (1)	7,0
Border	3 597 (5)	45,4	—	—
Rest of Cape	1 067 (4)	12,6	1 609 (25)	20,1
Total Cape	3 298 (22)	40,9	1 561 (27)	19,3
Johannesburg	3 321 (10)	47,9	2 212 (2)	27,5
Witwatersrand	1 010 (11)	12,0	688 (6)	7,9
Pretoria	2 555 (3)	33,2	1 321 (5)	16,8
Rest of Transvaal	—	—	1 390 (23)	20,3
Total Transvaal	2 166 (24)	29,6	1 309 (36)	18,2
Durban–Pietermaritzburg	3 480 (10)	51,6	—	—
Rest of Natal	3 007 (3)	51,5	413 (3)	6,1
Total Natal	3 371 (13)	51,6	413 (3)	6,1
Orange Free State	262 (1)	2,9	3 053 (12)	40,3
Total Union	2 810 (60)	38,1	1 630 (78)	21,5

Notes: [1] The figures in brackets represent the number of seats involved.
[2] The percentage column represents average percentage of constituency vote.

In so far as every vote over a majority of one is 'wasted', we can say that in its 60 seats fought and won, the United Party and its Labour ally 'wasted' 168 559 votes. The United Party 'wastage' then exceeded that of the Nationalists by over 40 000 votes;[29] and these, distributed over seats won only narrowly by the Nationalists, could have more than swung the balance in favour of the United Party.

For the picture to be complete, however, we need to depict the frequency of majorities gained by the respective parties according to size. This is shown in Table 22. Of the seats won by majorities of over 3 000 votes, it will be seen that in the Union as a whole the U.P./L.P. alliance won 27: 13 in the Cape, 7 in the Transvaal, 7 in Natal. While again in the Union as a whole only 11 H.N.P./A.P. majorities were of this size: 2 in the Cape, 2 in the Transvaal, and 7 in the O.F.S., the traditional Nationalist stronghold.

Table 22

PARTY MAJORITIES ACCORDING TO SIZE

	Cape		*Transvaal*		*Natal*		*O.F.S.*		*Union*	
	U.P./ L.P.	H.N.P./ A.P.	U.P./ L.P.	H.N.P./ A.P.	U.P./ L.P.	H.N.P./ A.P.	U.P./ L.P.	H.N.P./ A.P.	U.P./ L.P.	H.N.P./ A.P.
6 000–6 999	3	—	1	—	—	—	—	—	4	—
5 000–5 999	2	—	1	—	1	—	—	—	4	—
4 000–4 999	3	—	2	1	4	—	—	—	9	1
3 000–3 999	5	2	3	1	2	—	—	7	10	10
2 000–2 999	2	7	3	5	5	—	—	5	10	17
1 000–1 999	3	11	8	11	—	—	—	—	11	22
1–999	4	7	6	18	1	3	1	—	12	28

Of the 12 U.P./L.P. majorities of under 1 000, 6 were in the critical Witwatersrand region, and one was in the Pinetown constituency where the United Party was opposed by an anti-Nationalist independent. While of the 28 Nationalist majorities in the same category, 14 were in the rural areas of the Cape and the Transvaal. The critical Nationalist gains in these areas were generally won with only narrow majorities; and it was the narrowness of these majorities that raised the Opposition's hopes of reversing the 1948 electoral verdict in 1953.

4

The General Election of 1953: The Consolidation of Nationalist Power

INTRODUCTION

It was, as we have seen, only a slender majority that put the H.N.P. into power in 1948. Moreover, the more optimistic of the Nationalists' opponents could argue that the victory was due to the coincidence of a number of unfortunate accidents—the vagaries of the electoral system, the mood of post-war disillusionment with the U.P. Government, a desire for change, and so on—but that, in any case, it was unlikely to be of lasting significance. Some took the view that the Nationalist Government 'should be given a chance', presumably hoping that the acquisition of power would tame the beast. Others, and their numbers no doubt grew as the former view was increasingly shown to be deluded, clung to the hope that as the Nationalists came to show themselves in their true colours the voters would recoil and turn once more to the security of the United Party blanket.

During their first term of office the Nationalists indeed disdained to conceal their aims or to disguise the character of their regime. They proceeded to strengthen and to add to the existing segregationist structures in South Africa, and in doing so to transform them into a system which justified the distinguishing new name of 'apartheid'. The Government's uncompromising determination to create a new legal system to govern race relations in the country in spite of the narrowness and apparent tenuousness of its majority may have been due to a real sense of commitment to its objectives and a readiness to pursue them regardless of possible electoral costs. More probably in the light of the efficiency of the Party's organization, it calculated that it would not in the end have to pay the price of defeat at the next election. It had come into power on the strength of the Afrikaner vote, and if it retained its dominant share of that vote it could afford to ignore the opposition of English-speaking voters, however vociferous it might be, and to react aggressively to the opposition of the largely voteless non-white peoples of the country.

If the Government did have this kind of confidence in its position, the Opposition forces among the white population for their part made the most strenuous efforts to overthrow it. As a result the campaign in 1953 was the most tumultuous, and indeed the most critical, of all the campaigns in the post-war period, with the campaign which preceded the referendum in 1960 as the only possible exception.

Opposition to the Government was not of course confined to the Opposition on the parliamentary and electoral levels—an opposition largely identified with sections of the white population. The growing volume of apartheid legislation[1] ran directly counter to the aspirations and demands of the non-white sections—Africans, Asians, and Coloureds alike—stimulated and strengthened as these were by the heightened nationalism that characterized the post-war world, particularly in Asia and Africa, and supported as they also were by an increasingly sympathetic world opinion. In the late 1960s overt political conflict became so widespread a phenomenon in the world that a new term to describe it came into vogue—the politics of confrontation. Typically in this new-style politics, the confrontation is initially provoked by those who are outside the power structure. Confrontation, however, marked the politics of South Africa in the 1950s; it was already rampant in this period before the 1953 elections. But when one considers the general state of non-white political opinion as well as the world situation, it may well be argued that it was the Government's programme of apartheid legislation that provoked the confrontation. It was to this that the non-white movements responded with the massive Defiance Campaign, with boycotts, and with riots and sporadic acts of other forms of violence. In sum, the period of the Nationalists' first term of office was marked by a degree of unrest and violent disturbance that had been unknown in South Africa for decades.[2] This too was a situation on which the electorate was called upon to pass judgement.

The Government itself reacted to the non-white protests with, according to one's point of view, either decisiveness or ruthlessness. The main weapons which the Nationalist regime has used to suppress and intimidate its opponents were forged in this period. They were the Suppression of Communism Act (No. 44, 1950), the Public Safety Act (No. 3, 1953), and the Criminal Law Amendment Act (No. 8, 1953). These Acts created a wide new range of offences, conferred on the administration a discretion in the application of many of their provisions that was both excessively broad and beyond the reach of the courts, and laid down extremely severe penalties for offences defined in them. In consequence the scope of the laws extended beyond the hard-core militants and, at least potentially, seriously threatened the civil liberties of all South Africans, whatever their race or colour.[3] The Government defended these new laws on grounds that have since become over-familiar, namely that they were required in defence of law and order in the land. On this too the election provided the opportunity for the electorate to declare its mind.

There was yet another issue that was highly critical both from the point of view of the outcome of the election and from the point of view of South Africa's future political path. This was the whole constitutional issue. It arose from legislation that proposed to extend the concept of apartheid to the voting rights of the Coloureds (the Separate Representation of Voters Act, 1951). The procedures adopted were contrary to the special procedures specified in the so-called 'entrenched clauses' of the South African Act for the protection both of the franchise qualifications and the equality of status of the two official languages in the Union.[4] The Government's action, therefore, also had direct implications for the equality of status of the two official languages, and thus in effect for the position of the English-speaking section in South Africa. Out of the ensuing constitutional struggle a direct conflict threatened between the Cabinet and Parliament on the one hand and the courts on the other, and was only finally averted by a temporary tactical retreat on the part of the Government.[5] These constitutional issues aroused the fiercest controversy among the electorate in the whole period. The attempted removal of the Coloureds from the common roll violated one of the crucial agreements leading to the formation of the Union, as well as solemn assurances given by General Hertzog as Prime Minister in 1931.[6] The action of the Government in ignoring the procedures laid down in the Act of Union, and its subsequent attempt to circumvent the judgment of the Appellate Division of the Supreme Court[7] by passing the notorious High Court of Parliament Act, combined to arouse the most bitter resistance and to bring forth renewed charges of a ruthless disregard for the principles of the rule of law. It was in this atmosphere that the Torch Commando was born, and it in turn added to the heat of conflict by means of protest marches and massive public rallies. And it was at the height of this controversy too that the election took place.

In sum, the first five years of Nationalist rule had been marked by a growing intensity of political activity, of group emotion, and indeed of conflict. The Government's determination to push through to the achievement of its objectives seemed merely to harden as opposition increased. The issues, however, were clear; and they called for an equally clear verdict on the part of the voters.

THE CONTESTANTS

(a) The alignment of forces

In 1953 for the first time since Hertzog and Smuts had joined forces the Nationalist political forces stood united in a single political party, the National Party, formed by the merger between Malan's Nationalists and Havenga's Afrikaner Party in August 1951. The Nationalist victories in the South West Africa elections in 1950 had robbed the Afrikaner Party of its bargaining power and thus destroyed the basis of its continued independence. It was, therefore, faced with only two alternatives: to merge or be crushed out of existence. What delayed the merger was not any critical difference in policy or attitude, but the thorny 'internal' problem of the relationship between the Afrikaner Party and the Ossewa Brandwag. In the end, as the 'solution' of that problem suggests, the alternatives before the Afrikaner Party had not after all been so clearly divided. It might be truer to say that the Afrikaner Party was submerged by, rather than merged with, the National Party; for the new constitution of the National Party required all members 'to forswear allegiance to any other political organization, including the Ossewa Brandwag'.[8] Later, too, when it came to the nomination contests for the 1953 elections, the former members of the Afrikaner Party were all swept aside, and only Havenga remained.[9] Finally, when in 1954 Dr Malan retired, contrary to his hopes and Havenga's expectations, it was not Havenga but Strijdom, the 'Lion of the North', whom the Party chose as its new Leader. But the significance of that move was not so much the final elimination of Afrikaner Party influence as the outward mark of the shift of real political power from the Cape to the Transvaal.

In spite of these remaining tensions the National Party could face the 1953 elections with greater internal strength and cohesion than at any other time over the previous twenty years. Moreover it was now the single, unchallenged expression of the political life of the Afrikaner people. Little wonder that its candidates proclaimed with a sense of lyrical exultation the Nationalist election 'psalm':

NATIONALISM MEANS:
Love for what is your own:
Your own nation
Your own citizenship
Your own South Africa
The love of the American for America
The love of the Scotsman for Scotland
The love of the Britisher for Britain
The love of the South African for South Africa—
Our motto: Love what is your own—South Africa—
our home and fatherland.[10]

But what they immediately wanted to evoke was the love of the Afrikaner people—the majority of the electorate—for its 'own' party; the National Party. And in this they were remarkably successful.

On the Opposition side an entirely new element was injected into the situation with the formation of the War Veterans Torch Commando, commonly known simply as the Torch Commando.[11] The immediate cause that called it into being was the Government's handling of the Separate Representation of Voters Act, and the constitutional crisis in its various aspects continued to be the Torch Commando's principal target.

At its first National Congress in June 1951, however, it adopted the following five principles, indicative of a much broader concern:

1. To uphold the letter and the spirit of the solemn compacts entered upon at the time of Union as moral obligations of trust and honour binding upon Parliament and the people.
2. To secure the repeal of any measures enacted in violation of such obligations.
3. To protect the freedom of the individual in worship, language and speech and to ensure his rights of free access to the Courts.
4. To eliminate all forms of totalitarianism, whether Fascist or Communist.
5. To promote racial harmony in the Union.[12]

The sense of *élan* that distinguished the Torch Commando at its best, its image of crisp organization, its enthusiasm, and its fervour, as well as the importance of the issues that it confronted, all no doubt contributed to its rapid growth to approximately a quarter of a million members. It was under the banner of the Torch Commando that the most massive demonstrations, at least among the white electorate, against the Government's policies and actions took place. Clearly it had become a force to be reckoned with; but what was not immediately clear was how that force would be applied. An early decision by the Commando's leadership, and it was a crucial one, was that the Commando would not form itself into a new political party. The obvious solution that remained was some form of working alliance covering the United Party, the Labour Party, and the Torch Commando. And this, in the end, was achieved despite the U.P.'s distrust of the 'excesses' of the Torch Commando and the latter's poor opinion of the effectiveness of the U.P.[13] In February 1952 Torch leaders themselves paved the way for an alliance. Its Leader, 'Sailor' Malan, stressed, 'Our role in no way conflicts with that of the parties. We have a common objective—to kick out the Government.'[14] And some days earlier a member of the Executive, Kane-Berman, had argued that it was 'imperative' to develop a 'united front'. After further discussions, in mid-April, Strauss, Leader of the United Party, was able to announce just this event. The United Democratic Front, consisting of the Torch Commando and the United and Labour Parties, had been born.[15]

There was, however, one issue that seriously threatened the solidarity of the United Front, although it was an issue that should be more firmly identified with Natal than the Torch Commando as a whole. This was the question of the Natal Stand. Natal had always been something of a maverick province. It was, prior to Union, the only one of the four colonies that had insisted on submitting the question of entering into the Union to a referendum. It had nurtured the Devolution movement in the 1930s, and Durban at least had gone on, in 1938, to repudiate Fusion, and with it Smuts, by returning five members of the Dominion Party. Typically it was regarded by the rest of South Africa as the last bastion of jingoism. Whether that stereotype was justified or not, it certainly placed great value on the British connection, while at the same time having a strong sense of its own identity.

The constitutional crisis, particularly in its bearings on the status of the English language, understandably had a very marked impact on Natal. One reaction is to be found in the resolution that was passed by the U.P.-dominated Provincial Council. After calling for a new National Convention to reaffirm the entrenched clauses, it went on to say that 'the very existence of the Union is now in danger and . . . unless the Act of Union is honoured both in spirit and in letter the State of Union cannot continue to exist but will be dissolved'.[16] Two days later at a mass rally in Durban of some 35 000 people, E. G. Ford, Chairman of the Coastal Region of the Torch Commando, made the terms of the Natal Stand quite explicit and removed at the same time all elements of ambiguity. 'Will you' ,he asked the crowd, 'remain in a Broederbond republic if it is declared on the pretext of the *volkswil*?' And when the crowd roared 'No!' he asked again, 'Are you prepared to take the consequences if Natal is forced to stand on her own?' And 'Yes!' came the reply.[17]

Neither the National Executive of the Torch Commando nor that of the U.P. could be expected to view the Natal Stand with any enthusiasm, for a considerable part of the strength of both bodies lay in Natal. Its secession, assuming that as a possibility, would therefore leave both of them fatally weakened. Moreover, the notion of a Natal secession was widely unpopular in the rest of the Union; so that to endorse it would be to risk being identified elsewhere with an unpopular cause. On the other hand, just because the Natal base in each body was so strong, neither could afford to ignore it. In the end the Torch Commando came nearer to accepting the

Natal Stand than did the U.P. At its First National Congress in July it adopted a resolution, not made public until six months later, that said in part:

If, in her efforts to save Union, Natal is forced to stand alone, the Torch Commando throughout South Africa and South West Africa affirms its readiness to support Natal to the full by whatsoever action the National Executive may deem necessary.[18]

The U.P., however, at its Union Congress in November resolutely refused to accept the possibility of unilateral action by Natal. A quarrel between the two bodies, which was particularly bitter at the provincial level in Natal, inevitably followed, and it was patched up only in January 1953, when the provincial executive of the Torch Commando finally agreed that it would support those United Front candidates who agreed to support the Natal Stand.[19] At the same time Douglas Mitchell, on behalf of the U.P. in Natal, and Raymond Arde, on behalf of the L.P., issued identical statements:

I am grateful for this evidence of the unity of our forces, and I welcome this opportunity to re-affirm on behalf of the United Party [Labour Party] candidates in Natal, their previous declaration made in the vow taken at Durban on 6 June 1952.[20]

By the time the election campaign got under way, then, the two opposing forces—the National Party and the United Front—stood at least outwardly united and in reasonable battle array. There is no doubt that of the two the National Party represented a far greater organizational strength as well as an incomparably greater ideological unity. Nevertheless the United Front probably represented a gain as far as the Opposition was concerned. The alliance with the Torch Commando may have alarmed and antagonized many Afrikaner voters, but most of those who reacted in this way would very likely have voted for the N.P. in any case. And the Commando did bring a moral fervour as well as an organizational capacity, along with a host of enthusiastic volunteer workers, to the aid of the United Front. So the lines were drawn, and there was nothing for it but for the battle to begin.

(*b*) *The campaign*

In the election campaign itself the constitutional crisis was the central issue. A typical expression of the United Party campaign under this head is found in their election pamphlet, *The Law of our Fathers*. The preface to that pamphlet reads:

Cold-bloodedly and without shame, the Nationalist Government, seeking means to keep itself in power, tried to violate our Constitution—a Constitution which was drafted by South Africans for South Africans and which

was and is an expression of the will of the people of South Africa.
The Nationalist leaders were thwarted—but they will try again if they get the chance.
They must not be given that chance.

It began by praising the Appellate Division, and the courts generally ('A Great Institution'), went on to point the contrast with the High Court of Parliament ('A Shameful Scene'—'Amidst scenes of buffoonery, they sat in the historic Raadzaal in Pretoria, aping judges'), condemned the Government's attempt to elevate politicians above judges ('Political Trickery'), briefly stated the rights and procedures contained in the entrenched clauses and the attempt by the Government to ignore them ('Here is the Trust!'), asserted that the existence of the entrenched clauses did not derogate from the supremacy of Parliament, and went on to quote the Chief Justice on South Africa's sovereignty. In one section, 'The Will of the People', it gave the figures for the 1948 election as evidence that the Government had never obtained the support of the *volkswil* and that the *volkswil* had not therefore been thwarted by the courts. It then dealt with the Nationalist contention that the South Africa Act was a British law and gave quotations from Hertzog and Swart from the 1931 debates acknowledging the validity of the entrenched clauses. The final section, 'The Consequences', claimed that if the Government were successful in its endeavours, any future government could abolish the equal status of one of the official languages, or disfranchise any section of the population, by bare majority.

The Government's answer to these charges was given, *inter alia*, in its pamphlet *Democracy in Danger*.[21] Its headings indicate the nature of its contents: 'The New Struggle', 'Supreme Authority', 'Parliament is Sovereign. It acts on behalf of the people, who are the supreme authority', 'Prior to 1931', 'Statute of Westminster', '1937 Judgment' (the case of *Ndlwana* v. *Hofmeyr*), 'Court Verdicts Upset' (giving examples of when United Party governments had passed legislation to 'set aside' court judgments), 'Another Principle Repudiated' (referring to the United Party's previous acceptance of separate rolls in the case of both Africans and Indians), 'Important Questions', in which it held that the entrenched clauses were the product of British pressure, denied that the Separate Representation of Voters Act was 'invalid, discriminatory and unjust', claimed that it was no more immoral than the Acts of 1936 and 1946 placing Africans and Indians on separate rolls, and went on to assert that the Appellate Division's judgment of 1952 itself constituted an attack on the Court. The pamphlet went on to deal with the implications of the judgment, claimed that the Government had a specific mandate for its actions, and stated that the Government proposed to introduce legislation to endorse the sovereignty of Parliament, to 'perpetuate' the existing apartheid legislation, and to 'ensure that the people's voice will remain the supreme voice in the land'. In this vein it concluded:

Save the Will of the People
Save Democracy
The National Government Represents the People

Undoubtedly the Nationalist case was clearer, simpler, and more suited to popular appeal. It might seem to the Opposition to contain gross distortions, but the reiterated emphasis, both here and in speeches, on the *volkswil*, the assertion that the Government, having received a mandate to implement apartheid, was bound not to let the matter drop, and the appeal to national pride by references to South Africa's status as a sovereign state and to the need to ensure the sovereignty of her Parliament, were sufficient, one must assume, to convince the electorate of the justice of its case.

In this controversy the Opposition was faced with the difficult task of asserting the priority of means over ends: a distinction too subtle for mass appeal. And its task was made all the more difficult because of the United Party's acceptance, however reluctantly, of certain means which others in the United Front condemned unequivocally.[22]

The National Party justified all it had done in the constitutional sphere on the ground that it was not only empowered, but required, to act in the way it had in terms of the mandate it had received in 1948, and went on to ask for a renewal of that mandate in order that it might complete its task—by means which it declined to disclose. As might be expected, both from its own record and from the course of events over the last few years, it laid considerable stress on the colour issue.[23] It also made considerable play with the Communist danger, alleging that the United Party received support from Communists, tried to prevent legislation against Communism, went so far as to protect Communists, and indeed condemned the Government's action against Communists[24] and urged that only the National Party could protect South Africa from Communism. The Party also produced a highly effective pamphlet, *Fruits of the National Regime*, setting out in detail the achievements of the Government; and certainly the Party had a rising tide of prosperity to aid it in its return trip to power.

For the United Party the main point of attack remained the constitutional issue, for which it could harness so much emotional support; but it attacked too, after its manner, on a broad front. It summed up the opposition to the Government's disregard for civil liberties with its slogan 'Vote for the Right to Vote Again'—a slogan which backfired on it in 1958. On the colour question it urged that the Government's ruthless policy had reduced overseas confidence in South Africa and imperilled her prosperity; and it made considerable play with its 'White Policy'—a programme of intensive immigration, envisaging the bringing in of 50 000 'selected immigrants' every year. But apart from that it had little to offer beyond a return to the 1936 policy of Hertzog and a more tactful handling of non-Europeans. The Party seemed indeed to be caught in the toils of its own history. The United Party also did its best to direct attention to economic issues and produced a plethora of optimistic nostrums.

Perhaps the United Party tried too hard. The Nationalists retaliated by producing a list of 52 promises made by the United Party and predicted that their fulfilment would cost the South African taxpayer an additional R200 000 000 per annum. What effect these blasts and counter-blasts had on the electorate is hard to say, but at most it was probably marginal. The real questions facing the country were: the state of the nation, apartheid, civil liberties, and the constitutional question.

(*c*) *The disposition of forces*

At first sight it might seem that the 1948 election was more closely fought than the 1953 one; for in 1948 there were only 12 unopposed candidates compared with 20 in 1953, and breaking these figures down, only 11 United Party candidates were unopposed in 1948 compared with 18 in 1953, and one National Party candidate was unopposed in 1948 and two in 1953. But these figures are misleading. It is more to the point to record that the United and Labour Parties between them had a total of 147 candidates in both elections, and that the Nationalist contingent rose from a total of 102 (including the Afrikaner Party) in 1948 to 130 in 1953.[25] Whereas, therefore, the Nationalists let 48 seats go by default in 1948, in 1953 it conceded only 19.

The areas of increased competition are equally interesting; for they show for the first time an assault on United Party strongholds. In the Cape Town–Port Elizabeth–Border areas the number of Nationalist candidates rose from 5 in 1948 to 18 in 1953; in the Johannesburg–Witwatersrand areas from 19 to 26; and in Natal from 3 to 12. Perhaps the most astonishing effort of all took place in the Durban seats which the National Party invaded for the first time. Of the 7 Durban seats only Durban Berea and Durban Musgrave were unopposed; all the rest were contested by the National Party. So widespread indeed was the Nationalist assault that one is forced to seek some reason. Quite obviously the Party had absolutely no chance, no hope, of winning many of these seats; why then disperse its energies and resources instead of concentrating on the marginal seats?

This question, however, may well arise from too narrow a focus. If we include the extent of the United Party engagement in our inquiry, we find the same phenomenon there—not, it is true, of widely increased participation, but of fighting apparently hopeless causes. In well over 30 seats contested by the United Party, the National Party had gained majorities of over 20% in the 1948 elections. But the reasons behind these apparently similar phenomena were probably rather different. For the United Party, or rather the United Front, this was an election that called for a supreme effort. The nature and effects of Nationalist policies, and the extent to which the Government had shown itself prepared to go, all alike called for the judgement of the electorate; and the United Front could well believe that, if that judgement did not now go against the Government, then it never would. It was in this sense a critical election; and it called for an all-out effort on the part of the United Front, if possible to win the election, if not, at least to make a demonstration of its massive support.

On the Government side it is unlikely that quite the same motives operated. It had demonstrated in 1948 that it could win elections without worrying about the United Party bastions; and it had consistently claimed that the number of seats won, rather than the number of votes cast, was the proper index of the 'popular will'. Moreover, it must have known, or it could have guessed, that to contest seats like Durban North would merely serve to boost the United Front's preponderance of votes. What is more likely is that the National Party was not seeking to demonstrate its total voting strength, but was, rather, trying to assess it; that it was using the election in other words as a trial run for a future referendum on the republican issue. But it was perhaps flying the flag as well as flying the kite. It was put to the author by prominent Durban members of the Party that the main reason it was contesting so many seats in Durban was to boost the morale of its besieged supporters; it would give them something to fight for, something to cheer.

At all events the two opposing forces were reasonably evenly balanced, with a United Front total of 147 as against the National Party's 130 candidates. What was quite extraordinary, indeed unprecedented, in the history of South African general elections, was the degree to which other possible contestants stood aside from the battle. South African elections have generally brought forth challenges from eccentrics, dissidents, champions of old causes revived and of new causes before their time. And perhaps nothing so much illustrates the critical nature of the 1953 elections and the crystallization of the issues then at stake as the fact that only four independents and one 'Liberal'[26] stood for election. This was in striking contrast to the 55 'others' in 1948. Of these five, one stood in the Cape Town area, two in the Johannesburg area, and two in Transvaal rural constituencies; and only one was in a straight fight with one of the main parties,[27] while all the rest were engaged in three-cornered contests, but with insignificant effect, as we shall see.

THE TURN-OUT

The total Union electorate at the time of the election was 1 597 923,[28] but this figure is reduced to 1 359 812 for the 129 seats actually contested. The turn-out among these voters was impressive. No less than 1 195 109,[29] or 87,9% voted: a striking improvement on the corresponding figure for 1948. Particularly noteworthy too was the consistency of voter turn-out. A probable explanation for the uniformly high percentage poll lies in the much larger than usual number of constituencies fought by the National Party; as we have seen, with only two exceptions the two major blocks confronted each other in every contested seat. Another explanation may be the far greater efficiency of the United Front organization when compared with 1948.

Table 23

VOTER PARTICIPATION PER PROVINCE

Province	*Electorate*	*Votes cast*	*% poll*
Cape	489 684	436 391	89,1
Transvaal	606 623	528 626	87,1
Natal	127 481	112 613	88,3
O.F.S..	136 024	117 479	86,4
Union	1 359 812	1 195 109	87,9

These figures do not suggest, as the 1948 figures suggested, that the United Front lagged in its efforts to bring out the vote. Some such suggestion does seem to emerge, it is true, from a comparison of the turn-out in United Front-held seats and National Party-held seats.

Table 24

PERCENTAGE POLL ACCORDING TO PARTY WINNING SEATS

Province	*U.F. seats*	*N.P. seats*
Cape	87,8%	90,0%
Transvaal . . .	86,0%	87,8%
Natal.	87,7%	93,6%
O.F.S.	—	86,4%

According to these figures, there was a higher percentage poll in Nationalist seats than there was in United Front seats in each of the three provinces in which both parties won seats. Nevertheless, the differences are relatively slight except in Natal, and there the National Party won only two seats, both of which it had won for the first time in the previous election. It was to be expected, therefore, that they would be particularly hotly contested. Moreover, the percentage poll in the O.F.S., which was completely captured by the National Party, was hardly higher than the figure for United Front seats in the Transvaal.

The over-all conclusion is that both parties conducted vigorous and highly efficient campaigns; and the electorate as a whole took the elections sufficiently seriously to respond to these efforts. There is no evidence to suggest that more drive and/or more efficiency on the part of the United Front would have brought about a different result in the elections.

THE RESULTS

(*a*) *In terms of seats*

For the supporters of the Government, the election results were a triumphant vindication of all that it had done or attempted, a vote of confidence, a renewal of its mandate. It meant that the Government could settle down on the course on which five years earlier it had somewhat precariously embarked. To an undetermined number of supporters it meant even more: the stamp of God's approval of the manner in which the Government was fulfilling His mission.[30] To the members of the United Front, however, the elections were a disaster. No convenient scapegoat was to hand, none, that is, apart from the impersonal and remote one of the electoral system. There was little escape from the uncomfortable and depressing conclusion that, at least as measured in terms of seats won, the electorate really did prefer the policies and administration of the National Party to those of the United Party.

The returns showed indeed a steady and depressing swing in favour of the National Party, where a reversal of the trend had been so ardently hoped for. Of the 149 Union seats, the National Party raised its representation from 79 seats to 88, while the United Front share dropped from 71 to 61 (later 62, after the Johannesburg City by-election). Compared with the position at 1948 and including the 3 'Natives' Representatives', the Government's majority rose from a meagre 5 to a sufficient 19, or, with the 6 South West Africa seats included, a formidable 25.

The over-all pattern of the distribution of party strengths remained much the same as in 1948: in the Cape a United Front prepon-

Table 25

RESULTS OF THE 1953 ELECTION ACCORDING TO SEATS[1]

Region	*U.F. seats*	*U.F. %*	*N.P. seats*	*N.P. %*	*Total*
Cape Town area	12 (7)	80,0	3	20,0	15 (7)
Port Elizabeth	3	60,0	2	40,0	5
Border	5	100,0	0	0,0	5
Rest of Cape	4	13,8	25 (2)	86,2	29 (2)
Total Cape	24 (7)	44,4	30 (2)	55,6	54 (9)
Johannesburg[2]	14 (8)	82,3	3	17,7	17 (8)
Witwatersrand	8	44,4	10	55,6	18
Pretoria	2	25,0	6	75,0	8
Rest of Transvaal	0	0,0	24	100,0	24
Total Transvaal[2]	24 (8)	35,8	43	64,2	67 (8)
Durban–Pietermaritzburg	10 (3)	100,0	0	0,0	10 (3)
Rest of Natal	3	60,0	2	40,0	5
Total Natal	13 (3)	86,7	2	13,3	15 (3)
Total O.F.S.	0	0,0	13	100,0	13
Total Union[2]	61 (18)	40,9	88 (2)	59,1	149 (20)

Notes: [1] The figures in brackets show the number of uncontested seats.
[2] The Johannesburg City by-election result is not included in these totals.

derance in the urban seats, and National Party preponderance in the rural areas. Yet there were Nationalist gains: its representation rose in the Cape Town area from one to three, in Port Elizabeth from one to two, and over all, though it fell from 26 to 25 in the rural Cape seats,[31] its total share of the Cape seats rose from 50,9% to 55,6%. In the Transvaal it gained an additional seat in each of the Johannesburg, Pretoria, and rural regions. Its most spectacular advance was in the Witwatersrand region, where it gained 4 seats, while the United Front lost 3. In consequence, its share of these seats rose from 35,3% to 55,6%; and this meant that only in the Johannesburg area did the United Front maintain a majority of seats. So far as Natal and the Orange Free State were concerned, the position remained virtually unchanged: in Natal the National Party lost a seat through redelimitation, but in the Free State it succeeded in capturing the United Party's last remaining seat of Bloemfontein City.

If we examine the results according to size of constituency, we see perhaps more clearly the tendency for the United Front's strength to cluster in the relatively small number of large constituencies. A comparison with the 1948 figures[32] shows a loss of United Front strength in the small rural seats, but at the same time a National Party advance in the larger seats.

As a result of the tendency revealed in this table, the average United Front constituency in the Cape was 8,7% larger than the average National Party seat, in the Transvaal there was an 8% difference, and in Natal an 18,5% difference.

Table 26

RESULTS ACCORDING TO SIZE OF CONSTITUENCY

Voters	*Cape*		*Transvaal*		*Natal*		*O.F.S.*		*Union*	
	U.F.	N.P.	U.F.	N.P.	U.F.	N.P.	U.F.	N.P.	U.F.	N.P.
12 000–12 999	11	3	—	1	—	—	—	1	11	5
11 000–11 999	7	5	21	13	6	—	—	2	34	20
10 000–10 999	4	10	2	6	4	—	—	5	10	21
9 000–9 999	2	12	1	10	3	2	—	5	6	29
8 000–8 999	—	—	—	13	—	—	—	—	—	13
Total	24	30	24	43	13	2	—	13	61	88

(*b*) *The results in terms of votes*

As Table 27 shows, the election results in terms of the votes actually cast for the respective parties by no means demonstrated the kind of disaster for the Opposition forces that they suffered in terms of seats won in the House of Assembly. Admittedly they constituted a setback: the United Front majority dropped from 104 159 to 15 195 votes, and, just as ominously, the National Party's share of the vote rose from 41,2% to 49,0%. Nevertheless the United Front's strength remained relatively stable. In 1948 it had gained 50,9% of the votes cast; in 1953 the figure was 50,2%. A new factor, however, was introduced into the 1953 elections: the virtual elimination of minor parties and independents. Where, in 1948, these together mustered 7,2% of the poll, in 1953 they polled no more than 0,1% of the poll. The increment in the Nationalists' share of the poll could be almost entirely accounted for, then, if it is assumed that those who voted for 'others' in 1948 now swung to the National Party in 1953. This would, however, be an unjustifiable assumption. Some S.A.P. and Central Group votes might perhaps be assigned to the Nationalists, but by far the greater majority of independents had been anti-Government. At a generous estimate, therefore, not more than 3% of this vote can be placed on the side of the Government; but on that basis the Nationalists' share of the vote would be raised to 44,2%, and the national swing in favour of the Government in the contested seats would have been 2,5%—and this when the Opposition had been hoping for a swing of that order in the opposite direction.

In the Cape Province the relative strength of the two parties remained remarkably little changed, with the exception of the Cape Town area, where the over-all Nationalist vote rose from 11,2% to 36,6%, while the Opposition vote correspondingly fell from 71,8% to 62,8%. This apparently striking Nationalist gain was, however, no doubt largely due to the fact that whereas in 1948 they entered only two candidates in 1953 they entered 10.[33]

Table 27

VOTES CAST PER PARTY IN CONTESTED SEATS, 1953

Region	*Reg. voters*	*Votes cast*	*% poll*	*Spoilt*	*%*
Cape Town area	97 542	84 540	86,7	517	0,6
Port Elizabeth	59 526	53 592	90,0	287	0,5
Border	55 910	49 437	88,4	264	0,5
Rest of Cape	276 706	248 822	89,9	1 876	0,8
Total Cape	489 684	436 391	89,1	2 944	0,7
Johannesburg	101 263	84 445	83,4	531	0,6
Witwatersrand	201 725	177 505	88,0	1 351	0,7
Pretoria	84 846	75 285	88,7	458	0,6
Rest of Transvaal	218 789	191 391	87,5	1 799	0,9
Total Transvaal	606 623	528 626	87,1	4 139	0,8
Durban–Pietermaritzburg	80 147	69 252	86,4	285	0,4
Rest of Natal	47 334	43 361	91,6	310	0,7
Total Natal	127 481	112 613	88,3	595	0,5
Total O.F.S.	136 024	117 479	86,4	842	0,7
Total Union	1 359 812	1 195 109	87,9	8 520	0,7

In the Transvaal the National Party edged its way up from 21,2% to 31,1% of the vote in the Johannesburg area, and from 40,2% to 47,7% in the Witwatersrand; but the United Front still retained a very substantial majority in the former and a majority, if a tenuous one, in the latter. Its real reversal was in the Pretoria constituencies where, from having a slight lead with 50,6% of the vote, it dropped to 45,4%. In the rural areas its fortunes also declined, but less spectacularly, from 39,8% to 37,6% of the vote. The total effect of these changes in the Transvaal, however, is seen when we compare the United and Labour Party majority of 24 542 votes in 1948 with the National Party majority of 14 966 votes in 1953.

The increase in the National Party's voting strength in the Durban–Pietermaritzburg seats, a rise from a meagre 2,6% of the votes to 15,5%, is, as in the case of Cape Town, mainly a consequence of the greatly increased number of candidates entered in that area. In the rural areas of Natal, although it was still in a clear minority, its share of the vote increased less dramatically perhaps, but more significantly, from 31,9% to 36,7% of the votes. Meanwhile, in the Orange Free State the hopelessness of the United Party's cause was once more demonstrated as its already low share of 29,4% of the vote dropped once more, to 28,2%.

These figures, however, do not take into account the uncontested seats. Estimates of the votes that would have accrued to the respective parties had these seats been contested are shown in Table 28. If these estimates are reasonably accurate, the United Party and its allies retained the support of the majority of voters in all the pro-

United Front	%	*N.P.*	%	*Others*	%	*Majority*	%
53 064 33 415 37 059 104 049	62,8 62,3 75,0 41,8	30 908 19 890 12 114 142 897	36,6 37,1 24,5 57,4	51 — — —	0,1 — — —	22 156 13 525 24 945 38 848	26,2 25,2 50,5 15,6
227 587	52,2	205 809	47,1	51	0,01	21 778	5,0
56 472 91 565 34 188 71 916	66,9 51,6 45,4 37,6	26 266 84 589 40 639 117 613	31,1 47,7 54,0 61,5	1 176 — — 63	1,4 — — 0,03	30 206 6 976 6 451 45 697	35,8 3,9 8,6 23,9
254 141	48,1	269 107	50,9	1 239	0,2	14 966	2,8
58 251 27 158	84,1 62,6	10 716 15 893	15,5 36,7	— —	— —	47 535 11 265	68,6 26,0
85 409	75,8	26 609	23,6	—	—	58 800	52,2
33 110	28,2	83 527	71,1	—	—	50 417	42,9
600 247	50,2	585 052	49,0	1 290	0,1	15 195	1,3

vinces except the Orange Free State, while for the Union as a whole it improved on its 1948 position by increasing its 53,3% of the vote to 54,7%. This rise is probably more than accounted for by the absence of third-party intervention in 1953. On the other hand the National Party showed a significant increase in strength in all

Table 28

ESTIMATED TOTAL VOTES, 1953
(N.P. and U.F. only)

Region	*Est. votes*	*Rej.*	*N.P.*	%	*U.F.*	%
Cape						
Cape Town area .	155 621	944	40 501	26,0	114 125	73,3
Port Elizabeth[1] .	53 592	287	19 890	37,1	33 415	62,4
Border[1] . . .	49 437	264	12 114	24,5	37 059	75,0
Rest of Cape . .	266 427	1 999	155 111	56,7	109 317	41,0
Total Cape. .	525 077	3 494	227 616	43,3	293 916	56,0
Transvaal						
Johannesburg .	160 500	988	34 079	21,2	124 257	56,0
Witwatersrand[1] .	177 505	1 351	84 589	47,7	91 565	51,6
Pretoria[1] . . .	75 285	458	40 639	54,0	34 188	45,4
Rest of Transvaal	191 391	1 799	117 613	61,5	71 916	37,6
Total Transvaal	604 681	4 596	276 920	45,8	321 926	53,2
Natal						
Durban–Pieter-maritzburg . .	96 579	395	13 346	13,8	82 838	85,8
Rest of Natal. .	43 361	310	15 893	36,7	27 158	62,6
Total Natal .	139 940	705	29 239	20,9	109 996	78,6
Total O.F.S. .	117 479	842	83 527	71,1	33 110	28,2
Total Union.	1 387 177	9 637	617 302	44,5	758 948	54,7

Note: [1] Regions in which all seats were contested.

provinces, and in the Union as a whole its estimated share of the votes rose from 39,4% to 44,5%. Some of these extra votes would have come from the dissident Nationalist-minded voters who abstained in 1948; some from Nationalists who voted for Nationalist-supported independents and minor parties, such as the C.G. and S.A.P.; some would have come from an increased share of votes from those newly registered; and some perhaps, but on the evidence probably not very many, from those who had voted for United Party or allied candidates in 1948.

By and large the evidence suggests, then, that the United Party and its allies retained the support of more than half the voters; but that the Nationalist support was gaining in cohesion and also in numerical strength. That this latter point is valid is further suggested by an examination of the uniformity of direction in the swing towards the National Party in seats contested in both elections.

(*c*) *The swing*

There were 84 contested seats in the 1953 election for which the swing in votes can be calculated, i.e. seats which were contested by both major parties in 1948 as well as in 1953. This figure is, as in 1948, less than it might have been were it not for the effects of redelimitation. In the Orange Free State, for example, where 12 of the 13 seats were contested by both parties in both elections, the number of comparable seats is reduced to 8, because 4 of the 1948 seats disappeared under the 1953 delimitation. Nevertheless these 84 seats are sufficient to indicate a general trend.

At first sight the figures might perhaps be thought to suggest the absence rather than the presence of any trend. In the Cape the swing in individual constituencies varied from 9,0% in favour of the United Party to 9,9% in favour of the National Party; in the Transvaal from 19,2% in favour of the United Party to 13,5% in favour of the National Party; in Natal from 1,0% in favour of the United Party to 11,7% in favour of the National Party. Only in the Orange Free State was the swing uniformly in favour of the National Party, and there it ranged from 0,4% to 14,9%. But if we look at the Cape, the Transvaal, and Natal more closely, we find that out of the 24 Cape seats for which a swing can be measured only 5 swung in favour of the United Party; in the Transvaal it was 12 out of 48, and in Natal 1 out of 4. In the Orange Free State, as we have seen, the swing was all in favour of the National Party. For the Union as a whole only 18 seats showed a swing in favour of the United Party.

In the Cape the average of the swing in the 24 constituencies was 2,0% in favour of the National Party; in the Transvaal it was 2,6%; in Natal 6,1%; and in the Orange Free State 5,9%. The average of the swing in all these 84 seats was 2,9% in favour of the Nationalists.

If we try to avoid the difficulties arising from the calculation of the swing in terms only of the 84 seats falling within this category, by calculating the swing in terms of the total votes cast in each province and in the Union as a whole, a fresh set of problems confronts us. In particular the relatively large number of minor party and independent candidates in 1948 and the much larger number of National Party candidates in 1953 are serious distorting factors. Under the circumstances the swing calculated in these terms can hardly be regarded as a precise measure of the movement of opinion. On this basis, however, and with reference only to contested seats, the swing in favour of the National Party was 4,7% in the Cape, 4,1% in the Transvaal, 2,0% in Natal, and 2,3% in the Orange Free State, while for the Union as a whole it was 3,6%.

These figures differ considerably from those obtained by averaging the swing in the 84 constituencies, but in view of the difficulties stated this is hardly surprising. In 1948 in the Cape there were only 33 Nationalist candidates (including those of the Afrikaner Party) compared with 45 in 1953; in the Transvaal there were only 50 in 1948 compared with 58 in 1953; in Natal there were only 5 compared with 12 in 1953. It is to be expected, therefore, that the increased number of candidates put into the field by the Nationalists in 1953 would bring them a greater share of the vote, and this no doubt is partly the reason why the swing measured in gross terms is so much greater particularly in the Cape and the Transvaal than the swing calculated on the basis of averages. But in Natal the reverse holds good, and here perhaps the effect of the minor party candidates in 1948 is most clearly seen; for in 1948 there were 14 candidates of this sort in Natal, gaining in total 17,3% of the vote, while there was none at all in 1953. The absence of these candidates in 1953 heavily favoured the United Party and no doubt largely accounts for the difference noted.

Conclusions as to the exact extent of the swing must in the light of these factors be tentative only. We can suggest, however, with some measure of probability that the swing in favour of the N.P. was between 2% and 3% for the Union as a whole,[34] and that this was broadly maintained in each of the four provinces. But it is beyond dispute that what movement of opinion there was between 1948 and 1953 was in favour of the National Party, and also that this movement was not yet very pronounced and was certainly less than it had been in the previous quinquennium.

(*d*) *The disparity between seats and votes*

The disparity between the seats won by the respective parties in the House of Assembly and the votes cast for them is illustrated in the tables below. In Table 29 the seats won are expressed as percentages of the 149 seats filled in the 1953 elections; in the next two columns the votes cast in the contested constituencies only are expressed as percentages; and finally the percentage votes estimated for the major parties if the uncontested seats are taken into account.

Table 29

PERCENTAGE OF SEATS COMPARED WITH PERCENTAGE OF VOTES

Region	*% seats won*		*% votes cast*		*% estimated votes*	
	U.F.	N.P.	U.F.	N.P.	U.F.	N.P.
Cape	44,4	55,6	52,2	47,1	56,0	43,3
Transvaal	35,8	64,2	48,1	50,9	53,2	45,8
Natal	86,7	13,3	75,8	23,6	78,6	20,9
O.F.S.	0	100,0	28,2	71,1	28,2	71,1
Union	40,9	59,1	50,2	49,0	54,7	44,5

As this table together with Table 30 reveals, the vagaries of the electoral system cost the United Front heavily. It should have won a majority in the Cape, as it should also have done in the Transvaal seats; it should have won at least some seats in the Orange Free State; and, allowing for its 'unearned' degree of success in Natal, it still should have enjoyed a majority in the Union as a whole.

Table 30

SEATS ACCORDING TO PROPORTION OF VOTES

Province	*Actual seats won*		*Seats proportional to votes cast*		*Seats proportional to estimated votes*	
	U.F.	N.P.	U.F.	N.P.	U.F.	N.P.
Cape	24	30	28	26	30	24
Transvaal	24	43	34	33	36	31
Natal	13	2	11	4	12	3
O.F.S.	0	13	4	9	4	9
Union	61	88	77	72	82	67

In terms of the state of opinion in the country, the United Front should in 1953 still have enjoyed a workable majority in Parliament. As it was, the considerable United Front support in the country largely went to waste. Table 31 gives an indication of how serious this wastage was, by showing the number of voters required to win each contested seat.

On this basis it took, for the Union as a whole, twice as many United Front supporters to win a seat as it did Nationalists; and in

Table 31

NUMBER OF VOTES REQUIRED TO WIN EACH CONTESTED SEAT

Province	*U.F.*	*N.P.*
Cape	13 393	7 350
Transvaal	15 884	6 258
Natal	8 451	13 305
O.F.S.	—	6 425
Union	13 959	6 803

the Transvaal, where the Nationalist wins were decisive, each Nationalist counted for more than two and a half times as much as each United Front voter.

(*e*) *Factors in the distortion of voting strengths*

(i) *The loading and unloading of constituencies*

Once more in 1953 the strength of the United Party was centred on the urban areas (plus rural Natal as well), and that of the National Party in the rural areas, although it made important gains in the Witwatersrand. Given the system of loading urban and unloading rural constituencies, the over-all effect was to reduce the weight of United Party voters as compared with Nationalist voters. As seen in Table 26, 45 of the United Front's total of 61 seats had over 11 000 voters, compared with 25 National Party seats in the same category. At the lower end of the scale 42 of the National Party seats had fewer than 10 000 voters, compared with only 6 United Front seats in that category. The effect of this on the average number of voters in constituencies won by the U.F. and N.P. respectively is shown in Table 32.

Table 32

AVERAGE SIZES OF UNITED FRONT AND NATIONAL PARTY SEATS (CONTESTED SEATS ONLY)

Province	(*a*) *U.F.*	(*b*) *N.P.*	*% by which* (*a*) *exceeds* (*b*)
Cape	11 467	10 546	8,7
Transvaal	11 106	9 975	11,3
Natal	10 908	9 203	18,5
O.F.S.	—	10 463	—

From these figures we may conclude that the system of loading and unloading, coupled with the general correspondence between rural (i.e. loaded) and N.P. seats on the one hand, and urban (i.e. unloaded) and U.F. seats on the other, was, as in 1948, a contributory factor in the distortion of voting strengths; although again it probably was not in itself decisive.

(ii) *The concentration of United Front support*

It was the concentration of the United Front's support in a relatively small number of constituencies that was its major electoral handicap. Even if we take, for the avoidance of all speculation, the figures for contested seats only, we arrive at the striking difference between average United Front majorities and National Party majorities set out in Table 33. Table 34 demonstrates the extent to which the U.F. majorities tended to cluster in the higher ranges, while the N.P. majorities clustered in the lower ranges.

Table 33

AVERAGE MAJORITIES, 1953

Area	U.F.			N.P.		
	Gross		%	*Gross*		%
Cape Town	5 311	(5)	51,5	1 467	(3)	13,2
Port Elizabeth	5 079	(3)	48,4	857	(2)	7,9
Border	4 989	(5)	50,0	—		—
Rest of Cape	2 164	(4)	22,3	2 065	(23)	23,0
Total Cape	4 435	(17)	43,6	1 915	(28)	20,9
Johannesburg	5 513	(6)	60,9	1 340	(3)	13,3
Witwatersrand	2 245	(8)	22,5	1 098	(10)	11,1
Pretoria	2 773	(2)	27,8	2 000	(6)	22,0
Rest of Transvaal	—		—	1 904	(24)	24,5
Total Transvaal	3 536	(16)	37,6	1 691	(43)	20,2
Durban–Pietermaritzburg	6 791	(7)	68,5	—		—
Rest of Natal	4 319	(3)	49,3	847	(2)	10,0
Total Natal	6 049	(10)	62,8	847	(2)	10,0
Orange Free State	—		—	3 878	(13)	44,0
Total Union	4 476	(43)	45,8	2 075	(86)	23,8

Note: The number of seats involved is given in brackets.

Table 34

DISTRIBUTION OF U.F. AND N.P. MAJORITIES ACCORDING TO SIZE

	Cape		*Transvaal*		*Natal*		*O.F.S.*		*Union*	
	U.F.	N.P.	U.F.	N.P.	U.F.	N.P.	U.F.	N.P.	U.F.	N.P.
8 000–8 999					1				1	
7 000–7 999			1		2				3	
6 000–6 999	5		2		3				10	
5 000–5 999	3		1		1			1	5	1
4 000–4 999	2		2	1	1			7	5	8
3 000–3 999	2	5	5	5	1			2	8	12
2 000–2 999	3	7	1	10	1			2	5	19
1 000–1 999	2	11	1	15		1		1	3	28
1–999		5	3	12		1			3	18

As these figures show, in the areas of the United Front's greatest strength its average majorities ranged from 48,4% to 68,5% of the votes cast, while only in the Orange Free State did the average Nationalist majority exceed 40%. In the Cape and Transvaal rural areas, where it gained such sweeping victories, its average majority was in each case below 25%. The contrasting pattern of United Front wins compared with those of the National Party is therefore remarkably apparent.

But what did this mean in terms of seats? If we regard majorities as, in effect, so many 'wasted' votes, we find that in its 43 contested seats the United Front 'wasted' 192 465 votes, compared with 178 419 votes 'wasted' in the 86 National Party majorities. This, however, is not the whole story, for here the uncontested seats cannot be left out of account. At a conservative estimate, we can allow a majority of 5 000 votes for each of the 18 United Front uncontested seats, and 2 000 votes for each of the two Nationalist uncontested seats. On this basis we may estimate that in effect the United Front 'wasted' 282 465 votes, and the National Party 182 419 votes. In other words there was a net 'loss' to the United Front of some 100 000 votes. We can therefore reasonably conclude that if these votes had been more evenly distributed they would have been more than sufficient to make up the United Front's deficiency in seats.

As things were, at this most critical stage of South Africa's political history, the National Government was returned to office with the substantially increased majority of 27 seats and claimed on this basis a clear and decisive mandate from the people. Even more clearly than in 1948, however, this result was a reversal of what was in fact the majority opinion: it reflected not 'the will of the people' but the combined effects of demographic factors and the electoral system's built-in capacity for distortion.

5

The General Election of 1958: The Call of the 'Tribal Drum'

INTRODUCTION

With the confidence it derived from its renewed majority in the 1953 election, it was hardly to be expected that the Nationalist Government would falter in the pursuit of its objectives or show a greater willingness to make compromises or seek reconciliation. Whether it was sincerely convinced of the moral or theological rectitude of its policies, despite the growing volume of criticism of clergymen (of almost all denominations), journalists, and academics, or whether it simply conceived them as pragmatically necessary we may not know, but it certainly stuck to them with every appearance of conviction. On the one hand, apartheid was given further elaboration and greater rigidity,[1] and on the other hand, and in consequence, the civil liberties of South Africans were yet further restricted.[2] And all this was in spite of continued, indeed mounting, opposition and unrest among the Africans and other non-white groups,[3] and in spite of its failure among the white electorate to extend the base of its support.

However the moral argument might rage, politics in South Africa was very obviously the politics of power. Within the electoral arena, that power came primarily from the Afrikaner group; and provided Afrikanerdom retained its cohesion, that was sufficient. Outside the parliamentary scene, with its electoral base secure, it could, in dealing with non-white opposition and overt unrest, rely on coercion without the necessity of moderating its efforts for fear of losing office. The Nationalists' main objective in 1958 was, in brief, to consolidate the cohesion of Afrikanerdom, to strengthen the image of the National Party as its champion, and so to make sure of the retention of political power. To that end it was not necessary for the Government to be able to demonstrate that its policies had gained, or were likely to gain, the approval of the non-white peoples. Indeed, greater electoral profit was more likely to accrue from the non-white opposition that was generated; for in that situation the Government was able to exhibit to the full its capacity to govern—to handle the situation—by its display of firmness.

Before and during the 1958 election campaign it was very obvious that the Nationalist Government had little perception of a need to carry the nation with it, to govern, in Burke's phrase, 'according to the sense and agreeably to the interests of the people'—that is, if 'nation' and 'people' be given a generalized connotation applying to South Africa as a whole. But this of course is where the whole point lay. For the Nationalists declined to apply this generalized connotation: 'the nation', 'the people', were simply equivalent terms for *die volk*. And in that sense, and that sense alone, Burke's task was accepted as 'a great and glorious object of government'—and let the rest go hang!

THE CONTESTANTS

(*a*) *The National Party*

Under the leadership of Dr Malan, the National Party had been welded into the most effective political organization that South Africa had yet known; it had a coherent philosophy, a profound commitment to its policies, it commanded the enthusiastic loyalty not only of its hard-core members but of the mass of its supporters at large, and it had created a highly efficient party bureaucracy. Nevertheless the Party was not entirely without its elements of tension. Dr Malan's own long political career came to an end when he resigned both as Prime Minister and as member of Parliament in November 1954. Before his resignation took effect, he made it quite clear that he hoped and expected that N. C. Havenga, the senior member of the Cabinet and former leader of the Afrikaner Party, would be elected as his successor. Havenga, although from the O.F.S. himself, was identified with the more moderate, predominantly Cape, element in the Party. The Transvaal contingent, now by far the largest in the caucus as well as the most militant, decided, however, to take the opportunity to assert its position and to nominate J. G. Strijdom, the 'Lion of the North'. Before caucus met it became apparent that Strijdom would be elected, and Havenga retired from the contest and shortly thereafter from politics, a bitter and a disappointed man.[4] To external appearances the Party, however, remained as united as before. Nevertheless the occasion marked, if in only a muted fashion, the first stirring of the inner conflict within the Party which was to culminate in the split between the *verligtes* and the *verkramptes*.

The other sign that inner harmony did not prevail within the Party to quite the degree projected by its external image was given in a rather enigmatic reference by Dr Albert Hertzog[5] to Dr Verwoerd, then Minister of Bantu Affairs. According to Hertzog, Verwoerd wished to resign his portfolio on the ground that he could not 'stand the suspicion of his own people'.[6] As Minister of Bantu Affairs, Dr Verwoerd was emerging not only as the 'strong man' of the Cabinet, but also as the one man who was reshaping the concept of apartheid in a way that would shift the emphasis away from the simple notion of *baasskap* (with which Strijdom himself was identified) towards the more complex notion of 'separate development'. At the same time he was under attack for creating an empire of unprecedented scale out of his department—a state within a state.[7] Dr Verwoerd himself offered the somewhat unconvincing explanation for his tentative withdrawal that he wished to make clear the distinction between the policy and the man.[8] The incident itself had taken place some months earlier, and in a letter written in August 1957 Dr Verwoerd had given the same reason: 'In my opinion', he wrote, 'it is injurious to any government for any specific government policy to become too much identified with the name of the person implementing it.'[9] His former private secretary, in citing the letter, accepts it, on the one hand, as proof that Verwoerd's wish to resign 'was not the result of fear of attacks, of which he had endured his full quota, from both friends and enemies';[10] but, on the other hand, he goes on to say that he 'nevertheless suspected the unintermittent attacks and opposition to which he [Verwoerd] had been constantly exposed, added to the sheer burden of work . . . were becoming too much for him'. On the evidence, then, there is reasonable ground for accepting the view that Verwoerd's talk of resigning was at least in part a response to divisions within the Party, and the further probability is that these divisions had at least as one of their focuses Verwoerd's policies as Minister of Bantu Affairs.

The probability that there were elements of division within the National Party adds another dimension to what was the main thrust of the Party's campaign—the call to unity among the Afrikaners. There were, as we shall see, other reasons for the specific nature of this appeal; but it would at the same time have the advantage of aborting the Party's incipient internal tensions and of promoting its by now usual demonstration of impressive solidarity.

Certainly the call to Afrikaner unity was loud and clear, with all the hypnotically insistent power of the tribal drum. It was the *Star* which, it would seem, first used this metaphor to describe the Nationalists' campaign, but *Die Transvaler* gladly accepted its aptness: 'The tribal drum beats for every *rasegte*[11] person . . . [and] when the National Party beats the tribal drum, it causes a voice to be heard which its people trust—the voice of the good shepherd who knows his own and whom his own know.'[12] The tribal drum is beaten as a call to the tribe to gather together and unite against some danger; and the Nationalist made clear the nature of the menace, while at the same time invoking the symbols of past Afrikaner struggles. Typical of this approach was a speech made by the Minister of Labour, Senator De Klerk, at Vryheid, in which he described the election as the 'second Battle of Blood River'[13] —that battle in which the Boers had finally destroyed the power of the Zulu. Two days later he elaborated on the same theme and then went on to press the other great Afrikaner trauma into service, saying that those who voted against the Government would be committing a 'greater treachery than the traitors in the second *Vryheidsoorlog*'[14] (Freedom War, i.e. the Anglo-Boer War). The United Party did its best to counter the appeals to Afrikaner exclusiveness in favour of a broader South Africanism; but at times it too directed its own appeal to Afrikaner sentiment. In this vein Sir De Villiers Graaff traced the principles of the United Party back to the old parties of the republics, and asserted that its roots lay 'deep in the history of the Afrikaner and in his cultural heritage'.[15] He pointed out that two-thirds of the United Party's candidates had Afrikaans names and claimed that in 1953 as many Afrikaners had voted for the U.P. as had English-speaking voters. But to the Nationalists these were people who were traitors to their own people. They were, as Mr Ben Schoeman stigmatized them, the kind of Afrikaner who was prepared to sing 'God Save the Queen' and wave the Union Jack.[16]

If the 1958 election was primarily a call to Afrikaner unity, the cause for which this unity was urged was, once again, a united defence against the Black Menace. The basic argument was that a Nationalist government was essential to the preservation of 'White civilization' in South Africa; and this cause was pressed from the opening salvoes[17] of the campaign to the final rumble.[18] The Prime Minister's own final appeal to the electors claimed that the U.P.'s policy would lead to the destruction of the 'White race' in South Africa, whereas the N.P.'s policy of apartheid would secure its survival, while at the same time being both fair and just.[19] There is probably little cause to doubt that to the bulk of the voters to whom the Nationalists appealed—though, it must be said, not to the intellectuals as represented, for example, by SABRA[20]—fairness and justice were equated simply with the maintenance of white dominance in the state and the economy. On the whole it was left to Dr Verwoerd to expound a more sophisticated version of apartheid.

While denying that the Government proposed to bring about a total territorial separation of the races in South Africa, Verwoerd promised a reversal of the urban migration of Africans—which meant of course a migration from the 'homelands' to the so-called 'white' areas. By always regarding the African urban dwellers as 'migrant workers' (that is, by denying them rights as settled residents) and by the rigid enforcement of influx control regulations, as well as by promoting border industries adjacent to the homelands, the Government, he insisted, would be able to restrict the number of non-whites in the white areas to only six million by the year 2 000.[21] What the utility of that achievement would be—assuming it were realized—remained, however, obscure.

The other main issue, used no doubt for its own sake, but also to rally all true Afrikaners behind the National Party, was the equally familiar—and equally reliable—one of the republic. It featured prominently in the N.P. manifesto, where it was stated that the republic would be achieved as soon as there was proof that an adequate majority of the white voters favoured it.[22] To that end the N.P. was eager not only to enlarge its parliamentary majority but also to win what it so far had not achieved—a majority of votes. 'We must get', Ben Schoeman urged, 'the biggest number of votes, for that number will indicate how far we have advanced on the path to a republic.'[23] *Die Burger* stated that the feeling was developing among 'republican Afrikanerdom' that 'we have waited almost long enough'.[24] And the Prime Minister assured his supporters, 'the day of the republic is approaching much faster than the United Party realizes'.[25]

The republican issue was clearly linked too to the Government's request for a mandate to lower the voting age for white voters from twenty-one to eighteen; for the change would undoubtedly increase the Nationalist vote—in this context a vote for the republic—since not only were the Afrikaner youth more thoroughly indoctrinated in the Afrikaner myths, but they also outnumbered their English-speaking age-group peers. It was left, however, to the Minister of Defence, Mr Erasmus, to raise the question in a politically neutral way. 'As Minister of Defence', he said, 'I feel very much at liberty to ask this, for if I may call on a boy and a girl of eighteen years to defend their people, should they not also be in a position to make their cross?'[26]

(*b*) *The United Party*

If there were some indications of tensions within the National Party, as we have suggested there were, it must be admitted that they were rather of the kind that engage the clue-hunting enthusiasm of Kremlinologists. In the case of the United Party, on the other hand, the divisions were quite patent. Six U.P. rebels had been expelled from the U.P. after the general election in 1953 for having private discussions with Dr Malan in order to seek a formula which would enable them to vote for the Coloured Voters Bill, and they set themselves up as a new party—the Conservative Party. Later, nine members of the U.P. threatened to resign, over the failure of the Party to undertake to restore the voting rights of Coloureds. Although only one of this group actually resigned at the time, this division set the scene for the later split in 1959 which led to the creation of the Progressive Party. Meanwhile, also back in 1953, the disintegration of the United Front produced the Union Federal Party and provided further evidence for the weakening hold of the U.P. over its supporters.

Beset by these divisions, the U.P. drifted into a position vis-à-vis the Nationalist Government that was popularly described as 'Me too, only not so loud'. Its major strategy appeared to be the negative one of provoking the minimum amount of alienation of voters from it, and its tactics to be directed to avoid confrontation on controversial issues on which conservative opinion was likely to be consolidated on the one side. Inevitably, as a result, its performance in Parliament was lack-lustre, described by *Die Vaderland* as 'colourless and dispirited'[27] and by *Die Transvaler* as 'exhausted or already stricken paralysed'.[28] Under these circumstances it was hardly to be expected that its election campaign would generate much excitement. Nor did it. Indeed the major excitement—if that is the word—associated with the campaign was the extraordinary outbreak of violence and rowdyism by means of which Nationalist supporters sought to break up United Party meetings.

On too many points, too, the United Party was put on the defensive. There was, for example, the case of Archbishop Joost de Blank, who described the policy of white domination as 'inhuman and un-Christian',[29] and who looked forward to the day 'when public opinion and the laws of the land make our [i.e. Anglican] great schools open for entry on the basis of ability, and not of colour'.[30] N.P. spokesmen and the Nationalist press immediately pounced on these statements as supporting a policy of complete racial integration and, by a process of easy association, then sought to stamp the United Party with that policy. The result, predictably, was an agonized disclaimer reiterated by U.P. speakers and the English press, and Sir De Villiers Graaff assured the voters that the Party continued to adhere to 'the traditional pattern of our country's life and development—a policy of social and residential separation'.[31]

Again, as the African National Congress called for 'mass action' on 14 April in the form of demonstrations, processions, and a stay-at-home strike, and the Government proceeded to put into effect massive preventive measures, the United Party's silence on the issues provided the Nationalists with another weapon of offence. The U.P.

was blamed for African unrest, it was allegedly silent in order to woo the liberal vote, and, most damaging of all, it was even linked with the A.N.C. with the assertion that it was supported by the A.N.C. because under a U.P. government the latter would be able to achieve its aims.[32] On these issues the U.P. once again reacted defensively, and in doing so tacitly acknowledged that had the charges been valid it would indeed have been culpable. Sir De Villiers Graaff castigated the attempt to link the party with the A.N.C. as 'dangerous and irresponsible', and he went on to say, 'The United Party will not tolerate disorder, illegal action or economic blackmail for the redress of political grievances'.[33]

On one issue the United Party did go over to the attack, and that concerned the personal position of Dr Verwoerd. As we have seen, Dr Verwoerd's position was probably a matter of some dissension within the National Party itself, and no doubt the U.P. hoped to capitalize on this as well as to use him as a bogy-man with which to frighten those who might otherwise be inclined to move their support to the Nationalists. Adding point to the attack was the state of Mr Strijdom's health, which was known to be poor. Verwoerd the empire-builder was then projected as being doubly dangerous. As Minister of Bantu Affairs he was portrayed as the man who was ruthlessly prepared to carve South Africa up in fulfilment of his goal of total territorial separation of the races; but, more than that, as the man who would be likely soon to succeed Strijdom when ill-health forced the latter to resign.[34] What effect the U.P. attacks on Verwoerd had on the wavering voters is not known, but it probably was not great. In so far, however, as they were aimed at Nationalist voters, they probably misfired, causing the N.P. to close its ranks rather than be lured into further division. Dr Verwoerd himself stated that the Prime Minister had asked him to stay in his present office, and he went on to say that he realized that the United Party had made him its major election target and that he accepted the challenge represented by its attacks.

The United Party was not, however, wholly negative in its stance. If somewhat nervously, it nevertheless made an attempt to project an alternative course for South African politics. In 1957 it had adopted its so-called Senate Plan which envisaged reducing the enlarged Senate (consequent to the 1955 Senate Act) from 89 to 50 and including in it 12 senators elected by African and Coloured voters. The new Senate would be accorded greater power so that 'both the representatives of the Europeans and of the non-Europeans would have a veto on important measures adversely affecting their interests'.[35] At that time too the United Party had pledged itself to restore the Coloured voters to the common roll, although significantly with a somewhat higher minimum qualification.[36] As a further ameliorative measure, the party proposed to give Africans the right to buy land in urban areas, thus giving them in some measure a sense of security.[37]

The United Party manifesto itself was a rather colourless document, concentrating almost exclusively on safe economic issues. It proposed to finance its capital programme with a less heavy reliance on the taxpayer by reducing government wastage, by saving money by rescinding expensive ideological measures such as the Population Register, by the more productive use of available labour resources, and by the general stimulation of the economy. In general, the Party's campaign was fairly described by the *Star* as placing 'bread and butter before ideology'.[38] There is little doubt, however, that it lacked the evocative appeal of the 'tribal drum'.

(*c*) *The Labour Party*

By 1958 the Labour Party had moved far away from the Party that had helped Hertzog in 1924 to form the first Nationalist Government. Its policies on the crucial non-European question were indeed now hardly less liberal than those of the Liberal Party itself.[39] By 1958 its stated policies included: 'equal opportunity for all South Africans and their protection against economic exploitation and unjust discrimination'; a minimum wage for all workers with no discrimination on grounds of sex, race, or colour; a comprehensive system of social security, free of any means test; free and compulsory education for children of all races; and the abolition of 'man-made inequalities in the material distribution of goods and income'. More specifically it advocated the repeal *inter alia* of the Suppression of Communism Act, the Group Areas Act, the Riotous Assemblies Act, and the Public Safety Act.

In the sphere of Parliamentary representation, the Labour Party stood for the extension of the system of Natives' Representatives to the other provinces, increasing the number from three to ten, and granting the Africans the right to elect their own people as members. It proposed too to restore the Coloured voters to the common roll and to extend these provisions to the other provinces.

Clearly the Labour Party had moved so far from the United Party that a repetition of the previous electoral alliances would have been meaningless. The two Labour candidates expressed their opposition to the idea of such an alliance in forthright terms: 'We would become the victims of political expediency, as were several members of the United Party in the case of the Public Safety Act, the Criminal Laws Amendment Act and the "Hanging Bill".'[40]

This decision involved both candidates in three-cornered fights with the United and National Parties, and thereby made almost certain the disappearance of the Party from the Parliamentary scene.

(d) The Liberal Party

The Liberal Party had been founded in 1953, shortly after the general election of that year, on the basis of the year-old Liberal Association—an association that had conceived its role in the furtherance of its racial policies along lines similar to that of the Fabian Society. The defeat of the United Front in 1953, however, persuaded its founding members to come out as a political party, less, it might be said, in the hope of winning seats than as a means of obtaining a public platform for the more effective dissemination of its views. Alan Paton, the National Chairman of the Party, elaborated on this educative role of the Party in a book written shortly after the election: the 'parliamentary duty' of the Party, he wrote,

> is to try to put its policies and principles before the white voters of the country; to try to persuade white voters that failure to change their attitudes can lead only to disaster; to uphold the claims of justice and to preach both the folly and the wrongness of race discrimination; to bring African and Indian and Coloured and European Liberals on to the election platforms, thus giving largely white audiences an opportunity to see that those values of which they wrongly suppose themselves to be the sole custodians, are supported by their fellow South Africans of other races, and to be reassured that a non-racial democracy is a valid and exciting choice.[41]

The Liberal Party was in 1958 the only multiracial political party, and its policy was directed to the removal of all race discrimination, with a universal adult franchise, without exception on grounds of race, sex, or colour, as its aim. In 1958, however, it still accepted that it might be necessary to adopt qualifications based on education, property, earning power, or 'a record of a decent and industrious life'; but these 'should apply for the minimum period necessary for a smooth transition to universal adult suffrage'.[42]

In conformity with its policy of attempting to provide a bridge between whites and non-whites, the Liberal Party not only admitted non-whites as members, but as a party it actively sought co-operation with the African National Congress and the South African Indian Congress. These activities, however, were hardly likely to add to its appeal to a white electorate. Herein indeed lies the fatal dilemma for all such parties in South Africa; to court the favour of one colour group is to court disaster with the other. Nevertheless at the time of the election the Liberal Party had four representatives in Parliament:

Mrs V. M. L. Ballinger and Mr Stanford (both Natives' Representatives in the House of Assembly) and Senators Rubin and W. Ballinger (representing Natives in the Senate).

(*e*) *The South African Bond*

Formed in the closing weeks of 1955, the South African Bond represented a response to the protest of the 'thirteen professors'—members of academic staffs of Pretoria University and of the University of South Africa—against the Government's manipulation of the constitution in order to secure the removal of the Coloured voters from the common roll. Recognizing the strength of the antipathy felt by many Afrikaners to the United Party, the Bond attempted to provide a home for conservative voters who had been repelled by the Nationalists' methods. Ideologically it fitted into the narrow territory left between the borders of the two major parties.[43]

Without any notable political figure to lead it, and with policies so marginally different from those of the two major parties, the Bond was doomed from the beginning. Nevertheless it has a certain significance as an expression of the 'plague on both your houses' attitude that periodically comes over many South Africans of varying political opinions, although usually with insufficient strength to alter their voting habits.

THE DISPOSITION OF FORCES

(*a*) *The major parties*

A feature of the election that received considerable comment, at any rate in the early stages of the campaign, was the drop in the number of Parliamentary candidates put into the field by the National Party. In 1948, it is true, they and their Afrikaner Party allies together had entered only 102 candidates; but in 1953 the number rose sharply to 130. In 1958 the Party contented itself with putting up only 119 candidates, thus allowing 31 seats, or just over 20% of the total, to go by default. The United Party, on the other hand, entered a candidate in every seat, even that of the retiring Speaker. There can be little doubt therefore of the seriousness of the United Party's intentions; but is there any corresponding cause to doubt those of the National Party?

It was the *Daily News* that extracted the last cent of political capital out of the National Party's concentration of forces. 'It has', it commented, 'of intent run away from a real test of public opinion, and is fighting on a narrow, selected front, wholly in keeping with its sectional character and approach.'[44] But the *Pretoria News*[45] highlighted the only real puzzle in the National Party's decision: the fact that it did not seem to square with its apparent intention of treating the election as a test-run for a referendum on the republic, or with its stress on the importance of securing the maximum possible number of votes.

Now, however, the boot was placed in the most unflattering shape that could be fashioned on the foot of the United Party. It was accused of treating the election as 'a kind of census; in a tottering world it must try to establish where it can scratch out every vote, any vote . . .'.[46] At the same time the areas of uncontested seats were made the subjects of scorn and vituperation, being stigmatized as 'island dwellers in the great South African community, blocks of people who seal themselves off hermetically from their fellow-men . . . and thus from the growth process towards patriotism'.[47]

Table 35

NUMBER OF CANDIDATES, 1958[1]

Region	*U.P.*	*L.P.*	*N.P.*	*Lib.*	*S.A.B.*	*Ind.*	*Total*
Cape Town area	14 (6)	—	6	1	—	1	22 (6)
Port Elizabeth	5 (2)	—	3	—	—	—	8 (2)
Border	5 (2)	—	3	—	—	—	8 (2)
Rest of Cape	28	—	28	—	—	—	56
Total Cape	52 (10)	—	40	1	—	1	94 (10)
Johannesburg	16 (6)	1	7	1	2	1	28 (6)
Witwatersrand	20 (1)	1	19	—	—	—	40 (1)
Pretoria	10	—	10	—	—	2	22
Rest of Transvaal	22	—	22	—	—	1	45
Total Transvaal	68 (7)	2	58	1	2	4	135 (7)
Durban–Pietermaritzburg	11 (7)	—	3	1	—	—	15 (7)
Rest of Natal	5	—	4	—	—	1	10
Total Natal	16 (7)	—	7	1	—	1	25 (7)
O.F.S.	14	—	14	—	—	2	30
Total Union	150 (24)	2	119	3	2	8	284 (24)

Note: [1] Figures in brackets represent unopposed candidates.

As Table 35 shows, the seats that the National Party refrained from contesting were predominantly in the urban areas traditionally loyal to the United Party. In the Cape Town area it thus contested only 6 out of 14 seats; in the Johannesburg area only 7 out of 16, and in the Durban–Pietermaritzburg complex only 3 out of 11. These three regions combined commanded 41 seats and the Nationalists contested only 16. Apart from its avowed declaration of securing the maximum number of votes, this concentration of forces was, however, entirely rational. Of the seats it conceded in 1958, there were in fact few that it had contested in 1953, and then only with meagre success even from the point of view of vote-gathering.

(*b*) *Minor parties and independents*

In striking contrast with the 1953 election, when the fringes of opinion were largely left without candidates to vote for, the 1958 election would seem to have brought forward a more than adequate variety. In addition to the five parties already mentioned, candidates offered themselves under the banners of the Christian Democratic Party and the Republican Party, and there was one Independent Conservative as well as plain independents of varying persuasions and idiosyncrasies. In all, however, independent and minor party candidates totalled only 15, and these contested only 14 seats. These were distributed as follows: Labour Party, 2; Liberal Party, 3; South African Bond, 2; Christian Democrat, 1; Republican, 1; Independent Conservative, 1; independents, 5.

The intervention of these candidates[48] resulted in three-cornered fights in seven constituencies, in only one of which, Orange Grove, was there no Nationalist candidate. Of these seven seats, only one was won on a minority vote. That was Benoni, where the United Party gained only 47,6% of the vote, but as the Labour and United Parties were both more strongly opposed to the National Party than they were to each other, this cannot be regarded as a split-vote result. In all the other seats the winning candidate secured a handsome over-all majority. This is, indeed, indicative of the degree of support that these minor party candidates secured. Eleven of them lost their deposits,[49] and these, sadly enough, included Mr Alex Hepple, the courageous leader of the Labour Party. Their impact on the election was therefore negligible, although they did force the United Party to fight seven seats that might otherwise have been uncontested.

THE TURN-OUT

Although the 1958 election lacked the political excitement of that of 1953, there was little evidence of this in the turn-out of voters to the polls. For the Union as a whole 1 135 402 people[50] voted in the 126 contested seats, giving a poll of 89,6% of the 1 267 142 voters registered in those seats. The provincial figures are given in Table 36.

Table 36

VOTER PARTICIPATION PER PROVINCE

Province	*Electorate*	*Votes cast*	*% poll*
Cape	413 173	373 960	90,5
Transvaal	625 358	559 507	89,5
Natal	89 498	77 957	87,1
O.F.S.	139 113	123 978	89,6
Union	1 267 142	1 135 402	89,6

These figures reveal a remarkable uniformity of achievement. The Cape, Transvaal, and Orange Free State indeed recorded a higher percentage poll than in 1953, when the figures for those three provinces were 89,1%, 87,1%, and 86,4% respectively. In Natal, however, the percentage poll fell from 88,3% to 87,1%; but even there this drop is readily explicable. In fact relatively low percentages were recorded in only three seats: Durban Umlazi, where the poll fell from 87,7% in 1953 to 85,9%; Pietermaritzburg District, which was unopposed in 1953, recorded only 75,7%; and Natal South Coast, where there was a drop from 89,0% to 78,6%. Of these three seats Umlazi was the only one in which there was a Nationalist candidate in both elections.

What these figures on voter participation suggest is first that although the issues of the 1958 election were neither new nor exciting there remained a remarkably solid commitment on the part of the supporters of both parties. At the same time, it must be said that the organization of both parties was of a very high order, and there must have been very few voters who were prepared to vote at all who were not caught in the net of one party or the other.

Table 37

PERCENTAGE POLL ACCORDING TO PARTY WINNING SEAT

Province	*U.P. seats*	*N.P. seats*
Cape	85,8	91,9
Transvaal	86,3	90,2
Natal	85,3	94,1
O.F.S.	—	89,1

The figures in Table 37 may indicate that, as many observers believe, there is a greater proportion of really enthusiastic supporters among those who vote for the National Party than is the case with United Party voters. They also may be taken to reflect the tendency for higher polls to occur in the more closely contested seats; and certainly the average Nationalist majority, while showing a steady increase, still remained significantly below the average United Party majority.

THE RESULTS

(*a*) *In terms of seats*

As Table 38 shows, the 1958 elections not only wiped out all representatives of minor parties and independents for the first time since Union, they also inflicted a severe defeat on the United Party. In spite of all its efforts, it gained only just over one-third of the 'ordinary'[51] seats of the House of Assembly. The National Party, on the other hand, had scored a really impressive victory, and there is little wonder that the Party regarded the results not only as a triumph but as a vindication of its policies. In a victory celebration in Pretoria the Prime Minister claimed that the results showed that the people of South Africa realized that the United Party's policy of integration would bring disaster to South Africa, and also that the republic was nearer than people thought. He went on to reveal the

Table 38

RESULTS OF THE 1958 ELECTIONS ACCORDING TO SEATS[1]

Region	U.P.		N.P.		Others	*Total*
	Seats	%	*Seats*	%	*Seats*	
Cape Town area	10 (6)	71,4	4	28,6	0	14 (6)
Port Elizabeth	3 (2)	60,0	2	40,0	0	5 (2)
Border	5 (2)	100,0	0	0,0	0	5 (2)
Rest of Cape	1	3,6	27	96,4	0	28
Total Cape	19 (10)	36,5	33	63,5	0	52 (10)
Johannesburg	13 (6)	81,25	3	18,75	0	16 (6)
Witwatersrand	5 (1)	25,0	15	75,0	0	20 (1)
Pretoria	2	20,0	8	80,0	0	10
Rest of Transvaal	0	0,0	22	100,0	0	22
Total Transvaal	20 (7)	29,4	48	70,6	0	68 (7)
Durban–Pietermaritzburg	11 (7)	100,0	0	0,0	0	11 (7)
Rest of Natal	3	60,0	2	40,0	0	5
Total Natal	14 (7)	87,5	2	12,5	0	16 (7)
O.F.S.	0	0,0	14	100,0	0	14
Total Union	53 (24)	35,3	97	64,7	0	150 (24)

Note: [1] Figures in brackets represent uncontested seats.

political motive behind the proposals for an eighteen-year-old franchise; asserting that the youth were on the side of the Nationalists, he asked, 'But what is going to happen to the United Party when we shortly give the franchise to the eighteen-year-olds too?'[52]

But the predominant theme of post-election Nationalist speeches and comment was that referred to by the *Cape Argus* as 'cooing notes from the other side'[53]—the wooing of the English-speaking voter. The Prime Minister in his national broadcast, the Minister of Justice, Mr C. R. Swart, the Minister of Transport, Mr Schoeman, *Die Transvaler*, *Die Burger*, *Die Oosterlig*, all joined in the chorus, claiming that more English-speaking voters had voted for the National Party than ever before, urging that the National Party was truly national, and extending a welcome to English-speaking South Africans to the Party.

Stanley Uys, the acute political commentator on the *Sunday Times*, blamed, however, the 'disastrous delimitation' for the size of the United Party defeat, although he also felt that the United Party's 'bread-and-butter campaign was anaemic stuff compared with the emotion and racialism of the Nationalist Party's campaign'.[54] But probably the most sombre comment came from the *Star*: 'For those, who, like ourselves, believe that these policies can only deepen South Africa's racial crisis and aggravate its economic difficulties there is little to do except watch and wait and keep the light of liberty and justice burning.'[55]

Delimitation certainly seems to have been a factor in the *size* of the Nationalist majority. Gwendolen Carter has pointed out that of the 7 seats that the Delimitation Commission had abolished 5 had been held by the United Party, and two by the Nationalists, whereas in the 7 new seats it was the National Party that won 5 to the United Party's 2.[56] But even where the name was retained, the boundaries were sometimes so drastically redrawn that in effect new constituencies were created. Kimberley North and Hottentots Holland are both outstanding examples of this procedure; and in the latter constituency the Leader of the United Party, Sir De Villiers Graaff, was himself defeated in spite of an heroic 96,4% poll.[57]

Taking the immediately subsequent by-election in Johannesburg City into account, the 1953 elections had given the National Party 88 seats against 62 seats for the United Front. In 1958 the Nationalists gained 9 more seats at the expense of the United Party. The delimitation had given Natal and the Orange Free State an additional seat each, which, given the political pattern of those two provinces, meant an additional seat to the United Party in Natal, and an additional seat to the National Party in the Orange Free State. These, then, cancelled each other out.

Those two seats had been taken from the Cape, which was now left with only 52 seats. Specifically, the Cape Town area lost a seat, as did the Cape rural areas. The *status quo* was maintained in the Port Elizabeth and Border areas, both in regard to the total number of seats and their distribution between the two parties. In the Cape Town area the United Party lost two seats, while the National Party gained one; and in the rural areas the United Party lost three seats, while the Nationalists gained two. Over all in the Cape, then, the United Party lost five seats, and the National Party gained three.

In the Transvaal the total number of constituencies remained at 68, but the Johannesburg area lost two seats as did the Transvaal rural areas, and these were added to the Witwatersrand and Pretoria regions respectively. Almost inevitably the two seats surrendered by Johannesburg were at the expense of the United Party; and since the National Party had won a clean sweep in the rural areas, the two seats surrendered there were necessarily Nationalist seats. In Pretoria the two new seats were both won by the Nationalists, and the United Party retained the two seats it had won in 1953.

It was in the Witwatersrand, however, that the most striking change in the balance of political forces was recorded. In 1948 the United Party had held 11 out of the then 17 seats; in 1953 it dropped to 8 out of 18 seats; but in 1958 it could retain only 5 out of 20 seats. If it is true, as is often held, that the political centre of gravity in South Africa lies in the Witwatersrand, then this massive shift demonstrates more clearly than in any other area the Nationalist 'take-over' in the country.

In spite of the Nationalist gains in the Pretoria and Witwatersrand areas the results given in Table 38 still suggest that, broadly speaking, the United Party remained the predominant urban party and the National Party the predominant rural party. Of the 81 seats that may be roughly placed in the major urban areas, the United Party won 49 and the Nationalists 32, whereas, of the remaining 69 seats, the United Party won 4 to the Nationalists' 65. If we restrict ourselves to the three principal urban areas of Cape Town, Johannesburg, and Durban, however, we find that the United Party won 31 seats out of 38. These, and their counterparts in East London and Pietermaritzburg and the Natal South Coast, were the real 'island dwellers in the great South African community' of whom *Die Transvaler* had complained.

If we tabulate the results in terms of size of seats, as shown in Table 39, a somewhat different view emerges. From this table it certainly remains clear that the United Party's strength lay predominantly in the larger urban constituencies, but it appears that the Nationalist range was broader than suggested by Table 38. The picture is still one of a party rooted solidly in the rural constituencies, but it also shows how it had spread its support into the urban areas. Sectional in appeal it certainly remained, but as the Afrikaner had moved into urban and peri-urban areas, the Party was able to gain the 'look', at least, of a truly national party.

Table 39

RESULTS ACCORDING TO SIZE OF CONSTITUENCY

Size of constituency	*Cape*		*Transvaal*		*Natal*		*O.F.S.*		*Union*	
	U.P.	N.P.	U.P.	N.P.	U.P.	N.P.	U.P.	N.P.	U.P.	N.P.
12 000–12 999 . . .	1	—	—	2	—	—	—	—	1	2
11 000–11 999 . . .	7	4	6	13	8	—	—	3	21	20
10 000–10 999 . . .	9	8	14	10	1	—	—	2	24	20
9 000–9 999 . . .	2	6	—	8	4	1	—	6	6	21
8 000–8 999 . . .	—	15	—	15	1	1	—	3	1	4
Total	19	33	20	48	14	2	—	14	53	97

(*b*) *In terms of votes*

The figures given in Table 40, showing the results per region in terms of votes cast in the contested seats, indicate that the increased Nationalist majority in the House should not be written off as simply the expression of an even grosser distortion of the popular vote than that which occurred in 1953. In some respects, it is true, as we shall see, that the distortion was greater, but there was more to it than that: specifically, there was a continued movement in favour of the Nationalists.

Table 40

VOTES CAST PER PARTY IN CONTESTED SEATS, 1958[1]

Region	*Voters*	*Votes cast*	%	*Spoilt*	%
Cape Town area	87 993	75 520	85,8	557	0,7
Port Elizabeth	35 131	31 909	90,8	130	0,4
Border	31 685	27 905	88,1	148	0,5
Rest of Cape	258 364	238 626	92,4	1 515	0,6
Total Cape	413 173	373 960	90,5	2 350	0,6
Johannesburg	109 481	92 575	84,6	533	0,6
Witwatersrand	210 902	192 880	91,5	1 336	0,7
Pretoria	106 671	94 593	88,7	499	0,5
Rest of Transvaal	198 304	179 459	90,5	1 264	0,7
Total Transvaal	625 358	559 507	89,5	3 632	0,6
Durban–Pietermaritzburg	43 977	37 001	84,1	204	0,6
Rest of Natal	45 521	40 956	90,0	344	0,8
Total Natal	89 498	77 957	87,1	548	0,7
O.F.S.	139 113	123 978	89,1	827	0,7
Total Union	1 267 142	1 135 402	89,6	7 357	0,6

Notes: [1] While these figures are based on those given in 'Results of the Referendum . . . and of the Genera[l] Election . . . on the 16th April, 1958', op. cit., it will be noticed that the percentages of votes per part[y] in this table differ from those in the publication quoted. In the latter, the votes per party are express[ed] as percentages of valid votes; in this table, and throughout, these votes are expressed as percentage[s] of *total* votes cast.

In 1953 the United Front had gained 600 247 votes, or 50,2%, of the 1 195 109 votes cast, compared with the corresponding figures for the National Party of 585 052, or 49,0%. In 1958, out of 1 135 402 votes cast, the United Party vote dropped to 492 070 or 43,3%, while the Nationalist vote rose to 625 616, or 55,1%. Admittedly, only 18 United Party seats had been unopposed in 1953 against 24 in 1958, and the corrections which this factor necessitates will be examined later, but the shift indicated by the raw figures is too great to be discounted. Certainly it cannot be discounted by reference to the greater participation of minor parties, for this gave rise to an increase of only 9 000 votes in this category, and even if these had all been cast in favour of the United Party, they would hardly have affected the extent of the disaster.

In the Cape the most striking Nationalist gains were in the Port Elizabeth and rural areas. In the Port Elizabeth seats they increased their vote by 3 000 and their share of the polls from 37,1% to 52,1%. This was, however, an illusory gain, for in 1958 two out of the United Party's three seats were unopposed. No such comfort was available to the United Party with respect to the rural Cape seats. It is true that if the Nationalists' two unopposed seats are taken into account, the National Party would have bettered its 57,4% of the vote in this region in 1953. But its 64,8% in 1958 would still

U.P.	%	*N.P.*	%	*Others*	%	*Majority*	%
42 652 15 166 21 427 82 373	56,5 47,5 76,8 34,5	28 995 16 613 6 330 154 738	38,4 52,1 22,7 64,8	3 316 — — —	4,4 — — —	13 657 1 447 15 097 72 365	18,1 4,6 54,1 30,4
161 618	43,2	206 676	55,3	3 316	0,9	45 058	12,1
62 202 86 352 36 480 60 053[2]	67,2 44,8 38,6 33,5	25 701 103 496 57 529 118 057	27,8 53,7 60,8 65,8	4 139 1 696 85 85	4,5 0,8 0,1 —	36 501 17 144 21 049 58 004	39,4 8,9 22,3 32,2
245 087	43,8	304 783	54,5	6 005	1,1	59 699	10,7
28 690 23 973	77,5 58,5	7 503 16 347	20,3 39,9	604 292	1,6 0,7	21 187 7 626	57,3 18,6
52 663	67,6	23 850	30,6	896	1,1	28 813	37,0
32 702	26,4	90 307	72,8	142	0,1	57 605	46,5
492 070	43,3	625 616	55,1	10 359	0,9	133 546	11,8

[2] In the source quoted, this figure is erroneously given as 600 053.

have represented a considerable advance.

In the Transvaal the results, even in their raw form, were less alarming. Over all the Nationalists improved their vote from 269 107 to 304 783 and their percentage from 50,9 to 54,5, while the United Party vote fell from 254 141 to 245 087. But this did not indicate a swing of such catastrophic proportions. In the Johannesburg area the United Party actually improved on its 1953 position. In the Transvaal rural areas it still retained the support of over a third of the voters, although its share of the vote fell from 37,6% to 33,5%. But in the Witwatersrand and Pretoria areas the tale of woe was resumed. In the former its vote shrank by nearly 5 000 while the National Party received an increment of some 19 000, and in the process the United Party percentage fell from 51,5% to 44,8%, while that of the National Party correspondingly rose from 47,7% to 53,7%. And in the Pretoria seats the story was repeated. From 45,4% of the votes in 1953 the United Party dropped to 38,6% in 1958, while the National Party went from a 54,0% share of the vote in 1953 to an impressive 60,8% in 1958.

In Natal, where only 3 of the United Party's seats were unopposed in 1953 compared with 7 out of 14 in 1958, comparison of the raw voting figures is virtually meaningless. Of some significance, however, are the figures for the Orange Free State. In both elections all seats were contested, and in both the United Party failed to win a single seat. But in spite of the discouraging influence of the 1953 results, the swing in favour of the Nationalists was only a slight 1,6%.

In order to attempt to gauge more accurately the state of opinion in South Africa in 1958 and to assess the movement of opinion since 1953, it is necessary, as before, to estimate the votes that would have been cast for the two major parties if every seat had been contested. This is again done on the basis of estimated votes for the two major parties in the uncontested seats.

These estimates, added to the votes actually cast, yield the estimated total votes for the two major parties that are shown in Table 41.

Table 41

ESTIMATED TOTAL VOTES, 1958

Region	*Est. votes*	N.P.		U.P.	
		Votes	%	*Votes*	%
Cape					
Cape Town	131 489	37 779	28,9	89 446	68,5
Port Elizabeth	53 070	21 369	40,3	31 487	59,3
Border	46 311	11 376	24,6	34 695	74,9
Rest of Cape	238 626	154 738	64,8	82 373	34,5
Total Cape	469 496	225 262	48,0	238 001	50,7
Transvaal					
Johannesburg	149 298	32 082	21,5	112 269	75,2
Witwatersrand	202 805	106 548	52,5	93 265	46,0
Pretoria	94 593	57 529	60,8	36 480	38,6
Rest of Transvaal	179 459	118 057	65,8	60 053	33,5
Total Transvaal	626 155	314 216	50,2	302 067	48,2
Natal					
Durban–Pietermaritzburg	101 975	15 308	15,0	85 544	83,9
Rest of Natal	40 956	16 347	39,9	23 973	58,5
Total Natal	142 931	31 655	22,1	109 517	76,6
O.F.S.[1]	123 978	90 307	72,8	32 702	26,4
Union	1 362 560	661 440	48,5	682 287	50,1

Note: [1] All seats in the O.F.S. were contested.

These figures can be regarded as reasonably accurate. For one thing, the 1960 referendum gives us precise figures for a period very close in time to this election. Then, as a further guide, 12 out of the 20 uncontested seats were also contested in 1953, thus giving for these seats a trend in which the 1958 elections can be placed.[58] There can at least be reasonable certainty that in 1958 the United Party still retained a slight majority in the Union as a whole. Nevertheless the flow of opinion was plainly still running in favour of the National Party. Comparing the estimated votes for 1953 with those of 1958, we find, in the Union as a whole, a United Party majority of some 10% narrowing to one of approximately 1,5%; in the Cape it was reduced from over 12% to less than 2%; in the Transvaal a majority of over 7% was transformed into a 2% minority. That the United Party was reduced to desperately holding on to as much support as it could, is emphasized by a more specific investigation of the extent of the movement of opinion in terms of the swing.

(*c*) *The swing*

The number of seats for which the swing can be calculated in 1958 is 94, or over 60% of the 150 Union seats in the House of Assembly. Thus, while the same difficulties arising from delimitation that we have noted before still refer, the trend exhibited by the swing in these seats can be regarded as significant.

In the Cape there were 34 seats that are relevant, and 28 swung in favour of the National Party, with an average swing of 6,1%, compared with 6 seats which showed an average swing of 2,1% in favour of the United Party. The average swing in all 34 seats was 4,6% in favour of the Nationalists. In the Transvaal, out of 46 seats that are relevant, 41 swung towards the National Party, with an average swing of 5,9%, while 5 seats swung towards the United Party with an average swing of 1,6%. For all 46 seats the average swing was 5,1% in favour of the Nationalists. In Natal there were only 6 relevant seats; in one the *status quo* was precisely maintained, and in the other five the swing was all in favour of the Nationalists with an average of 4,8%. In the Orange Free State 8 seats showed a swing towards the National Party, the average swing being 3,6%.

Taking the Union as a whole, there were 82 seats that swung towards the Nationalists with an average swing of 5,7%; 11 seats that swung towards the United Party, with an average swing of 1,9%; and 1 seat in which there was no change. The average swing for all 94 seats was 4,7% in favour of the National Party.

On total voting figures in the 126 constituencies that were contested, the swing in favour of the Nationalists is shown as: 9,1% in the Cape, 4,0% in the Transvaal, 5,5% in Natal, 1,8% in the Orange Free State, and 6,5% in the Union as a whole. The figures in the Cape and Natal no doubt overestimate the real movement in opinion because of the greater proportion of uncontested United Party seats in 1958.[59] For this reason, in spite of the uncertainties involved in estimating voting strengths in uncontested seats, the estimated totals are likely to provide a more reliable guide. On this basis, we again find a swing in favour of the Nationalists in all four provinces: in the Cape of 5,0%; in the Transvaal of 4,7%; in Natal of 1,8%; in the Orange Free State, since all seats were contested, of 1,8% as before; and in the Union as a whole of 4,3%.

Allowing for the particular uncertainties referred to in Chapter 4 that arose in trying to calculate the swing between 1948 and 1953, it would appear that the swing in favour of the Nationalists between 1953 and 1958 was of a somewhat higher order than in the preceding period.

(d) The disparity between seats and votes

The swing in favour of the National Party may have been gathering momentum; but the United Party still commanded the support of the majority of the electorate. Yet, as we have seen, it was able to win barely more than a third of the ordinary seats in the House of Assembly. The distortion of the vote is shown in greater detail in Table 42, and with the increase in detail the number of anomalies multiply.

Table 42

PERCENTAGE SEATS WON COMPARED WITH PERCENTAGE VOTES

Province	*% seats won*		*% votes cast*		*% estimated votes*	
	U.P.	N.P.	U.P.	N.P.	U.P.	N.P.
Cape	36,5	63,5	43,2	55,3	50,7	48,0
Transvaal	29,4	70,6	43,8	54,5	48,2	50,2
Natal	87,5	12,5	67,6	30,6	76,6	22,1
O.F.S.	0	100,0	26,4	72,8	26,4	72,8
Union	35,3	64,7	43,3	55,1	50,1	48,5

These figures make interesting reading. Referring, first, only to the percentages of actual votes cast, we might notice that the United Party and National Party strengths were virtually identical in the Cape and the Transvaal; yet in the former province the United Party won 36,5% of the seats compared with 29,4% in the latter. Or we may compare Natal and the Orange Free State with reference again only to the percentages of actual votes. Here we find that the National Party, with only a slightly greater percentage of votes in Natal than the United Party gained in the Orange Free State, gained 12,5% of the seats in the former province compared with the total failure of the United Party in the latter. These comparisons are made even more striking by reference to the estimated voting totals. Referring to these figures, we find for instance that in the Cape the United Party won an estimated 50,7% of the vote while in the Transvaal the National Party achieved an estimated 50,2% of the vote. Yet in the former province the United Party won only 36,5% of the seats, while in the latter the National Party romped to triumph with 70,6% of the seats.

What this distortion cost the United Party in terms of seats is best illustrated by showing the number of seats each party would have won if seats had been proportionate to votes.

Table 43

SEATS ACCORDING TO PROPORTION OF VOTES

Province	*Actual seats won*		*Seats in proportion to:* (*a*) *Actual votes*		(*b*) *Estimated votes*	
	U.P.	N.P.	U.P.	N.P.	U.P.	N.P.
Cape	19	33	23	29	27	25
Transvaal	20	48	30	38	33	35
Natal	14	2	11	5	12	4
O.F.S.	0	14	4	10	4	10
Union	53	97	68	82	76	74

This gross disparity between seats and votes obviously involved a corresponding disparity in the weight of United Party and National Party votes, as is shown in Table 44.

Table 44

NUMBER OF VOTES REQUIRED TO WIN EACH CONTESTED SEAT

Province	*U.P.*	*N.P.*
Cape	17 958	6 263
Transvaal	18 853	6 350
Natal	7 523	11 925
O.F.S.	—	6 451
Union	16 965	6 450

A comparison of these figures with those of Table 31 suggests that for the United Party the law of diminishing returns was operating. Where in 1953, for the Union as a whole, each Nationalist voter had carried almost exactly twice the weight of a United Party voter, five years later he counted for over two and a half times as much as the United Party voter. It was a far cry indeed from the Benthamite principle: everyone to count for one, and no one to count for more than one.

(*e*) *Factors in the distortion of voting strengths*

The factors that operated to produce this disparity between votes and seats have been already identified in the analyses of 1948 and 1953 elections. It remains therefore merely to provide the details of their operation in 1958.

(i) *The loading and unloading of constituencies*

The figures given in Table 39 showed that while the smaller constituencies were won mainly by the National Party—25 out of the 32 seats with less than 10 000 voters—it had moved into the larger urban constituencies, formerly the area of United Party predominance, winning exactly half of the 44 seats with electorates of over 11 000. In spite of this the United Party constituencies continued on average to be considerably larger than those of the National Party, as is shown in the next table.

Table 45

A COMPARISON OF THE AVERAGE SIZES OF UNITED PARTY AND NATIONAL PARTY SEATS (CONTESTED SEATS ONLY)

Province	(*a*) *U.P.*	(*b*) *N.P.*	(*c*) *% by which (a) exceeds (b)*
Cape	10 821	9 569	13,1
Transvaal	10 878	10 099	7,7
Natal	10 191	9 082	12,2
O.F.S.	—	9 937	—

These figures show that in the Cape the gap in size between United Party and National Party seats rose from 8,7% in 1953 to 13,1% in 1958, due mainly to the loss of three United Party rural seats. On the other hand, in the Transvaal the difference in average size was reduced from 11,3% to 7,7% and this change was due no doubt to the spectacular advances of the National Party into the urban areas. As a result, where in 1953 the urban seats constituted only 44,2% of the National Party's holdings in the Transvaal, in 1958 they reached 54,2%. In Natal the gap between the parties' seats dropped from 18,5% to 12,2%; but this was not due to any change in the pattern of the parties' representation in that province; it was due, rather, to the creation of an additional urban seat which made possible a reduction of the average load on urban seats. Nevertheless, while the loading factor no doubt constituted an electoral handicap for the U.P., it was probably not the decisive one.

(ii) *The concentration of United Party support*

Undoubtedly the United Party's major handicap lay in the concentration of its support. The degree of concentration is shown clearly in Table 46.

It is apparent from these figures that the United Party continued to win its seats by very large majorities; but a comparison between the figures given here and the figures for 1953 given in Table 33 reveals a trend of almost equal significance, that is, that the National Party in its turn was beginning to win its seats by increasing majorities, and that this was true of every region.

Table 47, showing the frequency distribution of the party majorities, gives added confirmation of the tendency portrayed in Table 46 for the United Party to score larger majorities than the National Party. In comparing these figures for those for 1953 (Table 34) it would again appear that the Nationalists were increasing their majorities, that they were in fact not only extending their holdings

Table 46

AVERAGE MAJORITIES, 1958[1]

Area	U.P. Gross		U.P. %	N.P. Gross		N.P. %
Cape Town	4 835	(4)	54,1	2 250	(4)	22,9
Port Elizabeth	2 673	(1)	26,2	2 060	(2)	19,0
Border	5 032	(3)	53,8	—		—
Rest of Cape	13	(1)	0,1	2 681	(27)	32,3
Total Cape	4 125	(9)	44,9	2 591	(33)	30,3
Johannesburg	5 586	(7)	62,8	1 847	(3)	18,4
Witwatersrand	2 930	(4)	30,9	1 924	(15)	18,9
Pretoria	1 685	(2)	16,7	3 052	(8)	33,5
Rest of Transvaal	—		—	2 637	(22)	32,6
Total Transvaal	4 168	(13)	45,9	2 434	(48)	27,6
Durban–Pietermaritzburg	5 146	(4)	57,4	—		—
Rest of Natal	3 408	(3)	45,5	1 445	(2)	17,1
Total Natal	4 401	(7)	52,3	1 445	(2)	17,1
Orange Free State	—		—	4 115	(14)	47,5
Total Union	4 211	(29)	47,1	2 709	(97)	31,2

Note: [1] The number of seats involved is given in brackets.

but were also tightening their grip on those which they already had. And this holds good even if we add the two unopposed N.P. seats in the 1953 election to the upper majority ranges for that year. On the other hand, the comparison between Tables 34 and 47 would suggest that the U.P. majorities were tending to slip from the upper ranges to the middle ranges. This suggestion should, however, be treated with caution, since in 1958 U.P. candidates were unopposed in 24 seats, compared with 18 in 1953. If these unopposed seats were included the differences in the parties' respective distribution curves would be even more impressive.

Table 47

DISTRIBUTION OF U.P. AND N.P. MAJORITIES ACCORDING TO SIZE

	Cape		*Transvaal*		*Natal*		*O.F.S.*		*Union*	
	U.P.	N.P.	U.P.	N.P.	U.P.	N.P.	U.P.	N.P.	U.P.	N.P.
8 000–8 999	—	—	1	—	—	—	—	—	1	—
7 000–7 999	—	—	1	—	—	—	—	—	1	—
6 000–6 999	1	—	—	—	2	—	—	—	3	—
5 000–5 999	2	1	3	1	—	—	—	3	5	5
4 000–4 999	3	2	2	2	3	—	—	6	8	10
3 000–3 999	1	9	1	10	—	—	—	2	2	21
2 000–2 999	1	11	3	17	1	2	—	3	5	33
1 000–1 999	—	5	1	15	1	—	—	—	2	20
1–999	1	5	1	3	—	—	—	—	2	8

Gwendolen Carter, commenting on the 1958 elections, writes: 'Increasingly, South African delimitations are separating National and United Party supporters into different constituencies so that fewer elections are decided by narrow majorities.'[60] The conclusion is certainly true, as we have seen; and there are grounds for thinking that the reason here assigned is at least part of the answer, but it is also possible that this change represents a change in the proportions of United Party and National Party supporters in the country as a whole. This view is supported by the uniformity of the swing in favour of the National Party. The further conclusion is that whatever the reason more and more seats were seen in 1958 to be slipping from the possible grasp of the United Party. In 1958 the task before the United Party in order to gain a majority was to capture 14 of the 15 seats with majorities in 1953 of less than 10%. After 1958 the task confronting the United Party was not only to capture the 7 seats with majorities of less than 10%, but to win over a further 16 seats with majorities of between 10% and 20%—a far more formidable task.

And yet the United Party theoretically had the over-all majority to do it. If we take the uncontested seats into account, the estimated total number of votes gained from aggregating the United Party majorities is 276 593 votes compared with a corresponding 219 470 votes from National Party majorities. The United Party therefore had over 57 000 more votes than it needed to win its 53 seats. On the other hand there were 30 National Party seats with majorities of under 2 000, all of which theoretically could have gone to the United Party with a more strategically advantageous redistribution of its 'surplus' votes. This lay, however, outside the realm of political possibility. All the United Party could do was to glower with frustration at what it regarded as the National Party's ill-gotten gains. The National Party Government for its part was able to proceed on its task of reconstructing the social and political face of South Africa with full confidence in its ability to accomplish this task.

6

The 1960 Referendum: Afrikanerdom Triumphant

INTRODUCTION

The most deep-seated yearning of the committed Afrikaner nationalist had always been for the establishment of—in a sense the return to—a republic in South Africa. Only when that was achieved could the memory of the Treaty of Vereeniging be exorcized, and the Afrikaner nation be given its full corporate expression. When the 1958 election took place after ten years of Nationalist rule, it is hardly surprising that many of the party faithful had begun to feel that they had waited long enough, or that some of them indeed might have begun to wonder whether 'their' government had lost its sense of commitment to their national goal. There was considerable rejoicing among Afrikaner ranks therefore when it was finally announced that on 5 October 1960 the electorate would be given the opportunity to answer the simple question, 'Are you in favour of a republic for the Union?'

Although the question itself was a simple one, the issue was not. Apart from the counter-pulls of opposing sentiments, apart from the purely constitutional issue of the form of the state, and apart from the effect a republican constitution would have on South Africa's membership in the Commonwealth, there was as well the whole environing issue of the character of the Nationalist regime, and, more immediately, the background of traumatic events that took place in the months preceding the referendum—neither of which could avoid being in the mind of the voter as he cast his ballot.

In the slightly over two years that intervened between the 1958 election and the holding of the referendum there were four major events (using the word loosely) that were of particular significance and which need to be briefly recalled. The first occurred within three months of the election. It was the death of the Prime Minister, J. G. Strijdom, and the election on 2 September 1958 of Dr Verwoerd as his successor. The election was by the National Party parliamentary caucus, and Dr Verwoerd was opposed by two party leaders with far greater seniority than his own. C. R. Swart was one, Minister of Justice, Leader of the Party in the O.F.S., the man who had in effect destroyed General Hertzog politically at the historic H.N.P. provincial congress at Bloemfontein in 1940. The other was Dr Dönges, Minister of the Interior, Leader of the Party in the Cape, a man with a reputation for brilliance, courtesy, and charm, who represented the more moderate elements in the Party. In the event it took two ballots to determine the issue. In the first, the results were: Verwoerd 80, Dönges 52, Swart 41. Swart then withdrew and in the second ballot Dr Verwoerd succeeded with 98 votes to 75 for Dr Dönges [2] a triumph that was not only a personal one but one that also marked the ascendancy of the more militant Transvaal in the affairs of the Party. But it meant that at the head of both party and government was a man who would assert his will more effectively and more rigidly than perhaps any other Prime Minister in the history of the Union.

The next event, although its impact was marked at the time, was more evanescent in its effects. This was the famous 'wind of change' speech delivered before the combined Houses of Parliament by the British Prime Minister, Mr Harold Macmillan, on 3 February 1960. Breaking with the polite traditions that usually govern such formal occasions, Mr Macmillan dwelt rather on the widening gulf between South African policies and those of Britain, directed, as the latter were, to the achievement of a 'society . . . in which individual merit and individual merit alone, is the criterion for a man's advancement, whether political or economic'.[3] And he went on to warn South Africa that Britain might not be able to give the continued support and encouragement to South Africa 'as a fellow member of the Commonwealth' that she had hitherto: 'I hope you won't mind my saying frankly', he said, 'that there are some aspects of your policies which make it impossible for us to do this without being false to our own deep convictions about the political destinies of free men to which in our own territories we are trying to give effect.'[4] The sobering effect of this warning, particularly on the English-speaking section, is summed up in a *Cape Argus* comment: 'Mr Macmillan . . . has sounded what may be a final warning. We either recognise in South Africa that we are members one of another or we write our own world-wide rejection and doom.'[5] But Stanley Uys portrayed just as accurately the probable attitude of those who carried more weight in determining the country's political future: 'I think the Nationalists now will almost certainly start getting tougher and more intransigent. They believe they have nothing more to lose.'[6]

By far the most tragic of the series of events, and the most critical in its effects, particularly on world opinion, was the spate of demonstrations and riots at Sharpeville, Langa, Durban, and other centres which between 21 March and 9 April 1960 cost the lives of 83 non-whites and 3 African policemen, as well as injuries to 365 Africans, and 33 white and 26 non-white policemen. The 'Sharpeville Massacre' was, from the South African point of view, catastrophic in so far as its relations with the rest of the world were concerned and undoubtedly provided the kind of emotional shock that lay at the basis of South Africa's final failure to remain in the Commonwealth on becoming a republic. At home the immediate result was the familiar reaction of increased repression. A state of emergency was declared vesting the Government with vast powers,[8] and under the terms of the Unlawful Organisations Act, 1960, both the Pan-African Congress and the African National Congress were banned. On the other hand, at least for a time, the white regime seemed to pause and to re-examine the situation which had caused the tragedy. General Rademeyer, Commissioner of Police, announced a temporary suspension of the pass laws.[9] Mr Theo Gerdener, writing in *Die Nataller*, called for a more rapid application of separate development—the 'nearest thing to equal rights'.[10] And, most significantly of all, Mr Paul Sauer, then acting chairman of the Cabinet, in his famous speech at Humansdorp, stressed the need for a change in the application of apartheid, in particular, for the removal of unnecessary causes of frustration, the 'pinpricks' that encouraged Communist propaganda; for the revision of methods of enforcing the pass and liquor laws; for the need for higher wages; for the abandonment of the *baasskap* concept; and for a sound system of contact with Africans.[11] In short, while the fundamental character of the Government's policy remained unchanged, there seemed to be a readiness to adopt a more flexible approach to its application. As Dr Dönges summed it up: 'You can safely trust the Government to adapt its accepted policy to the demands of changing circumstances.'[12]

One of the significant elements in the situation derived from the fourth major event of this period—the attempted assassination of Dr Verwoerd on 9 April. What was significant was that it was in Dr Verwoerd's absence that a more conciliatory and flexible approach was being proposed by leading members of the Cabinet. Once the 'man of granite' returned to direct government policies, however, these encouraging suggestions were heard no more, and Dr Verwoerd, in his first address to Parliament after his recovery, made it clear that there would be no shift in the direction of government policy.[13] In this the Prime Minister no doubt accurately judged the hardening of attitudes in white South Africa—a hardening that amounted indeed to petrification, once the tragic outburst of violence succeeded the grant of independence to the Congo, and the stream of Belgian refugees into the Union began.

Another result of the attempt on Dr Verwoerd's life was that he was not able to attend the Conference of Commonwealth Prime Ministers in May 1960, and South Africa was therefore represented by its Minister for External Affairs, Mr Eric Louw. One can only speculate as to whether Dr Verwoerd's presence would have affected the outcome of that meeting, but it can at least be said that Mr Louw was widely regarded as one of the least ingratiating of South Africa's representatives.

Perhaps the most significant aspect of the incident, however, is that in effect it rendered Dr Verwoerd's position of dominance in cabinet and party virtually unassailable. To the fundamentalist Afrikaner his recovery from the point-blank assault was clearly a miracle. 'In this miraculous escape', comments *Die Burger*, 'all believers will see the hand of God himself. . . .'[14] And *Die Transvaler* wrote in similar vein, 'God called Dr Verwoerd to a special task and because this task is not yet fulfilled, He who disposes over life and death ordained that the attack should fail'.[15] So to attack Dr Verwoerd became almost a matter of heresy. And it was with this kind of strength behind him that he led the Government in its referendum campaign.

TECHNICAL QUESTIONS CONNECTED WITH THE REFERENDUM

(*a*) *The timing*

Understandably, in the light of the Nationalists' 1958 campaign and their subsequent victory, there was widespread speculation in the Union over the Government's next step towards its goal of a republic. Both Strijdom and his successor, Dr Verwoerd, were ardent republicans, and both considered it imperative to move forward as soon as possible.[16] As 1960, the semi-centennial anniversary of the Union, approached, there was quickening speculation that the Government would go to the electorate in one form or another at the peak of the celebrations, in order to profit from the mood of heightened emotion.

In view of the climate of speculation, it hardly came as a surprise that the Prime Minister should deal at some length with the whole republican issue shortly after the opening of Parliament in January 1960. The occasion was the reply to the Opposition motion of no confidence; but it did little, except in a negative way, to clarify the particular question of the timing of the referendum. Summing up his position on it, he stated:

> The undertaking which I give here, therefore, is that the date will not be before May 31 [i.e. Union Day]. I make no announcement as to any subsequent date and no insinuations and no inferences will be justified.

I do promise, however, that when the Government considers the time proper and right, it will give timeous notice to the people of South Africa, as to when the referendum will be held.[17]

Despite the Prime Minister's warning about 'insinuations' and 'inferences', the inference was in fact widely drawn that the referendum would in fact be held within the year. Why else go into the issue at such length?

There was one other factor relevant to that question, and that was the imminent arrival of the British Prime Minister. This would not affect the timing of the referendum itself, but it could have had an influence on the timing of Dr Verwoerd's speech. It is at least possible that, in raising the whole issue of a republic at that particular time, Dr Verwoerd was hoping that Mr Macmillan would give some public reassurance that South Africa would continue to be welcome as a member of the Commonwealth even if she became a republic. If that was indeed the hope, it was soon dispelled; for the general drift of Mr Macmillan's address was to the effect that South Africa was more of an embarrassment than an asset to the Commonwealth.

At all events, on 11 March 1960 the Referendum Bill was introduced into Parliament, and finally on 3 August 1960 the Prime Minister announced that the referendum would take place on 5 October. One can appreciate the feeling shared by both Verwoerd and Strijdom, when he was alive, that if the republic was not soon achieved 'the time would be past forever'.[18]

It was possible that with all the attributes of full sovereignity already possessed by South Africa, the point of becoming a republic might become somewhat dimmed in the minds of Afrikaners. Alternatively, the more ardent and aggressive republicans might become disenchanted with the Government and form a break-away group to achieve their purpose—thus threatening through division the Afrikaners' continued political hegemony. On the other hand, the Nationalists had still not demonstrated in 1958 that they commanded a majority of the popular vote and a sample poll later taken by the Party was still not hopeful.[19] It would seem that the decision to hold the referendum in 1960 was essentially the Prime Minister's own decision, and that it was to a large extent a gamble—although the Government did all it could to hedge its bets.

It was perhaps this sense of gambling that induced Dr Verwoerd to reverse himself (and not for the last time either) on what he had said in his obviously carefully prepared speech in Parliament on 20 January. Speaking to a group of Nationalist M.P.s' wives, he is reported to have said:

Our chances of winning are great, provided that we can harness all the forces of the people. If we do not win now, the fight becomes harder and

I am afraid, also more bitter. We are now fighting with gentle means. If we lose, we will fight harder and with a more forceful hand.[20]

The statement aroused, as can be imagined, a flurry of indignant, possibly fearful, speculation. What precisely did the Prime Minister mean, particularly in the last sentence of the quotation? He provided his own answer to this question in the Assembly a few days later. His position, he said—and he hoped to persuade the Party to adopt it—was this:

. . . if honourable members of the Opposition continue to regard the referendum as a fraud[21] and although we will in fact have this referendum . . . if we do not succeed then in the light of this attitude they adopt, and if it should be maintained, I would not be in favour of holding one referendum after another. I would prefer to say frankly that next time we will adopt the normal method adopted by all countries of allowing all decisions to be taken by the majority in a Parliament elected for that purpose.[22]

The stated condition was so vague as to be incapable of being tested objectively; nor was any period stipulated between the holding of the referendum and the holding of a fresh general election. If therefore the republic were rejected in the referendum, the country could expect that some time thereafter a general election would be held, and that if the Nationalists were returned to power they would use their parliamentary majority to pass the legislation necessary to establish a republic—regardless of whether or not their majority of seats reflected a majority of votes.

(*b*) *The size of the requisite majority*

In the National Party's Programme of Principles and Objectives, it is stated that

. . . a republic can be established only on the broad basis of the national will . . . [as expressed in] a special and definite mandate from the European electorate, and not merely by a parliamentary majority obtained as the result of an ordinary election.[23]

As we shall emphasize later, this principle confined the 'national will' to the 'European electorate'; but for our present purposes what is important is the phrase 'broad basis of the national will'. This phrase does suggest that at least a substantial majority should support the establishment of a republic; and this would indeed appear to be the interpretation placed on the phrase by both Malan and Strijdom. Verwoerd, however, was not a man to be bothered by niceties. For him a majority was a majority. The difference between him and Strijdom is explained by Verwoerd himself:

Advocate Strydom's [*sic*] second difficulty was his publicly stated conviction that the republic could not be brought about without a previously determined numerical majority either at a referendum or in Parliament. He would never say what he had in mind, although we argued frequently about this.

Verwoerd's main objection to a previously stipulated size of majority was that this would merely open up a further area of controversy, and he goes on:

Therefore I always pleaded for the principle of a bare majority; which one would have to admit meant a majority of one. This Advocate Strydom could not understand.[24]

This too was the position that Dr Verwoerd maintained in his 20 January speech in Parliament, when he said 'Majority will mean a bare majority, even if it is one vote. In other words, if there is a majority of one in favour, then Parliament will have to take the necessary legislative action to establish the republic.'[25]

It was natural that the Opposition should seize on Dr Verwoerd's blatant dilution of the principle of 'the broad basis of the national will' into a bare majority of one, and even more on his later total subversion of this principle when he argued that Parliament could enact what the majority might deny. The truth is that Verwoerd was not a convinced democrat, in the sense that he recognized any real validity in the majority. He had earlier said that 'false propaganda' might mislead those 'who would otherwise vote for a republic', and that the Government would have to take this into consideration; for people who were thus 'misled' would later come to realize that the republic was 'just and democratic'.[26]

(*c*) *The electorate*

If Dr Verwoerd did his best with respect to a majority in the referendum to turn his gamble into a certainty, he further hedged his bet with regard to the voters who would be allowed to participate in it. Three particular acts or decisions illustrate this.

In the first instance, as we have seen, the Government acted soon after the 1958 election to lower the minimum age for white voters from twenty-one to eighteen. According to one newspaper estimate, this would add an additional 150 000 new voters to the roll.[27] Since the median age of Afrikaners tends to be lower than that of the English-speaking section, there would be a larger proportion of Afrikaners in this group than in the electorate as a whole. Moreover, they would be more likely to vote more solidly in support of the Government and for the republic than the older age groups, for they would have been exposed more consistently to Nationalist indoctrination. All in all therefore the Government would expect a significant increment in its support from this move.

Furthermore, by restricting the vote in the referendum to whites, the Coloured voters (who now of course exercised their vote on a separate roll) were debarred from participating. Since Africans and Asians no longer had any form of representation in Parliament, they would in any case have been excluded even without this special provision. Clearly the 'Nation' whose will was to be expressed made no pretence at including anyone but whites.[28] These exclusions were attacked by both the United Party and the newly formed Progressive Party, the former directing its criticism particularly to the exclusion of the Coloureds, while the latter argued more inclusively for the participation of all sections of the population in the referendum. The Government, however, naturally had its way, and thus removed from the count a large number of voters who might be expected to vote against the republic.

Finally there was the question of whether voters in the territory of South West Africa should be included or not. On this issue, Dr Verwoerd had initially been quite categorical. The legal relationship between the Union and South West Africa meant, he said, that 'the voters of South West Africa will not be able to take part in this referendum, however much we would like to have their majority of votes for the republic'.[29] Oddly enough, the United Party in South Africa criticized this exclusion while its counterpart in South West Africa approved it; while the National Party in South West also dissented from its Union counterpart and pressed for the inclusion of the territory's voters. At all events, finding, he said, that the Opposition would be in agreement with the move, and pressed by the voters of South West Africa to recognize 'their right to vote as citizens', Dr Verwoerd changed his policy and on 9 March announced that the South West African voters would after all be permitted to vote. Whether his reasons were as stated or not, he again ensured a small but useful increment to his pro-republican vote.[30]

THE MAJOR ISSUES

(*a*) *Form of republic*

What could have been the most contentious as well as the most critical of all the issues involved in the referendum was in fact resolved before the campaign began. In so far as there was contention or even disagreement it took place privately within the National Party, rather than between the parties in public. There is no doubt, however, that much of the sting of republicanism was removed in the initial statement of Dr Verwoerd on 20 January, when he said,

'. . . there will be no radical changes in our parliamentary institutions or constitutional practices'. The major effect of the change he summed up in the statement, 'The monarch is replaced by the president'.[32] Although he did allow that the State might invest the president with 'extra privileges' not currently enjoyed by the Queen, the whole tenor of this part of his speech, including lengthy supporting arguments, was that the essential constitutional position of the president would be equivalent to the existing position of the monarch.

The significance of this issue lay in the mythologizing of the former Transvaal Republic that was widely current in Afrikaner circles, and which had prompted the yearning for a return to its institutional structures, including a president of the Paul Kruger type who both 'reigned and ruled'. If these notions were widely current among Nationalists, they were at the same time the focus of the suspicions and fears of the Opposition. These had, moreover, been sharpened during the war by the increasing prevalence at that time of Nazi or semi-Nazi type opinions,[33] and in particular by the publication of a Draft Republican Constitution in 1942. This constitution certainly had an authoritarian character together with disturbingly mystical overtones; 'the State President', for example, would be 'directly and only responsible to God'; he was to be 'altogether independent of any vote in Parliament'; he was empowered to appoint and dismiss the Prime Minister, to veto legislation and to dissolve Parliament; and he was given almost unrestricted power 'in time of national danger'.[34] Although the Draft had never been formally adopted by the National Party, leading Nationalists had been associated with its formulation, and *Die Transvaler*, then under the editorship of Dr Verwoerd, had generally endorsed it. Under the circumstances, the Opposition did its best to saddle the republic proposed in 1960 with the more obnoxious features of the Draft. Nevertheless, soon after becoming Prime Minister, Dr Verwoerd had in effect repudiated the Draft as a document that was still relevant. Acknowledging that he had been connected with the people who drew it up and had known of their work, he first of all denied that the National Party as such was 'connected' with it, and he then went on to say '. . . if I have anything to do with the matter it will not form the basis of any constitution drawn up in the future . . .'.[35]

That the position finally arrived at with regard to the form of the republic had been the subject of some internal dissension within the National Party, was later revealed—although in the blandest terms—by Dr Verwoerd. Moving the Second Reading of the Constitution Bill, he spoke of the 'sacrifices' which the Afrikaner had had to make 'of much of what he had earlier hoped would be characteristic of his republic', and of 'the great concessions' made 'for the sake of unity'.[36] It seems highly improbable that these 'sacrifices' and 'concessions' were either spontaneous or unanimous.

In spite of the Prime Minister's reassurances about the proposed general constitutional structure for the republic, the issue remained alive during the campaign at least in part because his assurances were only general. Until the text of the Draft Constitution was finally published, it was inevitable that speculation would continue, and that the Opposition would raise whatever frightening spectre that it had some hope of making plausible.

(*b*) *Commonwealth membership*

To English-speaking South Africans, and possibly indeed to a substantial number of Afrikaans-speakers, this issue was of paramount importance. There were the ties of long historical association, the sense of loyality and attachment to the Crown, of common struggles in the wars, of participation in the pursuit of common purposes, of sharing a common culture, including on the whole a common political culture, and of course the awareness of the economic benefits that derived from Commonwealth membership.

To the Nationalist, particularly the less sophisticated Nationalist, on the other hand, almost opposite sentiments prevailed. The Commonwealth was either identified with the British Empire or if the nature of the new Commonwealth was perceived, it tended to be perceived in terms of strident black nationalism which made South Africa the subject of attack wherever and whenever possible. In neither case was there cause to cherish association with the Commonwealth or a positive desire to retain membership in it. It is true that since 1948 successive Nationalist Prime Ministers had stressed the benefits of Commonwealth membership and the complete freedom and independence which South Africa enjoyed as a member, but it is doubtful whether the rank and file were entirely convinced. Memories die hard in South Africa, and memories of 1914 and 1939 were still lively and still for them symbolized South Africa's subordinate status.

It was in accordance with these notions that the National Party's Programme of Principles and Objectives stated:

> 10. It is convinced that the republican form of state, separated from the British Crown, is the form best adapted to the traditions, circumstances and aspirations of the South African nation, and is also the only effective guarantee that South Africa will not again be drawn into Great Britain's wars.[37]

The phrase 'separated from the British Crown' had generally been taken to mean a republic outside the Commonwealth. Indeed, until April 1949 when a formula was found to permit India to retain her membership on becoming a republic, it was simply assumed that a republican constitution and membership in the Commonwealth were mutually exclusive. Thus when the Republic of Ireland Act, 1948, came into effect that country ceased to be a member. The 1949 formula permitted 'acceptance of the King as the symbol of the free association of its independent member nations and as such the Head of the Commonwealth' in place of acceptance of a common allegiance to the Crown as the basis of membership. Henceforward republican status and membership were separate issues, requiring separate decisions.

That this was the case was accepted by the National Party. That did not mean that the two acts might not take place simultaneously. But Verwoerd has written, 'The preference of many of us was for a single process', and he went on:

> Advocate Strydom [*sic*], however, after considerable searching, came to the conclusion that under certain circumstances, two steps instead of one might well be necessary. Our arguments over this prepared me for what had to follow later.[38]

What 'had to follow later' was the decision—and it would seem the reluctant decision—to seek to remain within the Commonwealth on becoming a republic, at least for the time being. This decision, however, was not taken immediately. In his speech on 20 January, Dr Verwoerd gave only 'a clear and unequivocal promise, namely that before this referendum is held the country will be told whether it will be the policy of the government to remain a member of the Commonwealth, or not to remain a member'.[39] At the same time he went on to list the three considerations that would determine the Government's policy, namely the 'position in Britain', that is, whether the Labour Party was in power, 'the position within the Commonwealth', and the interests of South Africa. This statement therefore still left the issue in suspense, and the arguments he brought forward were hardly likely to appeal to those, on both sides of the fence, who wished to have a clear-cut statement of policy.

It was not until the beginning of August that the Prime Minister announced that the Government would ask formal permission from the other members for South Africa to retain its membership on becoming a republic, although at the same time he warned that if the results of the referendum were favourable but the other member countries were not prepared to give that permission, the Government would still go ahead to establish the republic.[40] These decisions were endorsed by both the Cabinet and the federal council of the National Party.[41] Subsequently, at a special union congress of the Party, a resolution was adopted that incorporated the main elements of Dr Verwoerd's statement.[42]

In view of the lateness of this decision—in itself an indication of the 'soul searching' that must have gone on in the party—when Mr Louw represented South Africa at the Commonwealth Conference in May, he had two suppositions to present to the meeting. What he sought was advance permission for South Africa to remain a member *if* the decision was taken in South Africa to become a republic, and *if* at that time South Africa wished to remain a member. The conditional nature of South Africa's request may have been a factor in the deferment of a decision by the Conference,[43] but it is more probable that substantive factors rather than the purely procedural one were behind it. There are some grounds for thinking that the U.K. High Commissioner in South Africa, Sir John Maud, had persuaded Mr Macmillan that a refusal to give advance agreement to South Africa's continued membership might influence enough voters to vote against the republic to defeat the Government in the referendum. On the other hand, particularly after Sharpeville, there had been talk overseas of actually expelling South Africa. In consequence, if the issue had been pressed to the point of a decision, it might even in 1960 have gone against South Africa—and this, no doubt, Mr Macmillan would have sought to avoid. Certainly the concluding paragraph in the communiqué on this issue was not encouraging from South Africa's point of view. After referring to the 'informal discussions' that took place on 'the racial situation' in the Union, it went on to say:

> The ministers emphasised that the Commonwealth itself is a multi-racial association and expressed the need to ensure good relations between all member states and peoples of the Commonwealth.[44]

The inference to be read into the guarded language used was that the policies pursued by the South African Government were not compatible with the new multiracial Commonwealth and consequently there was real doubt as to whether South Africa's application would be approved.

As may be expected, the Opposition made much of this issue. 'As sensible, prudent people', warned Sir De Villiers Graaff, 'we are forced to the conclusion that should we become a republic, our membership of the Commonwealth may well be placed in jeopardy and be subject to the veto of one or more of our most severe critics.'[45] Indeed, this became perhaps the major theme of the Opposition campaign. The value of the Commonwealth connection was reiterated again and again, and the proposal to establish a republic was thus portrayed as endangering that connection, and as placing the country at the mercy of its enemies.

In turn, the Government was forced to express a confidence on this question which perhaps it did not feel. At any rate, it certainly did its best to convince the country that a favourable outcome was assured. In a statement read in Parliament on his behalf by Dr Dönges, the Prime Minister stated that the question of whether South Africa was still welcome as a member was put to the meeting of Prime Ministers, and that 'with due regard to the existing unanimity rule, [it] was unambiguously answered in the affirmative'. And he went on to say, 'It is clear from this that it is the desire of member countries that South Africa should remain a member of the Commonwealth'.[46] In similar vein, in his broadcast to the nation on 3 August 1960, Dr Verwoerd said, 'The Government is convinced that consent will be given as has always been customary whenever such constitutional changes have taken place, and even when most extensive differences of opinion and policy have existed'.[47]

(*c*) *The republic and the regime*

From his first announcement on 20 January, the Prime Minister attempted to disengage the issue of the republic from other political issues. This, according to his statement, was the specific reason for referring the matter to a referendum rather than holding a special general election:

I want to say unequivocally that I do not believe that the decision should be obtained by means of an election. I want to announce, therefore, that this issue will be put to the electorate by way of a referendum. The reason for selecting this method is that this concerns an issue on which the nation should be able to decide the future unhampered by other complications.[48]

And he went on to point the conclusion:

I do not even want the question of confidence or no-confidence in a Government to be linked up with it. The Government is in power and will remain in power, so that nobody who votes a particular way need be afraid that in doing so he is throwing out his Government, and nobody who is not anxious to vote for the Government, need have the feeling that he cannot vote for the republic.[49]

This was to continue as a recurring theme of the Government's campaign. Obviously the Government was convinced that more republicans sheltered in the opposition kraal than the reverse—and this may well have been true. It would therefore pay the Government to emphasize the distinction between a vote in support of the Government and a vote in favour of the republic.

On the other hand, where the Government thought it would be to its own advantage it did not hesitate to introduce other issues. In particular, Dr Albert Hertzog,[50] and on several occasions Mr

Maree,[51] made the Government's racial policies a prime issue. And Dr Verwoerd himself, in his famous letter to the voters written two weeks before the referendum, ingeniously linked the republican issue to that of race and warned his readers, 'If we do not take this one step now, we ourselves possibly, but our children certainly, will experience all the suffering of the Whites who are being attacked in, and driven out of, one African territory after the other'.[52]

Indeed it would have been unreal to separate the question of the formal structure of the republic from the kind of regime under which it would operate. Apart from the Government's racial policies, there was also the question of the relations between English- and Afrikaans-speaking South Africans. Particularly in view of the subordinate role assigned to English in the 1942 Draft, but also in view of the practice followed by Nationalist governments since 1948 of promoting Afrikaners to key positions in the civil service, police and defence forces, there were fears among the English-speaking voters that the advent of the republic would further weaken their position. Moreover, the republican goal was a distinctively Afrikaner goal. This was openly acknowledged. 'The republic', wrote *Die Burger*, 'is in the final analysis primarily an Afrikaner ideal and an Afrikaner need. . . . [It] is . . . necessary to bring the patriotism of the Afrikaners to its full maturity and glory.'[53]

Nationalist leaders, however, made every effort to bring the English-speaking voter into the republican fold. In marked contrast to the sectional appeal made by the N.P. in its 1958 election campaign, the new theme was 'national unity'—i.e. English–Afrikaans co-operation. In his statement to the country immediately after his election as Leader of the N.P., Dr Verwoerd said:

> Above everything, I look forward to the happy day when all of us will be so joined together by a common patriotism into one people with two languages that political differences that might exist will no longer be based on sentiment.[54]

The N.P. referendum campaign was directed to persuading the electorate that only under a republic could this ideal of national unity be achieved. As things stood, it was argued, the English-speaking section continued to have divided loyalties, while Afrikaners, for their part, could not identify with a head of state who was 'always chosen from the heirs of the Royal family in another state, Britain'.[55] In consequence, the monarchy in South Africa was not the source of unity but of division. Consequently, Dr Verwoerd argued, 'if we wish to become one people—one people with two languages but with one national anthem, one flag and one country, we must be united by a symbol of honour from our own ranks.

This may only be a president who has grown up among us.'[56]

The theme was taken up by the Union congress of the Party in August, which adopted the following resolution:

> The Union Congress of the National Party extends the hand of friendship to all republicans outside its ranks and particularly to the English-speaking supporters of a republic who are not members of the National Party. They are assured that their support will appear as the greatest contribution to national unity.[57]

At the same time the extension of the hand of friendship carried not only the proviso that English-speaking South Africans join the ranks of the republicans, but also the warning that a failure to do so would be interpreted as evidence of hostility. In this vein *Die Burger* wrote: 'If they wish to regain their influence with us, influence for the good, they will have to free themselves of the suspicion, which among many Afrikaners is a bitter conviction, that their fundamental incentive in politics is still only a hatred of Boers.'[58] And in his speech on the Union Jubilee, after again making his plea for Anglophone co-operation in the establishment of a republic, the Prime Minister warned of the calamities that would follow if the 'political clashes' between the two language groups continued, and, as a means of avoiding these consequences, appealed to the English-speaking section 'to create a republic on the lines acceptable to all'.[59]

For the great majority of English-speaking voters what was being asked of them, however, was not co-operation with Afrikaans-speaking South Africans, but co-operation with a Government that was repugnant to them. 'The real reason for disunity in this country is the complete breakdown of trust between the Government-supporting groups and all other South Africans'—this was a typical response of the Opposition press. 'The present disunity in the country', the writer went on, 'is due to the 12 years of ever more sectional rule under which other sections have suffered increasing discrimination and exclusion.'[60]

Massive demonstrations in the major English-speaking centres of the Union indicated these appeals were not likely to induce it to abandon its opposition to the Government or to the republic that it advocated. Sir De Villiers Graaff ridiculed the idea that a republic would unite the two major white groups; it was not a republic but a miracle that was needed in order to accomplish this. 'If the Government are concerned with a split between the English-speaking and Afrikaans-speaking groups,' he asked, 'why have the Prime Minister and his party used so much restraint in the past in their efforts to bring them together?' Indeed, he argued, the National Party was the instrument of a 'narrow sectionalism', as the rigid enforcement of mother-tongue education in the Nationalist-controlled provinces demonstrated.[61] For the English-speaking people the reaction to the Nationalist overtures was in general that of 'Timeo Danaos . . .'.

Recollections of the violent opposition to the war effort, of the notorious 1942 'Draft Constitution' with its relegation of the English language to a subordinate position, the widespread belief that English-speaking citizens were discriminated against in the public services, as well as the mother-tongue education issue, were among the factors that made the English-speaking section suspicious of the proposed republic. And fears of this sort were probably a stronger influence on voting behaviour than a positive attachment to the Crown.

These suspicions were, however, secondary to those connected with the kind of republic contemplated and the kind of regime that would result. In this connection, Sir De Villiers Graaff warned: 'We know what Nationalist leaders advocated during the war years —that the franchise be restricted to national elements, that English should not have equal rights and that the President should have peculiar powers.'[62] The Opposition frequently referred to the proposed republic as the 'Broederbond Republic', implying that it would be dominated by a sinister secret society and be essentially anti-democratic in nature. Even after Dr Verwoerd's assurances to the contrary, Dr Steenkamp for the United Party continued to assert that the Broederbond was forcing Dr Verwoerd to keep the constitution of the proposed republic secret because they could not afford to make it public.[63]

There were, however, other fears, less extreme perhaps but still serious, and probably more widely felt than those expressed by Dr Steenkamp. These were summed up in the alternative appellation: a 'Verwoerd Republic', or as Dr Steytler expressed it, 'the wrong republic at the wrong time'.[64] The Nationalist regime had come to be identified in the minds of many people with a scant regard for constitutionality, a lack of sensitivity to the interests and opinions of any save their own supporters, and a steady erosion of civil liberties; and such people feared that support for a Nationalist-sponsored republic would perpetuate the evils that they saw. Dr Naicker, President of the South African Indian Congress,[65] and Mr Luthuli, President-General of the African National Congress,[66] both expressed fears of this kind, and Dr Steytler, for the Progressive Party, argued more broadly that any republic designed to maintain white domination was doomed to failure and would result in bringing about a situation like the Congo in South Africa.[67]

THE TURN-OUT

The arrangements for the referendum were simple and sensible. The only point to which exception might be taken was the provision that if the ballot paper were marked in some other way than a plain cross but in a way giving a clear indication of the voter's intention then the vote would still be counted as valid. Otherwise the referendum was conducted on virtually the same lines as a general election, the vote being counted for each Parliamentary constituency using the boundaries operative at the 1958 election. There was, therefore, a ready-made system of polling districts and electoral officers, and since no candidates as such were involved, the two major parties were empowered to appoint 'agents' to assist in the voting and scrutinizing procedures.[68]

Nevertheless, there were complicating factors: there was the problem of mobilizing the new 'teen-age' vote; there was the problem of ensuring maximum registration of voters; and there was the problem of creating an effective party machine in constituencies uncontested for a considerable time. These problems the parties tackled energetically and effectively.

Certainly the percentage poll was satisfactory. For the Union as a whole the percentage poll rose from 89,6% in 1958 to 90,9%, or if South West Africa, which had the lowest percentage poll, is included, 90,8%. Each of the four provinces, indeed, improved on its 1958 position.

Table 48

THE TURN-OUT PER PROVINCE

Province	*Electorate*	*Votes cast*	*% poll*	1958 *% poll*
Cape	591 298	544 083	92,0	90,5
Transvaal	818 047	734 930	89,8	89,5
Natal	193 103	178 585	92,5	87,1
O.F.S.	160 843	144 407	89,8	89,1
Union	1 763 291	1 602 005	90,9	89,6

These figures were perhaps all the more remarkable in view of the considerable increase in the number of registered voters. In 1958, the total electorate had been 1 532 179. There was, therefore, an increase of over 230 000 or approximately 15% over a period of two years.

What is also remarkable about the turn-out of voters in 1960 was the reversal of the trend noticed in previous elections: Natal, predominantly anti-Government and anti-republican, on this occasion was the scene of the heaviest turn-out, while the strongest centres of republicanism, the Transvaal and the Orange Free State, trailed the field, each with 89,8%. The improved turn-out in anti-republican centres is even more noticeable if we refer to the average percentage

Table 49

ANTI-REPUBLICAN AND REPUBLICAN PERCENTAGE POLLS

(The first column gives the average percentage poll in constituencies in which there was a majority against the republic; the second column, the average percentage poll where there was a majority for it. The 1958 figures are given in brackets)

Province	*Against*	*For*
Cape	91,8% (85,8)	92,2% (91,9)
Transvaal . . .	90,1% (86,0)	89,7% (90,4)
Natal.	92,8% (86,0)	92,4% (90,4)
O.F.S.	—	89,8% (89,1)

polls in anti-republican and republican constituencies respectively. These figures show that there was a much higher rate of improvement in the turn-out in anti-republican constituencies than there was in the republican constituencies. This fact provides supporting evidence for the suggestion made with regard to the earlier elections that the relatively low percentage recorded in Opposition seats was partly due to the absence in some of Nationalist candidates. In 1960 there was a major contest in every seat. The figures also demonstrate that the anti-republicans were just as eager to cast their negative votes as the republicans were to cast their affirmative ones.

But chiefly the turn-out was satisfactory in that with an over-all poll of nearly 91% it could not be said that the issue went by default. However narrow the eventual majority, at least it was a majority of a voting population that as nearly as may be reasonably expected can be equated with the statutory electorate (that is, the electorate for the purposes of the referendum).

THE RESULTS

(*a*) *The votes*

The tactical skill of the Nationalist Government is held in considerable respect in South Africa, even among the Opposition. It was therefore widely believed that the Government would not have risked such a serious setback to its prestige and to Nationalist aspirations as a defeat in the referendum would have constituted unless it had good grounds to believe that it would be successful. For this reason the results of the referendum came as no great surprise.

At all events, the results as shown in Table 60 justified the hopes of Dr Verwoerd and the gloom of the Opposition.

As expected, the Orange Free State and the rural areas of the Transvaal proved to be the most solid centres of republican support, with 76,3% and 71,0% of the votes respectively being cast in favour of the republic. The rural areas of the Cape with 67,2% and the

Table 50

RESULTS OF THE REFERENDUM[1]

Area	*Voters*	*Votes cast*	%	*Spoilt*	%	*For*	%	*Against*	%	*Majority*[2]	%
Cape Town	178 736	162 070	90,7	616	0,4	54 185	33,4	107 269	66,2	—53 084	32,8
Port Elizabeth	68 737	63 795	92,8	269	0,4	26 801	42,0	36 725	57,6	—9 924	15,6
Border	57 982	53 806	92,8	346	0,6	12 824	23,8	40 636	75,5	—27 812	51,7
Rest of Cape	285 843	264 412	92,5	1 650	0,6	177 608	67,2	85 154	32,2	+92 454	35,0
Total Cape	591 298	544 083	92,0	2 881	0,5	271 418	49,9	269 784	49,6	+1 634	0,3
Johannesburg	195 550	174 588	89,3	655	0,4	45 587	26,1	128 346	73,5	—82 759	47,4
Witwatersrand	258 996	233 494	90,2	932	0,4	132 155	56,6	100 407	43,0	+31 748	13,6
Pretoria	132 109	116 607	88,3	374	0,3	79 631	68,3	36 602	31,4	+43 029	36,9
Rest of Transvaal	231 391	210 241	90,9	1 296	0,6	149 259	71,0	59 686	28,4	+89 573	42,6
Total Transvaal	818 047	734 930	89,8	3 257	0,4	406 632	55,3	325 041	44,2	+81 591	11,1
Durban–Pietermaritzburg	141 884	131 116	92,4	481	0,4	21 757	16,6	108 878	83,0	—87 121	66,4
Rest of Natal	51 219	47 469	92,7	207	0,4	20 542	43,3	26 720	56,3	—6 178	13,0
Total Natal	193 103	178 585	92,5	688	0,4	42 299	23,7	135 598	75,9	—93 299	52,2
O.F.S.	160 843	144 407	89,8	798	0,6	110 171	76,3	33 438	23,2	+76 733	53,1
Total Union	1 763 291	1 602 005	90,9	7 624	0,4	830 520	51,8	763 861	47,7	+66 659	4,2
South West Africa	37 135	32 235	86,8	280	0,9	19 938	61,9	12 017	37,3	+7 921	24,6
Union and South West Africa	1 800 426	1 634 240	90,8	7 904	0,5	850 458	52,0	775 878	47,5	+74 580	4,5

Notes: [1] These figures are taken from Results of the 'Referendum held on the 5th October, 1960, and of the General Election of Members for the House of Assembly held on the 16th April, 1958'. An enclosure in the Union of South Africa, Bureau of Statistics, *Official Yearbook of the Union*, No. 30—1960, Pretoria, 1960–1. In this table, however, the votes for and against the republic are expressed in the relevant columns as percentages of the total votes cast and not as percentages of valid votes only, as in the work quoted.

[2] + indicates a majority in favour of the republic, and — indicates a majority against it.

Pretoria area with 68,3% affirmative votes were not far behind. The centres of opposition were, for their part, equally well-defined. The Durban–Pietermaritzburg seats cast 83,0% of their votes against a republic; of the Johannesburg votes, 73,5% were negative; of the Border seats, 75,5%; and of the Cape Town seats, 66,2%. In only three major regions of the Union was the vote reasonably close: Port Elizabeth with 57,6% against the republic; the Witwatersrand area (excluding Johannesburg) 56,6% in favour of it; and the rural areas of Natal, with 56,3% opposed to it.

Although there was a majority in favour of the republic, it was a slender one. Including the South West Africa vote it amounted to less than 75 000 votes out of 1 634 240 votes cast: a mere 4,5% of the total votes cast; while for the four provinces of the Union the majority was less than 70 000 out of more than 1 600 000 votes or 4,2%. It was on this basis that the Government decided to introduce legislation in Parliament to establish a republic in South Africa. It could, perhaps it should, have issued a statement to the effect that it had decided not to act on the referendum in view of the narrowness of the majority. The electorate had, however, been warned by the Prime Minister that a majority of one would be sufficient.

From the point of view of strict law, the Government not only could have refrained from enacting a republican constitution in spite of the majority recorded in the referendum in favour of a republic; it could equally have enacted a republican constitution even if the results of the referendum had been reversed. Nevertheless, from the point of view of political morality, it is unfortunate that this turning-point in South Africa's history should have been tainted by doubts as to its legitimacy. There is at least the suspicion that the Government manipulated the size and shape of the electorate in its own favour by reducing the age qualification, by excluding the Coloured voters, and by including South West Africa.

On the basis of the 1951 census figures, the 'teenage' vote probably added some 152 000 voters to the roll. Given the average proportion of Afrikaans-speaking to English-speaking at that age level of 63,5 to 33,5, some 46 000 more Afrikaans-speaking voters were added to the roll than English-speaking voters. If voting on the republican issue followed linguistic lines, the absence of these votes would then have reduced the republican majority to approximately 29 000 votes. In the 1958 elections there had been some 29 000 registered Coloured voters. As a result, at least partly, of a boycott less than 15 000 actually voted. But the reason for the boycott (resentment over the provision for separate representation) would not have applied to the referendum; and on the same line of reasoning, it is probable that there would have been a much higher proportion of registration among qualified Coloured voters.[69] If the Coloured voters had been included therefore—they were after all duly enfranchised citizens—this vote might well have been sufficient under the old franchise laws to produce an anti-republican majority, even with the inclusion of South West Africa in the vote. Without South West Africa there could have been little doubt about the outcome; and that South West Africa not being part of the Union of South Africa, was not really entitled to vote on the issue, even the Prime Minister himself had originally acknowledged. As it was, the inclusion of South West Africa added a bonus of nearly 8 000 votes to the republicans.

(*b*) *The swing*

In order to compare the voting figures in the referendum with those of the 1958 general election, it is necessary to use the estimated total votes for that election. A comparison on this basis shows that in the Cape the National Party vote of 225 262 votes in 1958 rose to a republican vote of 271 418 in 1960. The corresponding percentages were 48,0% in 1958 and 49,9% in 1960. In 1958 the United Party scored an estimated total vote of 238 001; in 1960 the anti-republican vote stood at 269 784. There was an estimated 50,7% of the votes in favour of the United Party in 1958, and this dropped to 49,6% against the republic two years later. On these total figures, there was, then, an estimated swing of 1,5% in favour of the Government.

The movement of opinion, measured on this basis, was much more pronounced in the Transvaal. In that province the National Party gained an estimated 314 126 votes or 50,2% of the total vote in 1958. In the referendum there were 406 632 votes cast in favour of the republic, or 55,3% of the vote. The United Party vote in 1958 was estimated at 302 067 or 48,2%; but in 1960 only 325 041 votes or 44,2% of the vote were cast against the republic; an over-all estimated swing of 4,6%.

Natal showed little change: 31 655 estimated votes for the National Party in 1958 and 42 299 votes for the republic in 1960. This represents an improvement from 22,1% of the vote to 23,7%. The United Party vote was estimated at 109 517 in the earlier year; and there were 135 598 anti-republican votes in the later, representing a slight fall in the percentage of the vote from 76,6% to 75,9%. Over all, this represents a swing of 1,2% towards the Government.

Since all seats were contested in the Orange Free State in 1958 there is no need to refer to estimated totals for that year. These totals show a gain for the Government: 110 171 votes in 1960 compared with 90 307 in 1958, while the United Party vote rose much more slowly from 32 702 to 33 438. This represented a percentage fall from 26,4% to 23,2% whereas the pro-Government percentage rose from 72,8% to 76,3%. There was therefore a swing of 3,4% towards the Government over these two years.

Taking the total figures for the whole Union, we find that the pro-Government vote rose from 661 350 estimated votes to 830 520, with a corresponding rise in its percentage of the total vote from 48,5% to 51,8%. Meanwhile, although the Opposition vote rose from 682 287 estimated votes in 1958 to 775 878 in 1960, its percentage of the total vote fell from 50,1% to 47,5%. Over all, then, throughout the Union there was an estimated swing in favour of the Government of 3,0%. Whatever doubts might be entertained about the validity of some of the referendum procedures as a basis for constitutional change, there can be no doubt on the basis of these figures that despite the political bitterness of the intervening two years the tide of opinion was still running strongly in favour of the Government.

(*c*) *Implications for party strengths*

The referendum was not combined with an election, and the constituency electoral machinery was no doubt used primarily for the sake of administrative convenience. Nevertheless the use of this machinery served at the same time to provide an interesting insight into electoral trends. In particular it gives an indication of how many seats the Nationalist and anti-Nationalist forces respectively would have won had the voting been conducted in terms of an election.

In spite of the swing in favour of the National Party if there had been a general election in 1960 the Nationalists would have won only one further seat from the Opposition. That was the Pretoria seat of Sunnyside. In 1958 the United Party had retained that seat with a majority of 614 votes, its share of the vote being 52,6%. In 1960, 57,4% of the voters voted for a republic, producing a majority of 2 050. The conditions there were, however, exceptional, The national increase in the electorate from 1958 to 1960 amounted to 15%. In Sunnyside the number of registered voters rose by 26,1%; and although the percentage poll fell from 92,4% to 89,8% the number of votes cast still showed an increase of 22,6%. This increase was probably largely due to the strong registration of Pretoria University students in that constituency, and since the student body is predominantly National-minded, their participation was probably largely responsible for the size of the republican majority.

If there was any comfort to be gained by the United Party it was from the Queenstown result. In 1958, with a 96,2% poll, Dr Steytler had held the seat for the Party with a hairbreadth majority of 13 votes.

In the meantime Dr Steytler had resigned from the United Party and joined the Progressive Party and, although he and the Progressives campaigned vigorously against the republic, there was the fear that the split would adversely affect the vote. On the contrary, with a 95,8% poll the anti-republican majority was increased to 121 votes, and the constituency was one of the few seats to show a swing away from the Government.

The Opposition success in Queenstown was more than counterbalanced by the results in the other four seats that could be regarded as marginal—one in the Cape and the other three in the Witwatersrand area. The Cape seat was Kimberley South. The United Party had been severely handicapped by delimitation in 1958 and lost the new seat of Kimberley South by 421 votes, a margin of 4,3% of the total vote. In 1960 the republican majority was doubled, reaching 968 votes, representing 8,6% of the total vote. In the Witwatersrand the Nationalists had captured the Boksburg seat in 1958 with a majority of 343 or 3,1% of the vote. In 1960 the corresponding figures were 1 070 and 8,4% respectively. In 1958 North West Rand had gone over to the National Party with a majority of 553 or 5,7% of the vote; in 1960 there was a majority for the republic of 1 731 or 14,8%. And Vereeniging, captured in 1958 by the Nationalists with a majority of 843 votes or 7,3% of the vote, recorded a solid majority in favour of the republic of 1 809 or 15,2% of the votes cast.

In general then, apart from the substantive issue itself, the referendum brought little comfort to the Opposition for it showed a continued movement of opinion in favour of the Government.

THE ESTABLISHMENT OF THE REPUBLIC

The results of the referendum were received with dismay by the opponents of the republic and with elation by its supporters. However minimal the constitutional changes that might follow in order to give effect to the referendum there was a feeling that, for better or for worse, depending on one's point of view, the country was about to take a critical and irrevocable step. To republicans of course the day of promise had arrived, and all other considerations were of minor importance. The anti-republicans, however, were anxious to save what they could from the wreck. Dr Steytler, for the Progressive Party, appealed to the Prime Minister to call a national convention, representing all racial and political groups, to help in the drafting of the new constitution[70]—a forlorn appeal indeed! Sir De Villiers Graaff, on behalf of the United Party, made a similar point although more negatively when he claimed that any republic established on the basis of the slender majority obtained in the referendum would 'in the nature of things, be a sectional republic'.

But the main burden of his response was that legislation should not be introduced to establish a republic until it was certain that South Africa would be able to remain in the Commonwealth.[71] Again, this was a forlorn appeal; for well before the referendum Dr Verwoerd had refused to contemplate any such deferment. And he made his position clear after the referendum when he said 'Seen both numerically and geographically, the decision is clearly final'.[72]

Some six weeks after the referendum the Prime Minister announced that the republic would be proclaimed on Union Day, 31 May 1961, henceforth to be known as Republic Day;[73] and early in the new session, in January 1961, he introduced the new Republic of South Africa Constitution Bill. The Bill, as promised, followed as closely as possible the existing constitutional structure—even to the extent of continuing to entrench the clauses governing the equal status of the official languages.[74] As Professor Kahn has commented, '. . . apart from establishing a republic and replacing the King and Governor-General by a President elected by the senators and members of the House of Assembly, it did not purport on the face of it to introduce any radical change in the structure of the State'.[75]

Nevertheless, before the Bill had passed through all its stages in Parliament, a radical change in the surrounding political situation had taken place. This occurred at the Commonwealth Prime Ministers' Conference, held in London in March. The full story of what took place there need not be told here,[76] but as is well known the upshot was that Dr Verwoerd felt compelled to withdraw South Africa's application to continue as a member on becoming a republic. In consequence, as the Bill passed through its final stages it was known that when the republican constitution came into effect South Africa would simultaneously cease to be a member of the Commonwealth.

If this was a defeat for the Prime Minister he skilfully turned it into an apparent triumph. As he stepped out of his aeroplane at Jan Smuts Airport, he was greeted by a 21-gun salute before a crowd variously estimated at between 40 000 and 60 000.[77] At the airport, Dr Verwoerd told the crowd, 'You may leave here full of hope. We have triumphed—not over another country, nor over Britain, but we have freed ourselves from the pressure of the Afro-Asian nations who were busy invading the Commonwealth. We were not prepared to allow these countries to dictate what our future should be. . . . Therefore, we now go forward alone. We are standing on our own feet.'[78]

This remained the Prime Minister's theme, and despite secessionist noises from Natal, in the end it paid off. On 31 May 1961 the Republic of South Africa came peacefully into being, although it was now outside the Commonwealth and, at least apparently, alone in a hostile world.

7

The General Election of 1961: The Threshold of a New Era?

INTRODUCTION

'We must realize', said Dr Verwoerd, 'that we are standing at the start of a new era.'[1] To many Afrikaners that may indeed have seemed to be the case, and it would be an era of hope and promise to which they looked forward. To many of the Opposition too the advent of the republic seemed to mark the beginning of a new era but one which they regarded with gloomier foreboding. It would however probably be more accurate to suggest that the old wine had merely been poured into a new bottle.

Be that as it may, the Government took the occasion to justify the holding of a fresh general election. In this vein, Mr Paul Sauer pointed out that the existing Parliament had been elected under the old, monarchical constitution, and that it was now appropriate to elect a new Parliament to represent the new Republic of South Africa.[2] Perhaps in a symbolic sense, the argument had some point, but it could have point only in a symbolic sense, for the composition of Parliament, the electorate, and the electoral system all remained as before. More substantive arguments were brought forward—from the need to wipe out the new Progressive Party, 'a dangerous party undermining the foundations of our existence in South Africa',[3] to the need to have a strong government in control without the interruption of a general election in 1963, the year in which, African nationalists claimed, the blacks would gain power.[4] The Prime Minister himself produced a whole battery of arguments: that it was necessary to demonstrate both at home and abroad that a strong, stable government would be in office for the next five years; that it would enable continuous attention to be given to the country's economic growth; that it would provide a five-year period uninterrupted by electoral contests in which national unity might grow; and that it would make possible 'sustained efforts' to deal with the country's racial problems.[5]

Certainly the country's racial problems were still very evident—and if a new era had dawned it had not extended to this most critical region of the country's political life. Throughout most of 1961 there were widespread disturbances, particularly in Pondoland where a state of emergency was subsequently declared, counterbalanced by police raids on an unprecedented scale. Indeed the country increasingly took on the aspect of being in a state of siege. At the same time overseas boycott movements against South Africa were mounting, there was an alarming outflow of investment capital, and unemployment was increasing to a disturbing level.

On the other hand, there were signs of a more liberal spirit abroad in the land. In 1959 Mr Japie Basson, the N.P. member for Namib (S.W.A.), had opposed the abolition of the Natives' Representatives in Parliament prior to the creation of the machinery envisaged in the Promotion of Bantu Self-government Act, and had subsequently been expelled from the Party for his act of independence and courage. This led to the birth of the National Union Party—a party that was still patently conservative in its general orientation, yet still patently to the left of the National Party. An even more serious split in the United Party in 1959 led to the formation of the Progressive Party which advocated a qualified form of multiracial democracy. And outside the party arena the dovecots of the Dutch Reformed Churches had been considerably fluttered by the participation of some of their prominent members in the Cottesloe Conference of the World Council of Churches, and in particular by their support for a resolution condemning discrimination.[6] Finally, even within the ranks of the National Party itself there were stirrings of discontent among the 'intellectuals', particularly with regard to the Government's policy towards Coloureds.

As a result, the 1961 general election, whatever other purposes it served, provided the opportunity for a grand debate on South Africa's racial policies. Other issues did enter into the debate, but these did not substantially affect the central issue. Moreover, perhaps because the outcome itself was not seriously in doubt, the participants succeeded for the most part, though with some exceptions, in avoiding both hysteria and sheer demagogy. On the whole, the issues were presented to the electorate with impressive clarity and definition; and equally impressive was the range of alternative policies: the clear-cut policy of a non-racial democracy of the Liberal Party uttered though it was in a small, if not still voice; the comprehensive scheme of checks and balances designed to protect a multiracial democracy from discrimination or group tyranny as presented by the Progressive Party; the policy of 'Ordered Advance' advocated by the United Party/National Union alliance, and, in some ways most revolutionary of all, the Bantustan policy propounded by the Government itself.

THE CONTESTING POLICIES

(*a*) *The National Party*

'The 1959 Parliament . . . set the newer tone of full political and partial territorial separation that was to mark the Verwoerd period.'[7] In particular the Promotion of Bantu Self-Government Act, 1959, marked the new direction, or at least the new emphasis, in government policies that Dr Verwoerd initiated. While on the one hand, the general apartheid apparatus was continued and, indeed extended, the new emphasis was now on the granting of political rights to the various African 'national' groups in their own 'homelands'. This included the notion that these might even develop into separate territorial states, a development which would involve the partition of the existing territory of South Africa.

The underlying thesis of the separate development concept was that a national entity was defined by its own culture of which the most obvious sign was its distinctive language, that each national entity developed a national self-consciousness which in turn, in the political area, generated the drive for national self-determination. In these terms, the inhabitants of South Africa were conceived as forming a multinational society comprising Whites, Coloureds, Indians, and, not just Africans, but North Sotho, South Sotho, Tswana, Zulu, Swazi, Tsonga, Venda, and Xhosa; and consequently each of these national entities should—'under the leadership of the White man'[8]—be enabled to develop their full national potential, i.e. ultimately complete autonomy or independence. In December 1960 Dr Verwoerd stated:

> We know that it cannot last forever that the one group can always be the servant of the other. We are decidedly not so stupid and un-Christian. In the implementation of our policy, we are prepared to take care of the growth and development of each group in its own sphere.[9]

These ideas formed the major part of the campaign that Dr Verwoerd led. Answering the United Party charge that he intended to 'carve up' South Africa, he replied, 'It is not we who wish to carve up South Africa; history has already carved it up'.[10] 'The whites', he said on another occasion, 'must eventually realize that in the end they could rule only over their own territory and over their own people, and that they would have to learn to maintain friendly relations with neighbouring black states'.[11] So he concluded, perhaps in response to the criticisms based on moral grounds that the Progressives and Liberals levelled at apartheid policies, that there was no policy more moral than that of the National Party.[12]

Of the many objections that have been raised against this Verwoerdian Grand Design, two might be mentioned at this stage. The first is that while it might sound theoretically plausible to propose a form of partition according to which each group would rule over only its own people, in fact, even on the Government's own over-optimistic projections, there would still be six million Africans living in the so-called white areas by the end of the century, and hence subject to the laws operative in them. Consequently, as the Opposition was quick to point out, it was facile, not to say fallacious, to talk of the whites in the projected 'White state'[13] ruling over only themselves. This remains a critical weakness of the Bantustan 'solution' to South Africa's racial problems; but the present regime still has been unable to improve on the pitifully weak efforts that Dr Verwoerd made to overcome it.

In the first place, he denied that Africans in white areas would be devoid of rights. They would, he argued, have rights pertaining to their own homelands—Xhosa living on the Rand, for example, would be able to vote in elections for the Transkei legislature.[14] The assumption behind this argument and therefore necessary to its validity is that the Africans living in these areas are mere sojourners. It is therefore logically essential for the Government to maintain its definition of such Africans as 'migrants', even though that definition lacks any observable correspondence with the facts.

In the second place Dr Verwoerd argued that in fact Africans living in urban areas would not be without rights. Apart from the rights referred to above, they would also have rights under a system of 'limited' local self-government, although it would always be 'under the guardianship of the White municipality which remains the owner of the land on which their residential areas are established'.[15] Here again the definition of African urban-dwellers as migrants is seen as crucial. Ownership of land is regarded as incompatible with their migrant status; and a full system of local self-government is, in its turn, regarded as incompatible with the absence of ownership of land. The 'rights' that remain can therefore hardly be regarded as substantial.

Finally Dr Verwoerd claimed that the economic development of the homelands through the border industry system would provide sufficient inducement to remain in the homelands to counteract the urban drift. Indeed programmes of economic development were central to the whole plan; for it is on this basis alone that the foundation can be built for the political superstructure envisaged. On this issue, however, the Government was caught in a number of political cross-currents. The Opposition insisted that economic development could go ahead only if white capital investment was encouraged in the homelands, a proposal which the Government rejected on ideological grounds. At the same time the Opposition—and academic economists—claimed that border industries were incapable of developing to the point where they could absorb the amount of labour needed to reverse the urban migration of the Africans. Moreover, while the more conservative, predominantly rural, supporters of the Government resisted the kinds of expenditures needed to give the policy the faintest glimmer of a hope of success, it was being pressed on its other flank to spend at a greatly accelerated rate. *Die Burger* was in the forefront in this latter campaign, declaring 'We even believe that the time is more than ripe for calculated risks in pace, scale and methods'.[16] On this issue, it may be said, the Government lacked the courage of its convictions, falling back on timid half-measures quite incapable of achieving their object.

The second major objection to the separate development plan that is particularly relevant to the election campaign was that while the plan was applied to the Coloureds, logically—according to the Government's own philosophy—it should not have been; for the Coloureds share the same language and culture with the whites. This was an issue which brought into the open divisions of opinion within the National Party itself. In July 1960 Dawie, the political commentator of *Die Burger*, wrote:

> The drive to a forward movement in Nationalist policy for the Coloureds is becoming stronger and stronger. The most dramatic idea of course is that the principle of representation of Coloureds by Coloureds in Parliament must be recognized, or put in other words: that the Coloured voters must be permitted to elect white or brown members. . . . My impression is that the National Party is already more than half-way in agreement with the principle, and can be completely won for it by strong leadership.[17]

At one point it seemed that this leadership might be forthcoming from an unexpected quarter. In September Mr De Wet Nel, Dr Verwoerd's apostle of separate development and Minister of Bantu Administration, was reported as conceding the eventual need for larger representation for the Coloureds and the possibility that they might be represented by Coloureds—although he did place these eventualities in the dim mists of the future.[18] Dr Verwoerd himself, however, remained immune to these doubts. Attributing the dispute to 'certain supporters of the republic . . . although they displayed liberalistic tendencies in the sphere of colour', he went on to prophesy in the familiar Verwoerdian fashion that a concession of this kind would lead step by step to 'biological assimilation' with the Coloureds and ultimately with Africans.[19] Undaunted, Dawie argued that since the Coloureds had 'no large homelands of their own' the kind of policy being applied to Africans could not be applied to them. 'They must remain represented in Parliament together with the white people', Dawie claimed, and logically, therefore, they should have the right to elect their own people to Parliament.[20] The position taken by *Die Burger* was supported by *Dagbreek en Sondagnuus*[21] and, though rather more timidly, by *Die Volksblad*,[22] and the controversy continued to simmer until into December.

Finally Dr Verwoerd issued a major policy statement on the position of the Coloureds. In this statement the notion of separate identity as applied to the Coloureds was re-emphasized, and was stated as the context within which their development would take place. To this end, Dr Verwoerd stated, a Ministry of Coloured Affairs would be established and the scope of the Coloured Council extended. In addition, a Coloured Development and Investment Corporation would be created, local government bodies in Coloured areas would be developed into full town councils, and housing programmes for Coloureds would be accelerated. The Prime Minister also proposed the holding of annual conferences between the Minister of Coloured Affairs and designated leaders of the Coloured people to consult on matters of common concern.[23] In short, the basic apartheid structure of separate political institutions was to be created for the Coloureds, whether or not they had a 'homeland' to serve as a territorial base, and whether or not they conformed to the accepted Nationalist doctrine of separate cultural identity. This policy was later officially endorsed by the Federal Council of the National Party, which reiterated the central Verwoerdian principle 'that a consistently applied policy of separate or autogenous development rests on a firm moral foundation as regards both Whites and Coloureds'.[24] While the 'intellectuals', as they were then referred to —they were later to become identified as *verligtes*—continued for a while to work for the acceptance of a more liberal Coloured policy, a heavily repressive speech by Dr Verwoerd in Parliament silenced them, for the time being at any rate; so that by the time the election campaign itself got under way the Party, at least publicly, was speaking once more with one voice—their master's voice. And the message was the Verwoerdian message, that the only policy that could at the same time preserve 'white civilization' in South Africa and maintain racial harmony was the policy of separate development applied to all racial or 'national' groups.

(*b*) *The United Party/National Union Alliance*

(i) *The United Party*

The United Party has often been accused, and continues to be accused, of lacking both intellectual vigour and moral firmness, of speaking with different voices according to the spokesman, the audience, or the circumstance, of being content to follow rather than to lead public opinion, of lacking any discernible ideological base, even of being a weaker, less clear echo of the Government. These accusations contain a measure of truth, although not quite the whole truth. That the Party is, of all the parties in South Africa, the most pragmatic is certainly true, and the distinction between pragmatism in action and political opportunism is not always clearly discernible. In many ways the United Party is, in orientation as well as in its support base, a party of the city, representing the businessman's notion of what is sensible in politics, limiting its vision to the short and medium range, ready to make accommodations in the interests of a stable society—and, its critics would say, in the interests of gathering votes.

If these are the characteristics of the United Party, they nevertheless do distinguish it from the National Party as far as a basic approach to politics is concerned. At the Union Congress of the United Party in 1959 Sir De Villiers Graaff, however, still felt it necessary to stress the policy issues that divided the two parties, and the eight-point programme announced by him in October 1960 provided a more specific content to these points of differentiation as well as accurately reflecting its pragmatic, middle-of-the-road position. The eight points were: (1) that the Coloureds should have the right of direct representation in Parliament;[25] (2) that artificial economic discrimination (e.g. job reservation) against Coloureds should be abolished; (3) that Asians be accepted as a permanent part of South Africa's population;[26] (4) that immediate attention should be given to the economic effects of the Group Areas Act on Asians; (5) that negotiations should be begun on the future political status of Asians; (6) that white capital and skills should be used to accelerate development of the Native Reserves;[27] (7) that urban African workers should be accepted as a permanent part of the urban population and not merely as migrants; and (8) that a stable urban African middle class should be fostered and given representation in Parliament.[28]

(ii) *The National Union*

The National Union was officially launched as a political party at a meeting in Bloemfontein in the beginning of May 1960. The prime mover in its creation as a new party was Mr J. (Japie) Basson, who had been expelled from the National Party as a result of his opposition to the abolition of Natives' Representatives by the Promotion of Bantu Self-Government Act, 1959. The objects of the new party were nicely calculated to occupy the relatively narrow strip of territory separating the two major parties—with the intention of weaning from the National Party those who, among its supporters, disagreed with the more restrictive and oppressive aspects of its policies, but who could not bring themselves to vote for the United Party.

In content, the Party's seven-point programme[29] overlapped extensively with the United Party's programme outlined above, although there were some differences. It did favour a republican form of government but with continued membership in the Commonwealth, and it omitted all reference to the Asians, to the future political status of Africans and to the race-federation idea expounded by the United Party. On the other hand the programme fairly represented the ideas of the more *verligte* elements of the National Party; but these elements remained at the time fairly thoroughly concealed.

We may then ask what in fact the new party hoped to accomplish. The points on which it differed from the United Party did not reflect major areas of conflict within the latter party. On these issues, therefore, there was no large number of United Party dissidents looking for a new political home. On the other hand, the more-or-less covert *verligte* supporters of the National Party could hardly be expected to switch party allegiance—if they did so at all—in such numbers as to bring the National Union to power on its own. The best that it could hope for, therefore, would be to form part of a coalition government with the United Party. But for that to happen it had to win seats; but, for the reasons stated above, it was difficult to see how it could do that in three-cornered contests with the two established parties. The logic of its situation pointed strongly in the direction of an electoral alliance with the United Party. The United Party for its part was not itself in so good a state that it could ignore the new party. It had already suffered the defection of many of its more liberal and able members to the Progressive Party, and it had suffered a sharp defeat in the referendum. Consequently it could not afford to accept the possibility of losing further ground in marginal seats through split anti-Government votes. Its own situation therefore tended in the direction of reaching some form of electoral agreement with the National Union.

(iii) *The Alliance*

The National Union was given a much-needed fillip to its stature on 15 July 1961, when it was announced that Mr H. A. Fagan had joined it and become its leader.[30] A former Minister of Native Affairs, Chief Justice of the Union from 1957 to 1959, and author of the Fagan Report, he had the status and experience which the party's leadership had hitherto lacked. Before Mr Fagan had actually joined the party, he had been included in its group of delegates who met with United Party representatives early in July in order to negotiate an agreement.[31]

This agreement was quickly reached. It included, as expected, an electoral alliance. According to its terms, the two parties would not contest the same seats, and one safe seat as well as several more doubtful ones were allocated to the National Union. As well, Mr Fagan was promised one of the Natal senatorial seats when Mr M. Mitchell was elected to the House of Assembly. The agreement, however, went beyond a purely electoral alliance, for it also included an agreed statement of common principles:

(i) 'The fullest co-operation and partnership in a joint responsibility of English- and Afrikaans-speaking citizens in the government of our country.'

(ii) Recognition and acceptance of the Republic 'as an accomplished fact which marks the end of old divisions'.

(iii) 'The right of self-determination of the white man as the bearer of Western civilization and the Western way of life', together with 'satisfactory political opportunities for our different non-White groups . . .'.

(iv) Goodwill and co-operation between White and non-White, and the 'elimination from our legislation and administration . . . of those things which offend against the dignity of the non-White groups'.

(v) Acceptance of the view that differences of opinion over 'immediate policy with respect to the representation of the various non-White groups' in Parliament, need not constitute an obstacle to co-operation on the 'urgent and pressing matters on which there was full agreement'.

(vi) 'Acceptance of a race federation in which all groups will be represented in the Central Parliament . . . on a basis which provides justice for all groups.'

(vii) The development of the Reserves, within the framework of a race federation, with the aid of White capital and skill; the recognition of an established Bantu class in the White urban areas; a 'more rational and sympathetic application of such measures as the pass laws'; and 'controlled freehold title for responsible urbanised Bantu'.

(viii) Effective machinery 'for mutual consultation between the different race groups'.

(ix) Agreement to work for 'a rapid increase in the tempo of economic and industrial development, and an improvement in the standards of living of all sections of the population'.[32]

This programme of 'Ordered Advance' was rather more conservative than the United Party's programme, mainly by virtue of omissions from the latter document. Nevertheless its acceptance clearly moved the National Union farther away from the National Party, and sufficiently close to the United Party to make it no longer a matter of surprise when it abandoned its separate identity and merged with the United Party in June 1962.[33]

(*c*) *The Progressive Party*

The split between the Progressives and the United Party took place at the United Party's Union Congress held in Bloemfontein in August 1959. The Congress had been preceded by further statements by the Prime Minister on the eventual independence of the Bantustans, which consequently made necessary a redefinition of the United Party's own policies on racial issues. There is evidence that the liberal wing of the United Party began to press for a statement of policy that was in their view more in line with the needs of the post-war world and, in particular, more sympathetic to the aspirations of the Union's non-white peoples. Mr Harry Lawrence, who had been a member of the United Party since its inception and before that a member of the old South African Party, has written:

> Some months before that fateful Congress my own views were made perfectly clear to the leader and the caucus of the United Party, namely that the party had failed to face unequivocally the necessary implications which must flow from accepting the multi-racial State in preference to Dr Verwoerd's pipedream of Partition.[34]

As the time of the Congress drew nearer, rumours increased that the conservative wing of the Party was hoping to use the Congress to crush the dissidents or drive them out of the Party. Mr Douglas Mitchell, the leader of the Party in Natal, led the attack at the Congress, and, so it is said, against the wishes of Sir De Villiers Graaff himself, introduced a motion that stated, *inter alia:*

> 2. [This Congress] expresses its entire opposition to the acquisition and alienation of more land for the Government's avowed purpose of giving it to Bantu tribes, which under the Bantustan policy of the Government, are to form independent sovereign Bantu states, whether such land is today Crown land or in private ownership.[35]

This resolution, on the face of it, repudiated the 1936 Hertzog 'settlement', whereby the United Party Government under the premiership of General Hertzog passed legislation that removed the Africans in the Cape from the common roll and created in its place the system of Natives' Representatives[36] and at the same time made provision for increasing the land available for the Reserves.[37] The original protest signed by eleven members of the Party, including Mr S. F. Waterson who did not in the end resign, stated that the resolution was 'a clear breach of the promise given by the United

Party in 1936'.[38] Sir De Villiers Graaff defended the resolution on the grounds that while the Party was prepared to approve the purchase of further land for the use of Africans within the framework of the Union, it was not prepared to add to lands which would eventually fall outside the territory of the Union.[39] Typical of Nationalist reaction was the comment of *Die Burger* which prophesied a United Party campaign of 'cynical opportunism' based on 'the cry that Verwoerd wants to give their homes to the Natives'.[40] Dr Verwoerd simply announced that the Government would abide by the relevant clauses of the 1936 enactment and buy land near the 'Bantu areas' to complete the Reserves.[41]

Nevertheless, while this issue provided the breaking-point for the Progressives, there was more to it than that. More fundamentally they claimed that the Congress had failed 'to face up to the increasingly urgent problem of our multi-racial country'.[42] Mr Lawrence described the general character of the Congress as 'an attempt to outbid the Nationalists for the control of colour prejudice', and this, he said, 'made my continued membership of the United Party impossible'.[43] The Progressive group, in other words, clearly wished to move the United Party towards the adoption of policies more liberal than the Party as a whole was, for one reason or another, prepared to accept. Mr Mitchell's resolution was probably designed to purge the Party of this group as well as to serve as a campaign weapon against the Nationalists; but even if it had not been introduced the tensions in the Party would probably have soon reached breaking-point.

The Bloemfontein protest was, at all events, followed by a flurry of resignations. Within a week eleven M.P.s including Dr Jan Steytler, leader of the U.P. in the Cape, five members of provincial councils and two U.P. members of the Johannesburg City Council had resigned.[44] These resignations were shortly followed by those of J. G. N. Strauss, Sir De Villiers Graaff's predecessor as Leader of the United Party and Leader of the Opposition, and of H. F. Oppenheimer, former United Party M.P. and South Africa's leading industrialist. While on his return from overseas, H. G. Lawrence, Minister of Justice under General Smuts and, according to *Die Vaderland*, the United Party's 'most capable Parliamentarian and most skilful political strategist', also resigned from the party.[45]

Later in October it was announced that the group would form a political party and that it would hold its first congress in Johannesburg on 13 and 14 November. Dr Wilson, the spokesman for the group, stated that its policies would embody a new concept of multiracial government, and that it would constitute 'a real alternative to the partition plan of the Nationalists'.[46] At that congress, the new Progressive Party adopted six principles, of which the first three are the most important and distinctive:

1. The maintenance and extension of the values of Western Civilization, the protection of fundamental human rights and the safeguarding of the dignity and worth of the human person irrespective of race, colour or creed.
2. The assurance that no citizen of the Union of South Africa shall be debarred on grounds of race, religion, language or sex from making the contribution to our national life of which he or she may be capable.
3. The recognition that in the Union of South Africa there is one nation which embraces various groups differing in race, religion, language and traditions; that each such group is entitled to the protection of these things and of its right of participation in the government of the nation; and that understanding, tolerance and goodwill between the groups must be fostered.[47]

The other principles referred to the maintenance of the rule of law, the promotion of social progress, and the promotion of friendly external relations.[48]

The response of the Nationalist press and of United Party leaders to this new intrusion into the political arena was immediate and forthright. *Die Transvaler* particularly condemned the 'one nation' concept, although it probably read more into the concept than was intended. 'If words still mean anything', it wrote, 'it means that this party . . . seeks to create a new unity out of many races. Boer, Briton, Jew, Bantu, Indian and Coloured will all form "one nation" together. . . . This is the most open and fatal point of view ever adopted by a political party in our country.'[49] A few days later, the same paper attacked the Party as revolutionary: '. . . it is revolutionary because it wants to destroy the entire political, economic, educational and even social system and replace it by a totally different system.' It went on to warn: 'The white man does not intend to surrender his future voluntarily; and if in the final analysis it has to be defended, he will defend it with blood. The Progressive Party, therefore, cannot cherish any prospect at all of realising its multiracial nation with the approval of the voters.'[50]

The national executive of the United Party called on all those members who had been elected to Parliament as United Party candidates and who had since joined the Progressive Party to resign their seats.[51] It argued that the presence of the Progressives could only 'hinder and embarrass the United Party in its role as the only effective Opposition and the only alternative government', and declared that the Progressive policy of the abolition of the pass laws and influx control had created 'an unbridgeable gulf' between them and the United Party.[52]

Mr Douglas Mitchell, however, saw the split as involving a more fundamental issue than pass laws and influx control. Mr Mitchell's elaboration did show points of agreement between the parties: the right to own property, the development of a 'responsible' African middle class, and the extension of the franchise to this class. But pass laws and influx control would be relaxed only for this class, not abolished, and the representation of Africans would at least initially be restricted to eight M.P.s and six senators. 'But', and here was the main point, 'we are determined not to hand effective political power to the non-European, that is United Party policy. The liberals and the Liberal Progressives have shown that they have no objection to effective political power being given to the non-European.'[53] In short, while Mitchell was prepared to allow the possibility of further development of African representation beyond the total of fourteen representatives, he was not prepared, as both Progressives and Liberals were, to contemplate even the eventual situation of African representatives being in a majority in Parliament.

The final formulation of the Progressive Party's policies and programmes was subject to a long process of rumination, including, as it did, a so-called Commission of Experts under the chairmanship of Donald Molteno, Q.C., which was given the task of drafting constitutional proposals appropriate to the multiracial character of South African society.[54] Even the constitutional proposals that eventually emerged from the Molteno Commission and that, with some changes particularly to the proposed franchise laws, were accepted by the party, were subject ultimately to the over-riding principle that any future constitution for South Africa would have to be drafted by a new National Convention representative of all the major ethnic groups.

By the time of the 1961 general election its position was, however, sufficiently clear and unambiguous for it to be understandable to the electorate. It stood for a constitution in which a Bill of Rights, a federal structure, a reformed senate and a reconstituted judiciary, would make the abuse of power by the executive, or the domination of one or more racial groups over the others, more difficult. While there were differences over the details of the franchise, it proposed a qualified franchise, coupled with the rapid extension of educational and job opportunities to the non-white groups. In short, it aimed, as did the Liberal Party, at an integrated society which would not prescribe political participation or economic activity by reference to race or colour, or encourage the division of political parties on racial lines; and, like the Liberal Party again, it agreed that its policies would lead in the foreseeable future to a black government in South Africa. Unlike the Liberal Party, however, it proposed a transition period during which the various social groups would learn to adapt themselves to these goals and to acquire the appropriate attitudes; and it was for these purposes that the complicated constitutional proposals were conceived.

It might well be argued, then, that the coming into existence of the Progressive Party served to crystallize the debate on future policies for the new Republic in a way that nothing else perhaps could have succeeded so well in doing. Its policy, as we have seen, was novel and distinctive; it therefore added a new element to the discussion. But because it was new, it also shed a new light on the policies of the older parties. It was indeed the entry of the Progressives into the electoral lists that gave the 1961 election its particular character and its main interest.

(*d*) *The Liberal Party*

The Liberal Party's participation in the 1961 election campaign was, in a sense, even more tangential than it had been in 1958. By now it had abandoned its original support for a qualified franchise and had come to support the immediate granting of the vote to all adult South Africans regardless of race or colour. In addition, it continued to press for the end of all forms of racial discrimination and the entrenchment of a Bill of Rights modelled on the U.N. Declaration of Universal Rights. In taking these steps the Liberal Party succeeded in substantially increasing its African membership[55] but without making the same kind of gains among the white electorate.

The Party, indeed, had a two-pronged strategy. On the one hand it attempted to serve as a bridge-builder, to retain links with non-white political movements, partly at least in order to prevent a complete disenchantment among the latter with the values of liberalism. This in itself implied an educative role, and it remained, on the whole, an implied rather than a proclaimed role, one which by demonstration showed that whites could be the friends and allies of the other coloured groups, and that within the doctrines of liberalism could be found the means to reconcile the various interests of the diverse racial groups, and ultimately to form a truly non-racial democracy. At the same time, it sought to make the same demonstration and to teach the same lesson to the whites. In support of the first task it increasingly identified itself with the various protest movements of the non-whites, urged the Commonwealth Prime Ministers in 1961 to exclude South Africa from the Commonwealth, and generally supported all external moves to impose trade and other forms of boycott on South Africa. In the enhanced 'laager' mood that followed South Africa's withdrawal from the Commonwealth, and the stepped-up attacks in the United Nations, its position on these issues could not fail to alienate the mass of white voters.

The Liberal Party, however, was not really in the business of winning votes. It used the 1961 election as it had used the 1958 election as a means whereby it could enjoy a public platform in order to put its message across. In taking advantage of this opportunity, it not only used black speakers on its platforms, but also introduced at least some white South African voters to the novelty of being canvassed by Africans.[56] What it lacked was the support of any major organ of the press; indeed the coverage of Liberal Party speeches and meetings was meagre to the point of being negligible. It also lacked leaders of any direct political experience. What it did most notably possess was a deep-seated conviction in the rightness of its cause, and the honesty and courage to express it. But this was not enough to make any headway with the electorate.

(*e*) *The Conservative Workers Party*

Less than two months before the closing of nominations a new political party suddenly entered the lists. This was the Conservative Workers Party. Its emergence was hardly a threat to the major parties, nor did it contribute anything of significance to the ideological debate. It was rather an expression of protest and at the same time a reminder that man does not live by political faith alone, that, on the contrary, 'immediate economic interests weigh more heavily with the wage-earner than distant racial objectives'.[57]

That South Africa's economic position was less than healthy had only recently been admitted by Dr Dönges, Minister of Finance, although he was quick to insist that its bases remained sound. There were, however, balance of payment problems, and unemployment had increased. Dr Dönges's answer to these problems was the unpalatable prescription to work harder, to save more and to retain a sense of confidence.[58] This was no doubt sound advice, but it was unlikely to comfort those who were unemployed or lived under the threat of unemployment.

The *Sunday Times* reported that those involved in the formation of the new party included the assistant chief secretary of the Iron and Steel Workers Union, the general secretary of the Engine Drivers and Firemen's Association, and the district secretary of the Amalgamated Engineering Union—all, it claimed, leading ex-Nationalist trade unionists. The paper reported that the Party had decided to contest a number of seats because in its view the Government had betrayed the interests of the working classes; the grievances of the workers were subordinated to the Bantustan concept of apartheid: and instead of checking unemployment, the Government simply told them to tighten their belts.[59]

The aims of the Party included a comprehensive system of social security and welfare: free education, free hospital and medical services, a compulsory national pension scheme, national unemployment assurance on a larger scale, family allowances, and adequate housing for workers. It proposed that reasonable minimum wages be laid down for all sections of the community, and it urged that immigration be governed by the welfare of South African workers and, in particular, by the need to insure that it did not create a threat of unemployment.[60]

The Nationalist reaction to the Conservative Workers Party was characterized more by indignation than alarm. *Die Vaderland* claimed that since 1924 the National Party had demonstrated by word and by deed its concern for the workers.[61] And *Die Transvaler* declared, 'In the National Party the workers have a friend beyond compare'.[62] It is possible, nevertheless, that the intervention of the new party did result in greater attention being given to economic issues in the campaign than would otherwise have been the case. If so, it was the Party's only real contribution to the debate.

THE ELECTORAL CONTEST[63]

When nominations closed on 15 September, official confirmation was given to the general view that the 1961 general election represented a radical departure from the post-war pattern. This is clearly seen from the figures given in Table 51.

The most striking feature of these figures is the unprecedented number of uncontested seats: a total of 67 out of 150 seats in the Republic, or nearly 45%. Altogether, the United Party/National Union alliance put up 99 candidates, compared with the National Party's 104 candidates—the first time in the post-war period that the National Party entered more candidates than its major opponent. In all, there were 51 seats which the Alliance did not contest and which, in effect, it therefore conceded to the Nationalists, but in four of these the National Party was opposed by the Conservative Workers Party. The previous record for conceded seats in our period was in 1948 when 48 Government seats were conceded by the Nationalist opposition alliance. In 1961, however, the Nationalists in their turn conceded 46 seats to the United Party. The major parties thus acknowledged in their nomination policies the force of the trend that we discerned in the 1958 election, namely, that the electorate was becoming partitioned into two blocs of constituencies, the one composed of safe Nationalist seats, and the other of safe United Party seats, with very few left in the borderland. From the point of view of conserving their energies the Nationalists exploited

Table 51

NUMBER OF CANDIDATES, 1961

Region	Contested seats							Uncontested		
	U.P.	N.U.	N.P.	P.P.	Lib.	C.W.P.	Ind.	U.P./N.U.	N.P.	Total
Cape Town	8	1	2	5	1	—	2	3	2	24
Port Elizabeth	1	1	1	1	—	—	—	2	1	7
Border	3	—	—	2	—	—	1	2	—	8
Rest of Cape	10	3	13	2	—	—	—	—	15	43
Total Cape	22	5	16	10	1	—	3	7	18	82
Johannesburg	6	1	4	4	1	3	2	6	—	27
Witwatersrand	10	3	13	1	—	1	—	2	4	34
Pretoria	4	—	4	—	—	—	—	—	6	14
Rest of Transvaal	12	—	12	—	—	—	1	—	10	35
Total Transvaal	32	4	33	5	1	4	3	8	20	110
Durban–Pietermaritzburg	7	—	—	6	—	—	1	4	—	18
Rest of Natal	3	1	3	2[1]	—	—	1	1	—	11[1]
Total Natal	10	1	3	8[1]	—	—	2	5	—	29[1]
O.F.S.	5	—	5	—	—	—	—	—	9	19
Total Republic	69	10	57	22[1]	2	4	8	20	47	240[1]

Note: [1] These figures include a candidate who withdrew after the closing of nominations.

the situation more fully than the United Party. Of the seats won by the United Party in 1958 the National Party contested only Queenstown in the Cape, Bezuidenhout, Florida, Germiston District, Pretoria Rissik and Pretoria Sunnyside in the Transvaal, and Zululand in Natal. In the referendum, the Opposition had increased its majority in Queenstown from 13 votes to 121; but it still remained within reach of the National Party. Sunnyside had gone over to the Nationalists in the referendum. The Nationalist venture in both these seats proved to be successful in 1961. In short, the National Party contested only five seats in 1961 which they did not win, and in which they had little chance of winning. Even *Die Burger* was led to doubt whether this situation was 'a good thing for a democratic country' and to wonder whether a future delimitation commission might not 'create a few more mixed and doubtful constituencies'[64]—a rather novel task, certainly, for a judicial commission.

Because of this economical division of labour between the two major groups, the broad outline of what the results would be was apparent to everyone: it was certain that the Government would retain, and probably slightly increase, their majority. Points of considerable interest nevertheless remained. 'The main interest now', the *Daily News* commented, 'is to see what impact the new parties, the Progressives and the National Union, have so far had on the electorate.'[65]

The National Union, as a result of its alliance with the United Party, entered ten candidates. Mr Basson himself was given the safe Bezuidenhout seat to contest; but if there was prima facie little chance of its succeeding in the other nine seats, there was at least the opportunity of establishing whether it could win votes from the National Party.

The Progressive Party for its part stood less as an alternative government than as an alternative Opposition.[66] Only two of its candidates were engaged in fights with Nationalists: both of these were in safe National Party seats, and both involved three-cornered contests with the National Union. In general, the Progressives sought to avoid the charge of 'splitting the vote', and it was to this end that R. A. F. Swart withdrew his candidacy from the Zululand contest after the surprise last-minute nomination of a Nationalist candidate—but too late to prevent his name from appearing on the ballot paper. In Maitland Dr De Beer carried on the fight after the entry into the lists of Mr F. Waring, thinly disguised as an independent. Eighteen of the remaining nineteen seats contested by the Progressives were straight fights with the United Party, and in the nineteenth the third candidate was a hardly formidable independent.[67] If, however, the Progressive Party avoided the charge of 'splitting the vote', it could hardly avoid the alternative charge of being more concerned to fight the United Party than the National Party. The Progressive Party, Sir De Villiers Graaff alleged, had hindered the United Party in its fight against the Government through its 'assault in the rear'.[68]

As the electorate prepared to go to the polls, the contending parties made their last appeals. Only the National Party, the Prime Minister declared, had a policy which would enable the white man to retain control over national affairs; only the National Party was capable of bringing racial peace and the eventual end of racial discrimination because racial separation was the only way in which discrimination could be avoided. Under the policies of the opposition parties, on the other hand, either the non-whites would be discriminated against, or the Bantu would discriminate against the whites and the smaller racial groups. The National Party, for its part, would assure the growth of white unity, and by providing a stable government and by preserving white control, it would restore the confidence of investors.[69]

For the United Party, Sir De Villiers Graaff claimed that unless the Government was halted in its course it would proceed so far in the next five years in the dismemberment of South Africa that it would commit South Africa irrevocably. Moreover there was the danger that independent Bantustans would pursue a course of hostility to South Africa. The answer to South Africa's problems lay in the United Party's policy of 'a federation of races which shall be free from the fear, the shibboleths and the unreasoned prejudices of the past'.[70] And Mr Fagan reiterated these sentiments. The National Union/United Party agreement, he claimed, could serve as a basis for cordial co-operation between the white groups, and for 'creating, in consultation with the non-whites, a spirit of confidence and goodwill among all sections of the population and for the ringing in of a new period of tranquillity and prosperity for South Africa'.[71]

Dr Steytler told Progressive Party supporters: 'You will be making it clear to our non-white friends tomorrow that it is not necessary to indulge in boycotts and strikes to throw off the yoke of oppression. You will also be showing the world at large that South Africa is still the nation that produced great men like Botha and Smuts—that we are not a nation so depraved as to try to deny for all time the freedom of the individual.'[72]

THE TURN-OUT

The response of the electorate to the challenge of the new era and to the clearly defined choice of its ideological basis was disappointing. Perhaps it does not care to exercise its prerogative of choice too often; or perhaps it is more interested in a choice of government than in a choice of ideology, or, in the *Rand Daily Mail*'s terms, in a choice of Opposition. Possibly a combination of all these factors dampened the electorate's enthusiasm.

Table 52

VOTER PARTICIPATION BY PROVINCE

Province	*Electorate*	*Votes cast*	*% poll*
Cape	321 715	255 475	79,4
Transvaal	489 893	380 577	77,7
Natal	130 599	94 950	72,7
O.F.S.	69 990	54 154	77,4
Total	1 012 197	785 156	77,6

These figures hide wide variations. In a manner reminiscent of the 1948 election, there was, first of all, a considerable difference in the turn-out of voters in United Party-held seats from that in Nationalist seats. In the Cape only 68,4% of the voters in United Party seats cast their votes; in the Transvaal the figure was 72,1% and in Natal, 70,1%. The corresponding figures for voter participation in Nationalist seats were: in the Cape, 87,6%; in the Transvaal, 79,6%; in Natal, 86,6%; and in the Orange Free State, 77,4%. Even these figures represented a considerable drop from the 1958 level. Unfortunately, in the absence of any opinion surveys, one can only speculate whether in the Nationalist seats one factor in the relatively low percentage poll might not have been, to put it at its weakest, a lack of enthusiasm, perhaps even a certain doubt, about the new direction in Nationalist policies.

In the Opposition seats, an important factor in the low voting figures was probably the abstention of National Party supporters. The call had gone out to them to abstain from voting in constituencies in which there was no Nationalist candidate; no doubt large numbers of them adhered to this policy. If this was a factor, however, it was only one, and in most United Party seats it would probably not have produced a greater drop in the poll than 7% or 8%,[73] although in some seats it might have been greater. Other factors there certainly were. In the Cape Town area, for example, there were only three seats in which the poll exceeded 80%. These were Bellville and False Bay (both Nationalist seats), and Maitland where there was a three-cornered fight with the United Party, the Progressive Party, and Mr Waring as an 'independent', as the contestants. At the other extreme the poll in Simonstown, where there was a straight fight between the United Party and the Progressive Party, reached only 60,6%. But, again, in the critical contest at Queenstown the voting reached the record high of 97,2%.

In the Johannesburg area there were three seats which recorded a higher poll than 80%, but these were all the scenes of straight fights between the United and Progressive Parties. In Bezuidenhout, where Mr Basson gained the National Union's only seat, the poll was just under 72%; and in the three Nationalist seats in this area (all won in straight fights against the Conservative Workers Party) the percentage poll rose above the 70% mark in only one, and there it reached only 70,4%. The extreme low was recorded in the Witwatersrand seat of Benoni, where only 43,8% of the voters bothered to vote in the United Party/Progressive Party contest. Meanwhile in the Transvaal *platteland* seats polls in excess of 80% were regularly recorded; only two seats fell short of that mark, and in these the poll remained over 78%.

In Natal the percentage poll varied from 48,5% in Durban Central, where the independent candidate polled only 504 votes in his fight against the United Party, to 87,0% in Zululand, where the United Party held off the Nationalist challenge. In the two Nationalist-held seats of Newcastle and Vryheid the poll was over 86% in both cases. Among the seats which saw straight fights between the United and Progressive Parties, the poll varied from 53,8% to 77,6%. In the Orange Free State, however, where all the seats were won, as expected, by the National Party, the poll varied from 72,2% to 84,7%; and in every case fewer votes were recorded for both the National Party and the United Party than were cast in the 1960 referendum contest.

Certain tentative conclusions seem possible: in general there was wide agreement that there was little danger from the one point of view, or hope from the other, that the Government would be defeated. Moreover in very few seats in which there were contests between the National Party and the United Party/National Union alliance was there much likelihood of a reversal in the results. Indeed there was only one really exciting contest between the major opponents, and that was at Queenstown, where, as we have seen, a record poll was recorded. There was no trend towards a higher poll in the seats in which the National Union was engaged. The National Party/Conservative Workers Party contests generally failed to rouse either excitement or enthusiasm. By and large there was a relatively low poll in the United Party/Progressive Party contests.

As we have seen, the 1961 election was an election fought over important and clearly established issues; it was not really fought over the fate of the government. Rather poll-weary as it was, the electorate as a whole failed to respond to the challenge of the issues presented to it.

THE RESULTS

(a) In terms of seats

The broad outlines of the election were foreknown: the Government would be returned to power possibly with a slightly, but only slightly, larger majority, certainly with a majority not more than slightly dented. But areas of interest remained within these limits. Would the National Union pull off the occasional coup? Would the Progressive Party break the United Party's hold in its urban fortresses? Would the Conservative Workers Party spring a surprise? The results gave blunt answers to these questions: the National Union won only the one safe seat given it by the United Party; the Progressives did win one seat, but again that was all. And all the minor candidates—Conservative Workers, Liberals, Theocrats, and independents—went down to defeat.

Over all, the Nationalists won two more seats from the United Party. Their success in Sunnyside, Pretoria, was expected, since the Government had gained a majority in this constituency in the referendum. In the 1961 election the Government majority increased from 2 050 votes to 2 727 votes, and it therefore became established as a safe Nationalist seat. The other loss to the United Party was the gallant constituency of Queenstown which had twice avoided defeat by the narrowest of margins: in 1958, by 13 votes; in 1960, by 121 votes. But in 1961 the National Party edged in with a majority of 369.

For the United Party, its main consolation was that in spite of the referendum set-back, and in spite of the fight on two fronts that it had been obliged to wage, it had, on the whole, held its own. The measure of its success was perhaps accurately reflected in the Pretoria seat of Rissik. Deprived of its one other Pretoria constituency of Sunnyside, it still held out in Rissik, although its majority fell to a mere 564 votes—less than half its 1960 majority which, in its turn, was less than half the 1958 majority.

(b) The results in terms of votes

The gross voting figures per party and per region are provided in Table 54. Unfortunately, however, these figures tell us less than usual about the relative voting strengths of the competing parties. As we have already seen, the map of the electoral battle is a patchy affair indeed. There were, to recapitulate, 4 seats in which the Conservative Workers Party opposed the Nationalists; 10 in which the National Union opposed the Nationalists, but in 2 of these there were also Progressive candidates; 43 in which the United Party opposed the Nationalists; 20 (excluding Mr Swart's withdrawn candidacy) in which the United Party opposed the Progressives; 2 in

Table 53

RESULTS OF THE 1961 ELECTION IN TERMS OF SEATS[1]

Region	U.P.		N.U.		P.P.		N.P.		Total
	Seats	%	*Seats*	%	*Seats*	%	*Seats*	%	
Cape Town	10 (3)	71,4	—	—	—	—	4 (2)	29,6	14 (5)
Port Elizabeth	3 (2)	60,0	—	—	—	—	2 (1)	40,0	5 (3)
Border	5 (2)	100,0	—	—	—	—	—	—	5 (2)
Rest of Cape	—	—	—	—	—	—	28 (15)	100,0	28 (15)
Total Cape	18 (7)	34,6	—	—	—	—	34 (18)	65,4	52 (25)
Johannesburg	11 (6)	68,75	1	6,25	1	6,25	3	18,75	16 (6)
Witwatersrand	5 (2)	25,0	—	—	—	—	15 (4)	75,0	20 (6)
Pretoria	1	10,0	—	—	—	—	9 (6)	90,0	10 (6)
Rest of Transvaal	—	—	—	—	—	—	22 (10)	100,0	22 (10)
Total Transvaal	17 (8)	25,0	1	1,5	1	1,5	49 (20)	72,1	68 (28)
Durban–Pietermaritzburg	11 (4)	100,0	—	—	—	—	—	—	11 (4)
Rest of Natal	3 (1)	60,0	—	—	—	—	2	40,0	5 (1)
Total Natal	14 (5)	87,5	—	—	—	—	2	12,5	16 (5)
O.F.S.	—	—	—	—	—	—	14 (9)	100,0	14 (9)
Total Republic	49 (20)	32,7	1	0,67	1	0,67	99 (47)	66,0	150 (67)

Note: [1] Figures in brackets are for uncontested seats.

which the United Party opposed the Liberals; and 4 in which the United Party was engaged only against independents. With this kind of kaleidoscope involved, gross totals mean little, and percentages even less.

Before an attempt is made to give a more accurate representation of the respective strengths of the parties, two preliminary matters can be cleared up. These refer to the performance of the National Union and of the Conservative Workers Party respectively. One of the points of interest, it will be recalled, was whether either or both of these movements would constitute a threat to the solidarity of Nationalist support. As far as the National Union was concerned, its electoral alliance with the United Party cast it in a supporting role with respect to the latter party, and it was therefore unlikely that its success in garnering votes would vary very substantially from that of its senior partner. This was in fact confirmed by the results. If we exclude Bezuidenhout (the seat allocated to Japie Basson), which the United Party had won by acclamation in 1958, the average percentage vote gained by the National Party in the nine remaining seats was 63,8 %, compared with an average pro-republic vote in 1960 of 61,9 %, and an average Nationalist vote in 1958 of 58,4 %. In the Bezuidenhout constituency, Basson won 76,4 % of the votes, while in 1960 the anti-republican vote had represented 78,3 % of the votes cast.

The picture was very different for the Conservative Workers Party. In the four seats which it contested—all in the Transvaal—the average percentage of the votes cast that were in favour of the

Table 54

VOTES CAST PER PARTY IN CONTESTED SEATS, 1961

Region	*Voters*	*Votes cast*	%	*Rej.*	%
Cape Town area	114 495	83 882	73,3	453	0,5
Port Elizabeth	27 031	19 923	73,7	103	0,5
Border	36 809	23 413	63,6	162	0,7
Rest of Cape	143 380	128 257	89,5	643	0,5
Total Cape	321 715	255 475	79,4	1 361	0,5
Johannesburg	121 353	86 203	71,0	498	0,6
Witwatersrand	180 714	140 307	77,6	647	0,5
Pretoria	58 991	47 625	80,7	238	0,5
Rest of Transvaal	128 835	106 442	82,6	607	0,6
Total Transvaal	489 893	380 577	77,7	1 990	0,5
Durban–Pietermaritzburg	87 806	59 095	67,3	516	0,9
Rest of Natal	42 793	35 855	83,8	333	0,9
Total Natal	130 599	94 950	72,7	849	0,9
Total O.F.S.	69 990	54 154	77,4	178	0,3
Total Republic	1 012 197	785 156	77,6	4 378	0,6

Nationalists was 73,1%, compared with corresponding figures of 64,5% and 59,5% for 1960 and 1958 respectively. The C.W.P., therefore, did not prove itself able to draw any appreciable number of its supporters away from the National Party; indeed it seems that the United Party itself would have fared somewhat better.

To turn once more to our major concern; under the peculiar circumstances of the 1961 election, a more accurate picture of relative party strengths is given by representing the votes cast in favour of the respective parties as percentages of the total votes cast in the constituencies that those parties contested, instead of as percentages of the total votes cast in the various regions.

Here the percentage vote needs to be read in conjunction with the number of seats involved. In the Cape Town constituencies, for example, the raw figure given in Table 54 of 17,9% of the votes obviously underestimates the Nationalist strength, because these votes were recorded in only two out of nine contested seats. On the other hand, 65,5% exaggerates the Nationalist strength unless it is again recalled that these votes were recorded in only two seats. What these figures indicate, therefore, is the degree of spread, or conversely of concentration, of the voting strength of the parties. and on this evidence it is plain that the National Party was extending its strength much more widely throughout the country than was generally supposed.

With regard to the Alliance, the figures given in Table 55 correct the downward distortion of its strength shown in the figures given in Table 53, particularly in the rural Cape and Johannesburg regions.

U.P.	%	*N.U.*	%	*N.P.*	%	*P.P.*	%	*Others*	%
46 115	55,0	3 781	4,5	15 005	17,9	11 799	14,1	6 729	8,0
5 896	30,0	3 995	20,1	6 763	33,9	3 166	15,9	—	—
18 280	78,1	—	—	—	—	3 694	15,8	1 277	5,5
38 360	29,9	7 697	6,0	80 330	62,6	1 227	1,0	—	—
08 651	42,5	15 473	6,1	102 098	40,0	19 886	7,8	8 006	3,1
31 080	36,1	6 507	7,5	19 472	22,6	19 807	23,0	8 839	10,3
41 504	29,6	13 989	10,0	80 821	57,6	1 293	0,9	2 053	1,5
17 802	37,4	—	—	29 585	62,1	—	—	—	—
32 008	30,1	—	—	73 719	69,3	—	—	108	0,1
22 394	32,2	20 496	5,4	203 597	53,5	21 100	5,5	11 000	2,9
35 109	59,4	—	—	—	—	22 966	38,9	504	0,9
14 458	40,3	2 804	7,8	15 674	43,7	2 471	6,9	115	0,3
49 567	52,2	2 804	3,0	15 674	16,5	25 437	26,8	619	0,7
14 877	27,5	—	—	39 099	72,2	—	—	—	—
95 489	37,6	38 773	4,9	360 468	45,9	66 423	8,5	19 625	2,5

Table 55

THE PERCENTAGE OF THE VOTES CAST IN FAVOUR OF EACH PARTY IN THE CONSTITUENCIES CONTESTED BY IT[1]

Region	*N.P.*	*U.P./N.U.*	*P.P.*
Cape Town	65,5 (2)	59,5 (9)	26,9 (5)
Port Elizabeth	62,7 (1)	49,6 (2)	34,7 (1)
Border	—	78,1 (3)	23,0 (2)
Rest of Cape	62,6 (13)	35,9 (13)	6,0 (2)
Total Cape	63,0 (16)	48,6 (27)	22,2 (10)
Johannesburg	60,2 (4)	60,5 (7)	48,6 (4)
Witwatersrand	70,1 (13)	42,0 (13)	24,4 (1)
Pretoria	62,1 (4)	37,4 (4)	—
Rest of Transvaal	69,3 (12)	30,1 (12)	—
Total Transvaal	63,3 (33)	41,0 (36)	45,8 (5)
Durban–Pietermaritzburg	—	59,4 (7)	43,2 (6)
Rest of Natal	55,4 (3)	48,1 (4)	31,4 (1)[2]
Total Natal	55,4 (3)	55,2 (11)	41,7 (7)[2]
O.F.S.	72,2 (5)	27,5 (5)	—
Total Republic	63,7 (57)	44,4 (79)	33,8 (22)[2]

Notes: [1] Number of constituencies contested given in brackets.
[2] Excluding the votes cast for R. A. F. Swart, who withdrew prior to the election date.

Indeed, after four successive defeats at the national polls, the United Party retained an impressive resilience. If the National Party succeeded in taking two more of its seats, nevertheless it held firm. There was certainly no landslide away from it, either in terms of seats or in terms of votes. What it did not exhibit, however, was any capacity to fight back, to reclaim lost ground, and it is this capacity that is of critical political importance.

As for the Progressive Party, given the disadvantage imposed by the electoral system on third parties, given the prevailing environment of opinion and of circumstance, and given the habitual loyalties by now attached to the major parties, it did surprisingly well. To capture a seat, to win over 66 000 votes, to average over a third of the votes cast in the constituencies it fought, was no mean achievement. Its major strength, as is particularly apparent from the figures given in Table 55, were in the Johannesburg, Durban, and Pietermaritzburg areas, and in these areas it was in some ways unlucky not to win more than its one solitary seat. In Parktown, Johannesburg, it lost by only 85 votes, and in Pietermaritzburg District by only 175; and in five other seats in these regions the margin of defeat was less than a thousand.[74] In the Cape seats, however, it failed to show the strength expected, and men such as Harry Lawrence and Dr Steytler who had formerly been acknowledged leaders, powerful and popular, in the United Party, now could barely muster 30% of the vote. But on the whole the Progressive Party had left its mark on the 1961 election, and the frankness with which it presented what was, to most voters, the novel case for a multiracial democracy did not, in the end, secure its own obliteration. For a political party to survive as a political party it must win seats, or at least display a manifest potential to win seats. The Progressive Party in 1961 passed this test, but with no very great margin to spare.

Although the large number of uncontested seats together with the intervention of a relatively large number of 'other' candidates, particularly the Progressives, makes it impossible to assess the probable effect of the uncontested seats on the voting strengths of all the contending parties, an ingenious formula has been devised to indicate the probable over-all strength of the Government in the country. Using the 51 seats in the Republic in which there were straight fights between the National Party and the United Party/National Union alliance as means of comparison with the referendum results, we may apply the following formula, adapted from Stulz and Butler:[75]

$$\frac{\text{Percentage of voters favouring a republic in 51 relevant constituencies}}{\text{Percentage of voters favouring a republic in the country as a whole}} \text{ equals } \frac{\text{Percentage of voters supporting the Government in the same constituencies in 1961}}{\text{Percentage of voters supporting the Government in the country as a whole in 1961}}$$

As Stulz and Butler point out, this formula assumes that the movement of opinion in the selected 51 constituencies is representative of the movement of opinion in the country as a whole. In 1960 the percentage of voters favouring a republic in the 51 constituencies was 60,7%. The percentage of voters favouring a republic in the country as a whole, excluding South West Africa, was 51,8%. In the 1961 election the percentage of voters in the 51 constituencies who voted for the National Party was 62,7%. On this basis then, the conclusion is that in the Republic's 150 constituencies 53,5% of the electorate would have supported the National Party. Even if this figure is slightly inaccurate, the degree of inaccuracy can hardly be so great as to subvert the conclusion as stated by Stulz and Butler: 'that the National Party Government now enjoys the confidence of a majority of the electorate, 1961 being the first *general election* after World War II when a majority of the "projected" national electorate supported the Government.'[76]

(*c*) *The swing*

The swing can only be calculated in the 51 seats previously referred to in which there were straight fights between the National Party and the Alliance. On the total voting figure in these constituencies there was a swing of 2,0% in favour of the National Party in the year that elapsed between the holding of the referendum and the general election of 1961. There were, however, minor variations within the provinces. In the Cape in the relevant 14 constituencies there was an average swing of 2,1% in favour of the Nationalists. In the Transvaal there was an average swing of 1,7% in 29 constituencies; in Natal an average swing of 3,5% in 3 constituencies; and in the Orange Free State an average swing of 2,0%—all in favour of the National Party.

All together, there was a swing towards the National Party in 42 of these 51 seats, and a swing away from it in only 9. But in the former group the average swing was 2,6%, in the latter only 0,8%. In only two constituencies was there a swing of more than 1,0% away from the Nationalists, and one of these was Bezuidenhout, where Mr Basson brought about a swing of 2,9% away from the Government. On balance, indeed, the National Union came off slightly better than the United Party. In the 8 seats in which it featured, the average swing towards the National Party was 1,8%, compared with an average swing of 2,2% towards the Nationalists in the 43 seats in which the United Party was involved. This difference of 0,4% is so slight as to be insignificant, especially when the relatively small number of seats contested by the National Union is taken into account.

Although they have not been used for the purpose of calculating the average swing, the 4 seats in which there was a straight fight between the National Union and the Conservative Workers Party form a useful basis for comparison. For in these seats the average swing in favour of the National Party was 8,7%, the swing in all cases falling within the range 7,2% to 9,9%. In 1960 the average swing towards the Nationalists in these seats had been 4,9%—less than the provincial average. The smallness of this sample is offset, then, by the extremely large difference in the size of the swing recorded in it, and one may conclude that the Conservative Workers Party was less successful than the United Party would have been, and was certainly no enduring threat to the Government.

In sum, a steady swing of opinion in favour of the National Party Government continued during the twelve months in review. There was resistance to this movement, it is true, in some areas, but nowhere of sufficient strength seriously to impede the general movement. Dr Verwoerd and his colleagues had every reason to be satified with the outcome of the general election.

(d) The disparity between seats and votes

The disparity between seats and votes in 1961 presented the more familiar picture of the exaggeration of the voting majority frequently associated with the single-member constituency type of electoral system. No longer could the Opposition claim that the Government, far from representing the 'will of the people', actually ran counter to it, as determined by counting heads. Nevertheless, the exaggeration of the voting majority was extreme. If the estimate of 53,5% is an accurate assessment of the Government's real voting strength in the country, then this would have entitled it, on a strictly proportionate basis, to 80 out of the 150 seats. Even if we allow a 1,5% error and concede an improbably high 55% of the vote to the Government, this would still have given it only 83 seats against a combined Opposition strength of 67 seats. In short, a just reflection of the relative strengths of Government and Opposition would have been a Government majority, out of the 150 ordinary seats, of 10, and in any case not less than 8 or more than 16. As it was, the Government was presented with a majority over all other parties of 48, or, with the South West Africa seats added, of 54; although these figures may be reduced by the 4 Coloured Representatives.

What this cost the opposition parties may best be illustrated by comparing the number of voters required per party to return 1 member in contested elections. These figures are shown in Table 56.

(*e*) *Majority sizes*

The average majorities per party per region are shown in Table 57. One's first reaction to these figures, perhaps, is that there is something wrong. Instead of the familiar picture of much larger United Party majorities than National Party majorities, we find, if anything, the reverse. Unfortunately, the figures in Table 57 are not as informative as they might be. In the first place, it leaves out of account the large number of uncontested seats; and secondly in only 5 seats all together, 4 in the Transvaal and 1 in Natal, were the Alliance majorities scored over National Party candidates. In other words, out of the combined Opposition's total of 51 seats, only 5 were won in contests with the Government. Twenty of them were unopposed, and 26 were at the expense of one another. So far as the Opposition parties are concerned, therefore, their votes in contested seats were in a sense 'wasted' through competing for a large number of the same seats.

As the case of the Progressive Party amply demonstrates, on the over-all view, the greater the proportion of defeated candidates to total candidates, the greater the disparity between votes and seats won. For the Progressive Party only 1 out of 22 contesting candidates was successful; for the United Party/National Union alliance, 29 out of 79 (or 37%) were successful; for the National Party, 52 out of 57 (or 91%) were successful. The National Party

Table 56

NUMBER OF VOTES REQUIRED TO WIN EACH CONTESTED SEAT

Province	N.P.			U.P./N.U.			P.P.		
	Votes	*Seats*	*Votes per seat*	*Votes*	*Seats*	*Votes per seat*	*Votes*	*Seats*	*Votes per seat*
Cape	102 098	16	6 381	124 124	11	11 284	19 886	—	—
Transvaal	203 597	29	7 021	142 890	10	14 289	21 100	1	21 100
Natal	15 674	2	7 837	52 371	9	5 819	25 437	—	—
O.F.S.	39 099	5	7 820	14 877	—	—	—	—	—
Republic	360 468	52	6 932	334 262	30	11 142	66 423	1	66 423

Table 57

AVERAGE MAJORITIES, 1961

Region	N.P.		U.P./N.U.		P.P.	
	Votes	%	*Votes*	%	*Votes*	%
Cape Town	3 615	31,3	3 614	42,5	—	—
Port Elizabeth . . .	2 768	25,7	2 730	29,8	—	—
Border	—	—	4 436	57,8	—	—
Rest of Cape	2 636	26,8	—	—	—	—
Total Cape . . .	2 767	27,3	3 756	45,5	—	—
Johannesburg . . .	3 663	45,5	2 378	33,0	564	5,5
Witwatersrand . . .	2 926	29,4	2 538	32,3	—	—
Pretoria	4 116	35,5	564	4,4	—	—
Rest of Transvaal .	3 476	38,9	—	—	—	—
Total Transvaal. .	3 353	35,6	2 245	29,9	564	5,5
Durban–Pietermaritzburg	—	—	1 663	22,5	—	—
Rest of Natal. . . .	2 612	28,1	2 123	25,3	—	—
Total Natal . . .	2 612	28,1	1 765	23,1	—	—
O.F.S..	4 844	45,6	—	—	—	—
Republic. . . .	3 284	33,7	2 655	33,6	564	5,5

reaped the fruits of success. And as a result, the hundreds of thousands of voters who opposed the Government, comprising between 45% and 48% of the electorate, found themselves represented in Parliament by less than a third of the members elected on the common roll—an effective strength in Parliament far below that in the country as a whole.

(f) Post-election comment

What was particularly striking in the press comments on the election results was the readiness to write off the United Party. The *Rand Daily Mail*, which had supported the Progressive Party, held that the 'reorientation of South African politics is well under way, with a strengthening of both conservative and liberal wings of thought'. This had taken place, it argued, 'at the expense of the so-called political centre, with the United Party shedding support heavily on both flanks'.[77] *Die Volksblad* spoke of 'the centrifugal forces which threaten the United Party's existence' as 'already the most striking features of the Parliamentary election', and it foresaw that the process would be accelerated.[78] Indeed *Die Transvaler* found no further reason for the continued existence of the United Party.[79]

Sir De Villiers Graaff maintained perhaps a misplaced jauntiness in the face of these suggestions, going so far as to argue that the United Party was going back to Parliament with a much stronger team than before, with 'capable young men' replacing the former Progressive M.P.s:[80] a most ungenerous comment on the older Harry Lawrence and Dr Steytler, and on the young Dr De Beer and R. A. F. Swart, apart from the other members.

As for the Government, Dr Verwoerd declared: 'We shall continue with the erection of the building of the future, but this will take place carefully, although with a firm hand, for care must be taken that our non-white population will not be subjected to chaos or to the dictatorship of their own leaders because their progress was sought with great haste, merely to gain popularity.'[81] This could be taken to mean almost anything. All that seemed reasonably certain at the end of 1961 was that whatever policies were followed in South Africa, they would be policies laid down by a National Party Government. The Government might wonder, like the Psalmist, why 'the heathen rage'; but whether the 'heathen' be the white opposition or the voteless black, it was sure both of its own righteousness and of its might.

8

The General Election of 1966: Dr Verwoerd's Umbrella

INTRODUCTION

At the outset of the election campaign *Die Transvaler* observed in an editorial, 'Politically South Africans live in a new world and in a new country'.[1] Certainly great changes had taken place in the world since the last election, not least those in Africa. The war in Algeria had finally come to an end, and Algeria had gained its independence—with a consequent mass movement back to France of the French settlers.[2] More remotely, Burundi, the Gambia, and Rwanda also had gained their independence. But it was the events in Central and East Africa that had the greatest impact. In Central Africa the so-called, but never really actualized, policy of partnership disintegrated as the African opposition to Federation mounted and became increasingly militant in what were then Northern Rhodesia and Nyasaland. White South African opinion was at one with Welensky in his condemnation of Britain's acquiescence in the dissolution of the Federation and her granting of independence to Zambia and Malawi. Kenya's attainment of independence with Jomo Kenyatta at the head of the government was seen as further, and perhaps even more dramatic, demonstration of the way things were heading in Africa, and, more specifically, of Britain's abandonment of the interests of the whites in favour of the black majority. If independence was granted to Tanganyika and Uganda with little fuss, the revolution in Zanzibar raised fears of an African Cuba. Meanwhile, the formation of the Organisation of African Unity with its avowed intention to liberate the whole of Africa and the increasingly hostile resolutions adopted by the United Nations against South Africa and the other white regimes remaining in Africa contributed further to the sense of threat that beset the whites in South Africa, and consequently intensified their craving for security.

This disturbing image of the 'outside world' was, however, brought into sharpest focus by events in Rhodesia, culminating in Rhodesia's unilateral declaration of independence and Britain's imposition of sanctions against the Smith regime. While Britain's refusal to use force against the rebel government caused strong resentment in Black Africa, the punitive measures which she did adopt were seen by the whites of South Africa as proof that Britain had gone over into the camp of the 'enemy'. For English-speaking South Africans in particular, this perceived change in their relationship with Britain caused a bewilderment that amounted almost to trauma, and this in turn bred a resentment towards Britain and an enhanced consciousness of their own South African identity. Most of them had been brought up in the comfortable world of the old British Commonwealth and retained strong ties of sentiment with the 'mother country'. These ties had been weakened by the advent of that republic which they had so strongly opposed; but at least Britain for a while had still seemed friendly—part, if not the centre, of their cultural home. The events of the two or three years preceding the election shattered this comfortable illusion and produced what was undoubtedly an over-reaction to Britain's position.[3]

This, in brief, was the 'new world' in which South Africa found herself living in 1966. But was South Africa herself, as *Die Transvaler* asserted, 'a new country'? To most observers at that time the comment would hardly have seemed apt. Certainly the same basic features of the South African political system were not only as apparent as they had been five or six years previously, they were even more sharply delineated. So that if the observation did have any point, it would have to be in some idiosyncratic sense of the term. That this was indeed the case is seen in the reason *Die Transvaler* gave for its remark. In essence, it was that the old constitutional and other associated conflicts that had divided the two white language groups were now over. What remained was a conflict in which everyone—regardless of language affiliation—'who values the survival of civilisation' must participate. In the end the apparent observation of fact is found to be a subtle introduction to the Nationalist election campaign, with the heavy stress it came to place on the need for white unity. If one digs deeper one may indeed come to the conclusion that however the parties might set up Aunt Sallys and industriously shy coconuts (or chestnuts?) at them, the vast majority of white South Africans did feel that they were all on the same side and possibly that the debate between the two major parties was more formal than real. This at any rate was the view taken by Laurence Gandar, who referred to 'the collapsed state of our politics' being 'reflected in the public's almost complete lack of interest in it'. And he went on to speak of the 'spirit of the election' as 'one of resignation, as if it were something inconvenient and unpleasant that must be gone through with like a minor operation'.[4]

Yet in the previous four and a half years South Africa's political history had been, to say the least, as full of incident as ever. In the earlier part of this period riots, other acts of violence, and disturbances had continued to occur in various parts of the country, but notably at Langa, in the Rustenburg and Sibasa areas, in and around the Transkei, and near Johannesburg and Pretoria. For the most part these continued to be clashes between conflicting African groups and between Africans and the police, but in the most spectacular outbreaks of violence, the Paarl riots in 1962, and in the Bashee Bridge murders, violence was also specifically directed against whites.[5] During the latter part of the period, however, violent action more characteristically took the form of sabotage.

Associated with the use of violence were two militant African political organizations: *Umkonto we Sizwe* ('Spear of the Nation') and *Poqo* ('pure'), underground forms of the A.N.C. and the P.A.C. respectively, both of which were committed to the violent overthrow of the South African Government through such methods as sabotage or ultimately guerrilla warfare. It was *Poqo* that was most prominent in the violence during the first phase referred to; but on 1 May 1963 the police arrested hundreds of *Poqo* suspects and by June the Minister of Justice assured the country that *Poqo* had been smashed. At all events, from that time this type of violence virtually disappeared.

As has been stated, sabotage became increasingly common, and from the evidence of the Rivonia Trial it would appear that the Spear was the prime organization in this field. In the charge sheet at that trial, 193 acts of sabotage were listed as having been committed between 27 June 1962 and 9 October 1963 when the trial began. There was a fresh outbreak of acts of sabotage immediately after the handing down of the verdict (13 June 1964), but thereafter acts of sabotage ceased in any significant degree to disturb the peace and good order of the Republic, at least for the time being.

Instead of these forms of violence filling the pages of the South African press, case after case of political trials provided South Africans with almost daily reading matter. The most prominent of these were perhaps the Rivonia Trial in which eight men, including Nelson Mandela, were sentenced to life imprisonment, and the trial of Abraham Fischer, Q.C. (leading counsel in the Rivonia case), which was still in progress at the time of the 1966 election, and which finally ended in a life sentence being imposed on him as well. Some indication of the extensive nature of police action during this period may be gained from the fact that in the year ending on 30 June 1964 a total of 966 persons (including 942 Africans) were sentenced to terms of imprisonment under laws relating to the safety of the State and that, as at 20 September 1966, 1 310 persons were serving prison sentences for offences of the same nature.[6] One might add that on 1 August 1966 the Minister revealed that there were 125 persons detained under the '180-day' clause;[7] and that there were still others, including Robert Sobukwe, former leader of the P.A.C., who continued to be detained in prison, under the terms of the Suppression of Communism Act, after the expiration of the terms to which they had been sentenced.

On the legislative side of this unhappy picture we find yet more laws being enacted to tighten the security structures of the State. The most notable of these were: the General Laws Amendment Act, No. 76 of 1962 (the so-called 'Sabotage Act'), which included very wide definitions of sabotage, an extensive range of additional offences, the prescription of severe penalties and a further broadening of executive power; the General Laws Amendment Act, No. 37 of 1963, which *inter alia* empowered the Minister to order, under certain broadly framed conditions, the continued detention in prison of a person who had served his sentence, and further increased the police's powers of arrest and detention; the General Law Amendment Act, No. 80 of 1964, which provided for the possibility of sentencing recalcitrant witnesses to successive terms of twelve months' imprisonment, and compelled a suspected accomplice to a crime to give evidence for the prosecution even if the evidence might tend to incriminate him; the Criminal Procedure Amendment Act, No. 96 of 1965, which provided that State witnesses to specified types of crime might be detained incommunicado for up to 180 days; and the Suppression of Communism Amendment Act, No. 97 of 1965, which placed further restrictions on certain types of publication.

In addition to these security measures, the apartheid apparatus was further elaborated through such acts as the Native Law Amendment Act, No. 46 of 1962, the Bantu Laws Amendment Acts, No. 76 of 1963 and No. 42 of 1964, and the Group Areas Amendment Acts, No. 49 of 1962 and No. 56 of 1965. Undoubtedly the most important piece of legislation in the apartheid context, and perhaps generally, was the Transkei Constitution Act, No. 48 of 1963, which, with its subsequent amendments, provides the model for the Bantustan concept of separate development, that is, the concept of evolving independent states for each of the eight major Bantu language groups in South Africa. The Transkei Constitution Act did not, of course, confer independence on the Transkei; according to its title, it was an 'Act to confer self-government in the Transkei on the Bantu resident in the Transkei', but even that more modest description of intent must be viewed as an exaggeration of what the Act actually did. Nevertheless, what it did do was not insignificant;

and what it portended was still more significant.[8]

As if to give point to the Government's avowed intention of 'leading' the Bantustans to full independence, Britain was proceeding apace to grant independence to both Bechuanaland and Basutoland, and indeed the new states of Botswana and Lesotho were born within months of the holding of the general election.[9] Two other events in Africa also intruded on the South African electoral scene. These were the Nigerian and Ghanaian military coups which, taken together with the spate of coups during the preceding few months in Africa, were seen as demonstrations of the violence and instability that overtake nations when the people are not yet 'ready' for full self-government.

These then were the storm-winds that were threatening to deluge the South African voters in 1966: the virtual completion of the process of granting independence to the former dependent territories of Africa—a process now reaching into the heartland of South Africa itself; the increasing hostility to the southern white regimes on the part of the African states, both individually and jointly through the O.A.U.; the growing support among the nations of the world generally for the African cause; the apparent abandonment by Britain of the white man to whatever fate black majorities might have in store for him; indeed, a perceived positive hostility on Britain's part to the whites in Africa as exhibited by her refusal to grant independence to Southern Rhodesia and by her imposition of sanctions when the Rhodesian Government unilaterally declared Rhodesia to be independent. Beneath these gathering clouds, white South Africans saw themselves not only as isolated and alone, but, perhaps for the first time, as vulnerable. Meanwhile at home there was, to change the metaphor, the familiar point and counterpoint of sabotage and violence and of further repressive legislation and intense police activity.

THE CONTESTANTS

The date for the forthcoming general election was decided at the first Cabinet meeting of the New Year.[10] It was to be on 30 March 1966, which meant that Parliament would fall short of its full term by over six months—a matter of no particular significance in itself, although the Opposition tried to make what political capital it could out of the calling of what it called an early election.[11] Possibly the Opposition had the idea that the National Party had been given prior notice that the election would be early and had been able to get a stride ahead of its opposition in preparing for the campaign. This, however, is purely speculative, and the issue of the timing of the election was soon overlaid by more substantive issues, or at least by the business of getting suitable candidates into the field, setting up the appropriate organization structures and generally getting on with the business of running a campaign.

In this flurry of activity, the parties did suffer a handicap. The Twelfth Delimitation Commission had been required to create ten new electoral divisions, and in doing so it had inevitably made a large number of changes in the existing constituency boundaries, including the complete abolition of six previous constituencies. All these changes inevitably created problems as far as party organization was concerned.[12]

Whatever the problems, by the time that Nomination Day came around, no fewer than 345 candidates were nominated to contest the 160 seats in the Republic, the largest number of candidates in the field in all the general elections so far considered. Compared with the record number of 67 uncontested seats in 1961, there were only 18 at the time nominations closed in 1966. Of the candidates who were returned unopposed, 1 was a United Party member and the remaining 17 were Nationalists. In the period between the closing of nominations and election day the Nationalist candidate for Durban Umlazi was declared by the Natal Supreme Court to be disqualified on the ground that he had not resided in South Africa for the required five years, and his United Party opponent was declared elected. The election returns, therefore, show two United Party members as having been returned unopposed.

The two main parties, of course, were represented among the candidates in full force (see Table 58 below), and the Progressive Party again entered a fair number of candidates, four more in fact than in 1961. The Liberal Party, however, abstained from the contests; and in its place two new parties entered the lists, the Republican Party and the National Front—if indeed the latter merits the title of 'party'. Another new group, the Conservative National Party, which appeared to be the 1961 Conservative Workers Party in a new guise, entered one candidate, who features ignominiously along with three independents in our tables as 'Others'.

'It is clear', commented a *Rand Daily Mail* editorial, 'merely from the nominations that the centre of gravity of politics has moved substantially farther to the Right.'[13] The Republican Party and the Front were both conservative in orientation, and so indeed were all the 'Others'. As for the older parties, the same editorial went on to observe: 'The middle ground formerly occupied by the United Party has been largely vacated for there are issues on which the United Party now stands to the Right of the Nationalists. The Progressives, refusing as always to bow to expediency or compromise their principles are seen in splendid isolation.'

Table 58

NUMBER OF CANDIDATES, 1966[1]

Region	*No. of seats*	*U.P.*	*N.P.*	*P.P.*	*Rep.*	*Front.*	*Others*	*Total*
Cape Town	15	11	11 (4)	3	—	—	1	26 (4)
Port Elizabeth	6	6	6	1	—	—	1	14
Border	5	5	4	1	—	—	—	10
Rest of Cape	28	21	28 (7)	1	1	—	—	51 (7)
Total Cape	54	43	49 (11)	6	1	—	2	101 (11)
Johannesburg	16	16 (1)	9	8	—	—	—	33 (1)
Witwatersrand	21	18	21 (1)	2	4	—	—	45 (1)
Pretoria	12	7	12 (1)	1	5	—	1	26 (1)
Rest of Transvaal	24	24	24	—	9	—	1	58
Total Transvaal	73	65 (1)	66 (2)	11	18	—	2	162 (3)
Durban–Pietermaritzburg	12	12[2]	12[2]	6	—	9	—	39[2]
Rest of Natal	6	6	6	1	2	1	—	16
Total Natal	18	18[2]	18[2]	7	2	10	—	55[2]
Total O.F.S.	15	9	15 (4)	2	1	—	—	27 (4)
Republic	160	135 (1)[2]	148 (17)[2]	26	22	10	4	345 (18)[2]

Notes: [1] The figures in brackets represent unopposed candidates as at the time when nominations closed.
[2] These figures do not take into account the subsequent disqualification of the N.P. candidate for Umlazi.

THE CAMPAIGN

One of the curious features of the 1966 election campaign was that although much had occurred in the external world and in the domestic arena since the last election, and although there were real and pressing issues confronting the Government, at least the two major parties seemed to devote the bulk of their campaigns to attacks on each other's policies rather than to presenting policies directed to the needs of the time. Moreover, these ascriptions of policies to each other were couched in the most general terms, and their results depicted in terms of ultimate doom. This tendency to view policies not from the perspective of the compelling present needs but from that of possible ultimate eventualities, not only made the election debate 'unreal'—'synthetic and unconvincing' as Laurence Gandar described it[14]—but also made it easier for the parties, as Gandar had earlier written, 'to frighten the life out of anyone who might be thinking of voting for a rival party'.[15]

(*a*) *The United Party*

The United Party campaign was in effect opened with Sir De Villiers Graaff's speech on a motion of no confidence at the beginning of the new session. The main thrust of his speech was aimed at the Government's policy on Rhodesia. To the United Party this, no doubt, appeared to be an issue presented to it by a benevolent Providence as a means of capturing the maximum support. White South Africans, and particularly English-speaking South Africans, had the strongest sense of empathy with the white Rhodesian regime, and the Government's policy of carefully balanced neutrality on the issue hardly matched the public's emotional commitment. Sir De Villiers Graaff and other United Party spokesmen accordingly plunged into the arena with the proposal that South Africa align itself decisively on the side of the Smith regime both by according to that regime *de facto* recognition as the Government of Rhodesia, and by instituting an official programme of aid to Rhodesia.

The heavy emphasis that the United Party initially placed on the Rhodesian issue, led *Die Transvaler* to observe that the coming election might, in one respect, be unique in that 'for the first time an issue of an external nature may play a significant role' in it.[16] In rather more pessimistic vein, although not specifically confining his comment to the election, Laurence Gandar wrote: 'Whatever happens it [the Rhodesian affair] is going to drag on and on, playing on our emotions in one way or another. In other words, it is going to keep fuelling the fires of White nationalism here for a long time.'[17] While both comments have a measure of truth in them, *Die Transvaler's* prediction would, in the end, have to be modified; for if it remained valid, it did so only indirectly in the sense that the Rhodesian issue modified attitudes in the direction suggested by Laurence Gandar, and hence helped shape the voters' response to the parties' respective appeals. Specifically and directly, however, the Rhodesian question later came to be overshadowed by other issues. Possibly the United Party began to discover that its position was failing to attract the support expected of it. Certainly the United Party strategy evoked heavy criticism. *Die Burger*, echoing the main point made by the Prime Minister, argued that the South African Government could hardly put itself forward as a mediator between Britain and Rhodesia, as the United Party urged, if at the same time it embarked on a large-scale aid programme to Rhodesia.[18] Helen Suzman, for her part, termed the United Party policy 'utterly dishonest';[19] and the *Rand Daily Mail* was equally critical.[20] Moreover, Dr Verwoerd's exposition of Government policy was persuasive, and the policy itself, from the point of view of South African interests, sensible.

The main burden of the United Party's campaign came to centre on the question of race policies. Here again the United Party gave more attention to attacking the Bantustan policy of the Government as exemplified in the Transkei than to propounding its own proposals. Early in the campaign, the *Star* wrote:

> It is now clear, and is no longer denied, that the eventual aim of the policy is independent African states where the old Native Reserves now lie. . . . This is not the kind of proposition with which any political party, let alone the Nationalist Party, could have gone to the polls 10 years ago. It can probably do so now only because the voters just do not believe it.

And it went on to argue that it was the United Party's task to bring 'this fact home to the voters'.[21]

To this task indeed the United Party spokesmen devoted the greater part of their attack. The coups in Nigeria and Ghana added further, if fortuitous, ammunition to the Party's armoury. Vause Raw, a senior member of the United Party in Natal, used it in this way:

> In this process of surrendering White leadership to these areas and states [the Bantustans], Dr Verwoerd was not only treating the White man as expendable but was endangering the rest of South Africa as well as condemning the Africans to the same pattern of dictatorship which had scarred the history of the African continent in recent years.[22]

Sir De Villiers Graaff himself painted a picture of the National Party as the allies, even if unwitting, of 'Afro-Asians' and Communists. Declaring that the latter two groups would like the National Party to win the election, he argued:

Such a win would present them with the prospect, within South Africa's borders, of Black independent States which could easily be bribed—which would be 'little Cubas' offering launching pads for Communism.[23]

A final example of this aspect might come from Mr Douglas Mitchell, the leader of the Party in Natal, in an extract which gives the full flavour of his brand of politics:

We shall protect what is rightly ours, we shall not dispose of our heritage to immature Black politicians scarcely veneered with what some are pleased to call civilisation.[24]

In short, the United Party presented the Government's Bantustan policy as one which involved surrendering large parts of South Africa's territories to independent Black states, and, what is more, bringing the twin threats of militant black nationalism and of Communism right, as it were, into South Africa's own parlour. The United Party Afrikaans weekly, *Ons Land*, even went so far as to call this policy 'Kaffirboetie politics'.[25]

The United Party's own race policy still relied on its vaguely formulated concept of Race Federation, but in the 1966 campaign it made the concept sound even vaguer. For the most part, United Party spokesmen contented themselves with presenting only that part of it which permitted Africans to elect eight representatives to the House of Assembly, and six to the Senate. A statement by Vause Raw contained one of the few instances of a fuller explanation. In this statement he asserted that the United Party 'guaranteed' that political rights would not be increased beyond the numbers stated 'without a definite mandate from the electorate at a referendum or a special general election', and he also went on to say that 'each race should control its own domestic affairs as far as this is practicable but under the direction of a White-controlled Central Parliament'.[26]

For the most part, however, the United Party relied on its call for the preservation of 'White leadership' over *all* the territory of South Africa. So Marais Steyn, the leader of the party in the Transvaal, wrote, '. . . the United Party openly comes out for White leadership over the whole of South Africa'.[27] From Vause Raw we hear that 'The United Party . . . bases its race policy on the need to retain White leadership and political control over the whole of South Africa . . .'.[28] And Douglas Mitchell varied the wording only slightly: 'We want to see our country built up on enlightened White leadership and we have not the slightest intention of abandoning this leadership over the whole of South Africa.'[29] This then was the major issue on which the United Party waged its campaign. It did include other items—from the building of a sound economy and the improvement of agriculture to the introduction of TV and the institution of a State lottery; but 'White leadership' was the issue that it hammered up and down the country. And it was with the surrender of 'White leadership' that it charged both the National Party and the Progressive Party alike.

(*b*) *The National Party*

The National Party too saw danger for South Africa—more specifically for the white man in South Africa—lurking at every corner. A *Rand Daily Mail* editorial aptly summed up its election campaign in these words:

With arguments seldom rising above the level of abuse and a devil's auction of *swart gevaar* utterances, it has all the intellectual and inspirational content of a horror film.[30]

The most spine-tingling horror that the National Party conjured up for the electorate was variously referred to as 'liberalism' (*Die Transvaler's* favourite) or 'integration'. 'A victory for liberalism', wrote *Die Transvaler*, 'means the downfall of the White race.'[31] And it urged that it was the duty of everyone 'who values the survival of civilization' to join in the struggle which would 'determine whether there will still be a White race in South Africa in the future'.[32]

In line with this view of the future, the National Party apologists grouped all other parties, from the Republican Party to the Progressive Party, in the same camp, since all the other parties insisted on the principle of 'one homeland' (i.e. in Nationalist terms, the principle of integration). Speaking specifically to the United Party's policies, but in terms that applied to other parties as well, the Prime Minister said, 'The United Party desires one people and fatherland for all races, with one central parliament in which white leadership will supposedly be safeguarded', and this, he went on to say, on the experience of what has happened in the rest of Africa will mean that the 'central government will become increasingly black until it is completely black'.[33] The general argument behind this conclusion was that, whatever the intention of the party concerned, in an 'integrated' society the black majority must inevitably in the end gain control of political power. The difference between United Party and Progressive Party policies was only one of pace; the results, however, would be the same: 'black rule in South Africa', as Dr Verwoerd put it. He therefore concluded: 'They are both equally bad.'[34]

From another point of view, the National Party and the Progressive Party joined in condemning United Party policy. Both parties poured scorn on its proposal to limit African representation to eight M.P.s and six senators, with any extension to this representation made subject to approval by the electorate.

This is no plan [comments an editorial in *Die Burger*] for peaceful co-existence, but for a violent conflict between white and black, in which, moreover, the blacks will hold all the moral and dialectical trump-cards—presented to them by a party of white South Africans![35]

The National Party's prescription for avoiding this conflict was (and is), of course, the policy of Bantustans in accordance with the principle of separate development. This policy, argued *Die Burger*, is 'not to stand in the way of others' right of self-determination, but to direct it to those parts of the land that are regarded as inalienably the Bantu's own'.[36] In a later article *Die Burger* lauded the policy as one 'with deep roots in our past, but which also satisfies the best contemporary idealism'.[37] Speaking for the National Party in Natal, Mr Volker expressed this 'idealism' as follows:

We recognise that each group has an inherent desire and right to determine its own future in terms of its own standards, ability, initiative and requirements.

We desire that the White man should be ensured of controlling his own future permanently and consequently recognise that the non-Whites should be entitled to look forward to enjoying potentially those same rights in so far as they affect their future.[38]

Die Burger's reference to the policy as one with 'deep roots in our past' had two sides to it. On the one hand, 'the urge for self-determination and freedom' is one which Nationalists know well from their own historical experience.[39] On the other hand, and countering the charge that they proposed to surrender large areas of South African territory, they argued that they merely proposed to give formal recognition to historically sanctioned divisions. Thus Mr B. J. Vorster:

There have thus far been two South Africas. . . . For generations the white man has lived in his territory and the black man in his, where he has ruled himself, but not over whites. What can be more reasonable than that?[40]

The Bantustan policy, in short, envisaged a future in which each national group in South Africa exercised its independent right of self-determination in its own historically determined territory, in a spirit of co-operation and good neighbourliness with one another. As for the dangers which the United Party foresaw in such a system, *Die Volksblad*, for example, claimed that while the three protectorates were all about to become independent, 'relations between the Republic and the neighbouring black states are inclined to improve with the closer approach of their independence'.[41] And

Mr Volker argued that the United Party policy was ten times more dangerous 'especially as their aim is to limit the rights of the Bantu to a permanently inferior position'.[42]

Unfortunately, however, the National Party came more under attack from the right than from the left. And in reacting to right-wing criticism, Party spokesmen revealed the Great Divide between theory and practice. Mr M. C. Botha, Deputy Minister of Bantu Administration and Development, rejected United Party assertions that it was the defender of the interests of the whites while the Nationalist Government championed those of non-whites, by pointing out that since 1948 the Government had spent R4 million on non-white housing compared with R216 million for whites.[43] And Senator De Klerk was reported as saying,

Independence might come to the Transkei in 10, 20, 50 or 100 years—and in all there might eventually be two, three, four, seven or eight Black states in South Africa.[44]

With this kind of admission being made, it is little wonder that the *Cape Times* was moved to comment that 'the myth of separate nationhoods is receding farther into the mists . . .'.[45] It was a comforting doctrine, for on the one hand it promised to avoid the clash of competing nationalisms for control of the South African power-structure, and on the other hand it promised that there would be no sudden and disturbing change in the system.

What Dr Verwoerd and the National Party were offering was security: security from the storms that threatened from within, as well as from those that threatened from abroad. But with regard to the external threats, the Party was no more concerned with consistency than it was in expounding its Bantustan policy. On the one hand it did its best to assure the electorate that the external threats were either non-existent or rapidly diminishing, while on the other hand it insisted that only a National Party Government was strong enough to withstand these threats. In line with the first form of reassurance, Dr Verwoerd argued in the opening speech of his campaign that 'recent events in Nigeria and Ghana' were inducing the Western nations to have second thoughts, and that they might be coming to understand that South Africa and Rhodesia 'were after all right'.[46]

On the whole much more stress was placed on the dangers that threatened. Typical of this approach was the statement by Mr Ben Schoeman, Minister of Transport and leader of the Party in the Transvaal:

We are aware of what has happened elsewhere in Africa and are conscious of the attacks that will be mounted by our overseas enemies and by certain nations in order to destroy white political power and to hand South Africa over to a black majority.

Hence, he argued,

South Africa's future depends on a strong and determined Government that will not surrender the rights of the whites, while it deals honourably and justly with regard to the non-whites.[47]

This, really, was the message that was the core of the Nationalist campaign—the Verwoerd Government gave South Africa the 'strong and determined Government' that the country needed.

There was, however, a further implication to this appeal, and one that gave the 1966 election its particular flavour. What the Government sought to achieve in 1966 was not just its re-election to office; for that it would be re-elected was universally conceded, except, in public at least, by the United Party. No, what it really aimed at in 1966 was a massive capture of English-speaking votes. In this it was encouraged by the 1965 provincial elections, in which, for example, it was able to win 8 of the 25 seats in Natal. And it was for this reason that it made Natal its major target. Consequently Natal blinked in the limelight which it had last experienced, but for rather different reasons, in the bygone days of the Natal Stand.[48] In the event, the National Party, for the first time in its history, entered a candidate in every Natal seat, and waged a campaign that included intensive door-to-door canvassing as well as 85 public meetings,[49] compared with 86 slated for the Transvaal with four times the number of seats at stake.[50]

In this campaign to win over English-speaking votes, the National Party relied heavily on the need to confront the external dangers which threatened with a display of national unity. Speaking in Durban, Dr Verwoerd said:

We fight as a people [*volk*] for our survival, and there is now nothing so important as that we have the consciousness of strong internal unity. That is why it is so important that Afrikaans- and English-speaking people stand side by side in the struggle for our survival.[51]

This theme was taken up again and again. Senator A. E. Trollip, Minister of Labour and Immigration and one of the two English-speaking members of the Cabinet, stated, 'It is of the greatest importance for the survival of the whites in South Africa that a bond is tied between Afrikaans- and English-speaking South Africans', and he called on English-speaking voters to vote for the National Party in order to demonstrate their 'patriotism'.[52] Dr Diederichs asserted that the election would be 'a national demonstration of the unity of our people',[53] and Dr Verwoerd reiterated his call 'to show a unified front to the outside world'.[54]

Many observers began to be persuaded that the National Party campaign would, indeed, be successful, even if not to the full extent claimed by the Nationalists themselves. *Die Transvaler* saw the coming election as 'the swansong of the United Party in Natal' and claimed that the National Party could easily win 10 of Natal's 18 seats.[55] A special report by George Oliver in the *Rand Daily Mail* was headed 'Natal swings to Nats as U.P. fights for survival',[56] and an editorial in the latter paper attempted to analyse the reasons for the expected 'substantial Nationalist inroads' into this predominantly English-speaking province:

> Among the most important are the deepening conservatism in Natal on colour issues, the influx of large numbers of disillusioned and bitter Whites from newly independent African states, the growth of anti-British feeling especially since the application of sanctions against Rhodesia, the changed public image of Dr Verwoerd following his successful visits to Natal, the skilful public relations work of the Nationalist Administrator, the growing conservatism of the principal Natal morning newspaper and the unpopularity of the United Party's Natal leader, Mr Mitchell.[57]

Viewed from the perspective of 1960, the most surprising item in this catalogue would be the reference to Dr Verwoerd. Times had indeed changed! At Dr Verwoerd's rally in Durban, *Die Transvaler* stated that political observers said that they had never seen such enthusiasm at a political meeting,[58] and the *Natal Mercury* too, spoke of a 'wildly enthusiastic reception'.[59] Mr B. J. Vorster offered the opinion that 'no single person in the country has done more to bring the Afrikaans- and English-speaking people together than the Prime Minister, Dr Verwoerd'.[60] Gerald Shaw, commenting on the growing Verwoerd personality cult, wrote in the *Cape Times* that 'Dr Verwoerd is now seen as the saviour of the British betrayed White man in South Africa',[61] and in the *Natal Mercury* he wrote, 'The Nationalists, side-stepping the Bantustan issue, are trying to generate the sort of atmosphere in which a vote against Dr Verwoerd will be seen almost as a betrayal of South Africa'.[62]

With the hope that this would indeed be the view of English-speaking South Africans as well as of Afrikaners, the Nationalists marched confidently towards election day. And there were few who were prepared to doubt that it would be the triumph that they expected.

(*c*) *The Progressive Party*

In all this the Progressive Party saw little cause for cheer. The demise of the 1961 Constitution in Southern Rhodesia and the acceleration of the trend to the right there, had undermined, to a degree, their own plausibility. Moreover in South Africa itself the same right-ward trend had also been apparent since 1961, and was particularly exhibited in the Progressives' own poor showing in the 1965 provincial elections. If, too, the electorate's present mood was one of fearful apprehension of the future, it was unlikely to respond in large numbers to a party that advocated the rejection of so many habits of thought and of behaviour.

Acknowledging that the Government was hardly likely to be defeated, the Progressive Party argued that the election, in effect, was an election of the opposition.

> Surely then [Helen Suzman said] it would be the intelligent thing . . . to start voting for a real opposition.
>
> In 26 seats you have that opportunity. And what a shot in the arm it would be for the body politic in South Africa—semi-paralysed by prejudice and crippled with fear.[63]

It was in accordance with this election strategy as well as with its own principles that the Progressives attacked the National Party and the United Party with equal vigour. The United Party, Helen Suzman maintained, was 'beating the drum of racialism and prejudices as hard, if not harder, than the Nationalists'.[64] Both parties Dr Friedman said, 'basically . . . stand for White domination'.[65] And Dr Steytler expanded on the theme. 'If', he said, 'the South African electorate allowed itself to be engulfed in the mass psychology of White domination, then the White man would be called upon to pay the price.'[66]

In general the Progressives argued that the peace and stability which South Africa currently appeared to be enjoying were being bought at too great a price, and were, in any event, illusory. As Helen Suzman saw it, it was the non-whites who were 'paying a high price for this peace',[67] and, Dr Steytler insisted, the Progressive Party 'would continue to put forward its policy of freedom of opportunity and personal freedoms for as long as it could, for it was convinced that the future safety of South Africa lay not in more repression, but in these freedoms'.[68]

The Progressives' own policy remained much as it had been in 1961: a rigid constitution with checks and balances to prevent the growth of arbitrary executive power and the domination of one or more racial groups by another, a qualified franchise applying alike to all racial groups, increased opportunities for education and jobs for all, and the abandonment of racial discrimination. In the 1966 campaign, in propounding its own policies the Party laid greatest stress on the last two points. In an article in the *Rand Daily Mail* on the Progressive Party's 'race policy', Helen Suzman stated that the Party rejected 'racial discrimination and the concept of domination by one race over another'. She went on to argue that the Party, in fact, had 'no "race" policy as such'; it only had 'a policy for all the citizens of this land and not for any particular section'. In so far, however, as the division between the 'haves' and the 'have-nots' and the 'educated' and the 'illiterate' largely coincided with race divisions, the Progressive Party could be said to have a 'race policy' in the sense that it aimed 'to ensure equal opportunity for all in this land'.[69]

While the Progressive Party hoped, of course, to increase its representation, its first priority was to secure Helen Suzman's re-election in Houghton. 'It was imperative', said Dr Steytler, 'for the Progressive voice—the only voice of sanity and moderation—to be kept alive and be seen to grow in volume.'[70] The *Rand Daily Mail*, which had given support to the Progressive Party throughout the campaign, specifically called for Mrs Suzman's re-election, and in this it was followed by the other Johannesburg English newspapers even though they generally supported the United Party. The *Star*, for example, argued that she should be re-elected, because (1) she was 'an unusually good M.P.', and (2) it was 'important for the Progressive point of view to be represented in Parliament'.[71]

(*d*) *The Republican Party*

The Republican Party represented a group of right-wing Afrikaners who had hived off from the National Party. It looked back nostalgically to the simpler Strijdom doctrine of unadulterated white domination. The more sophisticated concept of separate freedoms was not for it: it smacked too much of a retreat from a position of strength. Led by Dr C. F. van der Merwe, a former professor of medicine at the University of Pretoria, it was mainly based in the Transvaal, although as Table 58 shows, it was not confined to it. Very probably it represented a body of Afrikaner opinion that far exceeded its membership, and indeed the support it finally received in votes.

The *Sunday Times* was rather overstating the case when it claimed that there were 'unmistakable signs of a swing away from the Nationalist Party to the extreme Right-wing Republican Party in a number of Nationalist constituencies in the Transvaal'.[72] Certainly the National Party reacted sensitively to the new party, and throughout the campaign its spokesmen and its press refused to dignify it with its official title, referring to it, instead, as the 'van der Merwe Group' or as 'the van der Merwe-ites'. The political commentator, Harry O'Connor, discussed this reaction in these terms:

> The reason can only be that the Republicans make no bones about the kind of Republic they want—no Bantustans, the White man boss and uninhibited reversion to the fashions of yesteryear in the terminology

used to describe non-Whites [i.e. Kaffirs].

And this, the Nationalists know, is a formula not lacking in appeal to a considerable portion of the electorate.[73]

Neels Natte, columnist in *Die Transvaler*, explained the refusal to use the title, Republican Party, as follows: 'The National Party is the true republican party in South Africa, and anyone who after the creation of the Republic presumes to harvest the credit by virtue of name-giving, deserves to be treated as all National newspapers treat the van der Merwe-group.'[74] Meanwhile there were reports in the Nationalist press that, for example, the Republican Party was actively supporting the United Party candidate against the National Party in Potchefstroom,[75] and, conversely, that United Party supporters had been instructed to vote for the Republican Party where it was involved in straight fights with the National Party.[76]

With these suggestions of an alliance between the Republican Party and the National Party's traditional foe, the United Party, the National Party clearly sought to keep the ranks of its own supporters firm, whatever their private views on Bantustans might be. To vote for such splinter-groups, the Prime Minister further warned, was playing right into the Opposition's hands.[77] While at the same time Mr Daan Nel warned: 'They [the Van der Merwe-ites] do not fight the U.P. They wage a fierce war against the National Party.'[78]

(*e*) *The Front*

Of the minor groups or parties to make their appearance in 1966, the most curious was The Front or—to give it what was apparently its full title—The National South African Republican Front.[79] *Die Transvaler* described it as 'a loose alliance of people who think alike';[80] apparently it had no real organizational structure, although it did have a Secretary, Mr John Wilkinson of Durban; and throughout the election campaign it held no public meetings. In its various policy statements it claimed to stand for 'continued White guardianship over the entire Republic' as well as for 'separate development'; but if the Transkei proved to be a success it would accept the creation of further Bantustans. At the same time, it would grant urban Africans the right to own freehold property and would do away, in general, with 'petty apartheid'. Like the United Party, it supported the introduction of television and the institution of a state lottery.[81] So, picking its morsels from both the National and the United Parties, it was no doubt, as *Die Transvaler* suggested, too amorphous to capture the imagination of the voters.[82] Certainly there was little expectation that it would have any impact on the results, even in Natal where, in the end, it concentrated its campaign.

THE TURN-OUT[83]

The response of the electorate to the election campaign measured in terms of its turn-out to vote gives some credence to Laurence Gandar's earlier description of the mood of the voters as being 'one of ennui or even resignation'.[84] Admittedly the parties were faced, as we have already noticed, with difficulties of organization, tracing the movements of voters, and so on, as a result of the changes in constituency boundaries. Nevertheless the percentage poll, as Table 59 shows, was far from impressive—far short of the kind registered during the more lively fifties.

Table 59

VOTER PARTICIPATION PER PROVINCE

Province	*Electorate*	*Votes cast*	*% poll*
Cape	499 512	398 658	79,8
Transvaal	861 679	635 822	73,8
Natal	200 101	156 878	78,4
O.F.S.	121 773	86 877	71,3
Republic	1 683 065	1 278 235	75,9

In 1958, for example, 89,6% of the registered voters in the Union as a whole recorded their votes; and even in 1961 the corresponding figure was 77,6%. What was particularly noteworthy was the low level of voter participation in the Transvaal and the O.F.S., traditionally provinces that take their politics seriously and consequently that normally show high percentage polls.

A picture that shows some interesting variations from that seen in the previous table is to be found in Table 60, which gives the percentage polls per province in constituencies won by the United Party, the National Party and the Progressive Party respectively.

Table 60

PERCENTAGE POLL ACCORDING TO PARTY WINNING SEAT

Province	*U.P. seats*	*N.P. seats*	*P.P. seats*
Cape	74,75	83,7	—
Transvaal	68,0	74,7	80,7
Natal	76,75	83,3	—
O.F.S.	—	71,3	—

What is particularly noticeable in these figures is that it was only in the Nationalist-held seats in the Cape and Natal that the turn-out rose above 80% of the registered voters. Admittedly Nationalist supporters were under instructions not to vote in constituencies in which there were no National Party candidates, and this no doubt accounts at least in part for the low poll in such constituencies; but it certainly plays no part in the low poll in the National Party's own seats in the Transvaal and O.F.S. One factor having a bearing on this phenomenon may be found in the fact that in Pretoria the United Party contested only 7 out of the 11 contested seats, all of which were won by the National Party, and the over-all poll in Pretoria was only 68,9%. But in the O.F.S. the United Party was involved in 9 of the 11 seats contested, and there, as we have seen, the poll was not much higher. Very probably the somewhat unenthusiastic response was a reflection in part of the rather unreal terms in which the election debate was conducted. But it would seem that the major cause for the decline in voter-interest was that the establishment of the Republic reduced the fires of Nationalist enthusiasm and at the same time took something of the steam out of the Opposition. At all events, Nationalist supporters did not apparently feel moved to march together for the cause of Bantustans in the numbers that had responded to the call to establish the Republic.

THE RESULTS

(*a*) *In terms of seats*

According to the *Sunday Tribune* early in the campaign, 'Dr Verwoerd could not lose this election if he tries'.[85] As we have seen, virtually all commentators made the same prediction in one form or another. Such excitement as there was, therefore, in waiting for the election results, centred on such questions as the size of the Government's majority, the extent to which the National Party would succeed in Natal, and the fate of a relatively small number of marginal constituencies. In fact, except for the Natal question mark, 'mild interest' would be a better term than 'excitement' even on these somewhat peripheral questions. There was, for example, general agreement that the National Party would capture most, if not all, of the 10 new seats; and the main speculation was whether it would reach 120 or more of the Republic's 160 seats—hardly a critical question. In view of this general consensus, the fate of this or that particular seat was, again, hardly likely to arouse more than local excitement.

It was only really over Natal, then, that anything approaching excitement could be generated. Would the National Party be able to breach the United Party's last provincial bastion? On 23 March *Die Transvaler* stated that the National Party was 'certain of victory' in 7 Natal seats, and this view was accepted by the *Natal Mercury* on 30 March the day of the election. Again on the same date, the *Rand Daily Mail* reported that the Nationalists claimed that they would win at least 7 seats, that they had a 'better-than-even' chance in 3 more, and a 'fighting chance' in yet another 3. It went on to say, 'Failure to substantiate these claims would be a bitter blow to the party'.

As far as the minor parties were concerned, no one expected either the Republican Party or the Front to come even close to winning a seat. Nor was there any expectation that the Progressive Party would improve its position. The only question of real interest was whether Helen Suzman would be able to retain Houghton for the Progressive Party.

The answers to these questions are to be seen in Table 61, showing the party standings after the election according to the major provincial regions.

Table 61

RESULTS OF THE 1966 ELECTIONS ACCORDING TO SEATS[1]

	U.P.		N.P.		P.P.		
Region	*Seats*	%	*Seats*	%	*Seats*	%	*Total*
Cape Town	9	60,0	6(4)	40,0	—	—	15(4)
Port Elizabeth	2	33,3	4	66,7	—	—	6
Border	5	100,0	—	—	—	—	5
Rest of Cape	—	—	28(7)	100,0	—	—	28(7)
Total Cape	16	29,6	38(11)	70,4	—	—	54(11)
Johannesburg	9(1)	56,25	6	37,5	1	6,25	16(1)
Witwatersrand	1	4,8	20(1)	95,2	—	—	21(1)
Pretoria	—	—	12(1)	100,0	—	—	12(1)
Rest of Transvaal	—	—	24	100,0	—	—	24
Total Transvaal	10(1)	13,7	62(2)	84,9	1	1,4	73(3)
Durban–Pietermaritzburg	11(1)	91,7	1	8,3	—	—	12(1)
Rest of Natal	2	33,3	4	66,7	—	—	6
Total Natal	13(1)	72,2	5	27,8	—	—	18(1)
O.F.S.	—	—	15(4)	100,0	—	—	15(4)
Total Republic	39(2)	24,4	120(17)	75,0	1	0,6	160(19)

Note: [1] Number of uncontested seats shown in brackets

On the main question, the answer was clear and unequivocal: the National Party had gained a resounding victory, which was enhanced by the 6 South West Africa seats. The United Party, for its part, came out of the election with only 39 of the 160 seats, compared with 49 out of 150 seats in 1961. The only seat which the United Party gained from the National Party was that of Pietermaritzburg City, where the incumbent Mr Howard Odell, after winning a narrow victory for the United Party over the Progressive candidate in 1961, had resigned from the United Party in 1963 and in the following year had defected to the National Party. Contrary to many predictions the United Party wrested the seat back again though with a narrow margin of only 52 votes.

In Natal in general the United Party fought a relatively successful containing action, in restricting the Nationalist holdings to five seats. Even at that, however, it was a matter of reducing losses rather than making gains; and it certainly was not a matter for rejoicing that the National Party now held four out of six rural Natal seats compared with two out of five in 1961.

Over all, if Table 61 is compared with Table 53 (showing the 1961 results), it will be seen that the National Party substantially increased its percentage of the seats in every region and in every province as a whole—excepting, that is, those areas where it already had won all the seats in a region or province. There could be little doubt, therefore, that the Party was triumphantly continuing its onward march.

But for the Progressives there was one cheering note: Mrs Suzman did manage to retain her seat.

(b) The results in terms of votes

With the main outlines of the election results known even before the election took place, the interest soon shifted from the returns in terms of seats to the actual voting figures. These are shown in Table 62.

Again, from this table, the story of the National Party's success is apparent. In total it gained 57,7% of the votes cast; and in addition it returned 17 unopposed members compared with only 2 unopposed United Party candidates. Consequently the percentage it gained of the votes cast would underestimate the extent of its support. As for the United Party, it retained majority support only in the Cape Town, Border, Johannesburg, and Durban–Pietermaritzburg regions; and, compared with 1961, the Party's share of the vote dropped sharply in almost every region, especially if the National Union's votes are added to its own in 1961. The Progressive Party, however, suffered even more severe cut-backs in its voting

Table 62

VOTES CAST PER PARTY IN CONTESTED SEATS, 1966

Region	*Reg. voters*	*Votes cast*	%	*Reject*	*U.P.*	%
Cape Town	146 508	106 422	72,7	586	67 837	63,7
Port Elizabeth	79 084	66 161	83,7	283	28 413	42,9
Border	58 100	43 980	75,7	414	28 155	64,0
Rest of Cape	215 820	182 095	84,4	1 008	55 141	30,
Total Cape	499 512	398 658	79,8	2 291	179 546	45,
Johannesburg	200 116	140 737	70,3	774	74 425	52,
Witwatersrand	265 939	203 206	76,4	917	63 680	31,
Pretoria	140 725	96 985	68,9	631	16 771	17,
Rest of Transvaal	254 899	194 894	76,5	1 428	45 526	23,
Total Transvaal	861 679	635 822	73,8	3 750	200 402	31,
Durban–Pietermaritzburg	137 322	104 383	76,0	446	59 894	57,
Rest of Natal	62 779	52 495	83,6	240	23 827	45,
Total Natal	200 101	156 878	78,4	686	83 721	53,
Total O.F.S.	121 773	86 877	71,3	517	13 146	15,
Republic	1 683 065	1 278 235	75,9	7 244	476 815	37,

strength, and, except for Mrs Suzman's heartening success appeared to be teetering on the verge of extinction. On the other hand, the Republican Party fared even worse, while The Front was revealed as the damp squib that it was.

As in the discussion on the 1961 election, the way in which the respective parties fared in the constituencies which they actually contested might provide a fairer picture of their respective strengths. Table 63 shows the votes recorded by the respective parties as a percentage of the total votes cast in seats contested by them, region by region.

The main differences between the figures in this table and those in Table 62 are: (i) the United Party is seen to have significantly more strength in the Pretoria area and somewhat more strength in the Witwatersrand and in the 'rest of the Transvaal' than the figures in Table 62 indicated; (ii) the National Party shows up much more strongly in Cape Town, Border, the Cape as a whole, Johannesburg, and the Republic as a whole; (iii) the Republican Party, while still seen as commanding negligible support, is made to look slightly more respectable in Pretoria and the O.F.S. (where, of course, it contested only one seat); (iv) the Progressive Party figures show a marked improvement throughout compared with those in Table 62 and, especially given the prevailing political atmosphere, may be considered to have received encouraging support in the Cape Town and Johannesburg regions, although elsewhere it clearly had a hard struggle ahead of it in order to make any significant impact on the electorate.

P.	%	R.P.	%	P.P.	%	Front	%	Others	%
64	27,8	—	—	6 694	6,3	—	—	1 741	1,6
30	50,8	—	—	906	1,4	—	—	2 929	4,4
31	32,6	—	—	1 080	2,5	—	—	—	—
01	68,9	129	0,1	416	0,2	—	—	—	—
26	50,9	129	0,03	9 096	2,3	—	—	4 670	1,2
06	33,5	—	—	18 432	13,1	—	—	—	—
47	66,1	1 824	0,9	2 438	1,2	—	—	—	—
52	76,9	3 237	3,3	858	0,9	—	—	936	1,0
77	74,3	2 033	1,0	—	—	—	—	1 130	0,6
82	63,0	7 094	1,1	21 728	3,4	—	—	2 066	0,3
24	33,9	—	—	7 145	6,8	1 474	1,4	—	—
15	52,4	324	0,6	537	1,0	52	0,1	—	—
39	40,1	324	0,2	7 682	4,9	1 526	1,0	—	—
38	82,1	665	0,8	1 211	1,4	—	—	—	—
85	57,7	8 212	0,6	39 717	3,1	1 526	0,1	6 736	0,5

Table 63

PERCENTAGE OF VOTES CAST FOR EACH PARTY IN CONSTITUENCIES CONTESTED BY IT, 1966[1]

Region	*U.P.*	*N.P.*	*R.P.*	*P.P.*	*Front*
Cape Town	63,7 (11)	41,7 (7)	—	24,1 (3)	—
Port Elizabeth	42,9 (6)	50,8 (6)	—	8,3 (1)	—
Border	64,0 (5)	39,8 (4)	—	13,5 (1)	—
Rest of Cape	30,3 (21)	68,9 (21)	1,3 (1)	4,3 (1)	—
Total Cape	45,0 (43)	57,1 (38)	1,3 (1)	16,1 (6)	—
Johannesburg	52,9 (15)	54,4 (9)	—	25,1 (8)	—
Witwatersrand	34,2 (18)	66,1 (20)	4,9 (4)	11,4 (2)	—
Pretoria	25,5 (7)	76,9 (11)	8,0 (5)	7,4 (1)	—
Rest of Transvaal	23,4 (24)	74,3 (24)	2,8 (9)	—	—
Total Transvaal	34,1 (64)	68,9 (64)	4,7 (18)	20,4 (11)	—
Durban–Pietermaritzburg	57,4 (11)	33,9 (11)	—	12,5 (6)	1,8 (9)
Rest of Natal	45,4 (6)	52,4 (6)	1,8 (2)	5,9 (1)	0,5 (1)
Total Natal	53,4 (17)	40,1 (17)	1,8 (2)	11,6 (7)	1,7 (10)
O.F.S.	18,4 (9)	82,1 (11)	9,0 (1)	7,3 (2)	—
Republic	39,3 (133)	62,5 (130)	4,4 (22)	16,2 (26)	1,7 (10)

Note: [1] Number of constituencies contested given in brackets.

The major questions with regard to the voting are, however, what the total support commanded by the Government was, and the extent to which that support had increased or decreased since 1961. This latter question will be examined in the next section. With regard to the first question, as has already been indicated, the pro-Government percentage of all votes cast in all the seats contested in the Republic (Table 62) is likely to under-represent the pro-Government support in that it does not take account of the 17 National Party candidates who were returned unopposed. On the other hand, the figures given in Table 63 tend to exaggerate the over-all strengths of the various parties, in that their support would tend to be greater in the seats that they contested than in those that they did not. As in previous elections, therefore, we need to make some assessment of the votes that might have gone to the respective parties in the uncontested seats. Here we encounter a fresh set of problems; in particular: the difficulty of making estimates for individual seats in terms of the average swing from 1961 to 1966, because so many seats were uncontested in 1961, and because, in any case, so many changes in constituency boundaries were made in 1966; and the difficulty created by the intrusion of a third party of significant size, the Progressive Party, that was opposed to both major parties.

In view of these difficulties it seems sensible again, as in 1961, to confine our estimates for uncontested seats to the votes that might have been cast for the National Party in them. In seats in which National Party candidates were returned unopposed I have assigned to the National Party the average percentage of votes cast for the Party in the seats which it won in the regions where the uncontested seats were situated. In the two seats in which the United

Party returned unopposed members, I have assigned to the National Party the average percentage of votes cast for that party in the seats which it lost in the regions concerned. In both cases, the estimated total votes are based on the average percentage poll in the respective regions. Finally, with some guidance from the 1970 election results, I have made some slight upward or downward adjustments where it has seemed to me—as, it must be admitted, an 'educated guess'—such adjustments are likely to represent the degree of support with greater accuracy. Table 64, then, reflects the support which the National Party enjoyed in 1966, when allowance is made for the uncontested seats in accordance with these methods.

Table 64

ESTIMATED TOTAL STRENGTH OF THE NATIONAL PARTY, 1966

Region	*Estimated total votes*	*Estimated N.P. votes*	*N.P. %*
Cape Town	144 668	58 249	40,3
Port Elizabeth[1]	66 161	33 630	50,8
Border[1]	43 980	14 331	32,6
Rest of Cape	239 517	168 468	70,3
Total Cape	494 326	274 678	55,6
Johannesburg	149 324	48 823	32,7
Witwatersrand	213 276	141 092	66,2
Pretoria	106 035	81 186	76,6
Rest of Transvaal[1]	194 894	144 777	74,3
Total Transvaal	663 529	415 878	62,7
Durban–Pietermaritzburg	114 064	38 493	33,7
Rest of Natal[1]	52 495	27 515	52,4
Total Natal	166 559	66 008	39,6
O.F.S.	119 028	97 284	81,7
Republic	1 443 442	853 848	59,2

Note: [1] In these regions all seats were contested.

Taking all three tables in this section into consideration, we may reasonably assume that close to 60% of the voters—at least those who might be assumed to cast their votes—supported the Government in 1966. On this basis it would seem that this represented an increase of 5% or 6% over 1961.

(c) *The swing*

The number of constituencies which were reasonably the same in 1966 as in 1961 and which were contested by the same parties in both elections was relatively small. Nevertheless, some indication of the movement of opinion among the electorate may be gained from them.

In the Cape there were eight constituencies in which the U.P./N.P. swing may be calculated. In all of these the swing continued in the direction of the National Party, and ranged from 1,9% (Port Elizabeth North and Queenstown) to 9,1% (Humansdorp), with an average of 5,1%. On the other hand in three seats the United and Progressive Parties fought each other in both elections, and in all of these the swing was towards the United Party, ranging in extent from 3,0% to 7,3%, with an average of 5,5%.

In the Transvaal there were 21 seats for which the swing can be calculated in U.P./N.P. contests. In only one of these, Wolmaransstad, was there a swing to the United Party, and that was of the order of 3,0%. In the other 20 the swing to the National Party continued, ranging in size from 1,2% to 20,2% and averaging 7,4%. In addition there were 4 seats in which the swing can be calculated for U.P./P.P. contests. In one of these (Houghton) there was a slight swing of 0,5% in favour of the Progressive Party; in the others the swing ranged from 9,8% to 25,5% in favour of the United Party.

There were only three seats in Natal for which the swing can be calculated. All showed a continued swing from the United Party to the National Party, and they ranged from 3,0% in Newcastle, through 4,9% in Vryheid, to 13,2% in Zululand. Again in the O.F.S. there were only three seats that can be used, and the swing in these was also all in favour of the Nationalists: 4,5% in Bloemfontein District, 5,2% in Odendaalsrus, and 10,5% in Welkom.

The uniformity of the trend in favour of the National Party is clear from these figures and confirms the picture given in Tables 62–64. It is equally clear that at the intermediate level there was a similar trend away from support for the Progressive Party towards the United Party. There can be little doubt, therefore, that in 1966 the general body of white opinion continued to move steadily to the right.

(*d*) *Comparison between seats and votes*

Table 65 shows for the three parties that won seats in the 1966 election the percentage of seats won in contested elections compared with the percentage of votes cast in favour of the respective parties. The table is restricted to contested seats in order to make comparisons with the voting figures possible.

As this table demonstrates, the usual consequence of the single-member constituency electoral system of favouring the victor continued to operate to the gain of the National Party in 1966. Nor is the result different if we compare the total number of seats (including uncontested seats) won by the National Party in the Republic as a whole with the estimated total votes cast for it, for the Party gained 75% of the 160 seats with an estimated 59,2% of the votes—a percentage vote which, on a strictly proportional basis, should have

Table 65

PERCENTAGE SEATS COMPARED WITH PERCENTAGE VOTES (CONTESTED SEATS ONLY)

Region	U.P. % Seats	U.P. % Votes	N.P. % Seats	N.P. % Votes	P.P. % Seats	P.P. % Votes
Cape Town	81,8	63,7	18,2	27,8	—	6,3
Port Elizabeth	33,3	42,9	66,7	50,8	—	1,4
Border	100,0	64,0	—	32,6	—	2,5
Rest of Cape	—	30,3	100,0	68,9	—	0,2
Total Cape	37,2	45,0	62,8	50,9	—	2,3
Johannesburg	53,3	52,9	40,0	33,5	6,7	13,1
Witwatersrand	5,0	31,3	95,0	66,1	—	1,2
Pretoria	—	17,3	100,0	76,9	—	0,9
Rest of Transvaal	—	23,4	100,0	74,3	—	—
Total Transvaal	12,9	31,5	85,7	63,0	1,4	3,4
Durban–Pietermaritzburg	90,9	57,4	9,1	33,9	—	6,8
Rest of Natal	33,3	45,4	66,7	52,4	—	1,0
Total Natal	70,6	53,4	29,4	40,1	—	4,9
Total O.F.S.	—	15,1	100,0	82,1	—	1,4
Republic	26,2	37,3	73,0	57,7	0,7	3,1

given the Nationalists only 95 seats as against the 120 which they actually won.

An indication of what this disparity between seats and votes cost the Opposition parties is given in Table 66.

If, for example, seats were allocated to the United Party in the ratio of one seat to the National Party average of 7 165 votes, the United Party would receive 67 seats—30 more seats than it in fact won. Given the electoral system, however, the business of political parties is not to accumulate votes, but to win seats. And the fact of the matter as far as the United Party is concerned is that in 1966 its support was confined to four main areas: Cape Town, Border, Johannesburg, and Durban–Pietermaritzburg. In the other areas it might win a few seats (in fact, only five), but it still received a relatively large number of votes (246 504 or 51,7% of the votes cast for it)—and these votes, as the figures show, largely went to waste. In the earlier elections discussed, the main factor in the disparity between the number of seats won by the United Party and the number of votes cast for it, was the very great difference in the size of United Party majorities compared with National Party majorities. In 1966 National Party majorities tended, if anything, to be larger than those of the United Party majorities. In the 21 'Rest of the Cape' seats, for example, the National Party majorities averaged 39,2%, in the 11 Pretoria seats they averaged 58,6%, and in the 24 'Rest of the Transvaal' seats, the average size of its majorities was 51,25%. The principal factor in the 'wastage' of United Parties votes, then,

Table 66

NUMBER OF VOTES REQUIRED TO WIN EACH CONTESTED SEAT

Province	N.P.			U.P.			P.P.		
	Votes	*Seats*	*Votes per seat*	*Votes*	*Seats*	*Votes per seat*	*Votes*	*Seats*	*Votes per seat*
Cape	202 926	27	7 516	179 546	16	11 222	9 096	—	—
Transvaal	400 782	60	6 680	200 402	9	22 267	21 728	1	21 728
Natal	62 939	5	12 588	83 721	12	6 977	7 682	—	—
O.F.S.	71 338	11	6 485	13 146	—	—	1 211	—	—
Republic	737 985	103	7 165	476 815	37	12 887	39 717	1	39 717

was, as indicated, the dispersion of its votes in a large number of unsuccessful contests.

POST-ELECTION COMMENT

We have seen that one of the main focuses of the National Party's campaign was its attempt to win the support of the English-speaking voters, particularly in Natal. In terms of actual seats won in Natal, the number they achieved fell far short of their more optimistic predictions—two short, still, of the seven 'certain victories' which represented their most modest hopes. *Die Transvaler* expressed the Nationalist reaction to the results in Natal in the second headline to their major news item: 'Disappointments in Natal.'[86] The Party, however, soon recovered its buoyancy. *Die Burger* talked of the elections as marking 'a breakthrough into the heart of the English-speaking voters in Natal'.[87] And Dr Verwoerd stated that he was 'convinced that throughout the country the English-speaking people had given more support than ever before to the Government and its policy and that this process would be extended'.[88]

On the principal outcome of the elections, however, Nationalist joy was unqualified. *Die Burger* proclaimed it to be 'the greatest election victory since the establishment of Union'.[89] While *Die Transvaler* interpreted the results as giving the Government 'an overwhelming mandate for the implementation of separate development in all spheres'.[90] As against that view the *Rand Daily Mail* suggested that 'the Nationalists won in spite of Bantustans rather than because of them'.[91] On the other hand, both papers united in rejoicing, although for different reasons, in the crushing defeat of the right-wing splinter groups.

One may certainly say that in 1966 the electorate moved more solidly than ever behind the National Party. But whether one concludes that this was a move to the right or to the left, forwards or backwards, might well depend on how much in earnest one believes the Government to be in its Bantustan policy, and how seriously one considers the electorate to have taken that policy. On that last point one suspects that the *Rand Daily Mail* was closer to the truth than *Die Transvaler*. Given the political environment, both internal and external, at the time, and given the whole tone in which the election issues were presented, it would seem, indeed, that the voters of South Africa were seeking shelter under Dr Verwoerd's umbrella from the storms that threatened.

9

The General Election of 1970: A House Divided . . . ?

INTRODUCTION

(*a*) *Growing division among Nationalist Afrikaners*

As a result of the 1966 general election, the National Party Government's grasp of political power seemed to be secure for the foreseeable future. Dr Verwoerd, himself, within the Government, among the Party and its supporters, and among the electorate at large, exercised a personal dominance more impressive perhaps than that enjoyed by any previous Prime Minister, General Smuts included. Yet if he could have foreseen the events that were to follow his assassination, he might well have echoed the Earl of Gloucester's jeremiad: 'We have seen the best of our time: machinations, hollowness, treachery, and all ruinous disorders, follow us disquietly to our graves.' At least as far as Afrikanerdom was concerned, there was deeper and more bitter division, both overt and covert, within three years of his death than there had been for twenty to twenty-five years. Yet, as we have already seen,[1] there were signs of disagreement among the Nationalists as far back as 1958; and it is by no means improbable that the dichotomy within the Party would have reached breaking-point sooner or later even under Dr Verwoerd.

Nevertheless the death of Dr Verwoerd and the succession of Mr Vorster, and the policies the latter came to pursue, were the immediate or precipitating causes of the split. At the time, however, the horrifying circumstances of Dr Verwoerd's assassination[2] seemed to draw at least the white people of South Africa together, not only in mourning his death, but also in recognizing the role he played, both actual and symbolic, in resisting the external pressures being exerted against South Africa. The panegyric appearing in *Die Transvaler* was, perhaps—and understandably—the loudest and clearest in its praise:

In him South African statesmanship undoubtedly reached a zenith which will not easily be improved upon. Gifted, with a clear and brilliant intellect such as possessed by few men, inspired with a firmness of principle which evoked respect from friend and foe, and born with all the characteristics which may be expected of the leader of a people, Dr Verwoerd has for a long time already achieved for himself an enduring place in the history of South Africa.[3]

The *Natal Mercury*, which usually reflects with a fair degree of accuracy the views of its English-speaking Durban readers, referred to Dr Verwoerd in similar terms, but that it recognized all was not well within the National Party was apparent when it asked:

Will there be found a leader with the breadth of vision, tenacity of purpose and strength of leadership capable of carrying forward a bequeathed ideal and at the same time holding together a Party of divergent elements?[4]

The two main *verligte* Nationalist newspapers at that time, *Die Burger* and *Die Beeld*, both made reference to these 'divergent elements' in the Party. Dawie[5] made the comment that by the end of his life 'there were more controls in his [Dr Verwoerd's] hands, and he personally directed more important matters—with startling accuracy and in surprising detail—than even the most dominating of his predecessors, namely, General Smuts'. But, Dawie went on to say,

. . . [he was] also in a way autocratic, with a strong sense of discipline, even in the nation's thinking. Dr Verwoerd, it seemed, was always aware of the centrifugal forces among Afrikaners, which had to be fought with unswerving demands to adhere to the orthodox 'line', and firm dismissal of 'deviating pleas' which could cause rifts.[6]

The editor of *Die Beeld*, Schalk Pienaar, also referred to 'centrifugal forces within the National movement', and went on to comment:

Dr Verwoerd, the creator of the new dispensation, which caused these stirrings, held an apprehending eye and a firm hand over them. Under his apprehension and authority the flutters did not become eruptions. In this respect, too, his disappearance brings uncertainties.[7]

The clear implication was that, without the unique authority that Dr Verwoerd had been able to establish for himself in the Nationalist movement, there might well already have been 'eruptions', and consequently, that it was at least 'uncertain' whether any successor to Dr Verwoerd would be able to prevent them.

The 'new dispensation' that Dr Verwoerd had initiated had four main elements. With regard to race policy, the concept of separate development applied to all four major ethnic groups (accepting for the moment the dubious proposition that the Coloureds constitute a distinct ethnic group), and extending to the acceptance of 'eventual' independence for the Bantustans, was a peculiarly Verwoerdian notion. Secondly, from 1961 on Dr Verwoerd laid particular emphasis on the need for English-speaking co-operation in the cause of national unity. Thirdly, largely in order to maintain rapid economic growth, it was under Dr Verwoerd's regime that the policy of promoting large-scale immigration was adopted. And finally, in the last few months of his life Dr Verwoerd began to lay the foundation of an 'outward' foreign policy, especially as applied to Black African states. Each of these elements of the 'new dispensation' provided occasion for dispute within the ranks of National Afrikanerdom. However, since the unifying objectives of Afrikaner control of the state structure and of the establishment of a republic in South Africa had by now been obtained, these questions loomed all the larger. And it was largely on these questions that, even before Dr Verwoerd's death, the conservative and more liberal Nationalist Afrikaners were divided.

Under these circumstances the selection of Dr Verwoerd's successor took on a particular significance. The two main candidates were Mr B. J. Vorster, then Minister of Justice, Police, and Prisons, a former member of the Ossewa Brandwag who had consequently been obliged to stand as an independent in the 1948 election, and Mr B. J. Schoeman, leader of the Party in the Transvaal, Minister of Transport, and Leader of the House of Assembly. Of the two Mr Schoeman was by far the more senior, both in the Cabinet and in the Party, and he was generally regarded as the more moderate; while Mr Vorster, largely due to the measures adopted within the area of his portfolios, tended to be identified as an 'extremist'. No doubt it was partly for this reason that the more right-wing elements rapidly formed an effective lobby on the latter's behalf; although, significantly, it is also reported that he received the support of the Cape, including that of the 'liberal' Mr Piet Cillie, editor of *Die Burger*.[8] J. H. P. Serfontein surmises, and it is a reasonable surmise, that the 'peculiar bitterness and venom' with which the *verkramptes* later waged their anti-Vorster campaign was the result of the feeling that they had been betrayed by their chosen champion. 'We have been sold-out was later the general feeling', he writes, 'among the Hertzog-group and many verkrampte Nationalists.'[9] At the time, however, the Vorster lobby was sufficiently effective to induce Mr Schoeman to withdraw his candidacy. So it was that on 13 September 1966 Mr Vorster was unanimously elected by the Parliamentary caucus to the post of Leader of the National Party, and thus he consequently became Prime Minister. That unanimity did not survive for long.

The latent divisions within the Party were first brought into the open, oddly enough, by the arch-conservative, holier-than-the-Nationalists, English-speaker, Mr S. E. D. Brown, editor of the *South African Observer*. In mid-July 1966 he began a 'witch-hunt' of 'liberalists' and 'liberal' tendencies among a number of prominent Afrikaners. This was, of course, while Dr Verwoerd was still Prime Minister; and Dr Verwoerd failed to respond to the challenge by Mr 'Japie' Basson (U.P. member for Bezuidenhout) to repudiate Mr Brown's tactics.[10] If Dr Verwoerd remained silent, Dawie in *Die Burger* and Mr Schalk Pienaar, editor of *Die Beeld*, did not. Dawie, for example, stated that 'solid healthy Afrikaner opinion' had long been opposed to the activities of Mr Brown 'and the mainly Northern clique that is connected with him';[11] and *Die Beeld* weighed in on 7 August 1966 against the paper which served 'as the mouthpiece . . . of a small group of Afrikaner Nationalists'.[12] These statements broadened the area of conflict into a press war with the Nasionale Pers (which controlled the two papers cited) becoming the primary target of right-wing attacks.

The cleavage became even more marked two months later (and a month after Dr Verwoerd's death) in that its nature was carefully articulated. Being thus brought into the open, it became even more difficult to ignore it. The person responsible was Professor W. J. de Klerk of Potchefstroom University, the occasion, a Youth Congress convened by the S.A. Bureau of Racial Affairs. It was in his address to the Youth Congress that Professor De Klerk first distinguished the categories of *verligte* and *verkrampte* Afrikaners,[13] and, although the definition of these terms has undergone subsequent change, they have become part of the common coinage of South African political terminology. That this has been so, has been because there are indeed these divisions among 'National-minded' Afrikaners: divisions relating to basic attitudes about the role and nature of Afrikanerdom and the posture it should adopt towards current and future problems.

This was the conflict that was to lead, towards the end of 1969, to the formation of the Herstigte Nasionale Party (H.N.P.).[14] Before that event, the battle between the opposing viewpoints raged in almost every sector of Afrikaner community life, taking in the press as well as almost every private association. From this point of view, it is particularly important to recall the basic pattern of the Afrikaner *risorgimento*, in which Afrikaner institutions—the Church, the Broederbond, language and culture associations, commercial institutions, etc.—were interlocked, with the common objectives of restoring to the Afrikaner his self-respect, of promoting the unity of Afrikanerdom, and of establishing and preserving the culture values and spiritual ideals of Afrikanerdom. Of this movement, the National Party was the political arm—the effective instrument by which the Afrikaner *volk* could achieve its various, but integrated goals. And it was because all aspects and institutions of Afrikaner life were integrated to such a high degree, and because, moreover, the National Party came to be recognized as the body which, in Aristotle's terms, 'comprehended' them all, that all these aspects and institutions came to be politicized. There could not, for the same reasons, be change in one area of life without that change having repercussions in all others. The divisions, therefore, between the *verligt* and the *verkrampt* penetrated into all parts of the Afrikaner Nationalist movement. As J. H. P. Serfontein has described it: 'This struggle is more than a purely political battle. It is a struggle that extends over every aspect of the National-Afrikaner community life—religion, culture, youth, art, the business world, sport and politics.'[15] It is impossible within the scope of this study to follow the intrigues and stratagems with which the struggle was carried on in the various Afrikaner organizations. It is a story both fascinating and instructive—essential, indeed, for an understanding of contemporary Nationalist Afrikanerdom; but at present there is no real alternative to J. H. P. Serfontein's *Die Verkrampte Aanslag*, and unfortunately that work is available only in Afrikaans. It must, however, suffice to say that the *verkrampte* attack on the 'liberalist' threats to National Afrikanerdom was mounted with both subtlety and vigour, and that the *verkramptes*, indeed, achieved for a while considerable success. Increasingly too, although covertly, the attacks were directed against Mr Vorster's leadership; so that behind the scenes something approaching a 'Vorster must go' campaign was being mounted. At the same time, the nucleus of this *verkrampte* movement was coming to be ever more clearly identified as the 'Pretoria circle', with Dr Albert Hertzog as its leader. This, then, was the significance of Mr Vorster's action in February 1968, when he relieved Dr Hertzog of his portfolio of Posts and Telegraphs—although he still retained him as a Minister of Health.[16]

A few months later Mr Vorster came under open, personal attack with the circulation of an anonymous 'smear-letter' among all Nationalist M.P.s and other prominent Afrikaners. It is alleged that the Security Police were used to uncover the authors;[17] at all events, uncovered they were, and expelled from the National Party and disqualified for life from ever rejoining it. There was, however, a remaining strong suspicion that the Hertzog group were also implicated; and within two months of the circulation of the letter Dr Hertzog was dismissed from the Cabinet.[18]

These actions did not resolve the issue. If anything, the conflict deepened. The chosen focus of the next phase of the *verkramptes*' campaign revolved around the nation-building policy (as applied to the whites) that was in the forefront of the National Party's strategy. As we have seen in the previous chapters, it was a policy that had been initiated by Dr Verwoerd, but it had been given even greater emphasis by Mr Vorster and had consequently come to be identified with him. Organically related to this policy was the acceptance of the need for greater pragmatism and flexibility in party outlook. Mr Paul Sauer had given clear expression to this typically *verligte* viewpoint in May 1968, when he declared:

> There are new ideas and norms in South Africa and the new South Africa will have to be fashioned in terms of these new ideas. . . . A new generation now leads South Africa and they think in terms of new things. The older generation will have to adapt themselves to this.[19]

This perspective of the National Party's contemporary role evoked an immediate response in both *Hoofstad* and *Die Vaderland.* In an article in *Hoofstad* on 3 January 1969, Dr Treurnicht argued that 'New norms and principles can mean only one thing, and that is the rejection of the Christian ethic and the customs and traditions that in the course of centuries have been built upon it'. And this rejection he clearly associated with the 'nation-building' policy; for, he further argued, 'there are few things that cause so much alarm and despondency among Afrikaners as the denial of *Afrikanerskap* on account of co-operation with the English-speakers'.[20]

This, then, was the background to Dr Hertzog's first speech in Parliament since his dismissal from the Cabinet. Of the Afrikaners, he said:

> We Afrikaans-speaking people are still mainly anchored in our church and our religion. We are still mainly Calvinists. We are permeated by that great complex of principles called Calvinism, that code of moral, ethical and religious principles. They form part of our pattern of life. They form part of our being, of our upbringing. We cannot be anything else.[21]

He then sharply differentiated the English-speaking section:

> . . . basically the English-speaking Afrikaner is liberal. . . . This liberalism forms part of the very being of our English-speaking friends. They can no more divorce themselves from that than we can divorce ourselves from our Calvinistic background.[22]

It was for this reason Dr Hertzog maintained that the English-speaking South Africans had not seen 'their way clear to identifying themselves with . . . those measures which were so absolutely and inexorably necessary if we wanted to maintain ourselves and a white civilization in South Africa'.[23] The inference, of course, was, if Afrikaners moved by a desire to co-operate with English-speakers (or for any reason) became infected with liberalism, they would be cutting themselves off from their roots, ceasing, in reality, to be Afrikaners. The further inference was that in thus denying their

Afrikanerskap they would be stripping themselves of their unique capability to maintain 'white civilization' in the face of the *swart gevaar.*

In saying all this, Dr Hertzog was in fact undermining one of the main planks of the Vorster programme. His speech was, therefore, an oblique attack on the Prime Minister's leadership. This was all the more apparent in Dr Hertzog's final paragraph, and particularly in the implied threat of the final sentence:

In the struggle which lies ahead for us . . . it will once more be the man who is the bearer of these wonderful Calvinistic principles who will fight at the forefront of the struggle for our civilisation. But there is a condition attached to this. This condition is that we shall be able to rely on him only as long as he is in fact the bearer of those Calvinistic principles. The moment he forsakes those principles his power will collapse.[24]

The reaction to this speech was considerable. *Die Burger*, for example, argued editorially that the National Party had for many years sought to break down the 'more or less artificial' barriers between the two language groups, and that consequently it had to foil any fresh attempts to put these groups into separate kraals. And, quoting from a pre-referendum speech by Dr Hertzog himself, it concluded, 'The time is indeed ripe to unite as one nation'.[25] In Parliament itself, Sir De Villiers Graaff pressed the point until both Mr Vorster and Mr Ben Schoeman, as leader of the National Party in the Transvaal, repudiated the imputations against English-speaking South Africans.[26]

In truth, however, Dr Hertzog was less concerned with attacking the English-speaking group than with reasserting the fundamental Calvinist direction of Afrikanerdom. It was essentially a battle over the 'soul' of Afrikanerdom, and only incidentally one over Afrikaans–English relations, that was being waged. This was made clear in a leading article in *Hoofstad* written by Dr Treurnicht on 30 April 1969. Complaining about the use of the pejorative term *weerbarstiges*[27] he claimed that it was these 'so-called *weerbarstiges*' who had given to the Afrikaner people their Christian character. 'The question is', he went on, 'who deviates from the principles and policy of the National Party and who rejects the Christian-National foundations of our whole social, educational, political and national life? Without being falsely pious: Who stands by the Lord and His Word?'[28] The conflict within *Afrikanerdom* could hardly be more provocatively stated. The implication as *Die Burger* saw it was that 'the *weerbarstiges* fight for Christendom, for the Lord and His Word, while the National Party . . . represents the power of darkness'. It then went on to state:

When elements who are thwarted in their political ambition and caught in their intrigues present themselves as saviours of Christendom, it is time for the decent Afrikanerdom to stand up in its dignity and honesty and to say, 'Thus far and no further'.[29]

From this point it seemed apparent that the final rupture between Dr Hertzog and his supporters and the National Party could no longer be avoided. As *Die Burger* saw it, their position in the National Party 'had become intolerable for men of honour and self-respect'.[30] Nevertheless it seemed that the Hertzog group were as reluctant to resign from the party as the party leadership was to expel them. And a week later an agreement was patched up, whereby Dr Hertzog undertook 'to clear away the confusions and false impressions' aroused by his 'Calvinism' speech.[31] There was general, if in some quarters rather qualified, rejoicing over the restoration of peace. But it did not last long. In the subsequent meetings that Dr Hertzog was to address, and at which he was supposed to 'clear away the confusions', he made little or no reference to them, and concentrated instead on further attacks on *Die Burger* and *Die Beeld* and on further expositions of his own political position. Nor was there any discernible pause in the propaganda that issued from his fellow-thinkers, such as Dr Piet Meyer and Dr Treurnicht and the writers in *Veg*.

In fact, the breaking-point was near, and in the Transvaal Congress of the National Party the party leadership finally struck. The strategy that Mr Ben Schoeman adopted was astute—and ruthless. The four most contentious issues in the Government's policies were to be presented in turn to the eleven hundred delegates; they were to be open to discussion, and then voted upon. Delegates might vote for the motion of approval, vote against it, or abstain; but, with the approval of Congress, the names of those voting against the motion as well as of those abstaining were to be recorded in the minutes.

The four issues put to the congress were: The outward 'foreign' policy towards African states, including the question of black diplomats; co-operation between Afrikaans- and English-speaking South Africans; the Government's sports policy, especially the Government's agreement to accept the inclusion of Maoris in the New Zealand rugby team shortly to visit the Republic; and the Government's immigration policy. Mr Gert Beetge, one of Dr Hertzog's strongest supporters, described the proposed procedure as a 'shock'—with some justification since there had been nothing on these lines on the agenda—and attempted unsuccessfully to have the debate postponed. In the debate that followed, three of the four policy-issues were unanimously adopted. The exception was the Government's sports policy. On that issue eleven members voted against it, and seven abstained. Mr Schoeman then warned the delegates that they were all now bound by the Congress's decisions and that steps would be taken against any member who did not accept them.[32]

These proceedings put the Hertzog group at a clear disadvantage. They would now either have to drop their criticisms of the Government's policies, with consequent loss of face; or if they persisted with them they would have to face almost certain expulsion, an eventuality that they had sought to avoid. Dr Hertzog, however, almost immediately issued a statement that put the question beyond doubt. Totally ignoring assertions by Mr Vorster and other ministers that he had approved the new sports policy in 1967, both in the Cabinet and in the caucus, he took as his starting-point the decision taken by the Cabinet under Dr Verwoerd in 1965 to refuse to accept 'mixed' teams from overseas. He thereby attempted to stamp Mr Vorster as the one who had deviated from established policy, who was destroying what Dr Verwoerd had wrought. And this applied to the whole apartheid system. It would not just be mixing on the rugby-field; it would extend to dinner-parties, dances, and other social occasions, leading to 'the systematic and speedy destruction of all apartheid, and the preservation of the white man in South Africa'.[33] As Dawie commented, this unexpected statement amounted to an invitation to the party to expel him.[34]

This was the stage at which Mr Vorster announced to the Orange Free State Congress on 16 September 1969 that a general election would be held in the first half of 1970. And this was both the background to, and the occasion for, the election. As far as Dr Hertzog himself was concerned, he met his expected fate four days later, when the Ermelo constituency committee formally expelled him from the National Party. On 8 October 1969 a rally attended by some 2 500 people was held in Pretoria and there it was decided to form a new party; and on 25 October the Herstigte Nasionale Party was formerly constituted. This, then, marked the beginning of a new, public, and even more bitter phase in the battle for Afrikanerdom. And in the ensuing election campaign this battle was fought with all the ferocity of a religious war.

(*b*) *Other developments*

Before we turn to the election campaign, it might be useful to pause and review just a few of the major landmarks of the Vorster regime, particularly in the light of the *verkramptes*' accusations of increasing 'liberalism'. It is a valid comment that under Mr Vorster's leadership the South African Government had made some attempt to escape from the so-called 'laager mentality' of its predecessors.

Nevertheless, to describe the Vorster regime as liberal in the normal sense of the term would be as far-fetched as to describe the Nixon administration as communist. The activities of 'terrorists' (or 'freedom fighters', depending on one's point of view) in South West Africa resulted in a further addition to South Africa's repressive legal structure—the Terrorism Act (No. 83 of 1967). Moreover, existing legislation was further tightened—e.g. by the Suppression of Communism Amendment Act (No. 24 of 1967) and the General Law Amendment Act (No. 101 of 1969). One of the outstanding pieces of legislation in this period too was the Public Service Amendment Act (No. 86 of 1969) which provided for the establishment of a Bureau of State Security (popularly known as BOSS) which was made directly responsible to the Prime Minister.[35]

The general apartheid edifice was constantly added to and given greater rigidity by means of such Acts as the Population Registration Amendment Acts (No. 64 of 1967 and No. 106 of 1969), the Prohibition of Mixed Marriages Amendment Act (No. 21 of 1968), and the Physical Planning and Utilization of Resources Act (No. 88 of 1967). Of particular importance was the Prohibition of Political Interference Act (No. 51 of 1968) which, *inter alia*, made it an offence to belong to a racially mixed political party, and to assist a political party which had members of a racial group other than one's own. It was in response to this Act that the Liberal Party decided to disband and that the Progressive Party 'under protest and compulsion' restricted its membership to whites only.[36] Companion legislation provided: in the Separate Representation of Voters Amendment Act (No. 50 of 1968), for the termination of Coloured representation both in the House of Assembly and in the Cape Provincial Council when these bodies were dissolved; in the Coloured Persons' Representative Council Act (No. 52 of 1968), for the establishment of a partly elected, partly nominated, Council with certain subordinate powers of legislation—to be exercised subject to the approval of the Minister of Coloured Affairs acting in consultation with the Minister of Finance and the provincial administrators. In addition, the South African Indian Council Act (No. 31 of 1968) gave statutory authority to a body established in 1964; but the Council remained wholly nominated and its powers purely advisory. During 1968 and 1969, also, six new Territorial Authorities were proclaimed: Ciskei, Lebowa, Basuto Ba Borwa, Tswana (now Bophuthatswana), Mashangana, and Venda; and shortly before the general election, a meeting of chiefs finally agreed to the establishment of a Territorial Authority for Zululand. In short, the concept of separate—or 'parallel'—development continued to be extended, if not in degree, at least in extent. It now brought in the Coloureds (still in itself a highly contentious issue even in Nationalist circles), Asians, the other seven main African linguistic (or 'ethnic') groups, and, as well, under the Development of Self-Government for Native Nations of South West Africa Act (No. 54 of 1968), the six 'Native nations' of the disputed territory.

None of this was very exciting to the South African electorate. There was no sign of any leap of creative imagination in Government policies. Despite being clothed in new terminology—such as 'parallel development', 'multi-national' state—it was still the same old apartheid that was being applied, and being applied with apparent disregard to the objective needs of the country. This was particularly disturbing in the economic sector. At the time of the general election, South Africa was standing on the brink of serious inflation.[37] And there was wide agreement that one of the major causes of this inflation was to be found in restrictive Government labour policies, such as job reservation and the controls contained in the Physical Planning Act. Typical of the many statements to this effect made at the time was the following caution contained in a *Financial Mail* editorial:

> . . . unless more labour is allowed in industry and the cities, and unless restrictions on skilled work are whistled away faster, South Africa could be heading for a massive wave of wage inflation.[38]

Nevertheless the Government appeared to be unmoved by these views; and Government Notice R531 of 3 April 1970, issued by Dr Koornhof, Deputy Minister of Bantu Administration, gave notice of the Minister's intention to exclude Africans from a further wide range of occupations.[39] At the same time, pointing up the gap between ideology and reality, the Government was of necessity compelled to grant a vast number of exemptions to its labour regulations; and the State-run South African Railways was foremost in the employment of blacks in jobs formerly held by whites.[40] It would appear that there was some validity in the view that the South African economy was being kept afloat in spite of rather than because of Government policies. But if it was afloat it was still being washed by the waves of inflation; and of this the public was very well aware, as it was of the fact that Government policies were, at least in part, to blame for the shrinking value of the rand.

THE TIMING OF THE ELECTION

A general election was not due in South Africa until 1971, and, as is apparent in this study, there has been a marked tendency in the post-war period (and, for that matter, since Union) for parliaments to serve their full term, except under very special circumstances. When, therefore, Mr Vorster announced on 16 September 1969 that a general election would be held early in the following year, he was sufficiently departing from an established position to rouse comment and to require an explanation. It was clear, indeed, that the timing both of the announcement itself and of the general election was decided upon as part of the National Party's strategy to crush the *verkramptes* as thoroughly and speedily as possible; but, of course, it is rare that a government openly admits that a general election is timed to serve purely party purposes.[41] And in making his announcement, Mr Vorster couched his explanation in terms of the national interest. It was, he argued, essential that the outside world should not gain the impression from the activities of Dr Hertzog and his associates that the Government and the National Party were weak and unstable.[42] But it was almost certainly the domestic situation—applied specifically to the Afrikaner National movement—which the Prime Minister really had in mind. His announcement followed hard on the heels of the Transvaal Congress's 'smelling out' of the *weerbarstiges*, but before formal action had been taken against them and hence before they had launched their new party; but once he had made his announcement both those subsequent events became inevitable. This is precisely what the National Party leadership wanted; for in driving the dissidents into the open and in placing them in a situation where they would be forced to engage in a trial of strength, they hoped to administer the *coup de grâce* to the rebellion.[43]

Related to this issue, indeed a part of it, was the question of Mr Vorster's leadership. This leadership had, as we have seen, been under attack, mostly, it is true—with the exception of the 'smear' letters—surreptitious or indirect, but no less severe for that, over at least the preceding two years. And this Mr Vorster himself indirectly acknowledged. He was reported as saying to the O.F.S. Congress, 'I wish to place myself at stake in [the] election. Any government and leader has the right to ask the nation for a decision. I am making use of that right.'[44] What was at stake, however, was only indirectly his position as Prime Minister; directly, it was his position as leader of the National Party.

Party considerations then were at the base of the decision to hold an early election. And consequently the election was perhaps most fundamentally an election to determine the future course of the National Party, or even of Afrikanerdom itself. In this sense, as far as the Party's primary objective was concerned, it was 1943 all over again. As *Die Beeld* commented, basically the election was not a trial of strength between Government and Opposition—and, to the extent that it was not, the United Party was not 'relevant' to it. On the contrary, it was a battle for 'the soul of Afrikanerdom'.[45]

THE CONTESTANTS

If we omit the Langlaagte constituency in the Transvaal where no election took place owing to the death of the Nationalist candidate after nominations closed, there were 159 seats at stake in the Republic in 1970. Of these, only 10 were uncontested, of which 6 returned United Party candidates and 4 National Party candidates. As Table 67 shows, an impressive total of 392 candidates were entered in the field; or, as far as contested seats only were concerned, 382 candidates contested 149 seats. In consequence there were 78 seats in which there were 3 or more candidates. The United Party alone entered a total of 144 candidates, and, if we omit the uncontested seats, it entered 138 candidates in the 149 seats in which there were contests. It might be said that this figure represented the extent of its financial resources rather than the extent of its hopes of winning seats. Nevertheless the increase of 19 candidates over its commitment in 1966 did perhaps suggest a resurgence of optimism in the United Party, a feeling that there was a possibility that at last the trend of the past twenty-two years might be reversed.

As far as the National Party was concerned, the drop from 148 candidates in 1966 to 138 candidates in 1970 was not in itself significant. What was significant, however, was that the drop in the number of seats contested by the party was principally due to the smaller number of candidates which it put forward in Natal. As we saw in the previous chapter, Natal was one of its major targets in 1966; for that was where it had hoped to make its most impressive gains among the English-speaking section. Consequently it entered a candidate in every constituency. In 1970, however, it did not put forward candidates in seven out of the eighteen seats in that province. This was, of course, a more realistic assessment of its areas of strength and weakness; and it cannot, therefore, be regarded as a sign that the party was 'writing off' Natal. On the contrary, in spite of the intense campaign it was forced to wage in the Transvaal, it made a major effort to win English-speaking support in the coastal province.

The main centre of interest in the nomination figures, however, was the impressive number of Herstigte Nasionale Party candidates. With 77 candidates in the Republic (plus an additional one in South West Africa), it served notice of the earnestness of its intentions; and it certainly represented a remarkable effort for so young a party. It was noteworthy that it concentrated its efforts mainly in the Transvaal, excepting, that is, the Johannesburg seats. After some initial speculation that it might do so, in the end it did not contest a single seat in Natal; and in the Cape urban areas it offered only a token showing. In general, then, the nominations reinforced

Table 67

NUMBER OF CANDIDATES, 1970[1]

Region	*No. of seats*	*U.P.*	*N.P.*	*P.P.*	*H.N.P.*	*Others*	*Total*
Cape Town	15	12 (1)	10 (2)	3	2	2	29 (3)
Port Elizabeth	6	6	6	1	—	—	13
Border	5	5 (2)	3	1	—	—	9 (2)
Rest of Cape	28	24	28 (2)	1	12	2	67 (2)
Total Cape	54	47 (3)	47 (4)	6	14	4	118 (7)
Johannesburg[2]	15	15	9	6	2	3	35
Witwatersrand	21	21	20	1	16	3	61
Pretoria	12	11	12	1	12	2	38
Rest of Transvaal	24	23	24	—	24	—	71
Total Transvaal	72	70	65	8	54	8	205
Durban–Pietermaritzburg	12	12 (3)	6	3	—	—	21 (3)
Rest of Natal	6	6	5	1	—	1	13
Total Natal	18	18 (3)	11	4	—	1	34 (3)
Total O.F.S.	15	9	15	1	9	1	35
Republic[2]	159	144 (6)	138 (4)	19	77	14	392 (10)

Notes: [1] Numbers of unopposed candidates are shown in brackets.
[2] These figures exclude Langlaagte, where the National Party candidate died after nominations had closed, and where a by-election had to be held.

the view of the new party as a predominantly Transvaal phenomenon.

While the Herstigte Nasionale Party was attempting a major thrust into the South African political scene, the Progressive Party, on the other hand, reduced its forces from twenty-six candidates in 1966 to nineteen in 1970, the main areas of reduction being in Johannesburg where it entered two fewer candidates, and in the Durban–Pietermaritzburg regions where it entered three as compared with its earlier six candidates.

The over-all picture presented purely in terms of nominations was that the country was moving even more to the right, especially if it is mentioned that the great majority of the candidates listed as 'others' also represented conservative, right-wing elements. Certainly the numbers ranged on the right in South Africa's particular political spectrum far outnumbered those on the left. Any such conclusion, however, based only on this evidence must stand subject to revision in terms both of the campaign waged and of the results. More properly, we might regard the evidence of the nominations as provisionally indicating a continued move to the right.

THE CAMPAIGN

(*a*) *The National Party*

The National Party's election manifesto was issued early in March. In it the Party promised the electorate that it would continue with the policy of separate development, maintain job security for whites vis-à-vis non-whites, maintain residential apartheid and provide adequate housing for all, promote and maintain diplomatic links and co-operation with neighbouring African states, improve the lot of the farmers, assist the needy and aged, continue with its programme of planned and selective immigration, maintain the 'absolute equality' of the two official languages, and promote a common and undivided loyalty to the Republic.[46]

In his own election message, the Prime Minister promised that the Government would guarantee security, create more employment opportunities (presumably for whites), improve educational facilities, solve the housing shortage, and eliminate tension, bitterness and hate.[47] The question of national security, given prominence in Mr Vorster's speech, was further emphasized by other leading spokesmen. Speaking earlier in Durban, for example, the Minister of Community Development, Mr Blaar Coetzee, listed five points on which the Government was asking for a mandate—all (even, in the context, the last one) bearing on this issue. These points, according to a press report, were: '. . . to maintain peace and order at all cost; to build a strong defence force to guard against foreign incursion; to make South Africa's economic position unassailable;

to make a permanent home for the whites in South Africa, and to have a united English and Afrikaans-speaking White nation.'[48]

In terms of its general place in the National Party's campaign, 'racial' policies tended to be given less prominence than in previous elections. Perhaps there was just not very much more to say. Certainly what was said had a rather stale, familiar ring to it. 'The nation we are building in this country', Mr Vorster insisted, 'is a nation of whites only.' But, he went on: 'The White people have the right to build a white nation in South Africa, but at the same time the Coloureds, Indians and Bantu had the right to maintain their identities.'[49] Dr Connie Mulder, Minister of Information, Social Welfare, Pensions, and Immigration, repeated, too, the promise of eventual complete independence for the homelands, agreeing that they would be free to join the United Nations or any other organization, although Africans in white areas would have no political rights in the latter areas.[50] Even the familiar measure of ambivalence towards homeland independence was again expressed, as when Mr Blaar Coetzee said that the Africans in the homelands would get independence 'if they have it in them, and this we must find out in the future'.[51]

Some United Party spokesmen tended to repeat the type of *swart gevaar* criticism of the Bantustan policy that they had used in the previous election, Mr Douglas Mitchell of Natal being a noted, and habitual, exponent of this viewpoint.[52] But as a whole, the United Party either stressed that the policy as a whole had failed already,[53] or attacked specific aspects of apartheid policies in terms of the suffering caused and the animosity and bitterness engendered by them.[54] On the whole this type of message was also found in Progressive Party criticisms.[55] The Herstigte Nasionale Party, on the other hand, called for a stricter application of apartheid,[56] and criticized the relaxations permitted in job reservation regulations as being only in the interests of 'big capitalists'.[57]

It was in response particularly to the claim that the apartheid policy had already failed that Mr M. C. Botha, Minister of Bantu Administration and Development, insisted that the tide of African movement into white areas had already turned, arguing that if migratory workers (a terminological sleight of hand that in fact destroyed his whole case) and 'foreign Bantu' were excluded there were more Africans now living in the homelands than in white areas.[58] In similar vein, Mr Vorster argued that South Africa enjoyed 'peace and quiet, because the various races have been grouped in separate areas', and, even more optimistically, he went on to predict that in seven years' time there would not be 'one single mixed area in the whole of South Africa'.[59]

The 'new look' South African foreign policy was also defended by Government spokesmen. Dr Hilgard Muller, Minister of Foreign Affairs, gave particular emphasis to the argument that South Africans were one of the peoples of Africa, and not simply offshoots of Europe, and that South Africa could therefore make a sound contribution to a rational world order by co-operating with other African states.[60] Much the same argument was presented by Dr Connie Mulder in Pretoria,[61] and by Mr Ben Schoeman speaking in Maraisburg, who further argued that it was in South Africa's interests to have friendly relations with as many Black states as possible.[62] As we have already seen, the promotion of friendly relations and diplomatic exchanges also featured in the Party's programme as laid down in its election manifesto. On the whole, however, it remained a somewhat marginal issue. The United Party did not contest the policy, but simply claimed that this had for a long time been its own policy, and that the National Party had at last taken it over.[63] Perhaps it was partly due to this claim—although there was much more to it than that—that Dr Hertzog gave the National Party the final insult by referring to it as 'Vorster-Sappe'.[64] And Mr Jaap Marais, the H.N.P. Deputy Leader, mourned: 'The tragic fact is that one has to support United Party policies if one wants to remain in the National Party.'[65]

Perhaps to balance the 'liberalism' of its foreign policy, National Party leaders laid considerable stress on the Communist threat to South Africa. Indeed, there is some justification for describing the 1970 election as the '*Rooi gevaar*' (Red menace) election in contrast to the '*swart gevaar*' (black menace) elections of the past. Apart from whatever perceptions the Government leaders might have had of the dangers to South Africa's security posed by 'Communism',[66] it was, from their point of view, an apparently well-chosen tactical ploy. It helped, perhaps, to distract attention from the lack of progress with regard to its homelands policy as well as from the inflationary economic situation, while at the same time it served as a counter to the H.N.P. accusation that it was succumbing to 'liberalism'. No doubt, too, it was hoped that the perception of threat would rally the voters behind the Government. A good example of this election tactic may be found in these words of the Prime Minister:

> The Communists are creeping over the world and are coming nearer, slowly but surely, and they force one concession after another. They realise that one of the most important outposts to make a world victory possible is to conquer the southernmost point in Africa and the sea route around the Cape. . . . The world should know, after April 22, that there was no division in the National Party and that the greatest majority of South Africa stood full square behind the National Party Government.[67]

The *Rooi gevaar* also gave added justification for those Government policies and measures which all Opposition parties (including even the H.N.P.) criticized as intimidatory, repressive and contrary to the democratic rights of citizens. Mr Blaar Coetzee was one of the foremost exponents of the Government's 'law and order' campaign. As we have already seen, it was first among the five points for which he said the National Party sought a mandate. A few days later he was asserting: 'We have people in South Africa feeding the terrorists with information', and he stated that if necessary the Government would extend the 180-day detention law to 1 000 days. 'We are quite clear and very blatant about this. We are coming to ask a mandate in order to maintain law and order in this country.'[68]

In spite of what we have said above, at least prima facie, the predominant theme of the Nationalist campaign was the theme of white unity, that is, of the need of the two white language groups to co-operate in the building of a white nation, with a common loyalty to South Africa. This was the message that Mr Vorster in particular carried up and down the country, repeating it in meeting after meeting. Thus, in the opening speech of his campaign he argued that it was 'criminal' to advocate only one official language in South Africa. The National Party believed, he said, that 'English and Afrikaans should co-operate without giving up either of their languages, cultures and traditions'. And he even went on to assert, almost heretically: 'We have one common thing which ties us to South Africa stronger than language and tradition and that is our common love for South Africa.'[69] Later he further insisted that he would continue to stand for the equality of the two official languages and for English–Afrikaans co-operation, 'even if I know that not one English speaker would vote for the National Party'.[70] At the same time, Mr Ben Schoeman, in arguing the need for a 'united nation', insisted that it must be based on mutual respect for each other's 'tradition, language and culture'. 'We do not want to Afrikanerize you,' he said, 'similarly we do not want to be Anglicized.'[71] This is, of course, the traditional Nationalist approach to 'white unity'. It is a concept which, if and when it is at all salient, is salient within the context of a persisting Afrikaner identity.

As we have previously stated, the strategy of seeking English-speaking support and co-operation had been initiated by Dr Verwoerd, but Mr Vorster gave this strategy even greater emphasis; and when he used such words as 'Let us build a nation in South Africa',[72] he was extending that strategy to a point that was considered dangerous and unacceptable by the *verkramptes*. As we have also indicated this was, in the eyes of the latter group, but one manifestation among many of a pragmatism that was neglectful of fundamental principles and hence contrary to the fundamental ethos of Afrikanerdom.[73] In consequence, Mr Vorster's own position as leader of the National Party was at stake in the election. And, indeed, Mr Vorster himself, in announcing the early election, had, as we have seen, made the question of his leadership an election issue.

Mr S. F. Waterson, a veteran United Party politician, wrote early in the campaign, 'The impression I have got is that Mr Vorster is fighting for his political life'.[74] This type of view was typical of many analyses of the election, at least among Opposition commentators. Generally it was not an issue that Nationalist spokesmen openly confronted in their campaign; although Dr Treurnicht, who had drawn back from his earlier flirtation with the *verkramptes*, apparently found it necessary to reassure his readers that Mr Vorster had demonstrated that he was a true Afrikaner who would never tolerate liberal tendencies in the National Party.[75] Moreover, it was noteworthy that Mr Vorster embarked on a very heavy personal campaign that took him right across the country but that concentrated heavily on the Transvaal. It was significant, too, that the widows of the three previous Nationalist Prime Ministers were pressed into service to introduce motions of confidence and to call for loyalty to the Party and to Mr Vorster.[76] Winding up his final week of campaigning with meetings in Johannesburg, Springs, Nigel, and Pretoria, Mr Vorster ended on a high note with the Pretoria meeting at which an audience of 8 000 was reported to be present, and which was acclaimed by *Hoofstad* as a 'brilliant, personal triumph'.[77] Be that as it might, in the 1970 election the personal position of the Party leader was a contentious and divisive issue among 'national-minded' Afrikaners, and this, in itself, was quite a new phenomenon in the post-war politics of Afrikanerdom. That the binding force of loyalty to the leader should be so weakened as to give rise to this situation was itself evidence of the depth of the political cleavage.

(*b*) *The Herstigte Nasionale Party*

The programme of principles of the new party was announced at the time of its founding, and its main points may be summarized as follows: a republican system of government combining the offices of Head of Government and Head of State, the stricter application of apartheid, the gearing of assistance for Africans and African areas to their 'development potential', no further extension of urban residential areas for non-whites, a cut-back on immigration, and the restriction of citizen rights for immigrants to those who can speak and write Afrikaans, the freeing of foreign and diplomatic relations from the influence of financial and commercial considerations, recognition of the cultural rights of English-speaking South Africans, and the protection of the small man against 'money power'.[78] This programme was, however, soon amended to include the claims that it was based on the infallible Word of God, and that it was the first unashamedly Afrikaans party, and to propose the recognition of Afrikaans as the sole official language of the Republic with English recognized only as a second language.[79]

In its election manifesto published five months later, it further elaborated on these points and added others. The Afrikaner section was presented as the oldest as well as the largest section of the white population—the only white 'nation' that had been born in the country— as well as the pre-eminent bearer of the Christian National view of life. Hence white unity must be based on the recognition of the Afrikaner as the national core, and Afrikaans—the language of the majority of the whites—must be accepted as the official language.

According to the manifesto, the Party further advocated: the stricter application of apartheid, the restriction of immigration, which should not be state-subsidized, to the numbers considered necessary, the full implementation of the principles of Christian National Education, the restriction of economic growth to a rate that would be governed by the availability of domestic white labour and domestic capital—since the inflow of foreign capital was making the Afrikaner the slave of foreign 'money-power', the stricter observance of Sunday including a ban on Sunday newspapers, and the remodelling of the Parliamentary and executive systems, including the abolition of the 'present inefficient separation' of the offices of heads of state and of government.

The Party also declared itself opposed to: mixed sport, the exchange of permanent diplomatic representatations with Black states, 'influence schemes' such as the American Field Service and the United States–South Africa Leadership Exchange Programme, the misuse of police power against legal political opponents, and the 'liberal tendencies' of the Nationalist Government.[80]

These documents taken together reveal the H.N.P. as a narrow, sectarian party appealing specifically to the most conservative, orthodox Calvinist (in the South African sense) Afrikaners. This was particularly well illustrated in its attitude to immigration. Under the headline 'A Catastrophe Threatens', *Die Afrikaner* stated that 'the Vorster Government' did not 'bother any more' about its promise to ensure that the existing proportion between Afrikaners and English-speakers would not be disturbed. Claiming that from 1964 to 1968 94% of immigrants reinforced the English-speaking sections while the Afrikaners recruited only 6% of them, it predicted that by

1986, or at the latest shortly before the turn of the century, Afrikaners would be outnumbered by English-speaking South Africans.[81] Not surprisingly, Dr Hertzog condemned current immigration practices as 'part of an old plot to destroy the Afrikaners'.[82]

Linked with this attack on immigration policies, was a distrust of the political reliability—even, perhaps, of the spiritual and moral fibre of the English-speaking section. This at least was implied when Dr Hertzog argued that the vast majority of immigrants who did not become assimilated with the Afrikaners came to form part of the 'permissive society'.[83] It was also apparent in his famous speech in the House of Assembly.[84] This, too, was the message of Mr Jaap Marais who said: 'Those Englishmen who bind themselves to English churches, English universities and English companies like the Chamber of Mines, we see as an enemy of the white man in South Africa in the political sense.'[85]

Not that the National Party was much better! According to Dr Hertzog, that Party had become, under Mr Vorster, a 'party of golf politics'.[86] Mr Leon Mare, the H.N.P. candidate in Sunnyside, Pretoria, alleged that the National Party had become a 'cosmopolitan' party, including non-Calvinists and non-Christians among its members; and he asked his audience whether they would feel at home in a party of 'unbelieving Portuguese'.[87] The H.N.P., on the other hand, debarred atheists, Roman Catholics, and Jews from membership in it.[88]

These charges, to the effect that the National Party had become frivolous, ungodly, cosmopolitan, and liberal, tended to enrage rather than amuse Nationalist supporters, and since they are not notable for their restraint at political meetings it is not surprising that H.N.P. meetings became the scenes of very unpleasant violence (euphemistically referred to as 'rowdyism'). One such meeting, to the dismay of the National Party leadership, was screened by a British television team.[89] In general, the whole phenomenon of the violent disruption of H.N.P. meetings was castigated by their press organ as demonstrating the moral decline of the National Party under Mr Vorster.

Further evidence of this, at least of the growing materialism if not actually of corruption, in the National Party and its increasing identification with capitalists, was found in the large loans alleged to have been made by the Land Bank.[90] It was revealed in March that the Land Bank had made a loan of R225 000 to a Mr A. T. K. Kolver (father of Mr Vorster's son-in-law) and a further loan of the same amount to a Mrs A. van der Nest (*neé* Kolver). In addition, the Bank had previously made loans of more than R60 000 to Mr Fanie Botha (Minister of Water Affairs) and of R118 000 to Mr

Jan Haak (Minister of Economic Affairs).[91] It was reported that Mr Vorster had asked Mr Haak to repay his loan immediately.[92] Meanwhile Mr Vorster announced that he would recommend the appointment of a judicial commission to investigate allegations involving the loans,[93] and he responded to a question at his Springs meeting on 14 March by stating that a policeman would call on the questioner the following day to take a sworn statement.[94] Opposition response to these disclosures and subsequent events was twofold. On the one hand there were reports of rumours and discontent among rank-and-file Nationalists about leading Nationalists who had grown rich,[95] and on the other hand both the United Party and the H.N.P. reacted strongly against what was termed 'intimidation of the most blatant kind'.[96]

The rigid and unswerving dogmatism of the H.N.P., with its insistence on the application of its own strict interpretation of the doctrines of Calvinism to all spheres of national life, and with, as one of the corollaries of this application, its relegation of the English-speaking section to a secondary political role in South Africa, aroused in both the major parties strong opposition to what was viewed as Afrikaner *baasskap*. The National Party declared such views to be a threat to 'white unity' and hence to 'white security' in South Africa. The United Party, however, used the H.N.P. as a stick with which to beat the National Party. Mr Andrew Pyper (United Party candidate for Durban Central) asserted that the whole of the past history of the National Party had conduced to the creation of the *verkramptes*: 'The Nationalists' underlying philosophy was division—with language separation in schools, professional organizations, and even in the party itself. The H.N.P. mentality was the logical outcome of this policy.'[97] And in his personal message to the voters, Sir De Villiers Graaff made much the same point, saying that the H.N.P. was simply carrying National Party policy 'to its logical extreme'.[98] The linkage between the H.N.P. and the National Party was also emphasized by the many commentators who predicted that the National Party (sometimes personified by Mr Vorster) would tend to become more *verligt* or more *verkrampt* depending on how the H.N.P. fared with the voters.

(*c*) *The United Party*

One of the major themes in the United Party campaign was its attack on the Government simply as a government. In previous years most white South Africans, even if they disagreed with Government policies, would privately concede that the Nationalist Government at least provided efficient administration. By 1970 this image of administrative efficiency had become somewhat tarnished, and the

United Party, perceiving this mood of disillusionment, portrayed a picture of governmental muddle, confusion, and general incompetence. Launching the Party's campaign, Sir De Villiers Graaff, for example, asserted that the Nationalist Government had become 'too stale, too disinterested [*sic*!], too arrogant and too inept to be further entrusted with the destiny of South Africa'.[99] And in his final message to the electorate, the United Party Leader elaborated on this theme: the Government had 'bungled' the economy, it had failed to provide adequate social services, it had 'brought chaos to the labour position', it lacked a sound agricultural policy, and it had not developed a satisfactory housing policy for the various sections of the population.[100]

In his pre-election analysis, Ormande Pollok, writing in the *Natal Mercury*, suggested a number of factors which 'could add up to a massive grievance vote' favouring the Opposition. Of these factors, all except three (Government sports policy, the 'telephone crisis'—the telephone system was notoriously inefficient—and 'Government arrogance'), fell within the economic issue-area. They included the inflationary trends, and the threatened slow-down in economic growth at least partly due to the manpower shortage (both of which we have referred to in the Introduction), the fall in Stock Exchange prices, the sales tax, and wage and salary grievances of railwaymen, and civil servants.[101] The United Party understandably sought to capitalize on these grievances by presenting, on the one hand, a picture, as we have seen, of Government bungling, and, on the other, by projecting itself as the party which would 'give our people fresh dynamism'.[102]

At the same time, these economic issues were related to race relations in the country. Speaking of the policy of separate development, the Leader of the Opposition asserted that 'where there is separation there is no development, and where there is development there is no separation'; and, declaring the policy to be 'in ruins', he further maintained:

> . . . that attempts to carry it out are a continual drag on the economic development of the country and that . . . the best way to ensure good race relations is to promote economic growth at a high level of prosperity.[103]

Before we turn to the United Party's own race policy in more detail, however, we might refer to another issue on which the Party laid considerable stress in its campaign, and this is the issue of civil rights. In this area, Sir De Villiers Graaff condemned the Government's 'disgraceful abuse' of power,[104] alleged that the Government had 'become more and more intolerant of legitimate opposition, and in doing so [had] invaded the privacy and intruded upon the rights of normal people',[105] and promised, 'We shall restrict the arbitrary powers of ministers and officials and safeguard your rights as individuals'.[106]

The United Party did use the occasion of the election to present a more careful and detailed picture of its own race policy. This was done, in particular, in a major speech by Sir De Villiers Graaff in the beginning of April, in which he dealt comprehensively with all major aspects of this policy. With respect to political rights, in accordance with the Party's concept of 'race federation', Sir De Villiers Graaff proposed that there should be six M.P.s and two senators (who might be white or Coloured) representing Coloured voters, eight M.P.s and six senators (who would all be white) representing Africans, and two M.P.s and one senator (all white) representing the Indian voters—thus making a total of sixteen M.P.s and nine senators. No change in the Parliamentary representation of any of these groups would be made 'without the approval of the White electorate in a special election or a referendum'. In addition, however, Sir De Villiers Graaff proposed the establishment of a 'communal council' for each race group, and a system of consultation between the various race groups and Parliament through a system of 'linking statutory committees on which elected M.P.s and members of communal councils would serve'.

As far as the Reserves, or homelands, were concerned, rapid economic development, using private white capital as well as Government investment, was envisaged; and it was proposed that the Reserves would become largely self-governing in their own affairs. The Party, however, remained 'totally opposed' to the Government's policy of leading them to full independence. While proposing to maintain influx control and pass laws for Africans, the Party promised to administer them 'humanely and realistically'. At the same time, it would accept urban African workers as permanent residents, provide separate residential, social, and educational facilities for them, grant them freehold title to their homes, improve their training facilities and their standard of living, and grant them 'a measure of local self-government'.[107]

The National Party, however, placed 'white unity' at the centre of its election campaign. If one may use the politicians' device of mixing one's metaphors, it hoped to use 'white unity' as a weapon with which to pulverize the H.N.P., and at the same time, and as a result, to steal the United Party's thunder. In countering this ploy, as in its response to the National Party's 'outward' foreign policy, the United Party spent much time in proving its own superior credentials.

Where the National Party seek national unity—solely because of fear that they are not strong enough to stand alone—we of the United Party seek our national unity as a result of love for and confidence in our fellow South Africans.[108]

At the same time, United Party spokesmen also threw doubts on the sincerity of the National Party's advocacy of national unity. Sir De Villiers Graaff, for example, asked how many National Party English-speaking M.P.s or senators there were, how many English-speaking Parliamentary candidates, and how many English-speaking members had been appointed to important public boards.[109] Marais Steyn, United Party Leader in the Transvaal, similarly called on Mr Vorster 'to show his sincerity on this vital issue by doing something about Government-appointed boards on which English-speaking South Africans are horribly under-represented . . .'.[110]

(*d*) *The Progressive Party*

In 1966 the Progressive Party had suffered a potentially disastrous set-back. The redoubtable Helen Suzman had, it is true, managed to retain her seat; but, to use one indicator of its decline, while in 1961 it had secured 33,8% of the total votes cast in the 22 constituencies which it had contested, in 1966 its share of the poll in the 26 constituencies which it fought fell to a low 16,2%. The 1970 election was, therefore, likely to be critical for it. If its share of the poll continued to show a marked decline, or if it lost its only seat, its capacity to survive as a political party might well be thought to be in danger. As we have seen above, it responded to this crisis election by concentrating its forces in a reduced number of seats (19). There is, to its credit, however, no real evidence to suggest that it compromised its principles in order to try to win back voter support. In general, its Programme of Principles and its proposals for a new constitutional structure, as outlined in Chapter 8 above, remained unaltered: it continued, basically, to advocate a racially integrated society, with, in consequence, integrated political and economic structures, but subject to the proviso—hence its rather complicated constitutional proposals—that no race group should be in a position to dominate politically the rest, and as a transition to majority rule it proposed a qualified franchise based on education and/or income.[111]

In its actual election campaign the Progressive Party laid a great deal of emphasis on the issue of civil liberties. This issue, as we have seen, was also stressed by the United Party; but the Progressives, seeking to carve a place in the elections, felt obliged not only to attack the Government's disregard for human values and its consequent abuse of powers, but also to cast doubts on the United Party's record in this area. In a letter to the *Natal Mercury*, Mrs Suzman listed the five 'most important' Acts conferring 'vast powers . . . to restrict the liberty of a citizen', namely, 'the Suppression of Communism Act, the Sabotage Act, the 90-day Detention Act', the '180-day Detention Act' and the Terrorism Act, and she went on to charge that the United Party opposed the first two measures, supported the third, opposed the fourth and supported the fifth.[112] Later Mrs Suzman stated, 'Unlike the United Party, I do not take fright just because a bill is entitled the Terrorism Bill. I look at its contents and when it is obvious that such a measure can lead to the grossest abuse, I have no hesitation in opposing it.'[113] In more general terms, Dr Jan Steytler vigorously argued that 'when you reject [a person] because of his colour you are practising the most virulent tyranny imaginable because a man cannot change his colour'.[114]

This last perspective, again, governed the Progressive Party's contribution to the debate on national unity. In the same speech referred to above, Dr Steytler argued for a national unity that comprehended not only whites, but 'all South Africans who qualify as citizens'. National unity, therefore, 'should include all races'.[115] Other issues covered in this broad-ranging speech included education-policy as it affected non-whites, the Communist threat and the future survival of the whites. On the educational issue, Dr Steytler said, 'We tell this Government that any country which uses education to hold down 80 per cent of the population instead of uplifting them cannot call itself either Christian or wise'. On the question of the white man's future, he castigated the false thinking that led to a belief that 'you can secure your future on bases other than co-operation', and with regard to Communism, he claimed that it was to be fought not 'by limiting freedom but by extending it'.

One of those who appeared frequently on Progressive platforms was Mr Harry Oppenheimer, Chairman of the giant Anglo American Corporation and South Africa's most powerful financial figure. His participation prompted Dr De Wet, Minister of Planning, Mines, and Health, to a rash threat. Unless Mr Oppenheimer gave an immediate assurance that his industries would not be used to promote racial integration, the Government, Dr De Wet said, would view his requests for African labour in a different light from those of other industries; he warned him that a new dispensation would start for him after the election.[116] The Opposition press reacted strongly to this statement, the *Rand Daily Mail* alleging, for example, that the Government had gone from intimidation to blackmail.[117] Dirk Richard, editor of *Dagbreek*, in categorizing the factors that led to the National Party's electoral set-back, described Dr De Wet's threat as 'the greatest blunder on the list'.[118] Significantly, Mr Vorster in his post-election Cabinet shuffle, removed the relevant portfolio of Planning from Dr De Wet's charge.[119]

(*e*) *Others*

Among the small cluster of the candidates anonymously and ignominiously labelled as 'Others', the only group marginally worth mentioning is the National Alliance Party. Under the leadership of Mr Blyth Thompson, a disillusioned English-speaking former member of the National Party, it entered four candidates in the election, all in the Transvaal.

The only real interest in Mr Thompson's new party and its participation in the election, lies in the potentially embarrassing way in which he attempted to tar the National Party with the Herstigte brush. He accused the National Party, for example, of not wanting 'too many English supporters' in case the party became 'dominated' by them[120]—a claim that may well have a measure of truth. He also referred to the appointment of Mr Horwood, former Principal of the University of Natal, to the Senate as a minor concession to the English-speaking section. 'Otherwise', he said, 'half of South Africa's white population is virtually disfranchised because they are not Afrikaans.'[121] Mr Thompson, himself, however, lacked any claim to political stature, and in consequence what he had to say made very little political impact.

THE TURN-OUT

The level of voter participation in the political process, as shown by the percentage poll, began its decline as we have seen in 1961. On the whole the downward trend persisted in 1966 (cf. Tables 52 and 60), and, as Table 68 shows, it continued further in 1970.

Table 68

VOTER PARTICIPATION PER PROVINCE, 1970

Province	*Electorate*	*Votes cast*	*% poll*
Cape	585 743	465 213	79,4
Transvaal	1 005 020	734 382	73,1
Natal	207 161	158 353	76,4
O.F.S.	179 978	120 390	66,9
Republic	1 977 902	1 478 469	74,7

The province in which the most marked decline in the turn-out occurred was the Orange Free State. Viewed in relation to the other provinces, its low 66,9% poll is extremely striking. Oddly enough, however, this is consistent with a pattern that suggests that the increasing voter apathy since 1960 is magnified in the O.F.S. In the 1960 referendum, a poll of 89,1% was recorded in that province, compared with the national average of 89,6%. In the three subsequent general elections, the percentage poll (with the national averages shown in brackets) was: 77,4 (77,6), 71,3 (75,9) and 66,9 (74,7). In the absence of hard evidence, it is impossible to say why this should be, but one guess, at any rate, is that the voters of the O.F.S. might have been the enthusiastic supporters of the National Party when it was identified with the struggle to establish a republic, and, in the area of race policies, with white *baasskap*, but that they have tended to become increasingly disenchanted with the newer concept of separate development. Some support for this 'guess' is found in the fact that the decline in voter participation has not been accompanied by a swing over to the United Party—a party which is identified with a more integrationist approach. Whether or not this supposition is accurate, however, one may hazard the view that the one important factor is the complete absence of any expectation that the United Party will even approach the voter support needed to win a seat in that province. Nevertheless, the voters turned out to cast their votes in the nine seats in which the two main parties were contestants to a much greater extent than they did in the six seats from which the United Party stood aloof. In the former seats the average poll was 70,3%, compared with 65,0% in the latter.

In one other respect, too, the figures relating to the turn-out conform to a general pattern. As Table 69 shows, the turn-out in seats won by the National Party was, with the exception of the Free State, appreciably higher than that in seats held by the United Party.

Table 69

PERCENTAGE POLL ACCORDING TO PARTY WINNING SEAT—1970

Province	*U.P. seats*	*N.P. seats*	*P.P. seats*
Cape	74,8%	82,3%	—
Transvaal	70,6%	73,6%	81,3%
Natal	75,6%	80,5%	—
O.F.S.	—	66,9%	—

Again one is led to the conjecture that, with the exception of the O.F.S., the United Party is either less effective in its organization or it generates less enthusiasm among its supporters; but these alternatives are not, of course, mutually exclusive.

THE RESULTS

(*a*) *In terms of seats*

As in 1966, only a miracle could have prevented another Nationalist victory in 1970, and no one expected that that particular miracle would be performed. Nor, at a slightly lower level of interest, did anyone really expect the newly formed H.N.P. to pull a seat out of the electoral hat. Nevertheless, there still remained areas of interested speculation. One of these related not to the seats that might be won by the H.N.P., but to the number of votes that it might be able to poll, for this was seen as providing a clue to the strength of the more extreme right-wing of Nationalist Afrikanerdom. This question will be dealt with in the next section, and discussion on it may appropriately be deferred until then.

Still in connection with the H.N.P., only less directly, there was speculation as to whether it would draw enough votes from National Party's supporters, particularly in the Transvaal, to let in United Party candidates in some of the three-cornered constituencies. At the other end of the spectrum, the election was regarded as critical for the Progressive Party. Would it be able to improve on its solitary seat in Parliament? Or, on the other hand, would it have taken away from it even that which it had? In the latter event, it would be difficult to see how it could continue to have meaningful existence as a political party.

With regard to the National Party itself, there were three main questions: Could it successfully fight off the Herstigte threat? Could it consolidate, or even improve on, its 1966 gains in Natal? Finally, if its fortunes showed a marked decline, could Mr Vorster retain his leadership of the Party, or would, as Ormande Pollok predicted, 'the long knives . . . be out and the infighting to find a successor . . . be on'?[122]

The election results as far as the seats won are concerned gave a clear answer to some of these questions, a hint with regard to others, but with regard to some it gave not even a hint. These results are shown in Table 70.

The great excitement, if one can call it that, occasioned by these results was that the United Party for the first time in a general election for twenty-seven years improved on its previous Parliamentary standing. From 39 seats in 1966, its representation rose to 47; while the National Party's strength fell from 120 in 1966 to 111 (although this figure was increased to 112 after the Langlaagte by-election in which the National Party retained its seat). There was, of course, much jubilation in United Party circles, where the results were seen as a substantial break-through. More will be said on this later, but in the meanwhile it should not be forgotten, as the Opposition tended to forget in the excitement of the moment, that the Government still retained a majority of 63 seats (or 64 after Langlaagte, and 70 with the South West Africa seats added). Clearly, if the United Party had started on the road to victory, it still had a long way to go!

On the other main issues, the H.N.P., as generally expected, failed

Table 70

RESULTS OF THE 1970 ELECTIONS ACCORDING TO SEATS[1]

Region	U.P.		N.P.		P.P.		Total
	Seats	%	*Seats*	%	*Seats*	%	
Cape Town	10 (1)	66,7	5 (2)	33,3	—	—	15 (3)
Port Elizabeth	3	50,0	3	50,0	—	—	6
Border	5 (2)	100,0	—	—	—	—	5 (2)
Rest of Cape	—	—	28 (1)	100,0	—	—	28 (1)
Total Cape	18 (3)	33,3	36 (3)	66,7	—	—	54 (6)
Johannesburg	11	73,3	3	20,0	1	6,7	15
Witwatersrand	3	14,3	18	85,7	—	—	21
Pretoria	—	—	12	100,0	—	—	12
Rest of Transvaal	—	—	24	100,0	—	—	24
Total Transvaal	14	19,4	57	79,2	1	1,4	72
Durban–Pietermaritzburg	12 (3)	100,0	—	—	—	—	12 (3)
Rest of Natal	3	50,0	3	50,0	—	—	6
Total Natal	15 (3)	83,3	3	16,7	—	—	18 (3)
O.F.S.	—	—	15	100,0	—	—	15
Total Republic	47 (6)	29,6	111 (3)	69,8	1	0,6	159 (9)

Note: [1] Number of unopposed seats included in brackets. The Johannesburg seat of Langlaagte, which was not contested until a subsequent by-election (when it was won by the N.P.), is not included.

to win a seat; Mrs Suzman retained her Houghton seat for the Progressive Party, but that remained the extent of that party's strength; and the National Party lost ground in Natal.

Comparing the 1970 with the 1966 results (Table 61), we see that the United Party won one seat from the Nationalists in Cape Town, one in Port Elizabeth, two in Johannesburg, two in the Witwatersrand, one in Durban, and one in rural Natal. Except for the Witwatersrand, the areas of National Party predominance remained staunch in their party choice. Put another way, one may say that the United Party gains, with one exception, occurred in urban areas, where the Party has generally been strong, and where, one should also add, either the English-speaking section of the population is in a majority, or there is a relative balance between the two language-groups. Notably, too, every seat won from the National Party by the United Party in 1970 had been a United Party seat in 1961. What the United Party succeeded in doing in 1970 was therefore winning back seats that it had lost in 1966; but, even at that, its strength still fell 3 short of the 50 seats that the U.P./N.U. alliance won in 1961. In that later year, we should also remember, there were still only 150 seats in the Republic. Consequently, where the U.P./N.U. alliance held 33,4% of the Republic seats in 1961, it held only 29,6% in 1970 (29,4% after Langlaagte). Nevertheless this was from its point of view an encouraging rise from the meagre 24,4% in 1966.

None of the seats won by the United Party was won on a split vote. Indeed only 2 of the 159 seats were won on a minority vote. These were Germiston District where the National Party's plurality was 186 votes, while the H.N.P. polled 315 votes; and the other was Randburg where the National Party gained a majority over the United Party of 145 votes while the National Alliance polled 294 votes. It seems safe to assume that the Germiston District result would have remained the same in the absence of a H.N.P. candidate, but one cannot be quite sure of this in Randburg. In the absence of a National Alliance candidate, those of its supporters who placed more emphasis on its 'Englishness' might either have voted for the United Party or have abstained; but those who placed the greater emphasis on their party's support for separate development might well have voted for the National Party. But whether in fact there were different sections such as these among its ranks, and, if so, what their respective numbers were, and how in fact they would have reacted, are questions beyond the realm even of speculation.

(b) The results in terms of votes

Since 1953 interest in South African general elections has tended to focus on the actual voting returns rather than on the number of seats won by the respective parties. This pattern is, of course, a reversal of the situation in most countries operating a parliamentary system, but the reason for it is well known to all students of South African politics. The National Party's initial, and continued, success depends on two things: the numerical majority possessed by Afrikaners among the white population, and the solidarity of the Afrikaner community, expressed politically by support for the National Party. In spite of gloomy H.N.P. predictions about the effects of immigration, the first of these factors is likely to persist for the foreseeable future. For as long, therefore, as the political process in South Africa is restricted to the whites, the National Party can be expected to win elections *provided that* the solidarity of Afrikanerdom is maintained. General election voting returns provide one means of assessing whether this condition persists, or whether, on the other hand, there are signs of waning solidarity or even of division. In 1970, with the background of the Nasionale–Herstigte split, there is particular interest in examining the results as shown in Table 71.

With the above thoughts in mind, one's eye focuses immediately on the H.N.P. column; and one can imagine the National Party's sigh of relief. Its over-all total of votes represented, it is true, a significant proportion of National-minded voters (6,2% of N.P. + H.N.P. votes); but the actual number of votes cast for it was far from alarming—especially when compared with the 249 732 votes by which the National Party total exceeded that of the United Party. Indeed, *Die Transvaler* claimed, although with a clearly propagandist purpose, that the H.N.P. had been eliminated as a political factor.[123] Others, however, were more cautious in their views, Willem van Heerden (former editor of *Dagbreek*) conceding, for example, that the H.N.P. vote probably did not represent the full potential of that party.[124] Dr Hertzog himself remained undaunted. He maintained that by the next election the party would be better organized: 'Then we'll see who is crushed'.[125] That prediction was no doubt sheer bravado; but so would be any contrary prediction that the divisions within Afrikanerdom will be healed and that the National Party's hold on power will continue to be unassailable.

If we turn to the voting returns for the two major parties, we find initially an amount of swing away from the National Party that would seem to confirm the impression gained from the results in terms of number of seats won. Most notably the National Party's share of the vote in 1970 dropped to 54,3% from the 57,7% gained in 1966; and from the Party's own perspective this represents a serious decline. Moreover, its majority over its main rival fell from 261 170, representing 20,4% of total votes cast, in 1966 to 249 732

Table 71

VOTES PER PARTY IN CONTESTED SEATS, 1970[1]

Region	Reg. voters	Votes cast	%	Reject	U.P.	%
Cape Town	172 080	133 749	77,7	741	71 441	53,4
Port Elizabeth	90 840	72 633	80,0	371	34 313	47,2
Border	42 577	32 440	76,2	173	19 073	58,8
Rest of Cape	280 246	226 391	80,8	1 571	65 297	28,8
Total Cape	585 743	465 213	79,4	2 856	190 124	40,9
Johannesburg	208 519	145 448	70,0	1 170	84 298	58,0
Witwatersrand	328 151	241 015	73,4	1 216	87 896	36,5
Pretoria	178 773	130 364	72,9	640	27 750	21,3
Rest of Transvaal	289 577	217 555	75,1	1 351	50 233	23,1
Total Transvaal	1 005 020	734 382	73,1	4 386	250 177	34,1
Durban–Pietermaritzburg	133 822	100 469	75,1	655	66 123	65,8
Rest of Natal	73 339	57 884	78,9	476	30 710	53,1
Total Natal	207 161	158 353	76,4	1 131	96 833	61,2
O.F.S.	179 978	120 521	66,9	1 250	16 146	13,4
Republic	1 977 902	1 478 469	74,7	9 623	553 280	37,4

Note: [1] These figures are taken, with one minor correction, from *The Government Gazette*, No. 2707, 15 May 1970. They do not include the Langlaagte by-election result.

in 1970, or 16,9% of total votes cast. The obverse side of this decline in Nationalist voting support was, then, a relative rise in the strength of the United Party. Nevertheless, for all its jubilation over the seats it had won back, United Party enthusiasm might well be tempered by the reflection that its own share of the total vote increased hardly at all—from 37,3% in 1966 to 37,4% in 1970. It would seem indeed that the fall-off in National Party support was largely due to some of its voters turning to the H.N.P., and that on the other hand the gains that the United Party did make in terms of new voter support were offset to a large degree by the even greater relative gains made by the Progressive Party, since that Party, with seven fewer candidates in the field, still increased its share of the vote from 3,1% to 3,5%.

Moreover, if we look at the results as a means of assessing the over-all political complexion of the country, we find little evidence of real change. In 1966 the combined total of National and Republican Party votes amounted to 58,3% of the votes and the combined total of United and Progressive Party votes to 40,4%. In 1970 the respective percentages, with the H.N.P. votes substituted for the Republican Party votes, were 57,9 and 40,9.

None of these differences in percentages of total votes for 1966 and 1970 provides precise measurements of change, however, because there was not the same number of candidates for each party in both elections who were involved in election contests. It is therefore necessary to look also at the figures contained in Table 72.

N.P.	%	H.N.P.	%	P.P.	%	Others	%
47 996	35,9	906	0,7	10 738	8,0	1 917	1,4
37 163	51,1	—	—	786	1,1	—	—
12 192	37,6	—	—	1 002	3,1	—	—
154 862	68,4	3 824	1,7	632	0,3	205	0,1
252 213	54,2	4 730	1,0	13 168	2,8	2 122	0,5
35 900	24,7	375	0,3	21 494	14,8	2 211	1,5
138 294	57,4	8 578	3,6	3 455	1,4	1 576	0,7
87 418	67,1	12 884	9,9	1 269	1,0	394	0,3
145 249	66,8	20 722	9,5	—	—	—	—
406 861	55,4	42 559	5,8	26 218	3,6	4 181	0,6
23 972	23,9	—	—	9 719	9,7	—	—
25 160	43,5	—	—	1 464	2,5	74	0,6
49 132	31,0	—	—	11 183	7,1	74	0,05
94 806	78,7	6 154	5,1	1 191	1,0	974	0,8
803 012	54,3	53 443	3,6	51 760	3,5	7 351	0,5

For the reasons noted on p. 174 above, these figures do not necessarily given a more accurate picture of the existing relative strengths of the political parties, but they are useful (*a*) in providing a corrective to the distortions inevitably reflected by the raw figures, and (*b*) in giving further indication of change. Table 72, therefore, should not only be read in conjunction with Table 71, but also in

Table 72

PERCENTAGE OF VOTES CAST FOR EACH PARTY IN CONSTITUENCIES CONTESTED BY IT, 1970[1]

Region	*U.P.*	*N.P.*	*H.N.P.*	*P.P.*
Cape Town	57,3 (11)	51,3 (8)	4,2 (2)	35,7 (3)
Port Elizabeth	47,2 (6)	51,1 (6)	—	7,9 (1)
Border	58,8 (3)	37,6 (3)	—	9,8 (1)
Rest of Cape	30,7 (24)	68,4 (26)	3,5 (12)	4,9 (1)
Total Cape	43,0 (44)	59,3 (43)	3,6 (14)	20,3 (6)
Johannesburg	58,0 (15)	42,0 (9)	1,9 (2)	35,2 (6)
Witwatersrand	36,5 (21)	60,8 (20)	4,9 (16)	25,7 (1)
Pretoria	22,8 (11)	67,1 (12)	9,9 (12)	8,1 (1)
Rest of Transvaal	23,9 (23)	66,8 (24)	9,5 (24)	—
Total Transvaal	34,9 (70)	61,6 (65)	7,8 (54)	29,1 (8)
Durban–Pietermaritzburg	65,8 (9)	35,5 (6)	—	29,5 (3)
Rest of Natal	53,1 (6)	50,0 (5)	—	19,4 (1)
Total Natal	61,2 (15)	41,7 (11)	—	27,6 (4)
O.F.S.	22,1 (9)	78,7 (15)	8,6 (9)	14,4 (1)
Republic	39,8 (138)	60,6 (134)	7,2 (77)	25,4 (19)

Note: [1] Number of constituencies contested given in brackets.

conjunction with Table 63, the corresponding table for 1966. Comparing Table 72 with Table 71, the most striking differences are the improved showing of both the National Party (60,6% compared with 54,3%) and the Progressive Party relative both to its own past performance (25,4% compared with 3,5%) and to the H.N.P. Table 72 also shows more clearly than Table 71 the areas in which the various parties found their main strength.

Using the figures in Tables 72 and 63 as a means of assessing change, we find again the most striking differences to be the decline in United Party support and the upsurge in Progressive Party support. As far as the United Party is concerned, it is clear that in certain areas it lost votes to the Progressive Party (Cape Town, Johannesburg, and Durban–Pinetown areas). It is also clear that it failed to make significant gains in its areas of weakness (the more rural areas of the Cape and the Transvaal), although its position did improve significantly if not substantially in the O.F.S. If we compare the tables in more detail, certain oddities appear. For example, it would appear that in the Cape Town seats the United Party lost votes to both the Progressive Party, whose share of the vote rose from 24,1% to 35,7%, and to the National Party, rising from 41,7% to 51,3%, while its own share of the votes dropped from 63,7% in 1966 to 57,3% in 1970. This picture, however, is not true with respect to the National Party, although it is with respect to the Progressive Party. This will be further elaborated on when we turn to the swing, but at this stage we may point out that in 1970 there were only two National Party seats in the area that were unopposed compared with four in 1966. Of the four unopposed Nationalist seats in 1966, one was again unopposed in 1970; but in the contests in the other three constituencies Nationalist votes totalled 25 509, averaging 78,0% of the votes cast. Moreover in Parow, where the National Party polled 8 473 votes, or 93,1% of the total, its opponent was not the United Party but the H.N.P. The effect, then, of the Nationalist contests in these four seats would be considerably to raise its percentage of the vote.

The areas of most marked apparent Nationalist decline also require closer scrutiny. These are Johannesburg, Witwatersrand, Pretoria, and 'Rest of Transvaal'. In Johannesburg the Nationalist share of the vote according to Table 72 was 42,0% in 1970, compared with 54,9% in 1966 (Table 63). Again certain corrections need to be made. In 1970 the National Party contested Hillbrow where it secured 14,2% of the vote, but in 1966 it did not enter a candidate in that seat. On the other hand in 1966 its candidate secured 69,5% of the vote in Langlaagte, and the results of the later by-election in that seat (where it polled 58,8% of the votes) are not included in Table 72.

If we restrict our comparison to the other eight seats which it contested in both elections, we find that its share of the vote in those seats fell from 53,8% in 1966 to 45,3% in 1970. This is a substantial drop which cannot be explained away. Certainly the intervention of the H.N.P. was not directly responsible, since its two candidates in these eight seats secured only 375 votes between them. It is worth noting, however, that the average percentage poll in these seats fell from 71,7% in 1966 to 67,3% in 1970. This fall in the percentage poll may suggest that part of the reason for the decline in National Party votes was that a substantial number of its supporters abstained from voting in 1970.[126]

In the Witwatersrand seats the National Party's share of the votes in the constituencies that it contested fell from 66,1% in 1966 to 60,8% in 1970. Part of this drop was due to the presence in the contests of 16 H.N.P. candidates. While the most successful H.N.P. candidate polled only 1 202 votes, or 10,0% of votes cast (in Vanderbijlpark) these 16 candidates all together gained 8 578 votes, no doubt at the expense of the National Party. In Vanderbijlpark too, the United Party entered a candidate where it had not in 1966; in consequence, in that seat alone, the National Party percentage of the votes cast dropped from 90,9 to 71,4. The same situation obtained also in Randburg, where the National Party share of the vote declined from 89,1% to 68,6%. On the other hand, its poor showing in North Rand in 1966 where it polled only 25,3% of the vote is not reflected in 1970 because it did not enter a candidate there in 1970; and in Vereeniging where its candidate had been unopposed in 1966 it polled 60,5% of the votes in 1970. These factors probably do not quite balance each other out, and one is probably safe in assuming that the National Party did in fact lose ground in the Witwatersrand area. There is also little doubt that the United Party gained ground: for of the 17 seats in which it opposed the National Party in both 1966 and 1970, its percentage of the votes cast increased in 13 and dropped in only 4, its largest increase being in Randburg from 35,5% in 1966 to 48,3% in 1970, while its largest decrease was only 5,7%, falling from 29,3% to 23,6%, in Nigel.

In the Pretoria seats the loss of National Party support (67,1% in 1970 compared with 76,9% in 1966) is not so clear. One main complicating factor in comparing the two elections in these seats is the contesting by the United Party of two of the seats reflected in Table 72 that it had not contested in 1966; and in those seats the National Party's share of the vote fell from 92,5% in 1966 to 71,9% in 1970, and from 84,3% to 69,0% respectively. The other main complicating factor here is that, unlike the situation in Johannesburg, the H.N.P. did poll a considerable number of votes, 12 884, whereas in 1966 the Republican Party had polled only 3 237 votes. The first of these factors suggests that Table 72 (like Table 71) exaggerates the extent of National Party decline in 1970. The second factor, especially when read alongside the percentage vote recorded by the United and Progressive Parties, suggests that where the National Party lost votes in Pretoria it was mainly to the H.N.P.

The explanation for the National Party's drop from 74,3% of the vote in 1966 (Table 63) to 66,8% in 1970 (Table 72) in the 'Rest of Transvaal' seats is clear and simple; for in these seats the H.N.P. polled 20 722 votes (or 9,5%), compared with the meagre 2 033 votes polled in 1966 by the Republican Party. In these seats, too, the United Party not only failed to increase its share of the vote, but on the contrary it suffered a marginal decline. The fall in the National Party's share in the vote was, therefore, due almost entirely to the defection of former supporters to the H.N.P. The decline in the percentage poll, from 76,5% to 75,1%, suggests again, however, that some of its voters also preferred not to vote in the 1970 election (if 76,5% of registered voters had voted in 1970, 9 971 more voters would have voted than actually did so).

The Nationalist share of the votes in the constituencies which it contested in the Free State declined from 82,1% to 78,7%, and this in spite of contesting the four seats in which it had been unopposed in 1966, and which would, presumably, help to inflate its percentage in 1970. The decline was again mainly due to H.N.P. intervention; but at the same time the United Party did improve its position, as a comparison of Tables 72 and 63 shows. The United Party improvement is also reflected in the fact that it increased its share of the vote in five of the six seats it fought against the Nationalists in both 1966 and 1970, and that in the one seat in which its share decreased it fell by only 0,1%.

While the H.N.P. was able to draw off votes from the National Party, particularly in the Transvaal and O.F.S., its over-all performance placed it more in the category of a nuisance than that of a menace. At the same time the resurgence of the Progressive Party raised the hope of a more enlightened attitude emerging in the South African electorate. It made striking gains in all the major urban centres with the exception of Pretoria, and as a result at least staved off the immediate threat of extinction. Moreover, in the 14 seats in which the United Party and the Progressive Party had fought each other in both elections, the Progressive Party percentage of votes cast improved in all but one. And in Sea Point it came within 231 votes of wresting the seat from the United Party. Nevertheless, in the end it was left with its solitary seat in Houghton, and it failed to make significant gains in the rural areas.

Finally, as far as this section is concerned, we need to take into account the ten seats in which candidates were returned unopposed, in order to arrive at a reasonable estimate of the total support enjoyed by the National Party in 1970. In arriving at the estimated National Party vote in these uncontested seats, we have taken into account (*a*) the average percentage poll in the region concerned, (*b*) the percentage of the vote gained by the National Party in the last contest, and (*c*) the average swing. Table 73 gives the results of these calculations.

Table 73

ESTIMATED TOTAL STRENGTH OF THE NATIONAL PARTY, 1970

Region	*Estimated total votes*	*Estimated N.P. votes*	*N.P. %*
Cape Town	166 371	65 934	39,6
Port Elizabeth[1]	72 633	37 163	51,1
Border	49 136	16 485	33,5
Rest of Cape	234 644	161 217	68,7
Total Cape	522 784	280 799	53,7
Johannesburg[1]	145 448	35 900	24,7
Witwatersrand[1]	241 015	138 294	57,4
Pretoria[1]	130 364	87 418	67,1
Rest of Transvaal[1]	217 555	145 249	66,8
Total Transvaal[1]	734 382	406 861	55,4
Durban–Pietermaritzburg	130 790	30 643	23,4
Rest of Natal[1]	57 884	25 160	43,5
Total Natal	188 674	55 803	29,6
O.F.S.[1]	120 521	94 806	78,7
Republic	1 566 361	838 269	53,5

Note: [1] In these regions all seats were contested.

If we compare these figures with those of Table 71, we find that according to our estimates the total National Party share of the vote is given as 53,5% as compared with 54,3% of the actual votes cast. This is to be expected, as we have to take account of only four unopposed National Party seats as against six unopposed United Party seats. In general, because of the relatively small number of unopposed seats, Table 73 shows no marked variations from Table 71, and for the same reason we may have reasonable confidence in its accuracy.

A comparison between Table 73 and Table 64 (the corresponding table for 1966) reveals a remarkable stability of National Party strength in all the Cape Province regions, although there is a slight decline in the rural Cape seats which is also reflected in the Cape total. There is on the other hand a serious decline in the Party's strength in all regions of the Transvaal, throughout Natal and the Orange Free State. In consequence the estimated strength of the

National Party fell from a height of 59,2% of voters in 1966 to 53,5% in 1970—a level which, at least theoretically, should render it potentially vulnerable once more to defeat. Interestingly enough this estimate of 53,5% is precisely the same percentage of the vote that we estimated as going to the National Party in 1961.[127] If both of these estimates are reasonably accurate the inference is that the National Party was back to its 1961 position, and one reason for this is clearly the division that had split its forces.

(*c*) *The swing*

The limiting condition which we have set throughout the study in the calculation of the swing in individual constituencies is that the constituencies should be contested by the same two parties, without the intervention of third parties, in both the relevant elections. In 1970, with the presence of 77 H.N.P. candidates and 19 Progressive candidates, apart from 9 'Others', this condition inevitably restricts the number of seats for which the swing can be calculated to a relatively small number; and it is with this in mind that more than usual attention has been given in the preceding analysis to the losses and gains in the voting strengths of the respective parties.

All together, within the Republic there were 40 seats in 1970 for which the swing can be calculated. On the provincial basis, there were 22 in the Cape, 10 in the Transvaal (but restricted to Johannesburg and the Witwatersrand), 6 in Natal, and 2 in the O.F.S. In terms of party pairings, 35 involved swings between the National and United Parties, and 5 between the United and Progressive Parties. Of the 22 relevant constituencies in the Cape, 19 showed a swing to the U.P. from the N.P. (4 in Cape Town, 3 in Port Elizabeth, 2 in the Border, and 10 in the Rest of the Cape). The average swing in these constituencies was 2,5%. The average swing in the two U.P./P.P. seats was 13,6% in favour of the Progressives (7,9% and 19,2%); and in the lone Cape seat which showed a swing to the Nationalists, the swing was an insignificant 0,25% from the United Party.

Of the relevant Transvaal seats, 5 showed a swing from the National Party to the United Party, with an average of 6,3%, 3 showed a swing from the United Party to the Progressive Party, with an average of 4,0%, and 2 swung from the United Party to the National Party, with an average of 0,55% (1,0% and 0,1%).

The 6 relevant seats in Natal and the 2 in the Orange Free State all demonstrated a swing from the National Party to the United Party. In Natal the average swing was 6,9% and in the O.F.S. it was 3,4%.

Although this total of 40 seats is limited to only a quarter of the

Republic's constituencies, and although it does not include at all the important Pretoria and rural Transvaal seats, nevertheless the clear trend apparent in them does give the lie to the view that the United Party's apparently improved position was due solely to the siphoning off of former Nationalist votes by the H.N.P.; and, in so far as the figures in Table 71 seem to support this latter view, it demonstrates the caution with which raw voting totals have to be regarded. This is the logic of the fact that throughout the Republic (excepting the two regions mentioned) 32 seats showed a swing from the National Party to the United Party, the average swing being 4,1%; while only 3 showed a continued swing to the National Party, averaging 0,45% per constituency. On the other hand in the 5 seats that showed a swing from the United Party to the Progressive Party, the average swing was 7,8%.

Comparison between Tables 73 and 64 suggests that the National Party lost over-all voting support to the extent of 5,7%. If allowance is made for the loss of Nationalist voters to the H.N.P., it would seem probable in the 35 seats for which the swing between the United Party and National Party can be calculated the average net swing of 3,6% to the United Party reflects with reasonable accuracy the general movement of voters from the National Party to the United Party. At the same time Tables 71–73, together with the evidence of the swing, all support the conclusion that there was a significant number of United Party voters who moved to (or back to?) the Progressive Party.

(*d*) *Comparison between seats and votes*

While, for the reason previously stated, it is legitimate in considering South African elections to focus attention mainly on votes rather than on seats, this same focus may tempt one to an unreal appreciation of the power situation in the country. Partly as a counter to that temptation, as well as providing an insight into the effects of the electoral system on representation, the figures in Table 74 illustrate the disparity between the proportion of seats won by the parties and the proportion of the votes cast for them respectively.

It is clear from this table that there continues to be a very wide disparity between seats and votes, and that a swing in voting behaviour sufficient to give the United Party a majority in votes would not necessarily be sufficient to give it a majority in seats. This is further indicated by the figures in Table 75.

It is apparent from these figures that the Opposition parties suffer from a built-in electoral handicap, which would probably require a very substantial voting swing to overcome. This is further apparent

Table 74

PERCENTAGE SEATS COMPARED WITH PERCENTAGE VOTES (CONTESTED SEATS ONLY)

Region	U.P. % *Seats*	U.P. % *Votes*	N.P. % *Seats*	N.P. % *Votes*	P.P. % *Seats*	P.P. % *Votes*
Cape Town	64,3	53,4	35,7	35,9	—	8,0
Port Elizabeth	50,0	47,2	50,0	51,1	—	1,1
Border	100,0	58,8	—	37,6	—	3,1
Rest of Cape	—	28,8	100,0	68,4	—	0,3
Total Cape	31,25	40,9	68,75	54,2	—	2,8
Johannesburg	73,3	58,0	20,0	24,7	6,7	14,8
Witwatersrand	14,3	36,5	85,7	57,4	—	1,4
Pretoria	—	21,3	100,0	67,1	—	1,0
Rest of Transvaal	—	23,1	100,0	66,8	—	—
Total Transvaal	19,4	34,1	79,2	55,4	1,4	3,6
Durban–Pietermaritzburg	100,0	65,8	—	23,9	—	9,7
Rest of Natal	50,0	53,1	50,0	43,5	—	2,5
Total Natal	80,0	61,2	20,0	31,0	—	7,1
O.F.S.	—	13,4	100,0	78,7	—	1,0
Republic	27,3	37,4	72,0	54,3	0,7	3,5

from the fact that, of the seats won in 1970 by majorities of less than 2 000, 14 were won by the National Party compared with 13 won by the United Party, and of the seats won by majorities greater than 2 000 but less than 3 000, 11 were won by the National Party, 3 by the United Party, and 1 by the Progressive Party. If all these seats were considered marginal, the Opposition parties would have to win all 24 seats in this category, and, to obtain an over-all majority, including South West Africa, win an additional 12, while still retaining all of its own marginal seats.

Table 75

NUMBER OF VOTES REQUIRED TO WIN EACH CONTESTED SEAT

Province	*U.P.*	*N.P.*	*P.P.*
Cape	12 675	7 643	—
Transvaal	17 870	7 138	26 218
Natal	8 069	16 377	—
O.F.S.	—	6 320	—
Republic	13 495	7 435	51 760

CONCLUSION

The United Party and Progressive Party both made substantial gains in 1970, thus reversing for the first time the uni-directional trend that was so clearly apparent from 1948 to 1966. This is in itself important, because it does demonstrate that the frequent assumption that there is a law of ever-increasing rigidity among white South Africans is not necessarily valid for all time. Moreover, while the split in Nationalist ranks that occurred both before and after the formation of the H.N.P. weakened the National Party and dissipated its electoral forces, the extent of support that the new party was able to draw off from the old was not sufficient to account for the gains made by the United Party. On the other hand, there is as we have seen reason to believe that this split was one factor at least in the substantial number of non-voters among former Nationalist supporters.

On the other side of the picture, we have stressed that the United Party still has a long way to go before it can entertain a reasonable hope of winning an election. In this respect one less hopeful aspect of the United Party gains in 1970 is found in the view that these were largely due to the return to its fold of those English-speaking voters who had abstained or strayed into Nationalist pastures in 1966.[128] The point is, of course, that before the United Party can win an election it must be able to win over a substantial number of Afrikaans voters; and that if it failed to do this in 1970, then it really did not make significant headway. The point is well taken; but, it is clear that there was a swing in, for example, the rural Cape seats to the United Party, which are seats in which Afrikaners predominate. In spite of the well-attested aversion of Afrikaner Nationalist voters to go so far as to change their party support to the United Party, at least a significant number of them have demonstrated their ability to overcome this aversion.

In spite of the bias in the South African electoral system in favour of the rural areas, the continuing and increasing movement of the population to the towns is altering the political map of South Africa. One of the big political question-marks, therefore, is the extent to which the increasingly urban character of the parliamentary seats will affect future voting behaviour. In this connection the focus of interest tends to lie with the young urban Afrikaners; for it is whether these voters continue to maintain the Nationalist establishment in power, or switch their support to one or other of the Opposition parties, or move off in a new direction of their own, which will largely determine the political future of South Africa—in so far, that is, as it lies with the white voters to determine it.

In the two years that have elapsed at the time of writing since the 1970 election, the signs are that the Nationalist Old Guard is seeking to keep control of the situation. Certainly there has been no major new direction set in any area of political issues, no demonstration of real *verligte* influence on Government policy. On the other hand, behind the party curtain the process of debate and critical questioning continues, and it is I think legitimate to doubt whether in this climate an attempt to reassert a neo-Verwoerdian cast to Nationalist opinion can succeed. It may be that the National Party will be able, as it was in the case of the H.N.P., to prevent new divisions erupting that will give the victory to the United Party; but it is the author's opinion that its success in doing so will depend on its ability to transform itself into a party that is more in tune with the 1970s than the 1930s. There is a proviso attached, however, to such a prediction, and that is that there is no overt external threat to the regime; for such a threat would surely lead to the unfurling, once more, of Dr Verwoerd's umbrella.

10

Conclusions

MAINTAINING, DEVIATING, AND CRITICAL ELECTIONS

In the period covered in this study there were seven general elections as well as the referendum on the republic. Except for the last general election (1970) where as we have seen there was a slight but significant swing away from the Government, the elections from 1948 on have been most obviously characterized by the massive increase in the strength of the National Party in Parliament. Two questions immediately arise. The first is: How has this come about? The second, entering a rather more speculative area, would inquire whether the Nationalist hold on Parliamentary power is as assured as it would now seem. A third question, much engaging the attention of external commentators, as to the prospects of toppling the Nationalists (or, more generally, the whites) from power by non-parliamentary means (whether employed by internal or external agents), is another question altogether, and clearly lies outside the scope of my present inquiry.

Before turning to examine the first question raised, we may however take note of an assumption that is frequently made with respect to the operation of electoral politics. This assumption is that the normal pattern under conditions where the voters are free to form competing political parties and are likewise free at periodic intervals to express their preferences among those parties, conforms to the 'swing of the pendulum' principle. Indeed it may be argued that this assumption underlies the establishment of representative institutions: it is assumed that preferences are likely to change and that therefore voting procedures should provide the institutional means whereby such changes in preferences may procure changes in governmental personnel and hence in governmental policies.[1] Nevertheless, the assumption, even if approximately valid for, say, the United Kingdom, is certainly not universally valid, as the experience of the so-called 'one party' states of the U.S.A. demonstrates.

Given the varieties and complexities of voting patterns in the United States, it is not surprising that students of this area of politics should have sought to uncover typologies of elections that would be useful in the deeper understanding of voting behaviour. V. O. Key Jr. pioneered this area with his concept of 'critical elections'[2]—a concept that has led to further explorations by subsequent scholars. A recent study that pursues Key's concept in greater depth substitutes the term 'eras of critical realignment' for the term 'critical elections', thus sensibly extending the temporal boundaries of the concept.[3] The concept is incorporated and perhaps diluted in Angus Campbell's typology of maintaining elections, deviating elections, and realigning elections. Although all these concepts have been devised to generate increased insights into the American political process, they are sufficiently suggestive to justify an inquiry into whether they might not similarly illuminate the events in South Africa that have been discussed in the preceding chapters.[4] A *maintaining election* Campbell defines as 'one in which the pattern of partisan attachments prevailing in the preceding period persists and is the primary influence on forces governing the vote'.[5] A *deviating election* is one in which 'the basic division of party loyalties is not seriously disturbed, but the influence of short-term forces on the vote is such that it brings about the defeat of the majority party. After the specific circumstances that deflected the vote from what we would expect on the basis of party disappear from the scene, the political balance returns to a level which more closely reflects the underlying division of partisan attachments.'[6] In a *realigning election* 'popular feeling associated with politics is sufficiently intense for the basic partisan commitments of a portion of the electorate to change, and a new party balance is created'.[7] In the words of Key, 'a more or less durable realignment'[8] takes place.

If we refer back to include the brief survey of pre-World War II elections contained in the Preface, we might on the basis of a prima facie inspection of the total data suggest that the elections from the formation of Union down to 1924 were maintaining elections; that the 1924 election was a realigning election and the 1929 election a maintaining election; that the 1933 election (ushering in the coalition that led to Fusion) was another realigning election, and the subsequent elections of 1938 and 1943 were maintaining elections; and finally that the 1948 election was a realigning election followed by a series of maintaining elections (i.e. down to and including 1970). This rather facile categorization, however, seems to veil rather than uncover the significance of our period. What is missing is clearly any reference to the underlying forces that produced these changes. A further problem is one which arises out of the very attempt to categorize social phenomena; for these phenomena are always more complex than the categories allow, and hence elements of more than one category are likely to be found in any single phenomenon.

If we look for example at the 1943 election—an election, it will be recalled, that enlarged the ruling United Party's majority and an election in which pre-existing party attachments would appear to have been dominant—while at first sight it would appear to fit the definition of a maintaining election, at the same time, at the level of the opposition, a process of realignment was, as we have seen, taking place. In further examining the characteristics of a realigning era, Campbell notes that they have been associated in the United States with 'great national crises'.[9] The years of 1939 to 1943 may certainly be described in these terms, and at two levels. At the national level there was the crisis associated with South Africa's participation in the war. This, however, might be described as a security crisis, involving a threat to the State itself. Although Campbell does not appear to take such crises into account (owing perhaps to his American focus), it seems reasonable to assume that crises of this type have a consolidating rather than a disjunctive effect, and consequently that elections taking place under circumstances that relate to an external threat would tend to be maintaining elections. The over-all pattern of the election results in 1943, then, would conform to that expectation.

But the period was also marked by crisis at another level. This was the internal crisis manifesting itself within the Afrikaner 'nation'. The withdrawal of General Hertzog and his followers from the United Party provided the opportunity to re-establish the political unity of Afrikanerdom, a unity which had been shattered by Fusion; and there was the fear that if the opportunity were not seized and effective unity re-established, the spirit of Afrikaner nationalism would fade into a pale and ineffectual aspiration, a mere expression of piety. That danger apart, there was the further danger that the concept of a single 'South African nation', as represented by the United Party, would take root in people's minds and hence erode the distinctive spiritualities of Afrikanerdom. With respect then to the National Party's success in eliminating its Afrikaner rivals and in establishing its claim to be the political arm of Afrikanerdom, the 1943 election may be described, in part, as a realigning election.

This consideration relates to a further characteristic of realigning eras as noted by Campbell. 'The far reaching impact of the crises', he writes, '. . . is also likely to increase the political polarization of important segments of the electorate, usually along sectional or class lines.' And he goes on to argue: 'When an entire group polarizes around a new political standard, the pressures associated with group membership tend to hold the individual members to the group norm.'[10] From this perspective, and it would seem to be an apt one, the elections of 1943, 1948, and 1953 would together comprise an era of realignment, although the 1943 election should more accurately be called a transitional election. This becomes apparent if we take the areas of greatest concentration of Afrikaner population among the regions we have differentiated throughout this study, and look at the percentage of seats won by the National Party (or the H.N.P. as it still was in 1943 and 1948) in them over the period of these three elections.

Table 76

PERCENTAGE OF SEATS WON BY N.P. (OR H.N.P.) AND ALLIES IN AREAS OF AFRIKANER CONCENTRATION, 1943–53

Date	*Rest of Cape*	*Witwatersrand*	*Pretoria*	*Rest of Transvaal*	*O.F.S.*
1943 . .	57,6	—	25,0	34,8	92,8
1948 . .	83,9	35,3	62,3	100,0	92,3
1953 . .	86,2	55,6	75,0	100,0	100,0

If we allow for the fact that there were substantial numbers of English-speaking voters living on the Witwatersrand, it is clear that over these three elections the Afrikaner voters polarized massively around the National Party and hence provided it with the means to power.

In spite of the apparent conclusiveness of the figures in Table 76 above, there remains an element of artificiality in the demonstration. This sense of artificiality arises from the narrowness of the time span covered by the three elections, particularly in that it leaves the pre-1943 period out of account. If we extend our temporal perspective to include the main features of that period as described in the Preface, we may indeed find justification for arguing that the major era of electoral realignment was the upsurge of the National Party in 1921–4, and that the coalition–Fusion period (1933–43) was, to modify Campbell's topology slightly, a deviating era rather than an era of real realignment, with the basic party identifications becoming re-established among the electorate in the 1948 and 1953 elections and remaining dominant ever since.

DEMOGRAPHIC FACTORS IN SOUTH AFRICAN POLITICS

A serious defect in the Campbell topology is that in so far as its primary focus is on the formal outcome of elections it deflects attention away from the nexus between social and political forces and issues that determines those outcomes. Before attempting ourselves to outline an analytical system that more directly refers to that nexus within the context of South African politics, we should first bring into the discussion certain demographic features of the two major white language groups for, as has been argued throughout

Table 77

PERCENTAGE OF URBAN AND RURAL WHITE POPULATION WHO ARE AFRIKAANS- AND ENGLISH-SPEAKING RESPECTIVELY

	1936		1946		1951		1960	
	Afrikaans	*English*	*Afrikaans*	*English*	*Afrikaans*	*English*	*Afrikaans*	*English*
Cape								
Urban	42,9	51,4	48,3	48,6	49,7	46,8	52,3	43,7
Rural	85,3	13,3	84,6	14,5	82,6	16,2	83,8	15,2
Total	58,3	37,5	58,8	38,7	56,9	39,3	58,2	38,3
Transvaal								
Urban	40,7	51,4	50,1	45,3	52,7	42,2	56,5	36,8
Rural	87,0	10,7	83,9	13,2	86,0	11,6	87,6	10,0
Total	55,1	38,8	58,4	37,4	58,9	39,2	61,4	32,9
Natal								
Urban	14,6	81,5	19,1	78,2	20,0	76,5	21,9	73,0
Rural	37,8	50,9	34,3	55,2	33,6	55,4	36,1	53,6
Total	20,1	74,3	21,8	74,1	21,9	73,5	23,4	70,9
O.F.S.								
Urban	73,7	21,2	80,8	16,8	80,9	16,7	81,1	15,7
Rural	92,7	6,3	92,9	6,3	92,1	6,9	93,4	5,6
Total	84,0	13,1	86,7	11,7	84,8	13,3	84,0	13,3
S. Africa								
Urban	41,0	52,6	47,8	48,5	50,0	45,8	53,2	41,5
Rural	84,0	13,7	82,4	15,3	81,9	15,8	83,1	14,6
Total	55,9	39,1	57,3	39,4	56,9	39,3	58,1	37,1

this study, these groups are the basic constituencies of the major parties. Table 77 shows the percentage the Afrikaans- and English-speaking sections respectively formed of the total white population in the urban and rural areas, in the provinces and in South Africa as a whole, from 1936 to 1960. Table 78 concentrates on the Afrikaners and shows the increased urbanization that took place among them over that period by referring to the percentage of Afrikaners living in urban areas. Unfortunately up-dated figures are not available because the 1970 census did not require information with respect to home languages. There is, however, every reason to believe that the trends shown in these tables have persisted.

Two important inferences may be drawn from this table. The first is that, as far as South Africa as a whole is concerned, demographic factors continued over this period to favour the Afrikaner population, raising its percentage of the total white population from 55,9% in 1936 to 58,1% in 1960, while the percentage of English-speakers dropped correspondingly from 39,1% to 37,1%. In aggregate terms this means that while in 1936 the total Afrikaner population of 1 120 770 exceeded the total English-speaking population by 337 699, by 1960 the Afrikaner population had risen to 1 788 651, which was 646 817 more than the English-speaking total. The second fact of considerable importance that emerges is that where the Afrikaners were formerly in a minority in the urban areas of the Cape and Transvaal, by 1960 they formed a substantial majority in these areas. The same trend is clear with respect to the total urban population of South Africa: in 1936 Afrikaners formed only 41,0% of that population, and by 1960 this had risen to 53,2%. As a result we may speak not only of the urbanization of the Afrikaner but also of the 'Afrikanerization' of the urban areas.

The extent to which the movement of Afrikaners to the urban areas has affected the Afrikaner section as a whole may be readily seen from Table 78. This table renders the Afrikaner urban population as a percentage of the total number of Afrikaners with respect to the provinces and to South Africa as a whole.

Table 78

PERCENTAGE OF AFRIKANERS LIVING IN URBAN AREAS

	1936	1946	1951	1960
Cape	46,8	58,2	64,9	72,7
Transvaal	51,0	64,6	73,0	79,1
Natal	44,5	72,3	78,3	82,9
O.F.S.	58,6	66,4	62,0	73,8
S. Africa	47,8	60,4	68,9	76,5

Two facts are apparent from this table. The first is that the great majority of all Afrikaners now live in towns; and the second is that this development largely took place during and after World War II. With these facts in mind we may now turn to examine the pattern of voting behaviour during this period.

CHANGING PATTERNS IN PARTY SUPPORT

The first area that we shall look at is that of levels of participation in the elections covered. Two levels of activity are associated with participation. The first refers to the number of parties and candidates—and the number of seats left uncontested—in the respective elections. A somewhat compressed set of figures relating to this level of participation is provided in Table 79.

Table 79

NUMBER OF CANDIDATES ENTERED BY THE RESPECTIVE PARTIES

Party	1943	1948	1953	1958	1961	1966	1970
U.P. (plus allies[1])	152	147	147	150	99	135	144
N.P. (plus allies[2])	109	102	130	119	104	148	138
Afrikaner Party	22	—	—	—	—	—	—
Liberal Party	—	—	—	3	2	—	—
Progressive Party	—	—	—	—	22	26	19
Republican Party	—	—	—	—	—	22	—
Herstigte N.P.	—	—	—	—	—	—	77
Others	42	55	5	12	12	14	14
Uncontested seats	18	12	20	24	67	18	10

Notes: [1] These comprised the Dominion and Labour Parties in 1943, the Labour Party in 1948 and 1953, and the National Union in 1961.
[2] These comprised the Afrikaner Party in 1948.

For the present we shall restrict our comment on this table to two observations. With respect to the number of uncontested seats, it would seem that a small number of these are most frequently associated with a large number of minor party and/or independent candidates. In 1943, apart from the U.P.'s allies there were 64 such candidates; in 1948, 55; in 1966, 62; in 1970, 110. On the other hand, in 1953 and 1958, where the number of uncontested seats also remained relatively low, there were only five and fifteen candidates respectively representing this group; while in 1961, when there was an unprecedently high number of uncontested seats, there were still 36 candidates from outside the two major parties. These three elections, then, represent departures from the rule suggested by the other four. Part at least of the reason for this discrepancy will be revealed by the figures given in the next table, and discussion on it will be deferred until then. The other observation that we might make at this stage is that it is clear from the above table that from the point of view of candidacies alone, South African politics have been dominated through our period by the two major parties; that is, to put it another way, that the South African electorate has apparently preferred to engage in politics through the medium of one or other of the National and United Parties. This was most clearly the case in 1953. Only in 1970, and then largely through the intervention of the Herstigte Nasionale Party, was there some departure from this general rule. In view of this rule, we might suggest that a possible index of the intensity of the electoral battle is the ratio of the sum of the candidates of the two major party groups to the number of seats at stake in a given election.[11] These ratios are tabulated below:

1943	*1948*	*1953*	*1958*	*1961*	*1966*	*1970*
1,74	1,66	1,86	1,79	1,35	1,77	1,77

It will be seen from this that our index varies significantly from the mean (1,71) in two elections: in 1953 when it is much higher than normal and in 1961 when it is much lower. This index provides a useful base of comparison with the more frequently used index, the percentage poll.

Table 80

PERCENTAGE POLL, 1943–70

Region	*Percentage poll*							
	1943	1948	1953	1958	1960[1]	1961	1966	1970
Cape Town area	75,6	77,0	86,7	85,8	90,7	73,3	72,7	77,7
Port Elizabeth	77,8	80,9	90,0	90,8	92,8	73,7	83,7	80,0
Border	67,0	77,9	88,4	88,1	92,8	63,6	75,7	76,2
Rest of Cape	85,1	87,1	89,9	92,4	92,5	89,5	84,4	80,8
Total Cape	81,9	83,2	89,1	90,5	92,0	79,4	79,8	79,4
Johannesburg	73,8	69,2	83,4	84,6	89,3	71,0	70,3	70,0
Witwatersrand	80,6	79,6	88,0	91,5	90,2	77,6	76,4	73,4
Pretoria	76,0	78,3	88,7	88,7	88,3	80,7	68,9	72,9
Rest of Transvaal	81,7	83,5	87,5	90,5	90,9	82,6	76,5	75,1
Total Transvaal	78,6	78,5	87,1	89,5	89,8	77,7	73,8	73,1
Durban–Pietermaritzburg	70,5	72,5	86,4	84,1	92,4	67,3	76,0	75,1
Rest of Natal	74,1	81,3	91,6	90,0	92,7	83,8	83,6	78,9
Total Natal	71,7	75,4	88,3	87,1	92,5	72,7	78,4	76,4
O.F.S.	82,6	83,5	86,4	89,1	89,8	77,4	71,3	66,9
Union/Republic	79,5	80,3	87,9	89,6	90,8	77,6	75,9	74,7

Note: [1] The 1960 figures are, of course, for the referendum.

The over-all profile of voter participation emerging out of Table 80 is one of continuing upsurge from 1943 through to the referendum in 1960, and thereafter one of persistent decline. The same profile, with very marginal variations, also holds good for the total provincial voting figures. The percentage poll in the Cape rose four points from 1961 to 1966; in the Transvaal there was a drop of one point in 1948; in Natal there was a drop of eight points in 1958, and a rise of 5,7 per cent in 1966; nevertheless, in each of the provinces and in South Africa as a whole, the lowest percentage poll recorded in the 1953–60 period was considerably higher than the highest percentage poll recorded either before or after that period. Indeed, this observation is valid in every one of the regions into which we have divided the provinces.

If we refer back from this observation to our previously suggested index of electoral intensity (which necessarily omits the 1960 referendum), the conclusion becomes irresistible that there was, indeed, something distinctive about the 1953–60 period; for that period gains high scores in terms of both indices. It also suggests that these indices are more reliable, in general, than the number of third party candidates, or, except in extreme variations (e.g. in 1961), the number of uncontested seats. In both 1953 and 1958, the battle was, as it were, left to the giants. This was not due to a decline in political interest; on the contrary, the battle was too intense to permit the luxury of third-party interventions. From 1961 on, however, that luxury is not only permitted, but for many it has been transformed into a necessity. Again, this suggests some kind of shift in the post-1960 period.

Burnham, in his examination of critical elections or critical realignments, states *inter alia* that they 'are characterized by abnormally high intensity',[12] and goes on to cite among the manifestations of high intensity an 'abnormally heavy voter participation for the time'.[13] From this point of view, at least, the 1953–60 period satisfies one of Burnham's indicators of critical elections. As I hope has been made apparent from the chapters on the 1953 and 1958 elections and the referendum, these were votes that were critical in a politically more substantive way than is suggested by Burnham's use of the term. This is not to depreciate the importance of the 1948 election, when the Nationalists (with the aid of the Afrikaner Party) took their great leap forward that carried them into power. A number of factors were present in that first post-war election that might have produced a deviating result rather than a durable realignment (or a durable reversion to the pre-Fusion alignment). The 1953 election together with the 1958 one made quite clear that a solidary Afrikaner nationalism had indeed been established, and the pro-republican vote in 1960 achieved for that solidarity its due reward, namely, the republic that was its major aspiration. These are the reasons, then, why the level of political intensity was so high on these three occasions.

If one looks simply at election *results* the pattern does not show the same peaking at the referendum. It is, at least until 1970, one of smooth progression, as the tabulation below suggests. The upper row represents the *estimated* percentage of the total projected votes won by the Nationalists (with Afrikaner Party votes added in 1948); the lower row, the percentage of seats won by them.

	1943	*1948*	*1953*	*1958*	*1960*	*1961*	*1966*	*1970*
N.P. % votes	33,4	39,4	44,5	48,5	52,0	53,5	59,2	53,5
N.P. % seats	28,7	52,7	59,1	64,7	n.a.	66,0	75,0	69,8

There are, however, patterns within this pattern. Table 81 reveals one of these variations, showing Nationalist and United Party seats (plus those of their respective allies) for each election classified according to whether they were urban or rural.

Table 81

PARTY SUPPORT IN URBAN AND RURAL SEATS

	N.P. (plus allies)		U.P. (plus allies)	
	Urban	*Rural*	*Urban*	*Rural*
1943	4	39	72	35
1948	16	63	63	8
1953	27	61	54	7
1958	36	61	49	4
1961	37	62	47	3
1966	54	66	37	2
1970	46	65	44	3

It is clear from this table that where at first the Nationalists were predominantly a rural-based party, they have, while maintaining their hold on rural areas—indeed extending it to a near monopoly—now achieved a much better balance between rural and urban support. The United Party on the other hand has since 1943 remained a mainly urban party, with its relatively respectable rural support dwindling through the period to virtual insignificance. These trends are brought out even more clearly if we render the figures given in Table 81 in percentages.

Table 82

PERCENTAGE OF URBAN AND RURAL SEATS WON BY THE NATIONAL AND UNITED PARTY RESPECTIVELY

	% of urban seats		*% of rural seats*	
	N.P.	U.P.	N.P.	U.P.
1943	5,3	94,7	52,7	47,3
1948	20,3	79,7	88,7	11,3
1953	33,3	66,7	89,7	10,3
1958	42,4	57,6	93,8	6,2
1961	43,5	55,3	95,4	4,6
1966	58,7	40,2	97,1	2,9
1970	50,5	48,4	95,6	4,4

A more specific plotting of the respective political 'territories' of the National and United Parties can be provided by reference to the regions which have been used in this study. Table 83 groups these regions into four major categories: (A) those in which the United Party (including its former allies) have maintained a persistent dominance: Cape Town, Border, Johannesburg, and Durban–Pietermaritzburg; (B) those in which former United Party dominance has been succeeded by a relative balance between the two major parties: Port Elizabeth and 'Rest of Natal'; (C) those in which former United Party dominance has been reversed, giving way to National Party dominance: the Witwatersrand and Pretoria; and (D) those in which the National Party moved from a majority position to a dominant one: 'Rest of Cape', 'Rest of Transvaal', and the Orange Free State.

Table 83

PERCENTAGE OF SEATS WITHIN FOUR REGIONAL GROUPS WON BY UNITED AND NATIONAL PARTIES RESPECTIVELY

Year	*A*		*B*		*C*		*D*	
	U.P.	N.P.	U.P.	N.P.	U.P.	N.P.	U.P.	N.P.
1943 .	97,8	2,2	100,0	0,0	91,3	8,7	46,15	53,85
1948 .	93,6	6,4	63,6	36,4	56,0	44,0	12,0	88,0
1953 .	87,2	12,8	60,0	40,0	38,5	61,5	8,1	91,9
1958 .	84,8	15,2	60,0	40,0	23,3	76,7	4,2	95,9
1961 .	82,6	15,2	60,0	40,0	20,0	80,0	1,4	98,6
1966 .	70,8	27,1	33,3	66,7	3,0	97,0	0,0	100,0
1970 .	80,9	17,0	50,0	50,0	9,1	90,9	0,0	100,0

What their respective 'territories' mean to the parties is brought out in the tabulations below. First we shall tabulate the percentage of all U.P. seats that comes from Group A, and then in the line below, from Groups A and B combined:

	1943	*1948*	*1953*	*1958*	*1961*	*1966*	*1970*
% U.P. seats from A	42,3	62,0	67,2	73,6	77,6	87,2	80,9
% U.P. seats from A+B	52,3	71,8	77,0	84,9	89,8	97,4	93,6

In the next tabulation, we perform the same operation *mutatis mutandis* for the National Party, i.e. the first line shows the percentage of all National Party seats that comes from Group D, and the second line, that comes from D and C combined.

	1943	*1948*	*1953*	*1968*	*1961*	*1966*	*1970*
% N.P. seats from D	93,0	77,2	70,5	64,9	64,6	55,8	60,4
% N.P. seats from D+C	97,7	96,2	88,6	88,7	88,9	82,5	87,4

Taking this second tabulation first, we see that the National Party, at least up until 1966, has leaned less and less heavily on its exclusive 'territories' (Group D); and this in turn is the obverse side of its successful invasion into former United Party regions (see Tables 82 and 83 above). At the same time, its boundaries as represented by D and C still remain limited by United Party bastions of strength. For the latter's part, we further see that as United Party support dwindled it was confined more and more tightly within its own enclaves. Even with its 1970 election success, its sorties out of these enclaves have failed to alter its general situation to a material degree.

The significance of these territorial considerations for the political structure of South Africa becomes apparent when it is realized that our four groups of regions represent a spectrum from Group A, in which the English-speakers are predominant, through to Group D in which Afrikaners are (even more heavily) predominant. It is therefore from the relatively 'mixed regions' (Groups B and C) and to some extent Group A, that shifts in party support are most likely to occur.

A SUGGESTED ANALYTICAL FRAMEWORK FOR THE STUDY OF SOUTH AFRICAN POLITICS

In a country such as South Africa, where group identities and group norms are powerful and persistent, it is useful to distinguish those factors that promote convergence between groups and those that promote divergence, namely, those that have a tendency to bring the groups together and those that have a tendency to keep them apart. In general it would be expected that factors tending to promote convergence will be those that de-emphasize inter-group boundaries. It may consequently further be expected that within a given group, unless such convergent factors operate more or less uniformly, they may have themselves a disruptive effect, as some elements of the group move towards convergence while others react negatively, seeking to reinforce the group solidarity which is thus threatened. The same ambivalence may also be found in divergent factors, that is, while the general effect of such factors will be to maintain or increase the distance *between* two groups, the general effect *within* each group will tend to convergence, to increased group distinctiveness and solidarity, although some members may react against this polarization by seeking to promote attitudes of accommodation. Since, moreover, social life over a period of time exhibits both continuities and discontinuities, it may also be expected that both sets of factors may be operative within a period, or even simultaneously. In a period, for example, that is generally characterized by divergence, there may also be present factors promoting convergence, and vice versa. Indeed, if the total society sustains a capacity for collective action (e.g. by means of a stable political system), one is led to assume *a fortiori* that there are at least some convergent factors at work powerful enough to countervail the disintegrative tendencies of the factors that promote divergence.

We now apply these general considerations to party politics in South Africa, and in particular to the elections under review. Clearly, among the phenomena that may be classed as 'factors' in the above context there may be found a wide variety of content: social forces and social structures, the economic system, the international system, as well as those that are more specifically political. As far as this study is concerned, however, it is necessary to confine ourselves to those which have a direct political content. The questions that we are asking are relatively narrow: Why is it that the great majority of Afrikaners since 1948 have come to vote, and have continued to vote, for the National Party, and the great majority of English-speakers for the United Party?[14] And: Is this division on a linguistic basis likely to persist? The second question is the same question as: Is there any likelihood that the Nationalist Government will be voted out of power? For, if the language groups continue to divide in their party support, the demographic factors referred to in this chapter must ensure the indefinite continuance of the Nationalist regime.

With regard to the first of these two questions, the explanations offered here are necessarily partial, not only because we limit our inquiry to political factors, but also because our inquiry is truncated in point of time. By the time our period begins, party allegiances had already been established for a large section of the population, and these had continuing relevance. Nevertheless, the handicap is not vital; for the fact remains that a large—indeed a decisive—number of Afrikaans-speaking voters did turn in 1948 and subsequent elections, from the United Party to the National Party: in other words a process of divergency had set in.

From 1948 through to 1966 there was as we have seen an ever-increasing percentage of voters voting for the National Party, producing for it a similarly rising share of the seats. At the same time, from 1961 there has been a sharp decline in the level of popular participation in elections. From 1948 to 1960 inclusive, then, we have rising levels of participation coupled by a rising percentage of votes cast for the National Party. In the 1961 and 1966 elections the level of participation fell, while the percentage of the voters who did turn out who voted for the National Party continued to rise. Finally, in 1970 the level of participation fell still further, but at the same time the Nationalist vote also suffered a decline. One can suggest in view of this that the fall-off in voter enthusiasm first in evidence in 1961 represented the starting-point of a trend that was finally reflected in a fall-off in the support of those who did vote for the National Party. If we combine the percentage poll in the various elections and the referendum and the percentage of the estimated total vote that went to the National Party—i.e. if we take a percentage of the total registered voters instead of the estimated total vote—we arrive at the following figures:

Estimated N.P. % of registered voters	*1943*	*1948*	*1953*	*1958*	*1960*	*1961*	*1966*	*1970*
	26,6	31,6	39,1	43,5	47,2	41,5	44,5	40,0

These percentages perhaps represent a more reliable indication of *active* political support for the National Party, and bring into relief the decline from 1961, although the rise again in 1966 suggests that the election had some idiosyncratic features—and this suggestion we shall examine later.

For the meanwhile, with respect to the period 1943–60, some explanation is required of why the voters turned in increasing numbers and with apparently increasing enthusiasm to the National Party. In order to do so we may turn to the types of issue presented to the electorate and consider the extent to which they tended to promote convergence or divergence respectively. For this purpose we may make use of the notion of issue-areas used by Rosenau in the study of international politics,[15] although for our purpose quite different issue-areas are appropriate. These are firstly *status* issues, in particular issues which bear on South Africa's international status (e.g. her relation to the Crown, her membership in the Commonwealth), on the role and nature of the constitution, and on the status of the several population groups in South Africa; secondly, *culture* issues, identified as those which bear on the nature, aspirations, identities, and inter-relationships of the two major white groups; thirdly *race* issues, treated separately although logically a sub-group of culture issues since they deal with the same elements although applied specifically to the various races of South Africa; fourthly *security* issues, relating to South African security from both internal and external threats; fifthly *economic* issues, which are self-explanatory. In addition, we may leave a residual category in which we may place issues that gained prominence in one election and then ceased to be relevant.

In the general elections of 1948 to 1958 and the 1960 referendum the first four issue-areas were all salient. With regard to the *status* issue-area, the republican issue was given mounting prominence by the National Party, and it appealed, as we have seen, to deep-seated *volk* aspirations; on the issue of South African membership in the Commonwealth, the National Party moved from being opposed to South Africa's continued membership (1943) to support during the referendum campaign that was both qualified and at a secondary level of priority; on constitutional questions, particularly as shown in the 1953 election, the National Party clearly subordinated the constitution to 'the will of the people' and hence regarded it simply as a political instrument; but it moved, after the referendum, to a form of constitution that would command the broadest consensus among the white electorate (except with regard to the head of state, it virtually retained the existing constitutional provisions intact); and finally, throughout this period it gave emphasis to giving the Afrikaner his 'due', entrenching Nationalist supporters in all areas of the Establishment, and to insisting on a more widespread use of the Afrikaans language. As opposed to these positions, the Opposition reacted by emphasizing the importance of the Commonwealth connection, giving it a very high place in its order of priorities; by vigorously opposing the establishment of a republic; by insisting on the primacy of the constitution (particularly the entrenched clauses); and by being constantly sensitive to any implied threat to the status of the English language. In short, almost every item within this issue-area served to promote divergence between the two language groups, and hence to attach those groups to the political parties with which they were respectively associated.

With regard to the *culture* issue-area, there is clearly an overlap with many of the status issues just mentioned, but there were other issues that went beyond questions of status. In particular, the National Party placed stress on the issue of Afrikaner unity to an increasing degree (i.e. in relation to other issues) from 1943, until in 1958 it came almost to dominate all others. In contrast, the United Party continued to present the principle of national unity (i.e. as between the two white groups). The United Party policy in this issue-area therefore represented a policy of convergence; whereas the sectional appeal of the National Party was directly aimed at divergence. No doubt one factor that inhibited the appeal of the United Party to Afrikaners to come into its 'national unity' fold was the spill-over effect of its opposition to the status issues with which national-minded Afrikaners identified; so that for all its claim to embrace both language groups it tended to be identified with the culture-values of the English-speaking section.

The *race* issue-area in its broadest connotation undoubtedly promotes convergence between the two white groups, and the 1943 to 1960 period is no exception. Both groups tended to see the events occurring in Black Africa (and in Asia) through the same lenses; both groups were at one in their determination to prevent the replication of these events in South Africa; and both the major political parties staked their claims as the true defenders of White Civilization. The major difference between the two parties at least until 1959 (the year of the passage of the Promotion of Bantu Self-government

Act) was that the National Party more consistently, more absolutely and more ruthlessly stood for, or appeared to stand for, a policy of white domination. Although the 'race memory' of the Afrikaners is more copiously furnished with the memory of past conflicts with the Africans, one would hesitate to ascribe to the Afrikaners national characteristics which would endow the National Party's posture on race issues with a peculiar attraction—particularly when that posture is identified with a harsh ruthlessness simply for the maintenance of white domination. Yet such an assumption would underlie the proposition that the National Party's race policies promoted divergence rather than convergence. It is sometimes jokingly said in South Africa that English-speaking voters vote against the National Party but are glad to have a National Party government in power, particularly in times of racial unrest. There may be an element of truth in the jibe. National Party policies were in line with the rural-conservative traditions of Afrikanerdom and also with the political traditions of the Boer Republic. They served therefore as supports for the identification of Afrikaners with that party. It is not clear, however, that they had a repellent effect on the mass of English-speaking voters, except in so far as other issues had a spill-over effect on this area.

Issues within the *security* issue-area were also prominent in this period. Events elsewhere in the African continent (particularly in Kenya and the Congo) emphasized the 'Black menace'; the Cold War was at its height; the outside world showed increasing hostility towards South Africa, culminating, after Sharpeville, with a strong (if temporary) movement in favour of boycotting all South African goods, and South Africa's forced withdrawal from the Commonwealth. Internally moreover it was a period marked by widespread and serious racial unrest and increasing violence. Again it might be argued that these events tended to promote convergence between the two white groups. On the other hand, such a convergence tendency would seem to have been restricted by the antipathy of the Opposition to the widespread infringements of common beliefs regarding the proper regard for civil liberties that the Government's counter-measures involved. In short, the particular form of the Government's responses in this area tended to maintain the distance between the two groups.

While *economic* issues were raised during this period, on the whole South Africa's persistently booming economy reduced their salience, and one cannot say that they had any profound effect on political divisions except in so far as satisfaction with the Government's performance persuaded some voters to vote for it or restrained others from voting against it. There is little to suggest from the study of the elections concerned that such hypothetical voters formed a significant percentage of the whole.

In review, then, we may say that issues in the status issue-area and the culture issue-area were probably those which were most powerful in attaching Afrikaner voters in increasing numbers to the National Party and in arousing their enthusiasm for it, and that issues in the race and security issue-areas probably supported this tendency. At the same time these same issue-areas were probably salient in reinforcing the attachment of English-speaking voters to the United Party, primarily in reaction to Nationalist policies with respect to them. By and large it is true to say, moreover, that the respective tendencies of the various issue-areas were mutually supporting; so that there was a minimal degree of cross-pressure operating on the voter that might encourage his withdrawal from the political process.

If we compare the post-1960 period with the pre-1960 period we find a marked decline in the salience of the two issue-areas which we have identified as having the highest salience in the earlier period. In the *status* issue-area, the constitutional issue had been resolved by the referendum, the Commonwealth issue had been resolved by the force of events, the status of Afrikaners as a group was assured. It is true that in early 1961 the United and Progressive Parties were still fighting to stave off the republic and rescue the Commonwealth connection, but by the time the election took place these were no longer viable issues. Then in the *culture* issue-area, the status issues now having been resolved, the Nationalist Government reversed its previous stance and proclaimed itself the champion of national unity and of co-operation between the two white groups. That is not to say, however, that it did not acknowledge itself to be a fundamentally Afrikaner government; but it did play down its sectional appeal in favour of a broader, national appeal (i.e. with respect to the white 'nation').

On the other hand, and in part accounting perhaps for the muting of the National Party's sectional appeal, both *race* and *security* issue-areas were dominant in both 1961 and 1966; and this applied to both the internal and external aspects of security issues. Straddling both issue-areas was the projected menace posed by 'Communism'. The external environment was, if anything, more hostile than before, manifesting itself in the economic sphere, by boycott movements, the outflow of capital, and the retarded rate of foreign capital investment in South Africa. Politically, it manifested itself in the dwindling support for South Africa in the United Nations while the resolutions passed there grew increasingly sharper. It was in this period, too, that the great leap forward occurred in the granting of independence to African territories, and that the Organization of African Unity was formed. Internally, racial unrest, riots, and disturbances continued, while the Rivonia Trials and the trial of Abraham Fischer kept the menace of Communism alive.

With respect to the *race* issue-area, the continued disturbances tended to support the racial conservatism of the white voters. Nevertheless they may also have served to prompt both major parties to fresh formulations of their race policies, or, as was the case of the National Party in particular, to give a new thrust to an already existing policy. The United Party brought out its Race Federation plan, but the complexities and ambiguities, not to say its general timidity, cannot be said to have aroused the enthusiasm of the voters. The Government for its part gave greater articulation and emphasis to the concept of 'separate development' with the ultimate goal of several independent 'Bantu homelands'. But except to the extent that these different proposals reflected differences in the political cultures of Afrikaans- and English-speaking South Africans (which is possible), they do not have a significant bearing on the convergence or divergence of the two white major language groups.

In 1961, one might say, party loyalties held; and the election is perhaps sufficiently described, to use Campbell's typology, by referring to it as a maintaining election. We thus note the drop-off in voter turn-out coupled with only a slight increase in the vote for the National Party. In 1966, however, the continued decline in voter turn-out was more than compensated for by a considerable increase in the vote for the National Party. Two idiosyncratic factors would appear to account for this. On the one hand, Britain's imposition of sanctions against the Smith regime in Rhodesia undermined one of the important supports in the maintenance of English-speaking South Africans' sense of cultural identity, thus facilitating convergence from their side—at a time, moreover, when the National Party was placing strong emphasis on its concept of national unity. Then, on the other hand, and contrary to all previous expectations, Dr Verwoerd was acquiring an aura of personal charisma for English-speaking South Africans as well as for Afrikaners. What was not clear in 1966 was what the long-term effects of these two factors would be.

The 1970 election results would appear to suggest that their effects were short-lived indeed, and that the political pattern reverted once more to the divergence type. But that is a short answer and, like most short answers, misleading. Other considerations, then, need to be brought forward. First, the Herstigte Nasionale Party revived in the sharpest manner issues in the culture issue-area that had been prominent in the hey-day of the National Party's evangelical campaign: the threat to the Afrikaner language, the dilution of Afrikaner spiritual and cultural values, the swamping of Afrikaners by the tide of immigrants, the twin threats of materialism and liberalism. These were issues that it used as weapons against the National Party. The National Party, for its part, under Mr Vorster, continued to speak in terms of national unity and inter-group co-operation. As we have seen, the Herstigtes did not succeed in winning many votes; but what they may well have done is, on the one hand, to have subjected Afrikaans voters to a degree of cross-pressure that led many of them to abstain from voting,[16] and, on the other hand, to have revived the suspicions of the English-speaking minority of an Afrikaner urge to domination, and hence to have restored their traditional attachment to the United Party.

Secondly, in 1970 the economic issue-area received increased prominence, specifically with reference to the unhealthy signs of inflation, and secondly, with reference to a general decline in the administration's image of efficiency and general good husbandry.[17] Again, these issues may well have added to the cross-pressures on Afrikaners, persuading some to vote for the Opposition and others to abstain, while they may at the same time have served to disillusion the 1966 English-speaking converts to the National Party.

Thirdly, Opposition party claims that the Government's Bantustan policy had failed, together with the failure of the National Party to give any fresh impetus to that policy, may have disillusioned some of even its own supporters. And finally, there is some reason to think that of the Afrikaners who switched to the United Party the majority came from the younger age groups.[18] At the same time there is also reason to believe that the new support for the Progressive Party came mainly from the younger English-speaking voters.[19] In these latter two suggestions there lies the hint that the traditional pattern of voting behaviour may be beginning to decline.

What has been suggested here is that it was the emphasis given to the status and culture issue-areas that was primarily responsible for imparting the characteristic of divergence to South African party politics; secondly, that the decline in the salience of these issue-areas since 1960 has resulted in the two major parties' heavier reliance on the pre-established loyalty (or habits) of their supporters; and finally, that a generational influence may be at work which could presage the advent of a new alignment of political forces, possibly cutting across—at least eventually—the linguistic barrier. The Herstigte Nasionale Party, the United Party and the Progressive Party all wait hopefully for some realignment; for, depending on its nature, all potentially stand to gain something from it. The National Party for its part has everything to lose, and there are signs already that its awareness of this fact is inclining it to attempt to revivify status and culture issues.

Of considerable importance to the prospect of further political realignment is the extent to which the process of urbanization is likely to modify the attitudes of National Afrikanerdom. As far as cultural identity is concerned, that process does not seem to have had any seriously impairing effect, largely no doubt because of the complex of social and cultural associations that have assisted in maintaining an Afrikaner social milieu even in the 'alien' towns. Nevertheless, protracted subjection to an urban environment, representing, as that environment does, an economic rather than a social nexus, raises the level of economic issues in the ordering of people's issue perceptions, and moreover provides a common framework of experience and perspective with respect to those issues. While there is no ground for supposing that this in turn tends to promote a uniform response to those issues, it does suggest that attempts by political parties to define themselves by reference to culture and status issues are likely to be regarded as both anachronistic and irrelevant to the salient issues of contemporary life. If the National Party adopts such a strategy, one cannot, therefore, predict for it more than a short-term success.

On the other hand the race issue-area is likely to be salient for both white voters and non-white non-voters for the foreseeable future. The effects of this salience are unpredictable, although several if–then propositions can be formulated. There is, however, at least this possibility, to say no more, that the emergence of spokesmen of stature in the various racial groups through institutions set up by the Government itself, able to articulate their peoples' aspirations and grievances, already has initiated a process, which can hardly be reversed, of political interaction among those groups. One would not elevate the present state of that interaction; it has not yet made any perceptible dent in the domination–subordination relationship. Yet these small beginnings, coupled with the inevitable further penetration of blacks into the economic system, create a situation in the seventies vastly different from that in the fifties. And that situation calls for responses from the leaders of the major parties that are more creative than the traditional policies of convergence and divergence, than the calls for 'white unity' or the preservation of Afrikaner identity. Perhaps not the next election, but the one after, will give some indication of whether those responses are likely to be forthcoming.

Notes

CHAPTER 1

1. Section 36.
2. Section 35(1).
3. The Asiatic Land Tenure and Indian Representation Act, No. 28 of 1946.
4. Women's Enfranchisement Act, No. 18 of 1930.
5. Franchise Laws Amendment Act, No. 41 of 1931.
6. Act No. 12 of 1936.
7. In 1935 there were 10 628 African voters registered in the Cape. H. R. Hahlo and Ellison Kahn, *The Union of South Africa: The development of its laws and constitution*, Stevens, London, 1960, 165, n.77.
8. South West Africa Affairs Amendment Act, No. 23 of 1949.
9. Act No. 30 of 1958.
10. Act No. 55 of 1952.
11. Act No. 83 of 1965.
12. Acts Nos. 20 of 1940, 10 of 1946, and 55 of 1952.
13. The relevant sections of the South Africa Act (as amended) were incorporated, with only minor changes and some re-ordering, in the Republic of South Africa Constitution Act, No. 32 of 1961 (sections 42 to 45).
14. South Africa Act, s. 41(1); Republic of South Africa Constitution Act s. 42(1).
15. South Africa Act, s. 40(2); Republic of South Africa Constitution Act, s. 43(2).
16. Ibid.
17. *Government Gazette Extraordinary*, Vol. 151, No. 3931, 13 February 1948.
18. *Government Gazette Extraordinary*, Vol. 171, No. 5009, 20 February 1953.
19. Ibid.
20. Ibid. Author's italics.
21. Report of the Twelfth Delimitation Commission. *Government Gazette Extraordinary*, Vol. 19, No. 1364, 7 February 1966.
22. Ibid.
23. Cited in ibid.
24. Ibid.

CHAPTER 2

1. C. M. van den Heever, *General J. B. M. Hertzog*, A. P. Boekhandel, Johannesburg, 1944, 704.
2. Hereafter, for the 1943 and 1948 elections, referred to as the H.N.P. (Herenigde Nasionale of Volksparty).
3. One newspaper estimated at the end of the election that 'not less than 95% of the soldiers voted for the war effort'. *Daily News*, 29 July 1943. The same paper in 1948 provided further details. According to the figures then given there were 148 355 soldiers on the roll, of whom 80 641 (or 54%) voted. To the United Party it attributed 62 756 votes, the Dominion Party 4 647, the Labour Party 6 909, independents 3 011, the H.N.P. 2 962. *Daily News*, 19 May 1948.
4. These figures exclude three Afrikaner Party candidates and five independents who withdrew too late for their names to be removed from the ballot papers.
5. *Daily News*, 30 July 1943.
6. There was considerable controversy during the election campaign in Durban as to whether (as claimed by the Labour Party) Col. Stallard, Leader of the Dominion Party, had forced an angry Smuts to concede these seats immediately prior to his being sworn in as a Minister, or whether (as

Stallard claimed) the agreement was proposed to him and he 'reluctantly accepted it'. *Natal Mercury*, 12 June 1943.

7. The seat won in September 1939 by Col. Stallard after the withdrawal of Senator Clarkson.
8. *Natal Mercury*, 7 June 1943.
9. In the case of Umlazi this came as a result of the intervention of a Nationalist candidate, an event which induced the warring 'partners' to reach an agreement whereby the Labour candidate withdrew in return for the withdrawal of the Dominionite candidate from Durban North.
10. These included Dr Vernon Shearer, who had won Durban Point for the Dominion Party in 1938, resigned from that party in order to join the United Party in November 1939, resigned from that party in order to fight the Dominion Party for the Point seat in 1943, and, on winning that seat, immediately rejoined the United Party. *Natal Mercury*, 9 June 1943, and *Daily News*, 29 July 1943.
11. *Natal Mercury*, 7 June 1943.
12. For a brilliant analysis of the conflicts and manoeuvres of the contending forces in Afrikaner nationalism during this period see Michael Roberts and A. E. G. Trollip, *The South African Opposition, 1939–1945*, Longmans, Green & Co., Cape Town, 1947.
13. That this would prove to be the case was at the time by no means certain. The *Natal Mercury* of 25 June 1943, for example, forecast nine Afrikaner Party victories.
14. e.g. Mr A. C. Curry in Zululand.
15. e.g. Dr Vernon Shearer.
16. According to Roberts and Trollip, eleven of the independent candidates in the Transvaal were '*Volkseenheidkandidate*', products of the movement for Afrikaner unity, and one an Independent Republican; op. cit., 150.
17. Voting figures are from the *Government Gazette*, Vol. 133, No. 3233, 13 August 1943.
18. The Free State is excepted; for there every seat was contested by the major parties.
19. This delay was due to the need to wait for the arrival and counting of votes cast by the armed forces serving outside South Africa.
20. The *Natal Mercury*, e.g., on 25 June 1943 forecast that the results would be: United Party 70; Labour Party 10; Dominion Party 6; pro-Government Independents 4; making a pro-Government total of 90. Against this it forecast a total opposition of 60, made up of 49 H.N.P., 9 Afrikaner Party, and 2 independents.
21. *Natal Mercury*, 2 August 1943.
22. See n. 10.
23. By polling less than one-fifth of the vote of the successful candidate.
24. Op. cit., 159, 160.
25. Op. cit., 161.
26. The best account of the relations between the Afrikaner Party and the H.N.P. during the period 1943–51 is to be found in Gwendolen M. Carter, *The Politics of Inequality: South Africa since 1948*, 2nd edn. rev., Frederick A. Praeger, New York, 1959, chap. 9.
27. For the other seven seats the C.P.'s average percentage of the poll was in fact 7,9%.
28. See Table 10. The percentage of the total votes cast that went to the Communist Party was 0,8%.
29. Of these eleven seats six were won by the H.N.P. and five by the Coalition.

CHAPTER 3

1. An electoral alliance between the two leaders, Dr Malan and Mr Havenga, had been announced as early as 21 March 1947.
2. Eric A. Walker, *A History of Southern Africa*, Longmans, Green and Co., London, new impression, 1965; and cf. W. K. Hancock, *Smuts: The Fields of Force*, Cambridge University Press, Cambridge, 1968, 467–71.

3. Walker, op. cit., 764.
4. *Natal Daily News*, 13 April 1948.
5. Hofmeyr also remained Minister of Education, but at his own request relinquished the Finance portfolio.
6. *House of Assembly Debates*, Vol. 62, 20 January 1948, 62.
7. The term was intended to cover, as is generally understood in terms of South Africa's political terminology, the white 'races' only.
8. *Report of the Native Laws Commission, 1946–1948*, U.G. 28/1948.
9. *Natal Daily News*, 22 May 1948.
10. 'Kaffirboetie' is a pejorative term whose nearest equivalent is the American 'nigger lover'.
11. Alan Paton, *Hofmeyr*, Oxford University Press, Cape Town, 1964, 482.
12. Ibid.
13. *Natal Daily News*, 18 May 1948.
14. Unless otherwise stated, this section excludes the Labour and Afrikaner Parties since they were allied to the U.P. and H.N.P. respectively.
15. See, e.g., *Natal Daily News*, 9 and 28 April 1948.
16. He polled only 267 votes and lost his deposit.
17. *Natal Daily News*, 27 May 1948. This was before all the results were finally available.
18. e.g. Mr. B. J. Vorster, now Prime Minister, stood as an independent in Brakpan, where he was defeated by only two votes.
19. They won two of these and in the other three were heavily defeated.
20. This was in Drakensberg, the only one of these seats where the percentage poll was lower than 80%. The Nationalist candidate gained only 23,4% of the votes.
21. In Vryheid, which the A.P. won from the U.P.
22. This view was supported by a number of party organizers with whom the author has spoken, who frequently contrasted the outstanding enthusiasm and efficiency of the 1953 election with previous elections.
23. In Pretoria Central, Pretoria District, and Pretoria West the N.P. majorities were: 507, 674, and 139 respectively.
24. Henry John May, *The South African Constitution*, 3rd edn., Juta & Co., Cape Town, 1955, 139.
25. Gwendolen M. Carter, *The Politics of Inequality: South Africa since 1948*, 2nd edn. rev., Frederick A. Praeger, New York, 1959, chap. 9.
26. Enid Lakeman and J. D. Lambert, *Voting in Democracies*, Faber & Faber, London, 1955, 69.
27. 62% of the United Party seats had over 10 000 voters, compared with 25,3% H.N.P. seats in the same category.
28. This is the explanation favoured both by Gwendolen Carter and by Lakeman and Lambert.
29. This number would be considerably increased if uncontested seats are included in the calculation.

CHAPTER 4

1. Some of the more important statutes passed in the Nationalist Government's first five years of office were: the Asiatic Laws Amendment Act, No. 47, 1948; the Prohibition of Mixed Marriages Act, No. 55, 1949; the Native Laws Amendments Acts, No. 56, 1949, and No. 54, 1952; the Immorality Amendment Act, No. 21, 1950; the Population Registration Act, No. 30, 1950; the Group Areas Act, No. 41, 1950; the Native Building Workers Act, No. 27, 1951; the prevention of Illegal Squatting Act, No. 52, 1951; The Bantu Authorities Act, No. 68, 1951; the Natives (Abolition of Passes and Co-ordination of Documents) Act, No. 67, 1952; the Bantu Education Act, No. 47, 1953.

   For accounts of these and other acts and a fuller discussion of them the following works are particularly useful: Edgar H. Brookes, *Apartheid: A Documentary Study of Modern South Africa*, Barnes and Noble, New York, 1968; Brian Bunting, *The Rise of the South African Reich*, rev. edn.,

Penguin Books, Harmondsworth, 1969; Gwendolen M. Carter, *The Politics of Inequality: South Africa since 1948*, 3rd rev. edn., Praeger, New York, 1962; H. J. May, *The South African Constitution*, 3rd edn.; Juta & Co., Cape Town, 1955.

2. The worst single riot was the anti-Indian riot in and around Durban in January 1949, in which 147 people were killed and 1 087 injured; but there were further riots and demonstrations in Krugersdorp, Randfontein, Newlands, and Benoni, and between 18 October and 7 November 1952 there were riots in Port Elizabeth, Johannesburg, Kimberley, and East London in which both whites and blacks died. It was in this period too that the Defiance Campaign, initiated jointly by the African National Congress and the South African Indian Congress, was prosecuted, resulting in the end in the arrest of over 8 500 passive resisters.
3. Cf. Raymond G. Ruiter, 'The Maintenance of the Security of the State', in H. J. May, op. cit., 343–53, and E. H. Brookes and J. B. Macaulay, *Civil Liberty in South Africa*, Oxford University Press, Cape Town, 1958.
4. Sections 35, 137 and 152.
5. For fuller accounts of the 'constitutional crisis' see Gwendolen M. Carter, op. cit., chap. 4, 119–44; Geoffrey Marshall, *Parliamentary Sovereignty and the Commonwealth*, Clarendon Press, Oxford, 1957, chap. XI, 139–248.
6. Gwendolen M. Carter, op. cit., 121.
7. The Appellate Division unanimously ruled in the case of *Harris* v. *Dönges* that the entrenched clauses of the South Africa Act were still binding and that consequently the Separate Representation of Voters Act, being passed in contravention of their provisions, was invalid. The High Court of Parliament Act which purported to establish Parliament as a final court of appeal on constitutional matters was itself declared invalid by the Appellate Division: *Minister of the Interior* v. *Harris* (1952).
8. Gwendolen Carter, op. cit., 248.
9. Ibid.
10. *The Facts: Replies to Slogans and Allegations of the United Party*, Part 1, published by the Information Services of the National Party of South Africa, November 1951.
11. The best brief account of the Torch Commando is to be found in Gwendolen Carter, op. cit., 303–33.
12. Ibid., 308.
13. The difficulties were further compounded by marked personality clashes between Natal leaders of the Torch Commando and D. E. Mitchell, Natal Provincial Leader of the U.P.
14. Quoted in Carter, op. cit., 315.
15. The Declaration of the United Front is printed in Carter, op. cit., 316–17.
16. The resolution is printed in its main part in Carter, op. cit., 441, n.40.
17. Ibid., 318.
18. Ibid., 320.
19. Ibid., 323.
20. *Natal Mercury*, 17 January 1953.
21. The Afrikaans title, *Red die Volkstem* (Save the People's Voice), was interestingly different.
22. Cf. the Torch Commando leaflet, *Public Safety Bill is Dictatorship.*
23. One of its slogans was 'Vote National and ensure White Domination!' In Natal one of its leaflets showed a map of the province under the caption '~~Natal~~ [*sic*] India in the year 2000?'
24. The last two allegations referred to the United Party's opposition to the legislation that debarred duly elected Communists from continuing to sit in Parliament and in the Cape Provincial Council.
25. Only 149 seats were filled in the 1953 elections, as the Labour Party candidate for Johannesburg City died shortly before the election date. A by-election was held in this constituency on 24 June, but the results of this by-election are not counted in the statistical analysis contained in this chapter.

26. The Liberal Party as such was officially constituted in May—a month after the election was held.
27. This was in the Johannesburg seat of Hospital where an independent opposed the United Party candidate.
28. This figure includes the voters registered in Johannesburg City at the time of the by-election.
29. The voting figures for this chapter are from the *Government Gazette Extraordinary*, No. 5057, 24 April 1953.
30. The author found a firm belief among at least the less sophisticated Nationalists in divine intervention on behalf of their party. It is a belief that is probably by no means outworn, although the *Verkramptes* must now be having some doubts on this score.
31. The region, however, had lost two seats in the delimitation.
32. See Table 17.
33. Moreover in 1948 16,2% of the vote in this region went to minor party candidates, compared with a negligible 0,06% in 1953.
34. If we use the total *estimated* votes for the two main parties in the two elections, however, the over-all swing is reduced to only 1,8%.

CHAPTER 5

1. In addition to works previously cited, see International Commission of Jurists, *South Africa and the Rule of Law*, International Commission of Jurists, Geneva, 1960.
2. Ibid.
3. During this period there continued to be riots and other violent disturbances —e.g. in the rural Transvaal areas of Zeerust and Sekhukhuneland, in African townships in or near Johannesburg, Benoni, Pretoria, Kroonstad, and Rustenburg, and in Thembuland—over such matters as the issuance of reference books, or 'passes', to African women, cattle-culling programmes, and the implementation of the Bantu Authorities Act. In addition there were also various forms of non-violent protest, ranging from the Congress of the People, which adopted the famous Freedom Charter, to the bus boycott in Johannesburg. See Muriel Horrell, *Action, Reaction and Counter-action: a review of Non-white opposition to the apartheid policy, counter-measures by the Government, and the eruption of new waves of unrest*, South African Institute of Race Relations, Johannesburg, 1963, 14–28. Fuller accounts are found in the issues for the relevant years of *A Survey of Race Relations in South Africa*, South African Institute of Race Relations, Johannesburg, annual. See also Mary Benson, *South Africa: The Struggle for a Birthright*, Penguin, Harmondsworth, 1966.
4. Gwendolen M. Carter, *The Politics of Inequality: South Africa since 1948*, 3rd rev. edn., Praeger, New York, 1962, 249; John Cope, *South Africa*, Ernest Benn, London, 1965, 133–4.
5. Dr Albert Hertzog, son of General Hertzog, was Minister of Posts and Telegraphs. He continued to be a centre of controversy until he finally split from the National Party to help found and to lead the Herstigte Nasionale Party. In the final confrontation one of Mr Vorster's allegations was that during Dr Verwoerd's premiership Hertzog had approached him to participate in a right-wing opposition to Dr Verwoerd. J. H. P. Serfontein, *Die Verkrampte Aanslag*, Human and Rousseau, Cape Town and Pretoria, 1970, 201.
6. *Evening News*, 22 March 1958; Jan Botha, *Verwoerd is Dead*, Books of Africa, Cape Town, 1967, 28.
7. *Die Transvaler*, 24 March 1958.
8. Quoted in Fred Barnard, *13 Years with Dr. H. F. Verwoerd*, Voortrekker-pers, Johannesburg, 1967, 46.
9. Ibid.
10. Ibid., 46–7.
11. *Rasegte* would be roughly translated as 'true-bred'.
12. *Die Transvaler*, 15 February 1958.

13. *Natal Daily News*, 8 March 1958.
14. *Die Transvaler*, 10 March 1958.
15. *Rand Daily Mail*, 21 February 1958.
16. *Die Transvaler*, 3 March 1958.
17. In, e.g., the speech by Mr C. R. Swart, then Minister of Justice, reported by *Die Burger*, 1 February 1958.
18. Cf. such headlines as one in *Die Transvaler*, 16 April 1958, 'South Africa Must Choose Today. A European or Non-European Country.'
19. *Die Transvaler*, 16 April 1958.
20. SABRA (the South African Bureau of Racial Affairs) is the Afrikaans-Nationalist counterpart of the South African Institute of Race Relations, but whereas the latter is committed to the concept of an integrated society, the former takes the policy of separate development as its point of departure.
21. *Die Burger*, 4 March 1958.
22. *Die Transvaler*, 15 March 1958.
23. *Die Transvaler*, 3 March 1958.
24. *Die Burger*, 27 February 1958.
25. *Die Vaderland*, 11 March 1958.
26. *Die Burger*, 27 February 1958.
27. *Die Vaderland*, 28 January 1958.
28. *Die Transvaler*, 4 February 1958.
29. *Cape Times*, 24 January 1958.
30. *Rand Daily Mail*, 25 January 1958.
31. *Star*, 7 February 1958.
32. *Die Transvaler*, 24 March 1958.
33. *Rand Daily Mail*, 25 March 1958.
34. The poor state of Mr Strijdom's health and the probability of his early retirement were one of the more important side-issues of the campaign.
35. Gwendolen M. Carter, op. cit., 440, c.11, n.3.
36. *Rand Daily Mail*, 16 August 1957.
37. *Pretoria News*, 5 March 1958.
38. *Star*, 20 February 1958.
39. For a brief description of the changes in Labour Party policies see Gwendolen M. Carter, op. cit., 340–45. See also D. W. Kruger, ed., *South African Parties and Policies: a select source book*, Bowes and Bowes, London, 1960, and the Labour Party statement in *Digest of South African Affairs*, Department of Information, Pretoria, Vol. 5, No. 5, 14 March 1958.
40. *Star*, 18 March 1958.
41. Alan Paton, *Hope for South Africa*, Pall Mall, London, 1958, 62.
42. Ibid., 66.
43. See the statement by the Bond in *Digest of South African Affairs*, op. cit.
44. *Daily News*, 13 March 1958.
45. *Pretoria News*, 13 March 1958.
46. *Die Vaderland*, 14 March 1958.
47. *Die Transvaler*, 14 March 1958.
48. Strictly speaking, in two constituencies, Benoni and Rosettenville, it was the United Party who intervened as they had previously been held by the Labour Party.
49. By gaining less than 20% of the votes cast for the successful candidate.
50. The figures on which this and the following chapter are based are taken from 'Results of the Referendum held on the 5th October, 1960, and of the General Election of Members for the House of Assembly held on 16th April, 1958' in *Official Year Book of the Union of South Africa and of Basutoland, Bechuanaland Protectorate and Swaziland*, No. 30, 1960, Government Printer, Pretoria, 1961.
51. i.e. excluding the South West African seats and the Natives' and Coloureds' Representatives.
52. *Die Vaderland*, 18 April 1958.
53. *Cape Argus*, 18 April 1958.
54. *Sunday Times*, 20 April 1958.

55. *Star*, 17 April 1958.
56. Gwendolen M. Carter, op. cit., 492.
57. The National Party majority was 898 votes.
58. There was a spate of speculation on the probable total votes per party in the popular press. In general, the Government-supporting press produced figures that gave the National Party a majority, and the Opposition press produced figures that purported to prove the reverse, although in the latter category the *Natal Mercury* was an exception, giving 709 096 votes to the National Party and 699 058 votes to the United Party.

    Gwendolen Carter, using the simple formula of allocating 85% of 85% of the voters to the winning party and 15% of 85% to the major opposing party, arrives at results remarkably close to those given in Table 41. On her estimates, the voting strength of the two major parties was as follows:

	U.P.	N.P.
Cape	51,89%	47,40%
Transvaal . . .	48,47%	50,56%
Natal	75,83%	23,55%
O.F.S.. . . .	26,55%	73,33%
Union	50,35%	48,90%

    The Union figures, however, include the voting figures for South West Africa, where the National Party was in a majority; so that if these are taken out her estimated Union figures would give a slightly higher percentage to the United Party.

    Gwendolen M. Carter, op. cit., Appendix V, Chart A.
59. The extent of the swing in the Cape in favour of the Nationalists was further enhanced by the removal of the Coloureds from the common roll.
60. Gwendolen M. Carter, op. cit., 492. The importance of the delimitation as a factor in the results is also stressed by R. R. Farquharson, 'South Africa 1958' in D. E. Butler, ed., *Elections Abroad*, Macmillan, London, 1959, 271–3.

CHAPTER 6

1. Strictly speaking, it was a plebiscite and not a referendum, because the result was not legally binding. The term is preferred, however, because it was the one generally used in South Africa and was given official sanction, as it were, in the title of the Referendum Act, 1960.
2. *Die Transvaler*, 3 September 1958.
3. *Souvenir of visit of the Rt. Hon. Harold Macmillan Prime Minister of the United Kingdom to the Houses of Parliament on Wednesday, 3rd February, 1960*. Printed on the Authority of Mr Speaker, Cape Times Ltd., Parow, 9.
4. Ibid., 11.
5. *Cape Argus*, 5 February 1960.
6. *Sunday Times*, 7 February 1960.
7. John Cope, *South Africa*, Ernest Benn, London, 1965, 150.
8. The declaration of the state of emergency was made under the terms of the Public Safety Act, 1953. Such a declaration empowers the Government to 'make regulations on almost any matter, and cause the summary arrest and detention of anyone'. H. R. Hahlo and Ellison Kahn, *The Union of South Africa: The Development of its Laws and Constitution*, Stevens & Sons, London, 1960, 134.
9. *Sunday Express*, 27 March 1960.
10. *Die Nataller*, 1 April 1960.
11. *Die Vaderland*, 20 April 1960.
12. *Die Burger*, 29 April 1960.
13. Alexander Hepple, *Verwoerd*, Penguin, Harmondsworth, 1967, 154–5.
14. *Die Burger*, 11 April 1960.
15. *Die Transvaler*, 12 April 1960.
16. Alexander Hepple, op. cit., 174.
17. A. N. Pelzer ed., *Verwoerd Speaks: Speeches 1948–1966*, APB Publishers, Johannesburg, 1966, 326.

18. Alexander Hepple, ibid.
19. *Die Transvaler*, 3 November 1960.
20. *Die Burger*, 16 March 1960.
21. The Opposition made this charge on the ground that the Coloureds were being excluded from the vote.
22. *House of Assembly Debates*, Vol. 104, 21 March 1960, col. 3769.
23. D. W. Krüger (ed.), *South African Parties and Policies 1910–1960: A Select Source Book*, Human and Rousseau, Cape Town, 1960, 96. This principle was reaffirmed at the Transvaal National Party Congress in November 1958. *Die Transvaler*, 14 November 1958.
24. Van Jaarsveld and Scholtz (eds.), *Die Republiek van Suid Afrika*, Johannesburg: Voortrekker Pers, 1966, quoted in Alexander Hepple, op. cit., 174.
25. *Verwoerd Speaks*, 325.
26. *Die Transvaler*, 8 November 1958.
27. *Die Nataller*, 8 August 1958.
28. For Afrikaners generally the term 'nation' has more of a psychocultural connotation than a legal connotation—e.g. the 'Boerenasie' or the 'Afrikaner nasie' did not and does not imply a legal status. The exclusion of certain sections of the population from participation in the expression of the national will would not therefore strike them as inherently paradoxical.
29. *Verwoerd Speaks*, 326.
30. The National Party vote in South West Africa in the 1958 general election had exceeded the United Party vote by 4 822.
31. *Verwoerd Speaks*, 332.
32. Ibid., 330.
33. Michael Roberts and A. E. G. Trollip, *The South African Opposition 1939–1945: An Essay in Contemporary History*, Longmans, Green & Co., London, 1947, *passim.*
34. The fullest readily available account of the Draft Constitution is to be found in Brian Bunting, *The Rise of the South African Reich*, rev. ed.; Penguin, Harmondsworth, 1969, 105–9.
35. *Verwoerd Speaks*, 169.
36. *House of Assembly Debates*, Vol. 106, 30 January 1961, cols. 325–26.
37. D. W. Krüger, op. cit., 96.
38. Quoted in Alexander Hepple, op. cit., 174.
39. *Verwoerd Speaks*, 333.
40. Ibid., 407–8.
41. *Star*, 3 August 1960.
42. *Die Transvaler*, 30 August 1960.
43. The relevant sentences of the communiqué read: 'The meeting noted a statement by the South African Minister of External Affairs that the Union Government intended to hold a referendum on the subject of South Africa becoming a republic. . . . In the event of South Africa deciding to become a republic and if the desire was subsequently expressed to remain a member of the Commonwealth, the meeting suggested that the South African Government should then ask for the consent of the other Commonwealth governments either at a meeting of Commonwealth Prime Ministers or, if this were not practicable, by correspondence'. U.K. Central Office of Information, *Commonwealth Survey*, Vol. 6, No. 11, 24 May 1960, 452.
44. Ibid.
45. *Rand Daily Mail*, 9 June 1960.
46. *House of Assembly Debates*, Vol. 105, 18 May 1960, col. 8073.
47. *Verwoerd Speaks*, 407.
48. Ibid., 324.
49. Ibid.
50. *Die Transvaler*, 23 September 1960.
51. See, e.g., *Die Oosterlig*, 23 September 1960, and *Die Transvaler*, 26 September 1960.
52. Alexander Hepple, op. cit., 178.
53. *Die Burger*, 2 September 1960.

54. *Verwoerd Speaks*, 162.
55. Ibid., 329.
56. Ibid., 382–3.
57. *Die Volksblad*, 31 August 1960.
58. *Die Burger*, 4 June 1960.
59. *Verwoerd Speaks*, 404.
60. *Cape Times*, 7 June 1960.
61. *Star*, 17 August 1960.
62. *Sunday Times*, 14 August 1960.
63. *Cape Times*, 23 September 1960.
64. *Cape Times*, 4 August 1960.
65. *Daily News*, 22 January 1960.
66. *Golden City Post*, 31 January 1960.
67. *Rand Daily Mail*, 26 September 1960.
68. The Progressive Party expressed its discontent at not being recognized for this purpose.
69. There had been 52 000 registered Coloured voters in 1945, and from 1948 to 1953 the number never fell below 47 000.
70. *Star*, 7 October 1960.
71. *Sunday Times*, 9 October 1960.
72. *Press Digest*, 13 October 1960, 406.
73. *Die Transvaler*, 22 November 1960.
74. Sections 108 and 118.
75. Ellison Kahn, *The New Constitution*, Stevens & Sons, London, 1962, 3.
76. The account given by Sir Robert Menzies (*Afternoon Light: Some Memories of Men and Events*, Cassell, London, 1967, 212–14), although succinct, is generally regarded as substantially accurate.
77. Compare *Die Vaderland*, 20 March 1961, and *Die Transvaler*, 21 March 1961.
78. *Verwoerd Speaks*, 516.

CHAPTER 7

1. *Die Transvaler*, 6 June 1961.
2. *Die Vaderland*, 25 September 1961.
3. This was the view expressed by Mr. B. J. Vorster, then Minister of Justice. *Rand Daily Mail*, 6 September 1961.
4. This was one of the reasons given by the Prime Minister. *Die Transvaler*, 12 August 1961.
5. *Rand Daily Mail*, 2 August 1961.
6. A fuller statement of the view that apartheid conflicted with the tenets of Christianity was contained in a book written by eleven Dutch Reformed Church theologians and published at about the same time. This was A. S. Geyser and others, *Delayed Action!* N.G. Kerkboekhandel, Pretoria, 1960. Taken together, the two events created a considerable stir.
7. Gwendolen M. Carter, Thomas Karis and Newell M. Stultz, *South Africa's Transkei: The Politics of Domestic Colonialism*, Northwestern University Press, Evanston, 1967, 51.
8. A. N. Pelzer, ed., *Verwoerd Speaks: Speeches 1948–1966*, APB Publishers, Johannesburg, 1966, 295.
9. *Die Transvaler*, 1 December 1960.
10. *Die Transvaler*, 11 September 1961.
11. *Die Transvaler*, 2 October 1961.
12. *Die Transvaler*, 5 October 1961.
13. *Verwoerd Speaks*, 279. According to the 1970 Census there were eight million Africans living in 'white' areas. Merle Lipton, 'Independent Bantustans?', *International Affairs*, Vol. 48, No. 1, January 1972, 2n.
14. Carter, Karis and Stultz, op. cit., 121.
15. *Verwoerd Speaks*, 276.
16. *Die Burger*, 28 March 1961.
17. *Die Burger*, 23 July 1960.
18. *Die Transvaler*, 20 September 1960.

19. *Die Transvaler*, 23 November 1960.
20. *Die Burger*, 26 November 1960.
21. *Dagbreek en Sondagnuus*, 26 November 1960 and 4 December 1960.
22. *Die Vaderland*, 3 December 1960.
23. *Die Vaderland*, 7 December 1960.
24. Alexander Hepple, *Verwoerd*, Penguin, Harmondsworth, 1967, 157.
25. 'The Coloureds should be placed on a common roll and be free to nominate and elect their own people to Parliament.' Sir De Villiers Graaff, 'South African Prospects', *Foreign Affairs*, Vol. 39, No. 4, July 1961, 678.
26. Although a Department of Indian Affairs was created in August 1961, it was only in the following year that the Government officially abandoned the concept of repatriation and announced its recognition of Asians as a permanent part of the South African population. Alex Hepple, *South Africa: A political and economic history*, Frederick A. Praeger, New York, 1966, 139.
27. This had in fact been recommended by the Tomlinson Commission, but had been rejected in the Government's *White Paper on the Development of Bantu Areas*, Fact Paper 10, May 1956.
28. *Sunday Times*, 30 October 1960.
29. *Cape Times*, 2 May 1960.
30. *Star*, 15 July 1961.
31. *Sunday Express*, 9 July 1961.
32. *Star*, 16 August 1961.
33. *Star*, 16 June 1962.
34. H. G. Lawrence, 'Race Relations—South Africa's Greatest Problem', *The Forum*, Vol. 8, No. 10, January 1960, 8.
35. *Cape Times*, 14 August 1959.
36. Representation of Natives Act, No. 12 of 1936.
37. Native Trust and Land Act, No. 18 of 1936. The eventual total extent of these lands would amount to 13,7% of the area of the Union.
38. *Cape Times*, 14 August 1959.
39. Ibid.
40. *Die Burger*, 15 August 1959.
41. *Die Transvaler*, 17 August 1959.
42. *Cape Times*, 14 August 1959.
43. H. G. Lawrence, ibid.
44. *Star*, 21 August 1959.
45. *Die Vaderland*, 16 September 1959.
46. *Star*, 20 October 1959.
47. *The Constitution, incorporating the Principles of the Party. Adopted at Inaugural Congress. 13th and 14th November, 1959.* [Progressive Party] Union Head Office, Johannesburg, 15 January 1960.
48. Ibid.
49. *Die Transvaler*, 14 November 1959.
50. *Die Transvaler*, 17 November 1959.
51. The M.P.s who resigned from the United Party to join the Progressive party were: R. Butcher, J. Cope, Z. de Beer, C. Eglin, I. S. Fourie, H. G. Lawrence, J. Steytler, Helen Suzman, R. A. F. Swart, C. van Ryneveld, O. Williams, and B. Wilson.
52. *Star*, 18 November 1959.
53. *Star*, 24 November 1959.
54. *Franchise Proposals and Constitutional Safeguards: A report prepared for The Progressive Party of South Africa by a Commission of Experts* (*Molteno Report* vol. 1), n.p., November 1960. (Volume II, *A Rigid Constitution, the Decentralization of Government and the Administration of Justice*, was published in August 1962.) The author was a member of this commission.
55. T. Karis, 'South Africa', in Gwendolen M. Carter, ed., *Five African States*, Cornell University Press, Ithaca, 1963, 533.
56. Ibid., 532.
57. *Rand Daily Mail*, 6 September 1961.
58. *Die Transvaler*, 18 August 1961.

59. *Sunday Times*, 3 September 1961.
60. *Rand Daily Mail*, 8 September 1961.
61. *Die Vaderland*, 8 September 1961.
62. *Die Transvaler*, 9 September 1961.
63. All figures relating to the election are taken from the official publication of the results in *The Government Gazette*, Vol. 11, No. 10, 10 November 1961.
64. *Die Burger*, 31 August 1961.
65. *Daily News*, 15 September 1961.
66. See the comment of the *Rand Daily Mail*, 20 September 1961: 'We are voting for an Opposition, not a Government, and we want the best we can get. . . . It is essential to send a Progressive Party team back to Parliament.'
67. To be precise, this candidate adopted the imposing, if novel, title of Theocrat.
68. *Sunday Times*, 15 October 1961.
69. *Dagbreek en Sondagnuus*, 15 October 1961.
70. *Sunday Times*, 15 October 1961.
71. Ibid.
72. *Rand Daily Mail*, 17 October 1961.
73. This is on the assumption that in these seats this group of voters would not comprise more than about 10% of the electorate.
74. These seats were: Johannesburg North, Orange Grove, Durban Berea, Durban Musgrave and Pietermaritzburg City.
75. Newell M. Stultz and Jeffrey Butler, 'The South African General Election of 1961', *Political Science Quarterly*, Vol. 78, No. 1, March 1963, 105–6.
76. Ibid., 107.
77. *Rand Daily Mail*, 19 October 1961.
78. *Die Volksblad*, 23 October 1961.
79. *Die Transvaler*, 21 October 1961.
80. *Die Transvaler*, 23 October 1961.
81. *Die Transvaler*, 21 October 1961.

CHAPTER 8

1. *Die Transvaler*, 3 February 1966.
2. The Algerian revolution and its consequences had a considerable impact on white opinion in South Africa, because after South Africa the second largest concentration of 'Europeans' in Africa lived in Algeria. Moreover, while the white settlers in Algeria were seen as being readily able to go back to France, the Afrikaners, as they frequently assert, have no other home than South Africa. The Algerian experience, therefore, re-emphasized in the Afrikaner mind particularly, but also in the minds of whites generally, the necessity, for the sake of their own security, of retaining control in South Africa.
3. A simple illustration of this reaction may be found in a question directed to the author when he was visiting South Africa in 1968 by an English-speaking South African friend: 'Why do the British hate us so much?'
4. *Rand Daily Mail*, 12 February 1966.
5. In the Paarl riots two white civilians were attacked and killed and five whites were killed in the Bashee River incident.
6. Muriel Horrell (comp.), *A Survey of Race Relations in South Africa: 1966*, South African Institute of Race Relations, Johannesburg, January 1967, 74–5.
7. Ibid., 77.
8. For a fuller analysis of the Transkei see Gwendolen M. Carter, Thomas Karis and Newell M. Stultz, *South Africa's Transkei: The Politics of Domestic Colonialism*, Northwestern University Press, Evanston, 1967; and see also Christopher R. Hill, *Bantustans: The Fragmentation of South Africa*, Oxford University Press, London, 1963. While it is almost unbearably tempting to enter into a lengthy discussion on this subject, I must manfully recognize that this is not the place for it. Nevertheless, I will permit myself to express a personal opinion that the tortoise-like pace of the development of the Bantustans is less a reflection on the sincerity of its architects than it is an indication of the restraining force of the combined opposition of the United

Party and of the right-wing elements of the National Party. Moreover, the mere fact of their existence, especially in the light of the principles of freedom and self-determination which they are supposed to express, may yet be of critical importance in the future course of South African politics.

9. In September and October 1966 respectively.
10. *Die Transvaler*, 19 January 1966.
11. Cf. the charge made by the Leader of the Opposition, Sir De Villiers Graaff: 'Now the party has advanced the election before its allotted time has run out—not to ask for a mandate, not to propose a solution to our problems to the public, but in order to try to get a blank cheque.' *Die Transvaler*, 1 March 1966.
12. These problems were aggravated by the fact that the Commissioners only signed their report on 20 December 1965, and that it was not published in the *Government Gazette* until 7 February 1966.
13. *Rand Daily Mail*, 1 March 1966.
14. *Rand Daily Mail*, 26 March 1966.
15. Ibid., 12 March 1966.
16. *Die Transvaler*, 12 February 1966.
17. *Rand Daily Mail*, 19 February 1966.
18. *Die Burger*, 28 January 1966.
19. *Rand Daily Mail*, 1 March 1966.
20. See, for example, the editorial of 26 January 1966.
21. *Star*, 4 February 1966.
22. *Rand Daily Mail*, 3 March 1966.
23. *Natal Mercury*, 23 March 1966.
24. *Natal Mercury*, 30 March 1966.
25. *Ons Land*, 11 February 1966.
26. *Natal Mercury*, 3 March 1966.
27. *Rand Daily Mail*, 14 March 1966.
28. *Natal Mercury*, 3 March 1966.
29. *Natal Mercury*, 30 March 1966.
30. *Rand Daily Mail*, 30 March 1966.
31. *Die Transvaler*, 31 January 1966.
32. *Die Transvaler*, 3 February 1966.
33. *Die Transvaler*, 14 March 1966.
34. *Die Transvaler*, 28 March 1966.
35. *Die Burger*, 28 March 1966.
36. Ibid.
37. *Die Burger*, 1 April 1966.
38. *Natal Mercury*, 3 March 1966.
39. *Die Burger*, 28 March 1966.
40. *Die Transvaler*, 25 February 1966.
41. *Die Volksblad*, 7 March 1966.
42. *Natal Mercury*, 3 March 1966.
43. *Die Transvaler*, 5 March 1966.
44. *Rand Daily Mail*, 23 March 1966.
45. *Cape Times*, 10 February 1966.
46. *Die Transvaler*, 1 March 1966.
47. *Die Transvaler*, 21 February 1966.
48. Typical of this interest was the main front page headline in the *Rand Daily Mail* on the day of the election, 30 March 1966: 'Natal is Focal Point.'
49. The numbers of public meetings scheduled per party in Natal were: N.P. 85; U.P. 64; P.P. 28. *Natal Mercury*, 8 March 1966.
50. *Die Transvaler*, 23 February 1966.
51. *Die Transvaler*, 5 March 1966.
52. *Die Transvaler*, 26 March 1966.
53. *Die Transvaler*, 22 March 1966.
54. *Die Transvaler*, 24 March 1966.
55. *Die Transvaler*, 23 February 1966.
56. *Rand Daily Mail*, 19 March 1966.

57. *Rand Daily Mail*, 22 March 1966.
58. *Die Transvaler*, 5 March 1966.
59. *Natal Mercury*, 5 March 1966.
60. *Die Transvaler*, 9 March 1966.
61. *Cape Times*, 5 March 1966.
62. *Natal Mercury*, 17 March 1966.
63. *Rand Daily Mail*, 26 March 1966.
64. *Rand Daily Mail*, 15 March 1966.
65. *Rand Daily Mail*, 3 March 1966.
66. *Rand Daily Mail*, 8 March 1966.
67. *Rand Daily Mail*, 1 March 1966.
68. *Rand Daily Mail*, 10 March 1966.
69. *Rand Daily Mail*, 16 March 1966.
70. *Rand Daily Mail*, 30 March 1966.
71. *Star*, 29 March 1966. On the first point, cf. the *Rand Daily Mail*, 26 March 1966, which reported that in five years Helen Suzman had made '119 notable speeches and asked more than 800 pertinent questions'.
72. *Sunday Times*, 13 February 1966.
73. *Rand Daily Mail*, 11 March 1966.
74. *Die Transvaler*, 8 March 1966.
75. *Die Transvaler*, 21 February 1966.
76. *Die Transvaler*, 10 March 1966.
77. *Die Transvaler*, 2 March 1966.
78. Ibid.
79. *Natal Mercury*, 20 January 1966.
80. *Die Transvaler*, 19 February 1966.
81. Cf. *Natal Mercury*, 20 January and 5 February 1966.
82. *Die Transvaler*, 19 February 1966.
83. All figures for the voting in the 1966 election are taken from *The Government Gazette*, No. 1426, 22 April 1966.
84. *Rand Daily Mail*, 22 January 1966.
85. *Sunday Tribune*, 13 February 1966.
86. *Die Transvaler*, 31 March 1966.
87. *Die Burger*, 31 March 1966.
88. *Die Volksblad*, 5 April 1966.
89. *Die Burger*, 1 April 1966.
90. *Die Transvaler*, 1 April 1966.
91. *Rand Daily Mail*, 1 April 1966.

CHAPTER 9

1. See 71–2 above.
2. For a graphic description of Dr Verwoerd's assassination, see *News/Check*, 9 September 1966.
3. *Die Transvaler*, 7 September 1966.
4. *Natal Mercury*, 9 September 1966.
5. 'Dawie' is the pseudonym of Mr Piet Cillie, editor of *Die Burger*.
6. *Die Burger*, 10 September 1966.
7. *Die Beeld*, 11 September 1966.
8. J. H. P. Serfontein, *Die Verkrampte Aanslag*, Human and Rousseau, Cape Town and Pretoria, 1970, p. 71. Citations from this work are translated by the author.
9. Ibid., 72.
10. *Debates of the House of Assembly*, Vol. 17, 2 August 1966, cols. 76–7.
11. See J. H. P. Serfontein, op. cit., 60.
12. See ibid., 61.
13. Professor De Klerk identified the *verligte* Afrikaners with those who promoted dangerous 'liberalist' tendencies in Afrikanerdom—and this is how their opponents still see them. The *verligtes* themselves, however, identify themselves more in accordance with Professor De Klerk's definition of 'positive' Afrikaners—i.e. those who retain the traditional Afrikaner

values while taking a positive attitude towards future developments. The *verkramptes* were defined by Professor De Klerk as those ultra-conservative Afrikaners who were opposed to all change *per se*. Significantly, he regarded them as just as much of a menace as the *verligtes*—as he defined the latter group.

14. Reconstituted National Party.
15. J. H. P. Serfontein, op. cit., 14–15.
16. The portfolio of Posts and Telegraphs was moreover a politically sensitive one. Dr Hertzog had made it a bastion of *verkramptheid*, due to the public demand for television on the one hand, and Dr. Hertzog's absolute opposition to it on the other. At the same time, the Chairman of the South African Broadcasting Corporation, Dr Piet Meyer, was also the Chairman of the Broederbond and was well known for his *verkrampte* views. It might be added that in December 1969—well after the supercession of Dr Hertzog—a Commission of Inquiry into Matters Relating to television in South Africa, under the chairmanship of Dr Meyer, was appointed. It recommended in favour of the establishment of a television system (see its report, RP 37/1971); but the report was not tabled until 27 April 1971, i.e. a year after the election under review.
17. See Serfontein, op. cit., 159.
18. *Die Burger*, 12 August 1968. It was on the following day that *Die Burger* announced the steps taken against the letter writers.
19. Quoted in J. H. P. Serfontein, op. cit., 155.
20. J. H. P. Serfontein, op. cit., 174–5. There is no equivalent English word for *Afrikanerskap*, but it implies the qualitative content of the concept of being an Afrikaner.
21. *House of Assembly Debates*, No. 10, 14 April 1969, col. 3880.
22. Ibid., col. 3882.
23. Ibid., col. 3883.
24. Ibid.
25. *Die Burger*, 17 April 1969.
26. J. H. P. Serfontein, op. cit., 193. *See also House of Assembly Debates*, No. 11, 22 April 1969, cols. 4515–17.
27. The closest English equivalent would probably be 'recalcitrants'. It carries with it the connotation of trouble-making.
28. Quoted in J. H. P. Serfontein, op. cit., 197.
29. *Die Burger*, 1 May 1969.
30. *Die Burger*, 15 May 1969.
31. J. H. P. Serfontein, op. cit., 205. See also *Die Beeld*, 25 May 1969.
32. J. H. P. Serfontein, op. cit., 212–15; *Die Burger*, 11 September 1969.
33. *Die Burger*, 13 September 1969.
34. Ibid.
35. One of the subsequent allegations made by the H.N.P. was that the Prime Minister used the state security system for party political purposes. See, e.g., the report of a speech by Dr Hertzog in the *Star*, 18 February 1970.
36. Muriel Horrell, *Legislation and Race Relations*, South African Institute of Race Relations, rev. ed., Johannesburg, 1971, 17–18.
37. The Minister of Finance disclosed in his Budget speech that the consumer price index had increased during the year ending 30 June 1970, by 4,1%. *House of Assembly Debates*, No. 4, 12 August 1970, col. 1530.
38. *Financial Mail*, Vol. XXXV, No. 6, 13 February 1970. For further comments in similar vein, see Muriel Horrell (comp.), *A Survey of Race Relations in South Africa: 1970*, South African Institute of Race Relations, Johannesburg, January 1971, 81–7, 94–8.
39. Muriel Horrell, op. cit., 88–92.
40. In July 1970, according to the Minister, there were 88 Coloureds, 101 Indians and 1 229 Africans holding jobs formerly held by white 'graded' staff, and 1 371 Coloureds, 140 Indians and 12 698 Africans doing work formerly performed by unskilled and 'ungraded' white workers: ibid., 121–2.

41. A partial exception may be found in the 1961 election, when, as we have seen, one reason given for the early dissolution was the expressed desire to eliminate the Progressive Party.
42. Muriel Horrell (comp.), *A Survey of Race Relations in South Africa: 1969*, Institute of Race Relations, Johannesburg, January 1970, 4; *The Friend*, 17 September 1969.
43. Cf. *Die Burger*, 17 September 1969.
44. *Die Transvaler*, 17 September 1969.
45. *Die Beeld*, 21 September 1969.
46. *Die Burger*, 6 March 1970.
47. *Die Transvaler*, 4 April 1970.
48. *Natal Mercury*, 17 March 1970.
49. *Natal Mercury*, 8 April 1970.
50. The *Argus*, 10 March 1970.
51. *Natal Mercury*, 17 March 1970.
52. Cf. a report in the *Daily News*, 9 April 1970.
53. e.g. Speeches by Mr Marais Steyn (*Natal Mercury*, 21 March 1970) and Sir De Villiers Graaff (*Natal Mercury*, 25 March 1970); and Sir De Villiers Graaff's final message to the electorate (*Natal Mercury*, 22 April 1970).
54. e.g. Speeches by Mr Etienne Malan (*Rand Daily Mail*, 9 April 1970) and Mr Mike Mitchell (*Natal Mercury*, 25 March 1970).
55. e.g. Speeches by Mr Colin Eglin (*Cape Argus*, 13 March 1970); Dr Jan Steytler (*Natal Mercury*, 20 March 1970), and Mr Harry Oppenheimer (the *Star*, 2 April 1970).
56. The Herstigte Nasionale Party election manifesto, *Die Afrikaner*, 10 April 1970.
57. Mr Gert Beetge, *Pretoria News*, 18 March 1970.
58. *Die Transvaler*, 1 April 1970. Official statistics, however, show that in 1970 there were 8 060 773 'Bantu' in 'white areas' (6 819 968 in 1960), compared with 6 994 179 in 'Bantu homelands' (4 107 954 in 1960). *Bulletin of Statistics. Quarter ended December 1971*, Department of Statistics, Pretoria, Vol. 5, No. 4. It may be pointed out, however, that this represents an increase over the ten-year period of 18,2% in the white areas, compared with an increase of 70,3% in the homelands.
59. *Natal Mercury*, 14 March 1970.
60. *Hoofstad*, 2 April 1970.
61. *Hoofstad*, 18 March 1970.
62. The *Star*, 9 April 1970.
63. e.g. Mr Marais Steyn (the *Star*, 11 March 1970), and Sir De Villiers Graaff (*Rand Daily Mail*, 16 March 1970).
64. *Die Transvaler*, 26 March 1970. 'Sappe' is still a Nationalist term for the United Party. It is derived from the initials of the pre-Fusion South African Party.
65. *Rand Daily Mail*, 26 March 1970.
66. It is, perhaps, significant that South African Government spokesmen continue to refer to 'Communism' in monolithic terms.
67. *Natal Mercury*, 25 March 1970.
68. *Rand Daily Mail*, 21 March 1970.
69. *Natal Mercury*, 14 March 1970.
70. *Natal Mercury*, 8 April 1970.
71. *Natal Mercury*, 21 April 1970.
72. *Die Transvaler*, 3 April 1970.
73. Mr S. E. D. Brown, e.g., referred to Mr Vorster's 'weak, vacillating and pragmatic leadership' (*S.A. Observer*, November 1969), and in the following month's edition, he accused Mr Vorster of handing over the National Party 'to the new-rich Afrikaners and liberals'. And cf. a pamphlet circulated by the H.N.P. in Sunnyside, Pretoria), accusing Mr Vorster of abandoning Calvinism (*Hoofstad*, 17 March 1970).
74. *Natal Mercury*, 27 February 1970.
75. *Hoofstad*, 9 April 1970.

76. The *Argus*, 4 April 1970; *Hoofstad*, 7 April 1970, and *Die Transvaler*, 14 April 1970.
77. *Hoofstad*, 21 April 1970.
78. *Sunday Times*, 26 October 1969; *Africa Research Bulletin, Political, Social and Cultural Series*, Vol. 6, No. 10, 15 November 1969, 1554.
79. *Cape Argus*, 7 November 1969.
80. *Natal Mercury*, 9 April 1970; *Die Afrikaner*, 10 April 1970.
81. *Die Afrikaner*, 20 February 1970.
82. *Natal Mercury*, 17 March 1970.
83. *Pretoria News*, 17 March 1970.
84. See above, 185.
85. *Rand Daily Mail*, 24 March 1970.
86. *Natal Mercury*, 17 March 1970. Presumably Mr Vorster's taste for golf was taken as a sign of incurable frivolity.
87. *Cape Argus*, 19 March 1970.
88. *Die Burger*, 14 March 1970.
89. *Die Transvaler*, 6 April 1970.
90. The Land Bank is a statutory body, established initially by Act of Parliament in 1912. While it is free of direct Government control, its Managing Director and members of the Board are appointed by the President, and it is represented in Parliament by the Minister of Finance.
91. *Sunday Times*, 22 March 1970; *Die Afrikaner*, 27 March 1970.
92. *Rand Daily Mail*, 20 March 1970. This loan to Mr Haak was listed by Mr Dirk Richard, editor of *Dagbreek*, as one of the factors contributing to the National Party's loss of support in the election (*Dagbreek*, 26 April 1970); and it is significant that in the post-election reshuffle of the Cabinet Mr Haak resigned (*Rand Daily Mail*, 12 May 1970).
93. *Die Vaderland*, 16 March 1970.
94. *Rand Daily Mail*, 18 March 1970.
95. See the article by J. H. P. Serfontein in the *Sunday Times*, 29 March 1970.
96. *Rand Daily Mail*, 18 March 1970.
97. *Natal Mercury*, 18 March 1970.
98. *Natal Mercury*, 9 April 1970.
99. *Cape Argus*, 25 February 1970.
100. *Natal Mercury*, 22 April 1970.
101. *Natal Mercury*, 21 April 1970.
102. Sir De Villiers Graaff, *Natal Mercury*, 22 April 1970.
103. *Natal Mercury*, 25 February 1970.
104. *Cape Argus*, 2 April 1970.
105. *Natal Mercury*, 22 April 1970.
106. *Natal Mercury*, 9 April 1970.
107. *Natal Mercury*, 3 April 1970; *Cape Argus*, 2 April 1970. A rather more *verkrampt* posture is to be seen in Senator Horak's statement that the United Party would 'maintain White leadership, by force of arms if necessary, over the whole of South Africa'. *Natal Mercury*, 15 April 1970.
108. Sir De Villiers Graaff, *Natal Mercury*, 21 March 1970.
109. The *Star*, 21 March 1970.
110. *Natal Mercury*, 16 April 1970.
111. These qualifications were: *either* Standard VIII on its own, *or* Standard VI plus *either* an income of R600 per year (for two consecutive years), *or* occupation of property worth R1 000 (also for two consecutive years), *or* literacy plus ownership of unencumbered property worth R1 000. These monetary qualifications were subject to review every five years in the light of the changing value of money.
112. *Natal Mercury*, 19 March 1970.
113. *Natal Mercury*, 14 April 1970.
114. *Natal Mercury*, 15 April 1970.
115. Ibid., and *Rand Daily Mail*, 15 April 1970.
116. *Rand Daily Mail*, 21 April 1970 and *Die Transvaler*, 22 April 1970.
117. *Rand Daily Mail*, 22 April 1970.

118. *Dagbreek*, 26 April 1970.
119. *Rand Daily Mail*, 12 May 1970.
120. *Natal Mercury*, 19 March 1970.
121. *Rand Daily Mail*, 18 March 1970.
122. *Natal Mercury*, 21 April 1970.
123. *Die Transvaler*, 23 April 1970.
124. *Dagbreek*, 26 April 1970.
125. The *Star*, 24 April 1970.
126. H. Lever, on the basis of a survey conducted in Johannesburg West and Jeppes, lists the three main reasons given by Nationalists before the election for abstaining or for indecision. These were 'lack of interest, the division or squabble within the National Party and the failure of Nationalists to implement promises'. He further suggests that the second reason might well have been a factor in the first. Subjected to 'cross-pressures' within the National movement, the former Nationalist voter might resolve his difficulty by 'an "out of the field response"; that is to lose interest as a voter'. Reinforcing this potential tendency, was the marked reluctance among Professor Levy's sample, to name any of the opposition parties as a possible second choice, H. Lever, 'Factors underlying change in the South African general election of 1970', in *The British Journal of Sociology*, Vol. XXIII, No. 2, June 1972, 239–40. This reason for abstentions among Nationalists is also favoured by Professor W. B. Vosloo, along with 'complacency regarding the outcome', and 'dissatisfaction at recent governmental performance'. Prof. W. B. Vosloo, 'The election of 1970 (or who really won?)' in *New Nation*, August 1970, 5. The present author, with no hard evidence to back his opinion, has a sense that both these authors underestimate the effect of increasing inflation on the Nationalist voter who yet remained reluctant to switch party allegiances.
127. See 145 above.
128. See, e.g., H. Lever, op. cit., 243, and Prof. W. B. Vosloo, op. cit., 5–6.

CHAPTER 10

1. For rhetorical purposes the assumption is stated in a grossly over-simplified form, and the argument deriving the representative system from this assumption is likewise over-simplified. For example, the 'swing of the pendulum' principle is vague, or even silent, on the subject of the time-span within which the swing is likely to occur. Again, representative institutions may more accurately be said to assume that if changes in voter preferences occur, they *may*, under conditions of open competition, result in shifts in voter support from one party to another resulting in changes of government; but, of course, the ruling party may itself adapt its policies to changing public preferences with sufficient success to remain in power.
2. V. O. Key, Jr., 'A Theory of Critical Elections', *Journal of Politics*, 17 February 1955.
3. Walter Dean Burnham, *Critical Elections and the Mainspring of American Politics*, W. W. Norton, New York, 1970.
4. J. M. Beck has also applied the typology to Canadian elections in his *Pendulum of Power: Canada's Federal Elections*, Prentice-Hall, Scarborough, 1968.
5. Angus Campbell, Philip E. Converse, Warren E. Miller, and Donald E. Stokes, *The American Voter*, John Wiley & Sons, New York, 1960, 531.
6. Angus Campbell, Philip E. Converse, Warren E. Miller, and Donald E. Stokes, *Elections and the Political Order*, John Wiley & Sons, New York, 1966, 69.
7. Ibid., 74.
8. V. O. Key, Jr., op. cit.
9. Campbell, *et al.*, *Elections and the Political Order*, 74.
10. Ibid., 75–6.
11. This ratio is suggested rather than simply the sum of the two major parties' candidates, because (*a*) in two elections (1953 and 1970) there was one seat

which was not at stake, and (*b*) because the total number of seats (excluding S.W.A.) was increased from 1966 from 150 to 160.

12. Walter Dean Burnham, op. cit., 6.
13. Ibid., 7–8.
14. Professor H. Lever of the Witwatersrand University found in 1966 that 84,7% of the Afrikaners sampled in the Johannesburg West constituency gave the National Party as their party of preference, compared with only 4,8% who preferred the United Party. In an election in which a relatively large number of English-speakers voted for the National Party, he still found only 16,3% of his English-speaking sample stating a preference for the National Party compared with 60,7% for the United Party. H. Lever, *The South African Voter: Some Aspects of Voting Behaviour*, Juta & Co., Ltd., Cape Town, 1972, 25.
15. See James Rosenau, *The Scientific Study of Foreign Policy*, The Free Press New York, (London: Collier-Macmillan), 1971, 47.
16. H. Lever, op, cit., 175.
17. Ibid., 212.
18. Ibid., 176.
19. Ibid., 166.

Index